BOB DYLAN
ANTHOLOGY VOLUME 2

20 YEARS OF ISIS

Published in 2005 by Chrome Dreams
PO Box 230, New Malden, Surrey, England

Executive Publishing Editor: Rob Johnstone
Editor: Derek Barker
Typesetting: Tracy Barker
Cover Design: Jon Storey [front] Sylwia Grzeszczuk [back]
Printed and bound in Great Britain by William Clowes Ltd, Beccles, Suffolk

A CIP record for this book is available from the British Library

ISBN 1 84240 309 5

BOB DYLAN
ANTHOLOGY VOLUME 2

20 YEARS OF ISIS

edited by

Derek Barker

THANKS AND ACKNOWLEDGMENTS

This book is the result of 20 years of writing about Bob Dylan and as such it would be impossible to thank all those who have contributed help and information throughout those years. I would, however, like to make special reference for all manor of reasons, to –

John Baldwin, Ben Clayton, Mark Carter, Mark Carver-Smith, Chris Cooper, Dave Dingle, Jim Gillan, Michael Gray, John Green, Clinton Heylin, Patrice Hamilton, John Hume, Jim Johnson, Les Kokay, Robert and Arlene Levinson, Henry Porter, Paula Radice, Phil & Ali Townsend, Kevin Williamson, Matthew Zuckerman.

Extraordinary thanks to –

The ever dependable Rob Johnstone and everyone else at my publisher, *Chrome Dreams*, Tracy Barker, Paul Comley, Ian Woodward, and to Lynne Sheridan at the Licensing Department at *Bob Dylan Music Company/Special Rider Music*, and to Jeff Rosen at *Special Rider Music* for his continuing help and understanding.

Photo Credits – Dennis Grice, John Hume, Phil Meiners, Giulio Molfese, Andrea Orlandi, Jens Winter, Frank Witt, IWC, ISIS Archive.

Permissions –

The editor of this anthology would like to express his sincere thanks to Bob Dylan and to the copyright owners listed below for their permissions to quote from material written and composed by Bob Dylan. Most of the quotations contained in this book are taken from Bob Dylan recordings, in some cases live performances, and may differ from those printed in *"Bob Dylan Lyrics 1962-2001"*. Any lyrics not credited below are for review, study or critical purposes.

'A Hard Rain's A-Gonna Fall', Copyright © 1963 by Warner Bros inc.; renewed 1991 by Special Rider Music. *'All Along The Watchtower'*, Copyright © 1968 Dwarf Music; renewed 1996 Dwarf Music. *'As I Went Out One Morning'*, Copyright © 1968 Dwarf Music; renewed 1996 Dwarf Music. *'Billy'*, Copyright © 1972 Rams Horn Music; renewed 2000 by Rams Horn Music. *'Bob Dylan's Dream'*, Copyright © 1963, 1964 by Warner Bros inc.; renewed 1991, 1992 by Special Rider Music. *'Buckets Of Rain'*, Copyright © 1974 Rams Horn Music; renewed 2002 by Rams Horn Music. *'Can't Wait'*, Copyright © 1997 by Special Rider Music. *'Changing Of The Guards'*, Copyright © 1978 by Special Rider Music. *'Cold Irons Bound'*, Copyright © 1997 by Special Rider Music. *'Dear Landlord'*, Copyright © 1968 Dwarf Music; renewed 1996 Dwarf Music. *'Dirt Road Blues'*, Copyright © 1997 by Special Rider Music. *'Don't Fall Apart On Me Tonight'*, Copyright © 1983 by Special Rider Music. *'Dusty Old Fairgrounds'*, Copyright © 1973 by Warner Bros inc.; renewed 2001 by Special Rider Music.

Contributors

Derek Barker founded the international Bob Dylan magazine *ISIS* in September 1985 and has edited this highly respected journal without interruption for the past 20 years. He was born at a very early age in Cheshire, England and now lives in Warwickshire with his wife Tracy, his stepdaughter Samantha and two cats.

Derek, a regular contributor to the BBC, has had his writings on Bob Dylan published in journals in Europe, the USA and Japan and has previously worked with *Chrome Dreams* on Dylan related CD and DVD projects, in which he also appeared. He also advises premier auction house Christie's on the authenticity of items of Dylan memorabilia.

Derek Barker first edited (in book form) a collection of writings from the back pages of *ISIS* in November 2001. The resulting book, *"ISIS: A Bob Dylan Anthology"* (*Helter Skelter* 2001) was released to universal rave reviews and a revised edition of the book (*Helter Skelter* 2004) remains in print.

Mike Daley is a professional musician and Ph.D candidate in musicology at York University in Toronto, Canada. His articles have been published in *Popular Music*, *Popular Music and Society* and elsewhere.

Mike's master's thesis, on Bob Dylan's early vocal style, won the York Thesis Prize for 1997. He is currently completing a doctoral dissertation on the emergence of an historical consciousness in early rock criticism. Some of his other work can be found at his website, www.mikedaley.net

Tony DeMeur is a singer/guitarist and a founder member of the legendary pub combo the "Fabulous Poodles". Debuting in 1977 with their eponymous album on *Pye* records, the Poodles gained cult status in the UK and had Top Forty hits in the USA where they supported Tom Petty, Sha Na Na and The Ramones.

James Dunlap is an attorney who has been practicing business law in Seattle, Washington for 20 years. He received a bachelor's degree in the humanities, with distinction, from Stanford University, where he briefly taught Western Civilization, and a master's degree in intellectual history from Princeton University. He received his law degree from Boalt Hall at the University of California at Berkeley. Mr. Dunlap has been listening to Bob Dylan since the beginning and has been a major contributor to *ISIS* magazine for the past two years.

Trevor Gibb is a young and extremely talented singer-songwriter guitarist. He lives in Heaton, Newcastle Upon Tyne, England. Visit his website at trevgibb.co.uk

Michael Gray grew up on Merseyside. At York University in the 1960s he studied under F. R. Leavis, and interviewed A. J. P. Taylor and Jimi Hendrix.

His pioneering study *"Song & Dance Man"*, published 1972 was the first critical study of Dylan's work. A second edition was published as *"The Art of Bob*

Dylan" in 1981 and 1982. He co-edited the collection *"All Across The Telegraph: A Bob Dylan Handbook"*, 1987. The massive *"Song & Dance Man III"*, *Cassell Academic*, 1999 (*Continuum*, US, 2000) is recognised as a classic work and is still selling.

He has given talks at Dylan conventions, was a plenary speaker at the first Robert Shelton Memorial Conference at Liverpool University, and keynote speaker there in 2001. Since 2000 he has given fifty Dylan talks (more like one-man shows than lectures) at festivals, arts centres & on US campuses. He is a *Guardian* obituarist for major figures in rock'n'roll, writes travel features for the *Telegraph* and is writing the first biography of Blind Willie McTell.

Patrice Hamilton is a ceramics artist who lives in Somerset, England. Patrice has been a subscriber to *ISIS* magazine since its inception and produced artwork for many of the magazine's early covers.

Peter Higginson is a 43 yr old ex-lecturer in English, now a writer living in Wolverhampton, England. He is a singer-songwriter guitarist who has a Bob Dylan tribute act and has supported Martin Carthy, Dick Gaughan and Steve Gibbons. A Catholic, conservative, and Dylan fan since *"Hard Rain"* (1976).

Ronnie Keohane is author of the book *"Dylan and the Frucht"*. Born in the Bronx in 1953 . . . Not Dead Yet.

Ian Meacock graduated with a degree in theology and has worked as an academic researcher. He lives in Glasgow, Scotland.

D. R. Neyret is originally from the Oakland/Berkeley area near San Francisco, USA but has been living in France for the last 10 years. She is a recent subscriber to *ISIS* and her essay *"In Search of Jokerman"* is a long time labour of love.

Adrian Richardson has been a subscriber to *ISIS* magazine from day one. He has been a fan of Bob Dylan since the beginning, and has seen him in concert around the world many hundreds of times. Jim Callaghan, Dylan's chief of security, has described him as *"Bob's biggest Fan"*.

Matthew Zuckerman has been a Dylan fan since the age of 13 (1969). Mother from Plymouth, England, father from Brooklyn, Matthew was born in Berlin and grew up in Bath. He went to live in Japan during the Thatcher years, where he worked as a teacher and writer – came back to Bath the month Blair was elected but claims no responsibility for that. Matthew writes for *The Bath Chronicle* (music, literature, arts and is their resident Mr Memory). He also writes for *Asahi Evening News* (music) and is the fiction editor for *Wingspan*, ANA's in-flight magazine. Matthew, who is married to Mieko and has two children, Naomi and Cecil, has also edited a number of poetry books and has been a regular contributor to *ISIS* magazine for many years.

These so-called connoisseurs of Bob Dylan music, I don't feel they know a thing or have an inkling of who I am or what I'm about. It's ludicrous, humorous and sad that such people have spent so much of their time thinking about who? Me? Get a life, please. You're wasting your own.

Bob Dylan

I'm in the amusement business. That goes along with theme parks, popcorn and horror shows.

Bob Dylan

I didn't really choose to do what you are seeing me do right now. It choose me. If I had any choice I would have been a scientist, an engineer or a doctor.

Bob Dylan

I didn't consciously pursue the Bob Dylan myth. It was given to me, by God. If I wasn't Bob Dylan, I'd probably think that Bob Dylan has a lot of answers myself.

Bob Dylan

I believe that instinct is what makes a genius a genius.

Bob Dylan

Just because you like my stuff doesn't mean I owe you anything.

Bob Dylan

All this talk about equality. The only thing people really have in common is that they are all going to die.

Bob Dylan

If you try to be anyone but yourself, you will fail; if you are not true to your own heart, you will fail. Then again, there's no success like failure.

Bob Dylan

I have weak eyes. Try them for yourself. See the world as Bob Dylan sees it.

Bob Dylan

On some of my earlier records, I sounded cross because I was poor. Lived on less ten cents a day in those times. Now I'm cross because I'm rich.

Bob Dylan

Being noticed can be a burden. Jesus got himself crucified because he got himself noticed. So I disappear a lot.

Bob Dylan

Any day above ground is a good day

Bob Dylan

CONTENTS

Editor's Introduction

On January 1st, 1985 the Internet's Domain Name System is created and on the same day the first British mobile phone call is made by comedian, Ernie Wise. The future impact of the mobile phone must somehow have been immediately obvious to British Telecom because just sixteen days after that phone call they announce their intended abolition of its celebrated red telephone boxes. March 4th sees Mohammed Al Fayed buy the world-famous London-based department-store, Harrods. On May 25th, Bangladesh is hit by a tropical cyclone and 10,000 people lose their lives. Four days later at the Heysel Stadium in Brussels, Belgium, 39 football fans die and hundreds more are injured when a concrete wall collapses under crowd pressure at the European Cup Final match between Liverpool and Juventus. On July 10th the Greenpeace vessel Rainbow Warrior is bombed and sunk in Auckland Harbour by French DGSE agents. Famine continues in Ethiopia and on July 13th the Live Aid benefit-concerts in the United Kingdom and United States raise over £50 million for famine relief. Two months later, on September 1st, a joint American-French expedition locates the wreck of the RMS Titanic. On September 19th an earthquake measuring 8.1 on the Richter scale hits Mexico City resulting in more than 9,000 dead and 30,000 injured. November sees the launch of *Microsoft* Windows 1.0. The volcano Nevado del Ruiz erupts in Colombia, killing an estimated 23,000 people.

In the world of music, the summer of 1985 sees the Second British Invasion of the USA. Madonna is the only American artist in a US Top Ten otherwise dominated by British acts. Music videos are the current fad, but thankfully the public soon realize that many of these faces, which look oh so pretty on film, don't actually cut it when it comes down to the music. In a world where the drum machine has become king, too much style and not enough substance is the order of the day. In Britain music cassettes are outselling vinyl albums for the first time ever. The U.S. Postal Service issues an Elvis Presley stamp commemorating what would have been the King's 50th birthday. A record-breaking 500 million stamps are sold. 1985 is the year of charity rock and a galaxy of stars unite as USA For Africa. The record, *'We Are The World'*, reaches #1 and sells four million copies, making it the biggest-selling single of the decade. Artists United Against Apartheid record *'Sun City'* to protest against South Africa's racist policies. A comment made by Bob Dylan at the US Live Aid concert results in Farm Aid. Bob Dylan appears at the concert, which is staged at the Memorial Stadium in Champaign, Illinois, and $10 million is raised to help American farmers. The concert takes place in September 1985.

It was during that September that the madness first took hold of me and I decided to produce a magazine devoted solely to the life and works of one man. Within a couple of weeks of that decision the first issue of *ISIS* was mailed out to a few friends. At the time, the *"Biograph"* box-set and *"Bob Dylan Lyrics"* were both still a month away from being released and Robert Shelton's pioneering biography about Bob Dylan was still unpublished.

Now, twenty years later, you are holding in your hand the second *ISIS* book. *"Anthology 2"*, a follow-up to the critically acclaimed and highly successful

"ISIS: A Bob Dylan Anthology" (*Helter Skelter* 2001), has been assembled to celebrate *"20 Years of ISIS"*. It is a best-of selection of essays and interviews from the magazine's considerable back pages, which can be read from cover to cover as a potted biography, or more appropriately, simply dipped into and read as individual essays.

Like the magazine from which they are taken, this anthology is an eclectic mix of writings on Bob Dylan in which in-depth articles are punctuated by stories of fans meeting their idol, or off the wall tales of Bob Dylan out trick-or-treating or organizing a prototype moustache before deciding to grow his own. It is this pot-pourri of styles that has kept *ISIS* magazine so popular for so many years and the resulting Anthology has something for everybody.

The marvellous thing about this Anthology is that it wasn't planned; it just happened. When I compiled the first *ISIS* Anthology in 2001, there was never any thought of a follow-up. In fact, nothing could have been further from my mind. It seems, however, that this project was bigger then me, and it quickly took on a life of its own. People soon began asking when the second volume would be out. It seems that everyone just assumed there would be a second volume. Everyone but me, that is! Then, in September 2003, while writing a new introduction for the revised edition of the first Anthology, I succumbed and announced that at some unspecified date in the future there would indeed be a volume two. The date that I later decided on was of course September 2005; our twentieth anniversary.

In previewing an upcoming concert in Hamburg, New York, in 2001, a journalist for the *Buffalo News* wrote an introduction to his article that has been adopted by Bob Dylan as a preamble to his concerts. What better way to open this circa 160,000-word anthology than with these 73 words. So, light the Nag Champa, sit back and enjoy the book.

"Ladies and gentleman, please welcome the poet laureate of rock 'n' roll. The voice of the promise of the sixties counterculture. The guy who forced folk into bed with rock, who donned makeup in the seventies and disappeared into a haze of substance abuse, who emerged to find Jesus, who was written off as a has-been in the late eighties-and who suddenly shifted gears, releasing some of the strongest music of his career beginning in the late nineties. Ladies and gentleman, please welcome Columbia Recording Artist, Bob Dylan".

Derek Barker, May 2005

"I've seen all these crazes come and go, and I don't think I'm more than a craze"

In Dylan's Minnesota Footsteps

Michael Gray

If you're travelin' in the North Country fair/Where the wind hits heavy on the borderline...

My first glimpses of Minnesota made me think of Newfoundland. The plane came down through heavy raincloud, and by the time we emerged beneath it, we were hovering just above wet suburban rooftops and pointy green trees. At Minneapolis's grey airport, the people waiting to meet arriving passengers stood in dirty pastel padded jackets and nylon anoraks, with collapsing Cabbage Patch Doll faces and a cheerful shared pastiness I remembered from Newfie communities.

The same boisterous underclass crowds the public buses that take you, if you're mad, to Bloomington's Mall of America (the USA's biggest), or else the other way, on the $1, half-hour ride to downtown St. Paul, Minneapolis's so-called Twin City. Every time I take a bus people banter on the same two topics: sports teams (the Vikings vs. the Packers) and Clinton's indiscretions. Bob Dylan, who rides in limousines now but knows these people of old, said presciently in 1983: *"America is a divided nation right now. It doesn't know whether to follow the President or the Green Bay Packers"*. Plus ça change, as they say up in Canada.

But Newfoundland is poor and white; Minnesota, headquarters of many a Fortune 500 corporation, including 3M and Honeywell, is growing richer faster than most other states, and is 11th in per capita income; and while the state is 94% Caucasian, the Twin Cities are 12% black and include a significant Hmong community brought here by charitable churches in the early 1990s.

The two downtowns are separated by the Mississippi River, that *"strong brown god"*, as T.S. Eliot called it, which, upstate from here, begins its epic journey from the frozen north all the way to New Orleans. St. Paul is its northernmost port.

Something else divides the Twin Cities, St. Paul claiming to be *"the last city of the East"* and Minneapolis *"first city of the West"*, or at any rate, the Mid-West.

It seems true. Minneapolis, far larger, blasts up at the big sky with ultramodern architecture clustered like gargantuan shining organ-pipes, rising to overlook the beginning of that prairie flatness, that heartland wilderness to the west.

Downtown St. Paul looks like a compressed chunk of Manhattan, with a core of old stone buildings in big pre-war blocks as wide as they are tall, like the splendidly-named and beautifully-finished Bockstruck's, set on flinty streets with iron lamposts, with smart, dark bars and the elegant ghost of F. Scott Fitzgerald, who was not only born and raised here but moved back again to write *"This Side of Paradise"*.

The two do fuse, though. Uptown St.Paul is west of the Mississippi, its Grand Avenue houses dithering between Eastern and mid-Western styles, while Minneapolis includes the unprairie-like Dinkytown, to walk through which now is like having a nightmare that it's the 1970s again. Litter-blown streets where sordid shops you wouldn't want to go in peter out into a bleakness of suburban villas turned over to frat houses. The students are mostly about 19, mostly already grossly overweight and with eyes as dead as doornails. You look in vain for anywhere you'd want to have a drink or something to eat. The bar I find is like some bad South London pub taken over by the Bodysnatchers. The 10 O'Clock Scholar is long gone but the Purple Onion remains. It is indistinguishable from a Howard Johnson's coffee-shop. The ghost of Bob Dylan is not here.

My/youth was spent wildly among the snowy hills an'/sky blue lakes, willow fields an abandoned open/pit mines. . .

Hibbing, of course, is the least populous and the most important place in Dylan's Minnesota past. I hired a car for next to nothing and set off from St.Paul up the old Highway 65 to see it. It was November, and snowy. Flat, frozen fields, Dutch-roof barns, loblolly pines and stripped silver birch trees, Lutheran churches, dilapidated fencing, pick-up trucks more frequent than cars. The timeless scenery of telegraph poles and roadside mailboxes, the aluminium-grey road stretching out flat ahead; and signs for Jumbo Leeches and Flathead Worms, and snowmobiles for sale. The sky was bright blue, a beautiful day. Where I stopped to breathe the air outside, a dead deer, bony but immaculate, lay on its side in the snowy grass six yards from the road.

I stopped at Rob's chalet-style place for coffee. The five men in there, all wearing check shirts or overhauls, were drinking bourbon & soda in ice-filled glasses, with beer chasers. As if on cue their conversation was immediately about hunting. *"I swear, I lit a cigarette and he's still lookin' at me. It's like he's sayin' I know you ain't got a licence. . ."* A notice proclaimed *"MEAT RAFFLE every Saturday"*.

A hundred miles north of St.Paul I passed through McGrath, pop. 62, with its Catholic Church, Calvary Presbyterian Church and Pliny Graveyard. Then trailer-homes and more white clapboard than before, more and more picturesque old barns, grain-elevators like cocktail-shakers. On the radio they were announcing a bear-dressing contest.

The closer I came to the Iron Range towns, the narrower and emptier the road grew, and the taller the trees, and the more the banks of snow pressed in from the verges. The whole hushed place turned into Winter Wonderland, and cocooned inside it, Hibbing shone and twinkled like the set for the 'Perry Como Christmas Special'.

It would have been in Canada but for a mistake on an historic map. Deep in snow but easy to move around, it epitomises pleasant, old-fashioned small-town life. It's not such a small town, either. At 186 square miles, its grid of leafy, spacious streets is the state's largest by area. The people are exceptionally equable, and make you welcome. It almost makes you wonder why Bob Dylan ever left.

He lived here from the age of six. To begin with, he slept on the floor in Grandma Florence's house; later, this elder son of Abraham Zimmerman the hardware-store owner sometimes went debt-collecting with him in the poorer parts of town. In the front room at 2425, 7th Avenue East, his boyhood home, Bob practised in his first and nameless beat group, survived his Bar Mitzvah party and stared out of the window dreaming of escape. It was a mere couple of blocks' walk to Hibbing High School.

And what a school. You'd never know it from anything Dylan's let slip, but iron ore built Hibbing a school of palatial grandeur that cost four million dollars in 1920-23, with a sanitised medieval castle exterior in brick and Indiana limestone, hand-moulded ceilings, a 75-foot-long oil painting in the library, marble steps with solid brass handrails and, in the 1825 seater auditorium, six Belgian crystal chandeliers now worth a quarter of a million each and a stage that can hold the Minnesota Symphony Orchestra.

In 1958, with his second group, the Golden Chords, Dylan stood hammerin' on Hibbing High School's 1922 Steinway Grand piano (breaking a pedal in the process) and shouting out rock'n'roll songs at the annual student concert . . . and got laughed at, up there on stage in an auditorium so lavish and ornate, and with such acoustic excellence, that it almost justifies Stephen Scobie's conceit that *"Every stage Bob Dylan has played on for the past thirty years has been, after Hibbing High School Auditorium, an anticlimax"*.

The hotel manager, Debra Jensen, rings her friend Larry Furlong, one of Bob's old classmates, and he readily agrees to show me around the school. Debby drives me over, and we meet Larry on the snowy steps outside the school.

Thin, nervous, likeable, a little morose, Larry neither exaggerates nor underplays his Dylan connections. We walk around inside, and I'm gasping at the sheer size of it all. Imagine how it was when you were new there. We stand in the huge library and Debby tells me that she still has nightmares about being little and finding her way around it. One class or activity, she says, would be in the basement and the next on the 4th floor, and they were allowed three minutes to get there. *"Gym class to choir was the killer"*, says Debby's brother Denny, who has joined us. He's acting as stage manager for the school production that's in rehearsal. I'm lucky, because this means everything's open and functioning backstage – and he asks if I'd like to see That Piano.

So we go to one side at the back of the stage, and Denny unlocks this long low cupboard door and we roll out that big black Steinway sideways, until it's right there, throbbing with history, in front of me. And then another gesture of generosity: I'm allowed to play it for a minute. Some sort of bluesy riff seems called for. It sounds great. I've never encountered so rich and deep a tone: it is a double thrill to play it. There I am, forty-odd years on, standing on that huge

15

stage, looking out into that impossibly glamorous auditorium, hearing that Steinway tone. Fantastic.

Larry offers me a guided tour of town, so we leave the others and the school, whose Principal, these days, is the aptly named Mr. Muster. Larry sits in the passenger seat and says *"turn left here, now first right. OK, see that building, that's where Abe's hardware store was"*, and so on. You can't beat this kind of helpfulness, it's extraordinary and precious.

A train line cuts the ground/showin' where the fathers an' mothers/of me an' my friends had picked/up an' moved from/north Hibbing/t'south Hibbing/old north Hibbing . . . I deserted/already dead/with its old stone courthouse/decayin' in the wind. . .

Bobby often explored North Hibbing's ghost-town, where everyone lived before they moved them two miles south to dig out the ore they were sitting on. Larry guides me there, and the whole place is just snow-covered ground. I'd never know a town had been there – I can't even see any remnants any more. We walk toward the edge of the vast, vast hole far down below us, filled like a lake of iron-brown water, and beyond it the huge orange sun is dropping onto the snowy hills.

Hibbing's got schools, churches, grocery stores an' a jail . . . high school football games and a movie house... corner bars with polka bands . . . Hibbing's a good ol' town.

Dylan's mixed feelings about Hibbing are expressed perfectly in that one last line from *'My Life in a Stolen Moment'*, and he and it have had a difficult relationship ever since he left. In fact Minnesota altogether has a problem with Dylan. They resent his having left: still resent his rudeness of forty years ago. Minnesotans here tell he was difficult despite being shown much tolerance; they feel he bit the hand that nurtured him and/or denied his roots. Invoking the stroppy teenager, they're determinedly unimpressed by the great artist.

Thought I'd shaken the wonder and the phantoms of my youth/Rainy days on the Great Lakes, walkin' the hills of old Duluth. . .

In consequence, to the soul's delight and the professional eye's puzzlement, there is no exploitation of Dylan's incandescent name by the Heritage Industry. Look at how poor Liverpool exploits Beatledom: it's one of the city's biggest revenue sources. Yet Dylan is conspicuously absent from Minnesota tourism bumph. Even Hibbing's 1991 coffee table puffery *"On The Move Since 1893"* manages only this:

"Some contemporary well-known natives include Rudy Perpich; Kevin McHale; Jeno Paulucci, founder of Jeno's Pizza; Bob Dylan, folk musician, songwriter; Roger Maris and Vincent Bugliosi, Charles Manson Trial prosecutor".

35 miles away, the Judy Garland Museum welcomes you to the Garland Birthplace Historic Home, Grand Rapids (*"It's a swell state, Minnesota . . . We lived in a white house with a garden. It's a beautiful, beautiful town"*, quoth Judy on the brochure in my Minnesota press-pack); in Duluth, Dylan's birthplace home is disregarded; in Hibbing, the many pilgrims who come to the 7th Avenue house must simply decide whether to ring the bell and disturb the present owner or not.

I spent an hour there, by appointment (courtesy of Debby again), attuning to Bob's adolescent ghost inside those walls, and staring out at cold-storage suburbia as he must so often have done. The easy-going owner, Greg French, will soon tire of this sort of thing, just as High School staff will tire of letting people like me stand on their stage. Quite rightly, Greg restricts visitors to the living-room. You can't go poking around in Bob's old bedroom any more. It's another adolescent's now.

When the Zimmerman house went on sale in 1989, the realtor had enquiries from all over the Dylan-fan world, and thought he'd make his fortune. This came to nothing, and Greg paid $45,000 for the flat-roofed, two-storey, 1940s property (in *"Mediterranean Moderne"* style) not because it was Dylan's but because it was the best bargain in the neighbourhood at the time.

Once, a state tourism "PR specialist" called, to ask Greg if he'd consider doing B&B. Er, that's it. Meanwhile there's nothing but a downtown bar-cafe called Zimmy's to cater to the swell of Dylan-visitors, a swell that cannot but rise.

This extraordinary non-exploitation might seem bizarrely nose-and-face syndrome: a collective sulking at least as immature as the Dylan who said *"You're boring, I'm off"* four decades ago.

This communal hurt is quite misplaced. Those who actually knew him in the past – ex-classmates like Larry and Margaret Toivola (who let me look through her now-priceless copy of that 1959 High School Yearbook) – feel neither spurned nor uncomprehending of Dylan's quantum-leap away. More importantly, Dylan has, as we know, written beautifully in poetry and song about these places and their wintry magic. In interviews too, he has often re-affirmed his pride in his formative Iron Range, North Country roots:

"I'm that color. I speak that way . . . My brains and feelings have come from there . . . The earth there is unusual, filled with ore . . . There's a magnetic attraction there: maybe thousands of years ago some planet bumped into the land there. There is a great spiritual quality throughout the mid-West. Very subtle, very strong, and that is where I grew up".

Yet for the present, before Heritage strikes, it's bliss to explore these places without encountering a Bob Dylan Experience.

Pleasingly, Hibbing was also the birthplace of Greyhound Buses, and to take the road from there to Duluth, as I did after an all-too-brief two days in Hibbing, was to follow their earliest route. By chance, halfway between the two, I stopped at the Wilbert Cafe, built in 1922 and the first stopping-off point there ever was for Greyhound buses. Italianburger and fries, $3.95. It was one of the worst meals I've eaten in my life, anywhere in the world.

Duluth is a scruffy, tough little city full of whiskery geezers hitting the precipitous streets that tumble down to the industrial waterfront where the wind comes off the water. Armed with Dave Engel's excellent book *"Dylan In Minnesota: Just Like Bob Zimmerman's Blues"*, I drove up and down the grid of shabby roads, looking for, and finding almost all of, the apartments and houses through which the Zimmerman family passed in stages when they lived here, becoming Americans and struggling to chase the Dream. A tough place to start.

And for Bob too. I find the dour, forbidding Nettleton elementary school where Bob shamed his father by having to be dragged the two blocks there kicking and screaming. The doors are locked. I peer through the dirty windows. It's so ordinary, so drab. The change when Bob moved to Hibbing High was some upgrade. There's no blue plaque on the wall here either. Yet for Abe, there was another school to compare these with. Dominating the heights of Duluth is the Victorian monstrosity that he attended as a child, Central High, with its ludicrous 300-foot tower – the whole building looking as if it's been built out of dogshit.

The lake is so huge it's like the sea, making Duluth feel like a seaport, with a constant wind, tough people, a slight sense of menace, or at least the sense that you better have your wits about you on these colourless and poverty-soaked streets.

The ore from Hibbing leaves Duluth by boat to Chicago and points east. In the opposite direction came the immigrants from Russia, the Ukraine and, as Dylan's grandparents did, from Lithuania, via Liverpool, New Brunswick, Montreal and Michigan and along the Great Lake to Superior, across the bay from Duluth. You can see it all from the windows of the fast-deteriorating house the Zimmermans lived in when Bob was a baby. The alley down the side is strewn with foul rubbish, including big lumps of raw meat that the rats haven't eaten yet.

Twilight on the frozen lake/North wind about to break/On footprints in the snow /Silence down below.

I drove back down from Duluth to St.Paul, deliberately taking Highway 61: a road now so displaced by Interstate 35 that for most of its Minnesota stretch these days it's merely a County Road. It's a delight to drive down, therefore: it runs through real, scruffy towns, not strip cities, and now that it's so underused except for local farmers' pick-ups, the constant eyesore of billboards has vanished. It runs through dolorous, fog-coloured forest, past little lakes with frozen edges and circles of ice around tiny islands of cliff and tree in the water, with small wooden jetties and tied-up boats: Coffee Lake, Moose Lake, Sand Lake. There are 10,000 of these frozen lakes in Minnesota.

Sometimes farmland asserts itself for a while and there are horses and big old barns and log-piles; more often the road is a dark, forlorn corridor with olive-green sides. It's always a surprise to find a clearing glimpsed beyond the trees. Inappropriately flimsy houses are camped from time to time along the road, their front-yard junk mixed up with their plastic decorative squirrels and fawns, lions and Santa Clauses. You have to dodge and weave and pay attention to keep a grip on 51 as its keeps getting entangled in interstates.

Across a pretty river lies Pine City, the least piney and largest place since Duluth. There's a whiff of the prairies here and the other side of town there it is: prairie landscape instead of the Great North Woods. Easy to imagine Bob riding this highway; you can still find on the radio, on the Oldies Stations, the very music he would have had blasting out when he came down for weekends in the big city.

Back in St.Paul, smart people hurry out of the street's icy wind into the warm Manhattan glamour of the Saint Paul Hotel, smiling as they adjust their overcoat collars. They're excited by winter: by its imminent, welcome drama. These people are proud that they endure this climate. Its heartland ruggedness, they like to think, puts its iron in their souls. *I'm used to four seasons/California's got but one.*

Published in *ISIS* issue #89, March, 2000

Hibbing High School Latin Club 1957 – Bobby Zimmerman front row, third from left

Launching the Search for What's Really Real:
Reflections on Young Dylan's Aesthetics and the Liner Notes for *"Joan Baez in Concert, Part 2"*

James Dunlap

In Bob Dylan's prose writings about his youth, he has repeatedly said that he thought of himself as somehow being different. Some have felt that Dylan's Jewish background and membership in the mercantile middle class made him a distinct minority in the small community of Hibbing, Minnesota, which consisted largely of blue-collar mine workers. An estrangement from his own family's middle-class values may, however, have been the largest difference he felt, causing him to change his name and invent himself anew.

It is obvious that Dylan was attracted to those in Hibbing who suffered or had less than he did. Bob's closest friend in high school, John Bucklen, came from a family that was dirt-poor. John's father, unemployed, had lost a leg in a railway accident, and his mother supported the family through her work as a seamstress. Bob's high school girlfriend, Echo Helstrom, was also unburdened by material things, coming from the "wrong side" of the tracks. She lived in a rustic shack near the cemetery, at the outskirts of town. Finally, Dylan's friend from Jewish summer camp, Larry Kegan, was paralyzed from the neck down from a swimming accident when Bob was sixteen. Dylan's mother had no doubt that Larry's sudden misfortune had a dramatic effect on Bob's outlook towards life.[1]

Bob may have first learned to face harsh reality from witnessing his father's hardships. At the outbreak of World War II, Abe Zimmerman was employed in Duluth by Standard Oil where he had worked his way up from a messenger to a supervisor. Athletic, with a young family and a valuable job that exempted him from wartime service, Abe led an active and meaningful life. However, the Zimmermans' lives dramatically changed after the war. In 1946, when Bobby was five, Abe contracted polio, which left him bedridden for much of the year. While he survived, Abraham Zimmerman emerged handicapped with a limp and diminished mobility. Without a job any longer at Standard Oil, the Zimmermans moved 70 miles to the northwest to be closer to Beatty's family, the Edelsteins. While Bob's family did well in Hibbing, they undoubtedly settled for less than they might have expected before Abe got sick, given his earlier rapid rise.

Perhaps as a result of his friends' and family's experiences, Dylan's different outlook on life was characterized by something that he called *"ugliness"*. He identified this ugliness vaguely with the harsh truths and raw emotions that are often suppressed by the polite society in which most people live. Like James Dean in *"Rebel Without a Cause"* (as well as in *"East of Eden"* and *"Giant"*), Dylan felt that much of the social conformity that appeared to represent normal behaviour was, in fact, a cover-up or disguise. Social reality, Dylan believed, is often not what appears on the surface. There may be something darker beneath.

Dylan wanted to overcome the false and boring *"prettiness"* that he seemed to equate with simplistic, small-town domestic values. For example, in *'Note to the Errand Boy as a Young Army Deserter'* from his novel *"Tarantula"*, Dylan asks a series of questions. He replies to each satirically with the answer, in effect, *"You don't want to know"*. You may get an answer that you'd rather not hear: *"[W]onder why granpa just sits there & watches yogi bear? Wonder why he just sits there & don't laugh? think about it kid, but don't ask your mother . . . wonder why frankie shot johnny? Go ahead, wonder, but don't ask your neighbor . . . wonder why youre always wearing your brother's clothes? Think about it kid, but don't ask your father"*.

Despite the cruelty of such pointed barbs, Dylan believed that a person's acknowledgment of the underlying "ugliness" in society was a necessary first step in overcoming hypocrisy. In his songs, as in the *"Tarantula"* excerpt, Dylan consistently asked tough questions, intending to force people to confront the contradictions in their lives. In some songs, he would ask such questions for idealistic political purposes, such as in *'Blowin' In The Wind'* (e.g., *"How many times must a man turn his head,/Pretending he just doesn't see?"*). He would also force the subjects of his songs to face tough questions by being brutally honest, such as in *'Positively Fourth Street'* (*"[Y]ou know . . . /You'd rather see me paralyzed/Why don't you come out just once/And scream it?"*) and, most famously, by ruthlessly questioning a poor little rich girl who's lost all she once had in *'Like A Rolling Stone'* (*"How does it FEEL . . . to be on your own?"*).

* * *

In the liner notes that Dylan wrote to *"Joan Baez In Concert, Part 2"* (1963), Bob made important confessions about how he viewed himself growing up in Hibbing. He described being drawn close to the railroad tracks as a young boy. Dylan explained that the railroad lines weren't pretty, but they had a certain harsh reality to them, *"filled with stink an' soot an' dust"*. In a kind of epiphany, Dylan decided he would henceforth seek out a reality that would emphasize and embody raw and primitive emotional values.

Most of the liner notes to Joan's album contrast Bob's commitment to "ugliness" with Joan's "pretty" voice (and, in a prescient manner, they also contrast his carelessness with her social compassion). In doing so, Dylan recalled how he developed his unusual aesthetic, based upon uncultivated, direct sensations. He explained that, since he was young, *"I'd judge beauty with these rules/An' accept it only 'f it was ugly . . . /For it's only then I'd understand/An' say 'yeah this's real'"*:

21

The only beauty's ugly, man
The crackin' shakin' breakin' sounds 're
The only beauty I understand . . .
Ain't no voice but an ugly voice
A the rest I don' give a damn
'F I can't feel it with my hand
Then don' wish me t' understand . . .

In the same liner notes, Dylan said that Hank Williams was his first idol. Bob gave his reasons: *"For he sang about the railroad lines/An' the iron bars an' rattlin' wheels/Left no doubt that they were real"*. In the 1940s, Williams' popularity arose, in part, because he sang directly about blue-collar sorrows and aspirations in a new way. Hank's songs were especially noted for the taboo subjects that they explored, like divorce, adultery and alcohol. He wasn't afraid to expose the "ugliness" that life often brought. Instead, he recognized that a special type of pride might underlie the pain and frustration in the lives of the simple patrons of a humble juke joint. The sound of Williams' voice was also raw, matching his lyrics.

Raw emotions and what's "really real" did not, however, always have to be painful. For instance, besides mournful ballads (*'I'm So Lonesome I Could Cry'*, *'Your Cheatin' Heart'*), Hank Williams wrote party songs for a Saturday night (*'Hey Good Lookin'*, *'Jambalaya (On The Bayou)'*). These songs embodied life's simple pleasures and freely expressed them. In *'Spanish Harlem Incident'*, Dylan tellingly used the image of a wildly dancing gypsy girl to express his admiration, similarly, for her ability to freely express herself. In closing the song, Dylan posed a question with familiar phrasing. He's looking for genuine raw emotions, and so he asks the young gypsy girl: *"I got to know, babe, will I be touching you/So I can tell if I'm really real"*.

* * *

In the liner notes for Joan's album, Dylan recalled lying down on the grass as a powerful and noisy train approached and then passed. In a mixture of excitement and fear, he pulled a large patch of grass from the earth. In an unusual confession, Dylan then described how, as a lonely little boy looking at the dead roots of overturned sod, he tried not to be bothered by the fact that he had caused such needless destruction: *"It's then that my eyes'd turn/Back t'my hands with stains a green/That lined my palms like blood that tells/I'd taken an not given in return"*.

Elsewhere in the liner notes, Bob describes an incident involving Joan from the early 1950s when she was living with her family in Baghdad. (Joan's father was working in Iraq for UNESCO, teaching and helping to establish a physics laboratory.) Joan tried to save a dog from slaughter. Implicitly, Dylan contrasts Joan's inherent goodness in trying to save an animal with his own careless acts in having *"taken and not given in return"*.

When he confessed, in the fall of 1963, to having violated the sanctity of nature's green carpet when he was a boy, Dylan appears to have been thinking of Walt Whitman's 19th century epic poem *'Leaves of Grass'*. It would be hard to imagine growing up in the 1950s and early '60s with an interest in the avant-garde, as Dylan had, and escaping the ubiquitous Whitman. As Dylan reached maturity in the late 1950s, Whitman's reputation was enjoying a renaissance, particularly among non-academics. The branches of much of post-World War II poetry in the U.S., including William Carlos Williams and Allen Ginsberg, could trace their roots to Whitman. His influence in literature resulted specifically from his innovations in the use of an extended poetic line (adopted by the Beats), his wide use of lists to compile multiple layers of rich images (also adopted by the Beats) and his distinctive colloquial American voice that he used simultaneously to celebrate himself, the earth and all of mankind. Over the years, Whitman's voice had also come to be associated with pacifism and sexual openness, important themes of the post-war generation. Among the leading members of the Beat Generation, Whitman was also admired as a dissenter who represented freedom.

Whitman's poem *'Leaves of Grass'* begins with a lengthy discourse on the beauty and meaning of a few blades of grass, which, as in Dylan's liner notes, includes an image of a child with a handful of sod. Somewhat improbably, Whitman ponders the sod and finds in it an example of equanimity in the way that the grass deals with people of different races. Whitman wrote:

> *A child said, What is the grass? Fetching it to me with full hands;*
> *How could I answer the child? . . . I do not know what it is any more than he.*
> *I guess it must be the flag of my disposition, out of hopeful green stuff woven.*
> *. . .*
> *And it means, Sprouting alike in broad zones and narrow zones,*
> *Growing among black folks as among white,*
> *. . . I give them the same, I receive them the same.*

Whitman thus gives a voice to the blades of grass, and they use that voice to say, in effect, that they are colour-blind: whether one is black or white makes no difference to the grass. Consciously or not, Dylan thus alludes to lines from Whitman's poem that put forth the ideal of equal treatment of the races. This would be particularly appropriate for Dylan to do in liner notes written for an album by Joan Baez. Baez, after all, was a leading pacifist and civil rights activist.

It is not hard to imagine that Dylan knew the lines he alludes to from *'Leaves of Grass'*. While the Whitman poem is dense and book-length, the specific lines from which Dylan draws occur at the very beginning of the poem. Drawn from the poem's title, the lines are also central to its meaning. Familiarity with those lines would not, therefore, necessarily presuppose a thorough and improbable knowledge of all of Whitman's work. By the time Dylan wrote the liner notes for Joan's album, he would have at least been familiar with Whitman through Jack Kerouac's poetry collection, *"Mexico City Blues"*, which his friend from Minneapolis, Dave Whitaker, had recommended.[2] Kerouac's poem refers to

Whitman's *'Leaves of Grass'* in the 168th Chorus, which reads: *"Whitman examined grass/and concluded/It to the be genesis/& juice, of pretty girls./"Hair of Graves," footsteps/Of Lost Children,/Forgotten park meadows,/–Looking over your shoulder/At the beautiful maidens–"*.

In addition to their equal treatment of races, Whitman described blades of grass growing from the bodies of young men that might be buried beneath them. Whitman's sentiment thus anticipated the spirit of the times almost a century after his poem was written: his was not unlike the sentiment of the then-popular folk song, written by Pete Seeger, *'Where Have All the Flowers Gone?'* (*"Where have all the soldiers gone?/They've gone to graveyards ev'ry one/ . . . Where have all the graveyards gone?/They're covered with flowers ev'ry one"*).[3]

Dylan apparently knows of Whitman and what he stood for. He also admires the good works of Joan Baez and sees them in relation to Whitman's generous sentiments of universal brotherhood. Joan, Walt Whitman and even leaves of grass give themselves equally to all, while Dylan describes himself, by way of contrast, as being guilty from having *"taken and not given in return"*.

* * *

In his liner notes for Joan Baez, Dylan acknowledged at the outset that his values did not match her high ethical standards or those of Walt Whitman. But that didn't seem to matter to him because, Dylan says, he's coming from a different place. He is like no one else that he knows.

Following his confession of past destructiveness, Dylan concludes his story about the grass and the train by likening himself to a person uniquely born with demonic visions:

> *An' I asked myself t' be my friend*
> *An' I walked my road like a frightened fox*
> *An' <u>I sung my song like a demon child</u>*
> *With a kick an' a curse*
> <u>*From inside my mother's womb*</u>

As in the case of Dylan's description of his tearing up grass, his self-portrayal as a demon child singing and cursing his mother may also have come from a poem. In *'Benediction'*, the French poet Charles Baudelaire wrote that when, *"[t]he Poet appears among us in this tired world,/His outraged mother, racked by blasphemies,/Clenches her fists to God"* and threatens to destroy the Poet.

Baudelaire explained that the Poet sees things differently from others. For that reason alone, the Poet is dangerous. And, because he is singled out from others on account of his unique visions, the Poet is doomed to lead a difficult life. The Poet is cursed, and he curses the world in return. Linked in an unholy matrimony with the devil, the Poet explores good and evil, drawn to visions of ugliness and danger largely as an escape from his boredom. In contrast to Dylan's depiction of the goodness of Joan Baez, Baudelaire's Poet (like Dylan himself) sees only falseness and boredom (or *"ennui"*) in the merely "pretty" and good.

Images linking the devil to the Poet (as well as to the readers of his poems) also inform the very first poem in Baudelaire's collection, *"The Flowers of Evil"*. In *'To the Reader'*, Baudelaire wrote of both the Poet and the readers who are drawn to him:

> *Who but the Devil pulls our waking-strings!*
> *Abominations lure us to their side;*
> *Each day we take another step to hell,*
> *Descending through the stench, unhorrified.*
>
> . . .
>
> *There's one supremely hideous and impure!*
>
> . . .
>
> *I mean Ennui! . . .*
> *How well you know this fastidious monster, reader,*
> *–Hypocrite reader, you!–my double! my brother!*

It is clear that Dylan was familiar with Baudelaire and French Symbolist poetry. One of Bob's first friends and mentors in Greenwich Village, Dave Van Ronk, described one of the most well-thumbed books in Dylan's collection, clearly identifiable as Angel Flores (ed.), *"An Anthology of French Poetry from Nerval to Valery in English Translation"* (*Doubleday Anchor*, 1958).[4] That anthology contained large selections from Baudelaire. The translations above were taken from it.

Baudelaire's relevance to avant-garde or left-wing movements in the late 1950s and early 1960s, like Whitman's, was widely recognized. In 1963, Jonas Mekas, the organizer of New York's radical Film-Makers' Cooperative, made an explicit connection between the avant-garde of his day and the French Symbolist poet. In his regular movie column for *The Village Voice*, Mekas described the bizarre sexual extravaganzas of then-current underground films. He called the notorious combination of amateur social realism and explicit sexual images *"Baudelairean Cinema"*:

"A world of flowers of evil, of illuminations, of torn and tortured flesh, a poetry which is at once beautiful and terrible, good and evil, delicate and dirty". [5]

In part, the association of Baudelaire with the avant-garde was on account of their joint identification with inappropriate thoughts, censorship and obscenity trials. Avant-garde writers were "in revolt" against conventional values. Government bans and customs seizures affected the distribution of several works that had been recommended to Bob by friends at college and that later influenced him, including Allen Ginsberg's *"Howl"* (obscenity trial successfully defended in 1957) and Henry Miller's *"Tropic of Cancer"* (ban of 1934 novel, lifted in 1961). Baudelaire preceded them all, as portions of his poetry collection were found in violation of public morality in 1857. In addition to a hefty fine, several of his poems were excised from subsequent editions of his collection, *"The Flowers of Evil"*.

Dylan, like Baudelaire, recognized that his thoughts, even as a child, were seditious, so he walked *"like a frightened fox"* and kept to himself. Later, in *'It's All Right Ma (I'm Only Bleeding)'* (September 1964), he would write, *"[I]f my thought-dreams could be seen/They'd probably put my head in a guillotine".*

* * *

Dylan would begin his career by pursing his visions of what he felt was "ugly" and real. As a 22-year-old looking back on his boyhood, he already saw how his ideals had taken shape. He compared and contrasted those ideals with those represented by the 19th century poets Whitman and Baudelaire. Both poets stood outside society, but they clearly pointed in different directions. Whitman, like Joan Baez, was an optimist and a dedicated reformer using self-publicity to affect progressive change, striving to move the state of mankind ever upward. Baudelaire, the stealthy decadent, instead probed the depths of men's souls (mostly his own) so as to expose complex psychological and often forbidden emotional states.

At times, Dylan seemed to embrace Whitman's perspective and that of Walt Whitman's mentor and inspiration, the transcendentalist Ralph Waldo Emerson. In songs like *'Blowin' In The Wind'* and *'The Times They Are A-Changin'"*, Dylan assumed a god's-eye perspective and prophesied the victory of equality and justice as though they were principles of nature and its inevitable evolution. In other songs, however, Dylan would play the role of the subversive gadfly, exposing, like Baudelaire, the hidden motives and dark thoughts of others. Even in progressive songs like *'With God On Our Side'*, Dylan would stand outside the confines of an organized political movement and explain that modern man may be no better than his forbears.

Dylan's rebelliousness, independence and attraction to the "ugly" and the forbidden had defined his departure from both Hibbing and, later, the so-called *"Folk Protest Movement"* associated with Joan Baez and Pete Seeger. However, by thereafter abandoning conventional rules altogether and giving limitless reign to his creative freedom, Dylan soon found himself trapped by endless circles of dangerous thoughts and images, leading to bluesy songs of excess such as *'Desolation Row'*, *'Stuck Inside Of Mobile With The Memphis Blues Again'* and *'Just Like Tom Thumb's Blues'*.

Dylan, like Baudelaire, would become acutely conscious of the oscillation between extremes, between seeking transcendence and allowing himself to fall woefully short. In the coming years, Dylan's song lyrics and introspective writings would reveal that he felt himself pushed and pulled from both above and below. The different directions are well represented by Walt Whitman and Charles Baudelaire, the two poets whose shadows lurk behind Bob Dylan's liner notes for *"Joan Baez In Concert Part 2"*.

[1] *'Robert Shelton Minnesota Transcripts Interview with Abe and Beatty Zimmerman'*, in Derek Barker, ed., *"Isis: A Bob Dylan Anthology"* Helter Skelter, 2001, 20.

[2] Dylan's early reading, including Kerouac's *'Mexico City Blues'* is disclosed in Clinton Heylin, *"Dylan: Behind the Shades Revisited" Viking*, 2000, 49.

[3] *'Where Have All the Flowers Gone'*, written by Pete Seeger in the early 1950s, was in fact inspired by a passage from Mikhail Sholokhov's novel *"And Quiet Flows the Don"*, with additional verses by Joe Hickerson. Hickerson's additional verses were required to complete the circle, from missing girls (via missing soldiers and graveyards) back to flowers and girls once again.

[4] Van Ronk's observation of Dylan's bookshelf is in both *"Bob Dylan: An Intimate Biography"*. *Grosset & Dunlap*, 1971 by Anthony Scaduto at 99-100 and Robert Shelton's *"No Direction Home: The Life and Music of Bob Dylan"*. *New English Library*, 1986, at 107. In Scaduto, Van Ronk is quoted as saying there was *"a volume of French poets from Nerval almost to the present. I think it ended at Apollinaire, and it included Rimbaud, and it was all well-thumbed with passages underlined and notes in the margins"*.

[5] Jonas Mekas' article on Baudelairean cinema is from *The Village Voice*, May 2, 1963, which is just prior to Dylan's first visit with Joan Baez at her California home. The liner notes were probably written later, in a September 1963 visit with Joan.

Published in *ISIS* issue #114, May 2004

Bob Dylan 1962

Stories in the Press

With numerous gold records to his credit, Dylan's most popular recordings include, *'Knockin' On Heavens Door'*, *'Like A Rolling Stone'*, *'The Times They Are A-Changing'*(sic), *'It Ain't Me Babe'*, *"Sgt. Pepper"*, *"Beggar's Banquet"* and *"Music From Big Pink"*.

The above is an extract from a press release published in the *Arizona Republic* announcing Bob Dylan's show at the University of Mississippi. When challenged re the accuracy of the above statement, Jan Robertson, director of the University News Department is quoted as saying: *"I'm not a Dylan fan. It looked accurate to me"*.

Taken from issue #34 of *ISIS* December 1990
Originally published in The *Arizona Republic* October 24, 1990

Nils Lofgren

Nils Lofgren: "I got an urgent call one day in 1985 – *'Bob needs to speak to you immediately!'* He was about to do a George Gershwin benefit so I figured, *'Great, he wants me to play with him'*. I went out and bought all the Gershwin records and tried to figure out, *'Now, which of these tunes might Bob do?'* Finally, I get hold of Bob on the phone and he says, *'Er, Nils, y'know that acoustic guitar you played with Bruce on the 'Fire' video? Man, that sounded great. Where can I get a guitar like that?'* All he wanted was to borrow my guitar; they flew someone down, collected it, and returned it the next week . . ."

The Wicked Messenger #2115 printed in issue #38 of *ISIS* August 1991
Originally published in *Vox*

Dylan's DNA

"Tangled up in Bob": A lengthy and interesting look at the *"strange and tender madness that is Dylanology"*. In one of the more frightening paragraphs, Dylan collector Mitch Blank recalls the day a fellow collector phoned him up to say that he had several of Dylan's cigarette butts!

Blank: *"What do I want Dylan's cigarette butts for?"* I asked this degenerate, and he said, *"Don't you see? Dylan's DNA is on those butts. Sometime in the future we'll be able to clone a whole new Bob Dylan. The ultimate collectible"*. I told him he was disgusting. You know, even for me, there's a limit.

Printed in issue #99 of *ISIS* November 2001
Originally published in *Rolling Stone* magazine

A Couple more Dylan Stories

Joe Henry was a member of the band in the Dharma and Greg episode with Dylan. He had been asked to do it by T-Bone Burnett, who put the band together. The musicians were all waiting on the set. *"Bob just kind of appeared. I don't think anyone saw him come in. He was shy but charming. The producer comes over and says, 'There's a little make-up room upstairs, if anyone wants make-up'. Bob turns to me and says, 'Well, I know you want to go get made up, so we should go together?' So there's this tiny room, two chairs, me and Bob sitting there with little bibs on. He says to the make-up woman, 'Can you make me a moustache?' She's like, 'I'm sorry?' Bob says, 'Can you make me a moustache?' So she starts scurrying around and matching his hair colour and makes this beautiful, theatrical fake moustache. Bob turns to me, 'Do you think this should be smaller?' So I say, 'I think he wants a thin, pencil moustache'. Bob says, 'Yeah, with a space in the middle'. So she makes a little Vincent Price moustache. 'What do you think of that, Joe?' 'I think it looks great'. And then he shrugs and says to the woman, 'I guess you should just take it off'"*.

It was only later that Henry realised that Dylan was trying out what became his new look but that's not the end of it. Sometime later, he ran into Jakob Dylan and told him about the incident in the TV studio. Henry: *"Jakob told me, 'At this point, my dad's lot in life is, he goes round and gives people Bob Dylan stories. Now you have one'"*.

The Wicked Messenger #5332, published in issue #111 of *ISIS* November 2003

Professor Christopher Ricks considers all of Dylan's shows to have a certain sadness because Dylan is the one person who has to be there, and the one person who can't go to a Bob Dylan show. *"It's sad"*, he says, *"In the way it's sad that Jane Austen couldn't read a Jane Austen novel"*. If there's one thing about Dylan that he actually isn't keen on it's his Clarke Gable moustache; *"I just don't think it looks good. Do you?"* He admits that he considered getting up a petition to send to Dylan that read: *"Mr. Dylan, please remove the stipple from your upper lip"*. *"I didn't send it"*, he admits, *"because my students said that it might hurt Dylan's feelings. But 'lip' and 'stipple' – I quite liked that"*.

Published in issue #119 of *ISIS* March 2005

In Dublin's Fair City

According to the *New Musical Express* this week, when Dylan threw his arms around Carole King after *'Real Real Gone'*, at the end of the final European show in Dublin, he did it so hard that she fell into the front of stage pit and broke her arm.

The Wicked Messenger #3112 Published in issue #61 of *ISIS* July 1991

someplace new, but he was often denied. For instance, in *'Poor Boy Blues'*, he addresses a train: *"Hey, stop you ol' train,/Let a poor boy ride./Cain't ya hear me cryin'?"* A similar song is *'Standing On The Highway'*, which tells about Bob's attempts to bum a ride: *"Nobody seem to know me,/Everybody pass me by"*. The song's lyrics conclude with what will become a familiar image of Dylan, alone, feeling like some kind of outcast: *"Well I'm standin' on the highway/Wonderin' where everybody went/ . . . Please mister, pick me up./I swear I ain't gonna kill nobody's kids"*.

Until he decided just who he would be, it was natural for Bob to feel as though he were standing outside alone, wanting to be recognized or given a ride to someplace new. As late as his novel *"Tarantula"* (substantially complete by 1966), he would depict himself writing to a fictional pen-pal: *"[I]f youre going to send me something, send me a key-I shall find the door to where it fits, if it takes me the rest of my life"*. Dylan often found himself seeking a key to that one special door, allowing him access to someplace that would make him complete. He needed to know where he belonged. For a time, Bob's girlfriend Suze Rotolo played that role for him.

* * *

For the first year of their relationship, Bob seemed to find with Suze many of the same things that he did with his friends from the Dinkytown district outside of the University of Minnesota. Like them, she was a nourishing source of his ideas. Often through her literary interests, Suze helped inform Dylan's thinking. He consumed her poetry books and those of her sister Carla, and Bob and Suze apparently read to each other aloud. Suze seemed to see his full potential as a writer, and she encouraged him to develop his talents. Dylan, in turn, absorbed Suze and her ideas to such an extent that, eventually, he felt that he could only see his true self in her. *"[A]h but Sue"*, Dylan once wrote, *"she knows me well/ perhaps too well/an' is above all/the true fortuneteller of my soul/I think perhaps the only one"*. (*"11 Outlined Epitaphs"*.)

As Dylan began to see himself more completely through Suze, he got increasingly possessive of her. She was not allowed to have her own life. *"There was a period when I was part of his possessions"*, said Suze. *"I don't think he wanted me to do anything separate from him. He wanted me to be completely one hundred percent a part of what he was"*.[3] In an important way, as his inspiration and a major source of his ideas, she was a part of who he was.

Bob's possessiveness was the principal cause of early strains in the couple's relationship (although Bob's infidelities, the pressure of his growing fame and their youth were also factors). One biographer who knew both Bob and Suze commented:

"Bob needed a woman who would be a mere reflection of himself. That is not an oversimplification nor is it exaggeration; it was felt by everyone who was close to Suze and Bob during the couple of years they bounced from one emotional crisis to another".[4]

Among Suze's interests that Bob absorbed was the poetry of Edna St. Vincent Millay.[5] Like Bob's early idols and the fictional heroes of his first songs, Millay lived life intensely. Bob and Suze were an impressionable couple just emerging from their teenage years, and Millay's general attitudes about relationships and how to think were undoubtedly influential on them. But Bob also appeared to learn something important about specific lyrical techniques from her poems. Millay's technique of the interior dialogue, in particular, would become a characteristic of Dylan's introspective song lyrics, as well.

Lessons from a Village Bohemian

Edna St. Vincent Millay was a dashing and unconventional personality, daring the authorities to expel her from Vassar College in the years before World War I. She moved to Greenwich Village in 1917, helping to create the legend of an American Bohemia there. Her lifestyle captivated the public. As a married woman, it was widely reported that her translation of the French poet Charles Baudelaire's scandalous poetry collection, *"The Flowers of Evil"*, was done with the help of her lover, a much younger man.

In her writings, Millay frequently defied the inevitability of death while, at the same time, being obsessed by it. The message of her most famous poem, *'First Fig'*, embodies Dylan's youthful credo. It could have been the epitaph for Bob's early fictional hero, Ramblin' Gamblin' Willie, in his song of that name. Millay's poem reads simply:

My candle burns at both ends;
It will not last the night;
But ah, my foes, and oh, my friends–
It gives a lovely light!

Millay's heightened awareness of death and its impact on how one lives, would have appealed to Suze. She was, after all, the daughter of a passionate humanitarian father who had died while still young. The poetry of Millay doubtless touched her on a personal level. Millay's world-view would affect any household of which Suze was a part.

As Millay aged, her poetry darkened with the unhappy knowledge of love's unpredictable changes, as well as the permanence of death. She tried to rejoice in love's impermanence, but she knew that death would win in the end. She simply and stubbornly refused to resign herself to it. In *'Moriturus'* Millay wrote: *"With* [Death's] *hand on my mouth/He shall drag me forth,/Shrieking to the south/And clutching at the north"*.

'Dirge Without Music' is another sonnet with a similar message. It begins: *"I am not resigned to the shutting away of loving hearts in the hard ground./So it is, and so it will be . . . but I am not resigned"*. In a surprising way, Millay's central themes share the same tragic awareness of life's brevity that attracted Boston's death-obsessed, black-clad motorcycle club members to Joan Baez's mournful Elizabethan ballads. That same awareness gave rise, as well, to the furtive

restlessness of key members of the Beat Generation as they abandoned tradition and security in exchange for the more intense experiences of a life on the road.

While maintaining the centrality of love as a theme, Millay's poems, like many of Dylan's introspective love songs, are noteworthy for their departure from traditional sentimentality. Her poems reflect the attitudes of a sexually active modern bohemian, debunking outdated concepts. For instance, the speaker of Millay's *'Well, I Have Lost You'* refuses to submit to the emotions generally associated with the break-up of a romantic relationship. The poet speculates that the relationship might have been prolonged, but only by force or, perhaps, by loving less or more strategically:

> *I was not one for keeping*
> *Rubbed in a cage a wing that would be free.*
> *If I had loved you less or played you slyly*
> *I might have held you for a summer more,*
> *But at the cost of words I value highly*
> *And no such summer as the one before.*

Much like Dylan in the title of his song, *'Don't Think Twice, It's All Right'*, Millay, in the end, coolly admits to having lost her lover fairly.

The poem *'Well, I Have Lost You'*, is also remarkable for its *"If . . . /then . . ."* structure. This structure, which Dylan followed in his song, *'Tomorrow Is A Long Time'*, amounts to an internalization of the narrative's drama. The poet (or singer-songwriter) poses a series of theoretical alternatives to consider. In this way, the narrator can conduct an interior dialogue with him – or herself.

Although it does not use the *"If . . . /then . . ."* structure, Millay's *'I, Being Born a Woman and Distressed'* also makes use of interior self-dialogue and includes important breakthroughs in technique. Reflecting its modernity, the poem contemplates the erotic impulse outside the context of love. In presenting a kind of debate on the issue, the poem uses a mixture of pronouns (*"I"s*, *"you"s* and *"we"s*). Its successive lines could easily be understood as representing the points of view of two different people in discussing their relationship. Thus, addressing an unspecified *"you"*, the woman begins by expressing her attraction to physical contact:

> *I, being born a woman and distressed*
> *By all the needs and notions of my kind,*
> *. . . feel a certain zest*
> *To bear your body's weight upon my breast.*

While acknowledging that intense feelings exist (speaking as *"I"*, a woman distressed), Millay concludes, however, with a steadfast refusal to submit to those feelings. The poet decides that she will no longer converse with her lover: *"I find this frenzy insufficient reason/For conversation when we meet again"*.

There are two aspects of Millay's poem that will later appear in the interior dialogue techniques that Dylan also employs with his lyrics. First, Millay has internalized the sonnet's drama by engaging in a discussion with two aspects of herself. One *"I"* longs for physical contact, but the other *"I"* resists it and prevails. Second, by the end of the poem, it becomes clear that the apparent addressee of some of these remarks is not actually present. Although it might seem so on the surface, the narrator's words are not actually part of a face-to-face encounter with a real person. In context, the phrase *"when next we meet again"* implies that such a meeting has yet to occur, and the other half of the *"we"* is absent. Thus, the woman's interior dialogue and use of pronouns has become quite complex: it is a way of both talking to different aspects of herself and imagining the presence of another person.

Through the use of interior dialogues, Millay was free to adopt many masks and assume varied stances. In the case of *'I, Being Born a Woman and Distressed'*, the dialogue represented a battle of her erotic impulses against her more objective brain. In another poem, *'Pity Me Not'*, Millay specifically recognizes that two aspects of herself were in conflict. She says that she knows love is no more than a *"great tide"* that strews *"fresh wreckage gathered in the gales"*. She also knows that love is not everlasting. In conclusion, she observes: *"Pity me that the heart is slow to learn/What the swift mind beholds at every turn"*.

Reflections of Both "You" and "Me"

In his song lyrics, Dylan, like Millay, frequently internalized his romantic dramas with interior dialogue. His first use of this technique appears in *'Tomorrow Is A Long Time'*, written in August of 1962. Fittingly, it's a song with origins in his relations with Suze. With Suze, Dylan had sought unity with someone else, to see himself reflected in her and she in him. However, during Suze's half-year absence from New York to study art in Italy, Bob's ability to *"know himself"* through her had obviously broken down. Not surprisingly, when alone, he was left to converse with no one but himself. With a model provided by Edna St. Vincent Millay, this technique of talking to himself in song is the most important aspect of *'Tomorrow Is A Long Time'*.

* * *

The first three verses of *'Tomorrow Is A Long Time'* firmly establish that Dylan's peace of mind requires the felt presence of his beloved. The singer then lectures to himself that if time moved more quickly (and *"tomorrow wasn't such a long time"*), then he wouldn't feel lonesome. At this point, both first person pronouns (*"I"s, "me"s* and *"my"s*) and second person pronouns (*"you"s*) appear in close proximity in the song's lyrics.

In order to interpret the song, the listener's first challenge is to identify and reconcile the use of multiple pronouns in a manner that will allow all the words and phrases to make sense together. One must reconcile, for instance, the use of pronouns in such phrases as, *"If I could hear her heart a-softly poundin'"* with their use in the immediately following phrase, *"Then lonesome would mean nothing to you at all"*. In *'Tomorrow Is A Long Time'*, the answer is, obviously, Dylan is talking to himself about her, his beloved. The singer has become both *"I"* and *"you"*. In a tender and assuring chorus, he says (being his reasonable, self-sufficient self) that if his true love were close beside him, then everything would be all right with *"you"* (his emotional, more dependent self). The song creates a fictional second self, Bob Dylan conversing with himself.

With his use of interior dialogue, Dylan would do more than merely talk to himself with his innovative use of pronouns. While simple and obvious on the surface, Dylan's new technique would also develop into a much more complex examination of a self-within-the-self with whom Dylan would communicate in order to achieve greater awareness of the problems he faces and his potential responses to them. Finally, he was learning to invent aspects of himself and project them outward as though they were separate persons.

As many have long suspected, some of Dylan's characters –from the Elephant Lady to, perhaps, Mr. Jones and Ramona and even his muse in her various guises –might be understood, at least on one level, as containing reflections of Dylan himself. Beginning with *'Tomorrow Is A Long Time'*, any analysis of Dylan's lyrics that include dialogue (and particularly mixed pronouns) may require a consideration of the underlying or hidden relationships of the songwriter to the song's narrative or potential messages. This leads to a search for the masks that Bob might be hiding behind. Dylan has acknowledged this aspect of his work. In a 1985 interview, he tried to explain it:

"Sometimes the 'you' in my songs is me talking to me. Other times I can be talking to somebody else. If I'm talking to me in a song, I'm not going to drop everything and say, alright, now I'm talking to you. It's up to you to figure out who's who. A lot of times it's 'you' talking to 'you'".[6]

When Dylan speaks of himself through different characters with multiple and different pronouns, his lyrical messages are often rendered deliberately vague and suggestive. This is part of his songs' appeal. Searches for "meaning" should not detract from the multiple levels on which his songs work. Nonetheless, there can be little doubt that Dylan frequently talks with different aspects of himself and, as in *'Tomorrow Is A Long Time'*, often does so without announcing his shifting points-of-view.

Of Fading Time and Echoes

'Tomorrow Is A Long Time' involves more than just innovative techniques involving shifting points-of-view. It also offers an important example of Dylan's earliest uses of literary sources for some of his recurring themes. In that song, the sources come from both Millay and Greek myth.

In the first verse of *'Tomorrow Is A Long Time'*, Dylan establishes that he needs some attribute of his beloved, like the sound of her heartbeat, to feel at home and make time pass more quickly. In addition to providing a model for the interior dialogue technique, Millay may have provided the source of Dylan's changing sense of time when apart from his beloved. In *'Time that is Pleased to Lengthen Out the Day'*, Millay explained that she was not fond of time when, apart from her lover, it made the days seem longer:

> *Time, that is pleased to lengthen out the day*
> *For grieving lovers parted or denied,*
> *And pleased to hurry the sweet hours away*
> *From such as lie enchanted side by side,*
> *Is not my kinsman.*

In Millay's poem, then, time is the enemy. As in her poem, the changing sense of passing time is a frequent theme in Dylan's love songs. In *'You're A Big Girl Now'*, Dylan sings, *"Time is a jet plane, it moves too fast/Oh, but what a shame if all we've shared can't last"*. The lyrics of *'If You See Her, Say Hello'* are similar: *"Sundown, yellow moon, I replay the past"*, and then he adds ironically, *"I know every scene by heart, they all went by so fast"*.

In *'Tomorrow Is A Long Time'*, after echoing Millay's sentiments about the passage of time, Dylan next confesses that, without his beloved, he has no sense of himself. He wastes away; he can't even see his *"reflection in the waters"*. In perhaps the most poignant two lines of the song, Dylan declares: *"I can't hear the echo of my footsteps/Or remember the sound of my own name"*. Bob may be metaphorically nothing without her, like a ghost that makes no sound as it walks. Dylan may be saying more literally that she would ordinarily follow alongside or behind him, much as the couple would shortly appear on the cover of *"The Freewheelin' Bob Dylan"*. In that photograph, Dylan's glance is self-effacing and downcast, hands-in-pocket with a James Dean-like shrug. Arm-and-arm with his more ebullient girlfriend, the two amble down the slushy streets of New York. In that case, the sound of Suze's footsteps would echo Bob's own, and he clearly would miss not hearing them.

The reference to an "echo" of footsteps, when viewed in the context of the immediately preceding image of the singer's reflection in water, together constitute an unmistakable allusion to the Greek myth of the beautiful youth, Narcissus. According to the myth, the nymph Echo fell in love with Narcissus, but he repulsed her. In grief, Echo pined away until she was nothing but a disembodied voice (hence, the meaning of the word "echo" that we use today). But the gods had their revenge on Narcissus. They cursed him so that he would fall in love with his own reflection in a forest pool (hence, the meaning of our word "narcissism"). There, transfixed by his image, Narcissus also wasted away. Like both the characters in the Greek myth, Bob, looking for his reflection, feels himself to be fading away.

Dylan's mention of the memory of his name may be particularly revealing. At almost precisely the time that *'Tomorrow Is A Long Time'* was being written, Bob was legally changing his name. Although he had abandoned "Zimmerman" for all practical purposes some years before, the young singer-songwriter would have felt the severity of taking legal action to mark a final divide with some aspect of his prior self. The lyric stating he can't *"remember the sound of my own name"* may thus suggest that the singer regards his prior real self (Zimmerman) as in the process of being forgotten or lost. It could also be that, as in the case of the Elephant Lady, his sense of himself is multi-faceted, with an outward façade and a true (if somewhat confused) inner self.

Who Bob was at any given moment may have depended on what role he was playing. With multiple evolving identities, Bob may have simply needed a context in which to give his name its meaning, such as it would have from Suze's lips. Like a hitchhiker wanting someone to stop, or a lost vagrant at an unanswered door, Dylan needs his beloved to validate him. In *'Tomorrow Is A Long Time'*, Dylan needs her to speak his name, as though the sound from her lips, and only her lips, represents who he is.

At the end of *'Tomorrow Is A Long Time'*, Bob turns to the natural world as an ideal of pure beauty that he tries to compare with his beloved. Dylan concludes that not even nature, and nothing else either, can compare with the exalted feeling that he associates with Suze's eyes:

> *There's beauty in the silver, singin' river,*
> *There's beauty in the sunrise in the sky,*
> *But none of these and nothing else can touch the beauty*
> *That I remember in my true love's eyes.*

Millay's poem *'Dirge Without Music'*, like *'Tomorrow Is A Long Time'*, contains lines that exalt a lover's beauty, and the beauty of a lover's eyes in particular, over all the abundance that nature offers. As she so often did, Millay was writing of death, thinking of a lover buried in the ground. She recognized that her lover's decaying body nourishes the earth from below, and flowers grow from it. Millay next wrote, *"Fragrant is the blossom. I know. But I do not approve./More precious was the light in your eyes than all the roses in the world"*.

In Dylan's song, it is perhaps significant that the memory of his lover's eyes is unparalleled, and not the direct apprehension of the eyes themselves. Of course his beloved is absent; that's a central point of the song. At the same time, Dylan seems to acknowledge, like Millay and the poet John Keats before her, that beauty is not fully appreciated in the immediate apprehension of it. Like Keats wrote of the nightingale's song, it is the memory of having experienced beauty that lives on and is cherished. However, an awareness that beauty is most highly cherished only after it has gone leads to an association of joy with melancholy, an emotion characteristic of High Romantic poetry as well as much of Dylan's work. In Dylan's work, as in Millay's, such awareness encouraged moods of tender nostalgia. Dylan's depiction of this mood is perhaps most clearly evident in *'Visions Of Johanna'* (1965), an early version of which contained a lyric referencing the *"nightingale's code"* (a probable allusion to Keats). Tender nostalgia is also evident in Dylan's later, sometimes maudlin songs like *'I'll Remember You'* (1985), *'Shooting Star'* (1989) and, more successfully, *'Standing In The Doorway'* (1997).

As in their shared moods of tender nostalgia, the influence of both Millay's techniques and her specific poems may be discerned throughout Dylan's career.

As a final example, Millay's *'Dirge Without Music'* may well have been the source of the title of one of Dylan's most recent albums, *"Time Out Of Mind"*. The album contains many songs about aging and death, such as *'Highlands'*, *'Trying To Get To Heaven'* and *'Not Dark Yet'*. The sentiment of Millay's poem is similar. The opening couplet reads in its entirety, together with its concluding lines, as follows:

> *I am not resigned to the shutting away of loving hearts in the hard ground.*
> *So it is, and so it will be, for so it has been, <u>time out of mind</u>:*
>
> *Down, down, down into the darkness of the grave*
> *Gently they go, the beautiful, the tender, the kind;*
>
> *I know. But I do not approve. And I am not resigned.*

* * *

From the very outset of his career, it appears that Dylan, like Narcissus, could not bear to journey through life without, somehow, seeing a reflection of himself. The problem was <u>how</u> to see himself. He discovered that, alone, the eye cannot see itself. The eye needs a mirror or a context, something external by which it might know itself. Having left Hibbing and his family background behind, he had lost much of the context in which his identity could be placed. With his girlfriend Suze beside him, he found for a time that he could see himself in her. With *'Tomorrow Is A Long Time'* and its innovative techniques, Dylan would embark on a more solitary, introspective journey of self-analysis and discovery in songwriting that would continue throughout his career and that would include some of his most satisfying songs.

Notes:

[1] As reported in David Ewen, *"Great Men of American Popular Song"*, rev. ed. *Prentice-Hall*, 1972, 356.

[2] Transcribed from a recording of Cynthia Gooding's *Folksinger's Choice* radio program on WBAI FM, New York, probably broadcast March 11, 1962 and first available as a bootleg CD from *Yellow Dog* and *Great Dane*.

[3] Balfour, Victoria . *"Rock Wives" Beech Tree Books*, 1986, 60.

[4] Scaduto, Anthony. *"Bob Dylan: An Intimate Biography" Grosset & Dunlap*, 1971, 124

[5] Balfour, *"Rock Wives"*, 55.

[6] Cohen, Scott. *Not Like a Rolling Stone Interview, Spin.* Vol. One, No. 8, December 1985.

Published in *ISIS* issue #113, March 2004

Close Encounters

Included in this anthology is a collection of Close Encounters with Bob Dylan. For the purpose of the anthology these encounters have been scientifically graded into the five categories below.

1: A close encounter of the *first kind* (CE-1): An off-stage sighting of Bob Dylan at close range (within 500 feet of the observer).

2: A close encounter of the *second kind* (CE-2): This brief encounter usually finds the Dylan spotter exchanging a *"thank you"* with The Man.

3: A close encounter of the *third kind* (CE-3): This encounter usually consists of a *"thank you"* and concludes with the person obtaining an autograph. These autographs can be signed with either hand but right-handed signatures are usually more refined and therefore often sell for greater sums of money.

4: A close encounter of the *fourth kind* (CE-4): This encounter results in a brief conversation with Bob. In this instance "brief" is quantified as being no more than ten words. The conversation may conclude with the person obtaining an autograph but this is not a prerequisite of a CE-4 encounter.

5: A close encounter of the *fifth kind* (CE-5): This encounter involves direct and extended communication between Bob Dylan and a mere mortal. This encounter may leave physical effects on the environment such as the uprooting of trees and might even cause vehicle engines to stall and car radios to stop playing. This rare and often controversial form of close encounter will almost certainly have massive and long-lasting effects on the recipient's psyche.

A Close Encounter of the First Kind
The Night After The Hurricane

Derek Barker

I've often been asked if I'd like to meet Bob Dylan. The answer is probably not! To meet and talk with him may destroy the mystique that has cloaked his persona and captivated me for so many years. The closest I came was in 1987, at Wembley Arena, and that wasn't even that close.

Friday October 16, 1987 dawned like any other day; at least until I ventured out into the devastation left behind by what later became known as the *"Great Storm"*. The storm, which ranks as the fourth most severe since UK records began, started at about 1am and continued through much of the night. Although the centre of the storm passed some distance to the north of the Royston Weather Station, air pressure there was nonetheless measured at the extremely low value of 964 mb. The storm, which caused an estimated £1.9 billion of damage and the unparalleled loss of 15 million trees, has, for several reasons, acquired a certain notoriety. Firstly, the severity of its onset caught weather forecasters unawares (no change there, then) with the result that adequate warning was not given. Secondly, it affected some of the most heavily populated parts of the country and so had a far greater effect on people and property than it might otherwise have had. Thirdly, it came after a very wet fortnight, which loosened tree roots whilst the trees were still in full leaf, leaving the tree population very vulnerable to the strains imposed upon it by the gale. In fact, the only saving grace was that the gale occurred at night whilst most people were safely tucked up in bed. As mentioned in the introduction, Dylan's presence can have physical effects on the environment and it would be noticeable that on the day of his arrival in London in 1991 the capital experienced its worst snows for many years.

Getting across London was a monumental task. Driving on many of the city's roads was impossible, many tube lines were closed and even walking around the countless fallen trees was difficult. Nevertheless, I had the entire day to get across London to Wembley so there was certainly no need for panic. More pressing was the fact that for some reason, now lost in the mists of time, I didn't have a ticket for the show!

In fact, I had to resort to buying my ticket for the concert from a tout. The ticket cost me just £17.50, for what I think was a £15 seat. The seat was on the right-hand side riser, but <u>very</u> close to the stage; in fact, almost level with the side of the stage. During Tom Petty's set, someone wearing an unmistakably tight-fitting grey hooded coat came and looked over the side PA. Although only fifteen feet or so from me, Dylan was still on the other side of the barrier that separated the backstage area from the public seating and after a short time he turned around and disappeared from sight. Unknown to me, Dylan then made his way from backstage to the public concourse, and from there climbed the first set of steps to the public gallery (south grand tier) and continued to watch the show from there!

I later discovered that Dylan had done this at all of the Wembley shows. Apparently, some nights he just sat down on the steps, while on other occasions he asked a steward to help find him a seat. On this night that seat was only a couple of rows from me! Remarkably, I didn't even know he was there, but my friend Mark spotted him and pointed. So close was I to Dylan that I thought Mark was looking and pointing at me. I even waved back! It was only after the event that I discovered the extended digit was aimed not at me, but at Mr Dylan.

Over the years, depending on how much beer has been consumed, Mark's tale of my close encounter with our hero has grown to one version that has Dylan sitting next to me and asking politely if I was enjoying the show. In this fantasy version of Mark's tale, I make no retort but move to another seat in the hope that this hooded vagrant will stop pestering me.

This piece contains extracts from Derek Barker's *"Temples in Flames"* tour account, published in issue #17 of *ISIS* in October 1987.

Bob Dylan 1965

The Freewheelin' Bob Dylan

Derek Barker

The Background

The story of Bob Dylan's first collection of original songs is a strange one. After his eponymous début album notched up sales of less than 5,000 copies, there were those at *Columbia Records* who would have been happy to offload the kid that some were already calling *"Hammond's Folly"*.

John Hammond Sr, *Columbia Records'* Director of Talent Acquisition, had championed Dylan since signing him to the label in October 1961. The two men had first met at the apartment of Ned O'Gorman in September when Dylan was working up harmonica for Carolyn Hester's first album on *Columbia*.

Hammond: *"I saw a kid in the peaked hat playing not terribly good harmonica but I was taken with him . . . I was sitting there thinking, 'What a wonderful character, playing guitar and blowing mouth harp, he's got to be an original'. It was one of those flashes. I thought, 'I gotta talk contract right away'"*.

Having previously worked in both sales and promotions, David Kapralik had recently been promoted to *Columbia's* Director of Artists & Repertoire where he replaced Mitch Miller.

Kapralik: *"John Hammond burst through* [my] *door like a bookie with a hot tip, he was delirious about the kid . . . the gist of it was that we had to sign Dylan immediately because he was going to be important – not just musically, but intellectually and politically as well. Not a* recording *artist, but recording* artist. *He seemed more excited about the kind of message Dylan conveyed and what he represented than about his music, which was so unusual . . . If another A&R man had brought Bob Dylan to me, I don't think I would have allowed him to be signed at that time. But with John I said, 'Go ahead'"*.

However, after the commercial failure of his first album (which incidentally, Kapralik had attempted to scupper) the Director of A&R began to file the necessary paperwork to end Dylan's contract with the company. When Hammond (already enraged that the label had not given the début album proper support and promotion) found out that A&R were considering dumping his protégé, he cornered David Kapralik in a corridor and began a vicious all-out verbal attack. Kapralik decided that if *"Bob Dylan meant that much to him, then so be it. Let the old guy fall on his own failures. In a few years, he reasoned, no one would remember the Bob Dylan name anyway"*.

The recording sessions for *"Freewheelin'"* commenced on April 24, 1962. The gap between the *"Bob Dylan"* album and *"The Freewheelin' Bob Dylan"* had been an unusually long fourteen months. The last session with John Hammond, which produced the withdrawn *"Freewheelin'"* album, took place on December 6, 1962. The final session that was organised to record the replacement tracks took place on April 24, 1963, exactly one year to the day from the first session. This was in marked contrast to his début album, which had been recorded at two sessions (November 20 and 22, 1961) and is reputed to have cost a mere $402.

Since taking over as Dylan's full-time manager, Albert Grossman had tried without success to liberate Dylan from his contract with *Columbia*. Even in 1962, Grossman was an extremely shrewd businessman and immediately saw that the contract, which Dylan had signed before Grossman took over as his manager, favoured the record company and not the artist. And while that was nothing new, Grossman believed he could negotiate a better deal elsewhere, and tried several ploys to extract Dylan from the contract. Grossman instructed his lawyer David Braun to draft a "disaffirment" letter stating that *Columbia's* contract with Dylan was null-and-void because it had been entered into when Dylan was under the age of twenty-one and without the consent of his parents.

Columbia's attorneys pointed out that Dylan had been in the studio several times since turning twenty-one and that in doing so he had automatically reaffirmed his contract with them. However, to save any further problems, and without Grossman's knowledge, John Hammond summoned Dylan to his office and requested that he reaffirm the original contract now he was of an age to do so. Much to Grossman's chagrin, Dylan did re-sign and the situation between Grossman and Hammond deteriorated. An infuriated Grossman quite rightly accused Hammond of being unethical; stating that having received the disaffirment letter, Hammond should have talked to Dylan through his lawyer.

Grossman was now adamant that his artist should no longer work with John Hammond, but dislodging a legendary producer, who had discovered amongst others Aretha Franklin, and was also the chairman's brother-in-law, would not be easy. The line from *'Mixed Up Confusion'*, *"there's too many people/And they're all too hard to please"* could well have been an observation by Dylan on the hassles that surrounded him during the making of *"The Freewheelin' Bob Dylan"*. Dylan's hassles, however, soon changed from producers and record labels to television censors.

The idea of booking Bob Dylan for a two-song slot on the *'The Ed Sullivan Show'* came from the programme's producer, Ed Sullivan's son-in-law, Bob Precht. Precht had heard Dylan's first album and was very impressed. He'd also seen Dylan perform in the Village and thought he could give the kid a chance, while providing something a little different for the *'Sullivan Show'*. Precht contacted Dylan and asked if he would attend an 'interview' at the station's West

57th Street office. Dylan duly attended the interview, played a few songs, was deemed suitable by the 'selection committee', and was told to be available for a rehearsal, which would take place a week before the actual show. Interestingly, this wasn't the first time that Dylan had been interviewed for the *'Sullivan Show'*. *The Music Corporation of America (MCA),* then a talent-booking agency, had contacted him with a view to getting him onto the show to coincide with the release of his first album. He had attended an interview, but had heard nothing further.

This time, however, Dylan made it past the committee stage and he went around the Village clubs telling all his friends to be sure to watch the show. The rehearsal was held at Studio 50 on Broadway and 54th Street. Amongst the other entertainers were Irving Berlin, Rip Taylor, and the Italian mouse puppet, Toppo Gigio. At around 3pm, the *CBS*-TV head of programme practices (the censor), Stowe Philips, told Precht that there was a problem with Dylan's act. The song *'Blowin' In The Wind'* was apparently OK, but they couldn't permit him to perform *'Talkin' John Birch Paranoid Blues'*.

Precht was told the song was simply too controversial and there was a chance that members of the John Birch Society who, in the song were being compared with Adolf Hitler, might take legal action against *CBS*-TV. Precht, who was keen to champion Dylan, consulted Sullivan over the matter. Sullivan had no objection to the song and couldn't see what all the fuss was about. However, he told Precht that Dylan must have some other material, *"so let's not take any chances. Get the kid to do another song".* When Precht put this option to Dylan, he apparently answered, *"No, this is what I want to do. If I can't play my song, I'd rather not appear on the show".*

The popular misconception is that Dylan's return to *Columbia* studio A, to record replacement tracks for his album, was brought about by 'The Sullivan Show's' refusal to air *'Talkin' John Birch'* But how so? *Columbia Records* weren't even aware which songs Dylan intended to sing on the *'Sullivan Show'* until he attended the rehearsal on the afternoon of May 12, which was eighteen days after he had cut the replacement songs!

Clearly then, *'The Ed Sullivan Show's'* decision re *'Talkin' John Birch'* could not have had any bearing on Dylan's extra recording session, and any notion that a young Bob Dylan had the clout to decide he wanted in some way to update an album that was aging before his eyes is surely misplaced. The very fact that *"The Freewheelin' Bob Dylan"* album exists as a rarity at all, is because it was already a finished product when someone decided it needed to be changed. A guy with 5,000 or so album sales under his belt would hardly have been in a position to demand the recall of an already finished product with a view to recording some new songs. After all, this would require his record company to allow him back into the studio to record, and then for them to re-master, re-press and re-package the album. And anyway, if Dylan himself had already rejected *'Talkin' John Birch'*, why on earth would he want to perform it on *'The Sullivan Show'*?

45

Dylan biographer Clinton Heylin suggests that Dylan's attempt to perform *'Talkin' John Birch'* on *CBS*-TV might have been a very deliberate act of confrontation (Bob Dylan confrontational! Surely not?)

Heylin: *"If he had managed to get it past the head of programme practices, as he might well have, Columbia Records and CBS-TV would have been made to look very stupid, and Dylan would have succeeded in publicly ridiculing the John Birch Society"*.

According to the publicist Billy James who accompanied Dylan to the TV rehearsal, Dylan was *"not too terribly disappointed"* about not appearing on the *'Sullivan Show'*. Could that have been because as Heylin suggests, Dylan was half expecting to be refused permission to perform the song? If Billy James' account is to be believed, Dylan seems to have remained remarkably laid back about missing his first chance to appear on national television, a privilege that was rarely afforded to folk singers.

However, according to biographer Anthony Scaduto, someone else who was present at the rehearsal said that when Dylan was told he couldn't perform the song because the Birchers might sue, Dylan shouted *"Are you out of your fucking mind. What the hell can they sue about?"*

More recently, the discovery of a letter to the F.C.C (Federal Communications Commission) in Washington, said by Robert Shelton to have been written by Dylan, seems to confirm that Dylan was upset by *CBS*-TVs decision to exclude his song. The prose style of the letter, which was dated May 16, 1963, makes clear that it was not written by Dylan himself but by one of his managers. However, it was in Dylan's name and this is part of what he wrote:

"One of the musical compositions in my repertoire relates to the John Birch Society. I have performed this musical composition throughout the country and it has met with considerable success".

The letter goes on to say that Sullivan and the production staff supported him but that *"they were all overruled, however, by the station representative"*.

The letter, which describes the conduct of *CBS*-TV as *"shocking and outrageous"*, asks the F.C.C to *"initiate appropriate proceedings"* and ends by suggesting *"a formal hearing at which I will be happy to testify"*. Dylan testifying in Washington – what a thought!

Heylin's confrontation theory presupposes that the song was already a contentious issue with his record label. It is of course possible that corporate lawyers at *Columbia Records* had already independently drawn the same conclusion as the *CBS-TV* "programme practices" people, i.e. that the song was too risqué. John Hammond, however, tells a different story:

"It was the CBS lawyers, not Columbia Records, who decided that the reference to Hitler involved every single member of the John Birch Society, therefore it was libellous, or some crap like that".

That being the case, being confrontational could not have been an issue for Dylan, because until the time of the TV rehearsals, there was no issue to be confrontational over. In his book *"Clive: Inside The Record Business"*, Clive Davis states that *'Talkin' John Birch'* was dropped after the television debacle, but that <u>he</u> was ultimately responsible for the song's removal from the album. Even though Hammond and Davis appear to tell contradictory stories, both tales are probably true. I believe Hammond is correct in saying it was the *CBS* lawyers who decided that the reference to Hitler might be libellous. But after lawyers at *CBS* raised the problem, it was Clive Davis (who at the time was head of legal affairs at *Columbia Records*) who decided to lose the song from the album. It would have been Davis who made the final decision regarding the album, but after the legal department at *CBS* had made noises, he probably had little choice; and anyway, he wasn't likely to stick his neck out for such a minor artist as Dylan.

Therefore, if we agree that Hammond and Davis are right about the axing of *'Talkin' John Birch'* taking place <u>after</u> the extra recording session, and that Dylan probably didn't have the clout to demand that the album be changed, the only conclusion left, is that it was *Columbia Records* who wanted the album improving/updating, and because the album was going to be recalled and delayed anyway, they could now also address this <u>new</u> issue of the potentially libellous *'Talkin' John Birch'*.

According to Robert Shelton, Dylan was far from calm when *Columbia Records* informed him that they were going to lose the track from his album, and he demanded to see Clive Davis. Dylan met with Davis who informed him that the axing of the song was a straightforward commercial decision and not a reflection on the quality of the artist's work. Nevertheless, Dylan was not impressed at being censored and stormed from the office.

Although Dylan objected strongly to losing *'Talkin' John Birch'* from the album, he was pleased to have had the opportunity to make other substitutions. After his return from England, he had talked with friends about the forthcoming *"Freewheelin'"* album saying:

"There's too many old-fashioned songs in there, stuff I tried to write like Woody. I'm goin' through changes. Need some more finger-pointin' songs in it, 'cause that's where my head's at right now".

Even if we accept the above suppositions, the question remains, why did *Columbia Records* decide to take the time and trouble to re-record such a minor artist? If you'll excuse the quip, the answer might be *'Blowin' In The Wind'*.

Although his first album had sold poorly, it nevertheless got good reviews in *Sing Out!*, *The Village Voice*, and *Little Sandy Review*. In fact, during the fourteen months it took him to complete *"Freewheelin'"* his reputation in folk circles had been steadily increasing. One of his new song's *'Blowin' In The Wind'*, was being talked about very favourably. The lyrics and music for the song were published in *Broadside* #6 (late May, 1962). The song was also published in the October 1962 issue of folk music's most prominent magazine *Sing Out!*.

Hammond: *"By this time, Bob had written 'Blowin' In The Wind' and Peter, Paul and Mary were convinced this was a master, as was I"*.

Peter, Paul and Mary's first album (released in March 1962) had been in the 'Top 10' for ten months and remained in the 'Top 20' for two years. Two singles from their album *'If I Had A Hammer'* and *'Lemon Tree'* were also hits. Consequently, they were flavour of the month and their willingness to record Dylan's *'Blowin' In The Wind'* probably helped convince *Columbia* that Dylan was not only worth hanging on to, but that maybe they should be putting a little more effort into cultivating the kid from Hibbing. If so, they were right to do so. Peter, Paul and Mary released *'Blowin' In The Wind'* on June 18, 1963 and it sold 320,000 copies in ten days!

One further point, at the time, other than *RCA*, *Columbia Records* were the only US record label that had full 'in house' facilities, i.e. A&R, producers, engineers, recording studios, mastering services, pressing plants, and even design facilities and in-house photographers. Therefore, most of the people who worked on *"The Freewheelin' Bob Dylan"* would have been salaried *Columbia* employees. Consequently, *Columbia* could re-do *"Freewheelin'"* quickly and with relatively little expense, a fact that is often overlooked when discussing the re-recording of this album.

At the time, unknown to almost everyone, Peter, Paul and Mary had a part interest in Bob Dylan! Roy Silver, who for a time managed up-and-coming comedian Bill Crosby, had signed a five-year management agreement with Dylan, after spotting him at the Gaslight Club during his residency there in June 1961.

When Grossman later bought out Silver's artists, which still included Bob Dylan; Peter, Paul and Mary put up 50% of the required $10,000. At the time Dylan had no knowledge of Peter, Paul and Mary's involvement. This deal would have been a double whammy for Grossman, because not only did he manage Peter, Paul and Mary, but the flawed *Columbia* contract, which he so wanted out of, was written in such a way that Dylan (and therefore Grossman) earned more money from songs written by Dylan and recorded by other artists, than songs written and recorded by Dylan himself! If Grossman couldn't get Dylan out of the *Columbia* contract, he sure as hell could manipulate it.

Dylan's growing reputation got a further boost when, twelve days before returning to the studio for the final recording session, he performed his first major solo concert. Promoter Harold Leventhal had booked him to appear at New York Town Hall. This was an extremely important booking for Dylan, and his audience of nine hundred included many prominent Village folkies, most of whom were impressed by Dylan's performance. To add to this, Robert Shelton dashed off another extremely positive review for *The New York Times*, by which time most of the sceptics at *Columbia Records* were beginning to change tack.

With Hammond gone and Tom Wilson now at the controls, Dylan was given the chance to update *"Freewheelin'"*. He recorded five new songs for possible inclusion on the album. *'Girl From The North Country'*, *'Masters Of War'*, *'Talkin' World War III Blues'*, *'Bob Dylan's Dream'* and *'Walls Of Redwing'*. All but *'Walls Of Redwing'* made it to the final album release.

It took Dylan twelve months, eight sessions and two producers, but in the end, an album that began with its feet firmly planted in the blues (the working title for the record was *"Bob Dylan's Blues"*) had slowly blossomed into an extremely creative and imaginative piece of original work.

The Songs

Work on Dylan's second album began with two recording sessions, which took place on April 24 and 25, 1962. These sessions were very blues biased (see list below) and demonstrated Dylan's penchant toward Robert Johnson and Big Joe Williams.

'(I Heard That) Lonesome Whistle' (Hank Williams/Jimmy Davis); *'Going To New Orleans'* (traditional); *'Milk Cow Blues'* (Kokomo Arnold), and *'Baby Please Don't Go'* (Big Joe Williams). The song *'Corrina, Corrina'* is based on a traditional American folk/blues song often performed by Mississippi John Hurt, Mance Lipscomb, Sleepy John Estes and others. Dylan, however, makes the song his own by changing the melody and mood, while also throwing in a chunk of Robert Johnson's *'Stones In My Pathway'* for good measure. Although it appears to be a Dylan composition, Michael Krogsgaard links *'Rocks And Gravel'* to Lenny Carr's *'Alabama Woman Blues'* and Brownie McGhee's *'Solid Road'*. Dylan said of this song:

"I learned one verse from Big Joe Williams, and the rest I put together out of lines that seemed to go with this story".

At any rate, the song is copyrighted Bob Dylan, but interestingly it isn't included in *"Lyrics 1962–1985"* or *"Lyrics 1962–2001"*. *'Corrina, Corrina'* and *'Rocks And Gravel'* are both later attempted with an improvised band set-up at three sessions in October and November. The late changes meant that none of the songs recorded at the first two sessions was included on the final album.

After a break of eleven weeks, Dylan's next visit to the studio on July 9, 1962 proved to be a far more rewarding exercise with *'Bob Dylan's Blues'*, *'Honey, Just Allow Me One More Chance'* (adapted by Dylan from a song by Henry Thomas), *'Down The Highway'*, and of course *'Blowin' In The Wind'* all making the final cut. It is however worth mentioning here that Dylan was never sure about the quality of *'Blowin' In The Wind'* and, if John Hammond is to be believed, Dylan considered leaving the song off the album! In 1966, Dylan said of the song:

"I was never satisfied with 'Blowin' In The Wind'. I wrote that in ten minutes".

One sad casualty from this session was Dylan's *'Worried Blues'* a song that he almost certainly adapted from folksinger and folksong collector, Hally Wood.

After another long break, this time of almost sixteen weeks, Dylan went back into the studio on October 26, 1962 for the first of three electric band sessions. Only three songs (*'Corrina, Corrina'*, *'Mixed-Up Confusion'* and Arthur Crudup's *'That's All Right, Mama'*) were attempted during a session that lasted three hours. The prime reason for the session seemed to be to record something for release as a 45-rpm single.

The same three songs were again attempted over three hours on November 1, only for Dylan to return on November 14 to try again! According to Dylan (after fifteen attempts at *'Mixed-Up Confusion'*) he stormed out of the session in disgust. If so, Dylan's annoyance may have been exasperated by the suggestion (by either Grossman or Hammond) that he attempt a Dixieland version of the song! At any rate when Dylan returned to the studio, only guitarist Bruce Langhorne remained. *'Mixed-Up Confusion'* was not re-attempted, and the session continued with only two acoustic guitars. The first number was *'Don't Think Twice, It's Alright'*, which Dylan and Langhorne nailed in a single take. *'Ballad Of Hollis Brown'* and *'Kingsport Town'* were both then attempted twice each, and the session closed with *'Whatcha Gonna Do'*.

Over the years, there has been speculation as to whether it was Dylan or Bruce Langhorne who played the main guitar part on *'Don't Think Twice, It's Alright'*. Some sceptics felt the guitar work was simply too good to be Dylan! Here's what Langhorne had to say to *ISIS* on November 14, 2002:

"I'm pushing the edges of memory here. If I remember correctly, he [Dylan] did play the guitar. I didn't play anything but ornaments. The bulk of the guitar playing is himself on that tune".

When Dylan returned to the studio on December 6, all thoughts of a backing group had disappeared. In the interim, however, a single had been selected from the three previous band sessions. The tracks that had been chosen for release were *'Mixed-Up Confusion'* and *'Corrina, Corrina'*.

The A-side, a piano driven *'Mixed-Up Confusion'*, had been recorded at the final band session on November 14 (take 13). This track is not to be confused with the rather ugly track (take 10) that was later used on both *"Masterpieces"* (1978) and *"Biograph"* (1985). It should also be noted that the single's B-side, *'Corrina, Corrina'*, again with backing band, is not the same take as included on *"The Freewheelin' Bob Dylan"* album.

As was the case with *'Milk Cow Blues'*, *'Corrina, Corrina'* has a hint of Elvis Presley about it. *'Mixed-Up Confusion'* is of course pure Elvis. Where was Dylan going with these sessions and whose idea was the single? We have already discussed Dylan's rapidly growing reputation in the folk circles, so why was the author of *'Blowin' In The Wind'* now trying to be Elvis Presley? Was Dylan still uncertain of his direction? Was he suddenly regressing to his rock and blues roots? Was, as has been suggested, the band sessions purely the brain-child of producer John Hammond, or was Dylan simply losing the plot?

As Clinton Heylin writes in *"Bob Dylan: The Recording Sessions"*:

"That Dylan himself, and presumably Albert Grossman (who was in attendance at these sessions), always intended 'Mixed-Up Confusion' to be an A-sided single seems self-evident. Their reasons remain harder to fathom".

'Mixed-Up Confusion'/'Corrina, Corrina' was released as a single in the USA on December 14, 1962, but was quickly withdrawn. The sensible choice for a single, *'Blowin' In The Wind'* backed with *'Don't Think Twice, It's Alright'*, was not released until September 1963, nearly two months after it had become a hit for Peter, Paul and Mary! Although as previously explained, Dylan's *Columbia* contract was written in such a way that he would have earned more from Peter, Paul and Mary covering the song than he would recording it himself! This would also explain Dylan's frequent visits to Witmark & Sons in July and December 1962, and February, March, April and May '63 to record demos for use by other artists.

The December session, said to have lasted for just one hour, yielded three songs that made it onto the *"Freewheelin'"* album; *'Oxford Town'*, *'I Shall Be Free'*, and *'A Hard Rain's A-Gonna Fall'*. Shortly after this session, and with the album supposedly in the can, Dylan went to England to work on the television play *"Madhouse On Castle Street"*. While in England the blotting paper man was exposed to a plethora of new songs and influences, the uppermost of which was Martin Carthy. Two months after his return to New York Dylan went back into the studio to update the *"Freewheelin'"* album and in doing so created a mega rarity.

The first new song that Dylan attempted at the April 24 session was *'Girl From The North Country'*. Along with *'Boots Of Spanish Leather'*, this song takes a large part of its melody from Martin Carthy's arrangement of the trad song *'Scarborough Fair'*. *'Boots'*, however, wouldn't see the light of day until the release of Dylan's third album, *"The Times They Are A-Changin'"*, released January 13, 1964. It has been mooted in some quarters that this extra *"Freewheelin'"* session was in fact scheduled as the first session for the *"Times"* album.

The idea for *'Bob Dylan's Dream'* is taken from the English folk ballad *'Lord Franklin's Lament'*, again learned from Martin Carthy.

Dylan: *"I ran into some people in England who really knew those* [traditional English] *songs . . . Martin Carthy's incredible. I learned a lot of stuff from Martin".*

In the *Guardian*, November 25, 2002, Martin Carthy said of Dylan: *"He has amazing intuition, he's up to his eyeballs in tradition and always has been".*

'Masters Of War' and *'Talking World War III Blues'* were worked up as the other replacements. As previously mentioned, *'Walls Of Redwing'* was the only song from this session that failed to make it onto the final album release.

The Records

As we all know, or at least we should know, it's the music that matters; but I guess most *ISIS* readers are also collectors of records, CDs, books, or other types of Bob ephemera. Most Dylan enthusiasts will therefore be aware of the ultra rare withdrawn *"Freewheelin'"* album, but did you know there are at least half-a-dozen different collectable versions of this album with values ranging between £300 and £20,000 (US$30,000+)?

The valuation of $30,000+ in the March 8, 2002 issue of *Goldmine* reaffirms the withdrawn <u>stereo</u> version of *"The Freewheelin'Bob Dylan"* as the world's most expensive 33-rpm vinyl record album. Some would argue that accolade belongs to the Beatles' 1966 "Butcher Cover" release *"Yesterday And Today"*. However, the value of the "Butcher Cover" albums is due purely to the "Livingston pedigree" and the pristine sealed state of the rare <u>covers</u>. The actual records are identical to the regular release. In the case of *"The Freewheelin' Bob Dylan"*, albums listing the incorrect tracks on the cover sell for a mere £100/$150, the real rarities are the records that actually <u>play</u> the four original withdrawn tracks.

It seems that before the changes to *"The Freewheelin' Bob Dylan"* were implemented, a small number of <u>records</u>, <u>record labels,</u> and radio station promo <u>timing strips</u> featuring the four original tracks were manufactured. However, in no cases did all of these three component parts ever appear together!

All copies of the deleted album were manufactured at *Columbia Records* plant in Los Angeles, but there is also a Canadian oddity. All known instances of <u>covers</u> that list the four deleted tracks came from *Columbia Records'* Canadian plant. It seems that these covers were made in advance of the record itself and that the Canadian plant never pressed any records containing the four original withdrawn tracks. *Columbia* Canada, however, continued to use this original misprinted cover until the early seventies! This means that if you find a copy of *"The Freewheelin' Bob Dylan"* that lists the missing tracks on the cover, unless it's been tampered with, the cover will house the regular LP only. Nevertheless, in near perfect condition, these Canadian covers are valued at around £100. Amazingly, there is a further fault with the Canadian covers. Track two, the withdrawn *'Rocks And Gravel'*, is mistakenly listed here as *'Solid Road'*.

There are four known variants of Radio Station promos of *"The Freewheelin' Bob Dylan"* and all four are of value. All of these white label records carry the words "Radio Station Copy – Not For Resale" on the label. The first is the standard release featuring the regular tracks on the timing strip, label, and LP itself, and as such this item has no real connection with the withdrawn album. However, this standard promo album is still worth around £300 (US$500).

Next up is a Radio Station promo with a "timing strip" that lists the original withdrawn tracks, but the record label and LP feature the replacement tracks. (The timing strip is pasted over the tracks listed on the front of the LP cover). The value of this item is around £500 (US$800).

The two remaining radio promos are real curios in that they play the reverse of what is stated on the labels, i.e. records with labels listing the replacement tracks always play the withdrawn tracks (The last two copies that were sold changed hands for $3,000. I'm not certain of the condition of these LPs, but $3,000 seems to me to be a gross under-valuation), while records with labels that list the withdrawn tracks always play the 'regular' replacement tracks! (value £1,000 – US$1,600). Both of these versions feature timing strips listing the withdrawn tracks.

The two remaining versions of the *"Freewheelin'"* album were destined for record stores. The mono version comes with the red *Columbia* "Guaranteed High Fidelity" record label. The label lists the regular replacement tracks but the LP plays the withdrawn tracks (value £7,500 – US$12,000). The final version is the ultra rare stereo edition. This album, which plays the withdrawn tracks, lists them on the red *Columbia* "360 Sound Stereo" label, but not on the album sleeve. Only two copies of this stereo album are known to exist. (value £20,000 – US$30,000+). The first stereo copy ever discovered was documented in *ISIS* magazine in *The Wicked Messenger* column (#2311 – March 28, 1992). This stereo LP was found by a collector in March 1992 in what was described as a *"record store junk shop"* on St. Marks Place in New York's Greenwich Village. The album, which was described as being in VG- condition, was bought for just $2. Within 24-hours of the find the new owner was offered $15,000 for the LP. The offer was turned down. Any thoughts that this stereo copy might be unique were quickly put to rest when six months later, in late 1992, a second copy came up for sale at auction. Ian Woodward, who reported the sale in *ISIS* in *The Wicked Messenger* #2755, takes up the story:

"In this instance, it is understood that the provenance of this disc is known: It was apparently sent by Columbia Records to a jazz records reviewer. This supports the view that these are early versions of the album, which were never on sale in regular record racks. The disc was apparently sold at auction and the price has not been disclosed, but it is understood to be in five figures".

It might seem remarkable that these two stereo copies of *"Freewheelin'"* should emerge at approximately the same time. In reality, however, it was probably the emergence of the New York copy, and its big money price tag, that prompted the discovery and sale of the second copy, which emerged in close proximity to its 'birth place' in California.

One further twist to the *"Freewheelin'"* saga is that when the original withdrawn albums were pressed, tracks three and six were reversed on the *vinyl LP* itself, which meant that *'A Hard Rain's Gonna Fall'* was the third track and *'Let Me Die In My Footsteps'* was the sixth and final track on side one. Because the record label did not reflect this mispressing, and in an attempt not to confuse radio station programmers and disc jockeys, a notice to that effect was included inside the sleeves of the promo albums. However, this notice didn't make it into all the promos, but in some cases it was mistakenly included with the regular pressings! These pressings didn't have the fault, so the erratum note would have made absolutely no sense to those reading it at the time.

The question that has never been properley answered is how could a major manufacturing plant manage to make so many mistakes? As I've already stated, every radio promo LP that plays the withdrawn tracks has a label to the contrary, and every promo label that lists the withdrawn tracks is fixed to an LP that doesn't play them! Then there is the incorrect fixing of the timing strips to the LP covers and spurious erratum notes. Surely, no manufacturing system could be that poor, or go so wrong?

Pete Howard, a Dylan collector and an ex-employee at *Columbia Records* Los Angeles manufacturing plant takes up the story:

Howard: "Here's my summation and theory of why and how so many *"Freewheelin'"* variations exist.

When I worked at the *Columbia Records* manufacturing plant, from 1976-80, I was almost the <u>only</u> music lover working there and certainly the <u>only</u> record collector. To everybody else, it was just a factory job. Sure, some people liked Barbra Streisand and a couple of hipsters liked Pink Floyd; but by and large, they could have just as easily been making shoes. I used to get laughed at when I'd take home every day LP slicks, label sheets, etc. by my favourite artists.

Everybody who worked there just went by numbers, not artist or LP names. So back in 1963, I'm sure you had a bunch of women on the LP assembly line with their hair up in curlers (sorry about the 1963 stereotyping) that slapped together all the components of either 'L 1986' or 'CS 8786'. They didn't know Bob Dylan from Bob Newhart, and didn't care.

So what happened, I'm speculating, is that once the order came down to stop the presses and destroy all the parts, only <u>some</u> of the parts (labels, lacquers, etc.) were destroyed, and others were left lying around. Then, when the new components arrived from the mastering lab/print shop etc., things got somewhat mixed up. Most pointedly, it appears that old 'metal parts' (the lacquers, stampers, etc.) were not all destroyed, and that several hundred records were made with new jackets, new labels but – oops – the old, wrong music. But none of those factory workers caught it . . . it just went right on through. It doesn't take long for one, two or three 'spindles' (holding 100 LPs each) to whisk through the manufacturing process, get shrink wrapped and get sent out the door".

So, Pete suggests that it is popular misconception that LPs were manufactured, shipped, and then recalled. It is far more likely that some component parts were made at the Los Angeles manufacturing plant (at that time situated near the corner of Santa Monica Blvd and Robertson Ave). And that after word came down to halt production, only <u>some</u> of these parts were destroyed, while others ended up being used. This is, in fact, the only scenario that makes complete sense.

How to Spot a Rare *"Freewheelin'"*

One way to spot a rare *"Freewheelin'"* (one that actually plays the withdrawn tracks), mono or stereo, is to look at the width of the last track on side one. If this track is the widest band on side one, then that track is *'A Hard Rain's A-Gonna*

Fall', and the LP is the regular and not the withdrawn version. You can also check the matrix or master numbers, which are scratched into the vinyl between the last track and the record label. The master number of the withdrawn LP is XLP-58717-1A (side two is marked XLP-58718-1A). In the case of the stereo release, the numbers would be XSM-58719-1A and XMS-58720-1A for side two. The important part of the number is the "1A" after the dash. This number means the record is a first edition pressing. If any other number follows the dash, forget it.

The easiest way of identifying the ultra rare stereo album, however, is simply to remove the LP from its sleeve. If the LP has a red *Columbia* "360 Sound Stereo" label (CS 8786) that lists the withdrawn tracks, you should place the record carefully to one side before leaping into the air and shouting "Oh blimey, look what I've found" or more likely, "F*%~in' Hell!" However, as only two copies of this ultra rare stereo edition have ever been discovered, it's probably not worth planning how you are going to spend your £20,000. However, Pete Howard certainly believes there are more copies out there.

Howard: "I think it's way too speculative, naive, and flies in the face of logic, to believe that only two stereo copies exist! As I've learned in 30-years of intense collecting, there's a huge difference between "in collectors' circles" and in the real world. Since *CBS* never manufactured less than 100 (one spindle) of anything, it defies logic that 98 stereos have been thrown away. It stands to reason that at least a couple more would exist in collections where people don't know what they have".

Exactly how many 'red label mono' copies (CL 1986), were made seems nearly impossible to answer. An educated guess would be 200-500. How many avoided being destroyed is wild speculation, but no more than two-dozen have emerged so far.

The Lost Songs

Forty years later, what is the situation with the four withdrawn songs? In 1999, *Classic Records*, an audiophile label based in California, investigated the idea of issuing a double album version of *"The Freewheelin' Bob Dylan"*. The proposal was that both discs would be 180-gram vinyl and that disc one would be the standard album release, while disc two would be the original withdrawn version containing the four rare tracks. The planned release never came to fruition and as a consequence only one of the four withdrawn tracks, *'Ramblin' Gamblin' Willie'*, has been officially released in full.

'Ramblin' Gamblin' Willie', or as it was listed on the withdrawn album, *'Gamblin' Willie's Dead Man's Hand'*, was released on *"The Bootleg Series Vols 1-3"* in 1991 in the same form that it appeared on the original withdrawn stereo *"Freewheelin'"* album. *'Let Me Die In My Footsteps'*, however, was edited for release on the *"Bootleg Series"* and the 3:33 version that appears there omits the fifth verse.

'Rocks And Gravel' remains unreleased, and although "The Bootleg Series Vols 1-3" does contain a version of 'Talkin' John Birch Blues', entitled 'Talkin' John Birch Paranoid Blues', this is a live performance from Carnegie Hall, New York, October 26, 1963, and not the version that was on the original "Freewheelin'" album.

The Vigotone bootleg CD, "The Freewheelin' Bob Dylan Outtakes", which was released in 1994, contains 25 of the studio takes recorded at the "Freewheelin'" sessions. The material on the Vigotone CD was re-released in 1999 by an unnamed CD manufacturer and again in 2001 by Original Masters Revisited. All three releases are identical and while they include three of the withdrawn tracks not officially released on "Freewheelin'", they do not include 'Ramblin' Gamblin' Willie', assumedly because that track had already been included on "The Bootleg Series Vols 1-3".

Notes:

The sources used to prepare this text are far too numerous to list here. However, Clinton Heylin's "Bob Dylan Behind The Shades: Take Two", and "Bob Dylan: The Recording Sessions" were, as always, invaluable. "No Direction Home: The Life & Music of Bob Dylan" by Robert Shelton, "Down The Highway: The Life Of Bob Dylan" by Howard Sounes, "Dylan – A Biography" by Bob Spitz, "Bob Dylan" by Anthony Scaduto and "Clive: Inside The Record Business" were also consulted.

The extract from the letter to F.C.C. comes from the Robert Shelton archive and is reproduced in part here with thanks to Ian Woodward.

Special thanks should also go to Tim Neely for his excellent piece in Goldmine (Vol 28–No.5–issue 564), and to guitarist Bruce Langhorne for his memories.

Finally, to Pete Howard, founder and editor of ICE Magazine (www.icemagazine.com) who generously gave me his time, provided me with numerous anecdotes and read through my piece before publication. To Ian Woodward who also read the piece before publication, and to Paul Comley for proofing.

THE FREEWHEELIN' BOB DYLAN PRICE GUIDE	
CL 1986 Canadian Release	
Cover With Withdrawn Tracks	£100
CL 1986 White Label "Radio Station Copy"	
Regular Promo. Std Tracks on Cover, Label & LP	£300
CL 1986 White Label "Radio Station Copy"	
Timing Strip List Withdrawn Tracks, Label lists & LP plays Std Tracks	£500
CL 1986 White Label "Radio Station Copy"	
Label & Timing Strip List Withdrawn Tracks, LP plays Std Tracks	£1,000
CL 1986 White Label "Radio Station Copy"	
Label Lists Std Tracks, Timing Strip & LP have Withdrawn Tracks	£2,000+
CL 1986 Red "Guaranteed High Fidelity" Mono	
Label Lists Std Tracks, LP Plays Withdrawn Tracks	£7,500
CS 8786 Red "360 Sound Stereo" Label	
Label Lists Withdrawn Tracks, LP Plays Withdrawn Tracks	£20,000+
All prices quoted above are for albums in mint or near mint condition	
The % listed below should be subtracted for albums in less than mint condition	
Mint or Near-Mint = prices as above	
Excellent - 20% Very Good - 50% Good - 70% Poor - 90%	

Ultra Rare LPs by Other Artists

Elvis Presley's 1957 *RCA "Christmas Album"* on red vinyl is valued at about $18,000, but Presley's most rare disc the *RCA Victor* radio station promo, *"Stay Away, Joe"*. All evidence indicates that only one copy exists and as this record has never been sold, there is no established value.

Manufactured by *Vee Jay Records*, before their rights to The Beatles expired on October 10, 1964, the LP *"Jolly What! The Beatles And Frank Ifield On Stage"* was originally released with a cover known by collectors as the "old man" cover. The LP was then released with a cover that featured a prominent drawing of The Beatles. This re-issue hardly made it to record stores and less than 100 copies are believed to have been made. The first time a 'factory sealed' copy turned up in collecting circles was in 1976 when a USA collector from the Northwest discovered three unopened stereo copies in the basement of a Midwest record store! In 1995, one of the three copies was sold for $22,000.

The Beatles and the Butcher

The original cover of The Beatles' 1966 US release *"Yesterday And Today"*, which featured a controversial photo of the group dressed in white butcher smocks with cuts of raw meat and dismembered body parts of dolls strewn about, is probably the most collectable album 'cover' ever. For obvious reasons the "Butcher Cover", as it became known, was quickly withdrawn and stock at *Capitol Records* was put to one side to have a new and more tasteful cover picture pasted over the offending photo. It is possible, though not recommended, to peel the replacement cover pic to reveal the original Butcher Cover. However, it is the so-called 'first state' albums that fetch the big money, i.e. those that escaped having a new cover-slick pasted over the original.

After the recall in 1966, the then President of *Capitol Records*, Alan Livingston, took home a box of the albums (five stereo and approximately nineteen mono) from the stock that was waiting to have the new "Trunk Cover" pasted over. In 1987, after twenty-one years in a closet, Livingston gave the box of records to his son Peter, who took some of them to a US Beatles Convention. Nearly every copy was sealed and even the shrink-rap was in pristine condition. Peter was asking $1,000 for mono copies and $2,500 for stereo. Within a matter of minutes all the copies that he'd taken to the convention were sold.

The remaining copies were soon sold, each one coming with a letter of authenticity written by Peter's father. Within a couple of years, the price for mono albums rocketed to $5,000. However, no stereo copies changed hands until the early nineties when one of the five known Livingston copies was sold to a Washington based US collector for $20,000 cash. This transaction established a world-record sale price for a vinyl album. In 1994 this copy was again sold, this time for $25,000 to a collector in California.

Published in *ISIS* issues #'s 106 and 114, January 2003 and May 2004

Pete Howard's Story

In the 1970s, Pete Howard had one of the finest Bob Dylan record collections in the world. He had "regular" and "promo" pressings of <u>every</u> Dylan record, including his rare first two singles. However, the biggest challenge of all, by far, was the original *"Freewheelin' Bob Dylan"*. Pete was very proud of the fact that he was the only person in the world to own <u>two</u> copies (that played the rare tracks) for a number of years, when almost nobody else he knew owned even one.

Pete Howard: "I made it my personal task to find out as much as I possibly could about the original *"Freewheelin'"* LP and it helped that A: I was based in Los Angeles, where the rare disc was manufactured and B: I worked for *CBS Records'* LP manufacturing division while at the height of my hobby (1976-1980).

Even with that favourable backdrop, there was very little to learn about this odd pressing, which had happened (then) a decade earlier. I spoke with many higher-up *CBS Records* executives, including producer John Hammond himself but nobody, even Hammond, could remember anything concrete about the pressing.

When I started collecting Dylan's records with earnest in the early seventies, an original *"Freewheelin'"* was indeed, without exaggeration, 'the holy Grail'. I just couldn't believe how rare this thing was, and that impression lasts to this day.

I'll never, ever forget the day that I finally got one (my first one). Since there was no Internet yet (still the early 70s) and collector's magazines like *Goldmine* were in their infancy, I drew up little signs and put them up at record stores all over Los Angeles. It seemed hopeless, but I had to start somewhere. This, of course, in addition to pulling out every used *"Freewheelin'"* (with a '60s label) that I ran across, holding my breath, taking out the LP and looking at the last band on Side One . . . it was always the darn "fat band" (*'Hard Rain'*).

But lo and behold, sometime in 1973 a fellow named John responded to my ad. He called me up and said he had the original *"Freewheelin'"*. Well, by now I'd heard this a thousand times, so I started out sceptical. I asked him to get the album and describe it to me on the 'phone. He did, and as it turned out, to my astonishment, it wasn't a phoney false alarm. He had the real McCoy; and was willing to sell it – maybe.

I went over to his Los Angeles apartment, we engaged in small talk, and he eventually pulled out the record. Imagine trying to carry on any conversation when you first lay eyes on a record that you want more than anything in the world.

I remember him saying, in trying to coax up the price, *"You <u>know</u> this is going to be worth a couple of hundred dollars someday"*. And then offering it to me for $50. I actually hesitated, because I didn't want to jump at it and say "yes!" which might have scared him off. So I thought for a while and counter-offered $45. You have to remember: this was a lot of money 30 years ago. You could eat for several days on $5.

Well, John further blew my already blown mind by pulling out a Beatles' *"Yesterday And Today"* butcher cover. *"If I throw this in, would you go the $50?"*

I said *"yes"*, and walked away with my head in a daze. I don't mean to gloat, because I've had my share of bad deals over the decades, but I do realize it was the best transaction of my record-collecting life. It just happened to have happened before any price guides, etc. had been conceived and written".

Published in *ISIS* issue #114, May 2004

White label Radio Promo sides 1 and 2
The labels list the withdrawn tracks
therefore the record would play the regular tracks

One of the only 2 known stereo LPs to contain and play the withdrawn tracks.

White label Radio Promo sides 1 and 2
The labels list the regular tracks
therefore the record would play the withdrawn tracks

Stories in the Press

It seems that Bob Dylan has ordered such a clamp-down on his security he was barred from getting into one of his own concerts.

The rock legend's handlers told security at a recent concert in Oregon that absolutely no one could get backstage without an official pass.

It turns out that Dylan himself – who was without his laminate – was refused entry by the literal-minded guards at the Jackson County Exposition Center, reports the *Oregon Mail Tribune*. Dylan was finally allowed in after the guards' supervisor, Chris Borovansky, came over and ushered Dylan inside. *"I told them they did a great job"*, Borovansky said, adding that he later qualified the *"no-pass"* rule: *"There's no exception"*, he said. *"Except for one"*.

Published in issue #99 of *ISIS* November 2001

Fans Fall For Pop Wind-Up

Rumours that Bob was to play at a pub in Plymouth started to circulate after a national newspaper listed the concert in their gig guide! The gig was announced by Plymouth rock music promoters Graham Deykin and Paul Meredith who sent out flyers stating that Robert Zimmerman would be appearing at the Britannia pub, Milehouse, on April 1st, 1996. The date was of course the giveaway.

At least one national newspaper and Channel 4 Teletext included the date in their listings, which resulted in pub landlord, Ian Mellor, being bombarded with callers asking about the gig.

Promoter Graham Deykin said: *"It was Paul's idea, I told him not to do it. I'm amazed that so many people fell for it – one man rang me to ask if he could go and when I told him to check the date he said he was free that night"*.

Published in issue #66 of *ISIS* May 1996

Dylan on the Internet

In the October 1999 issue of *Mojo*, there was a Dylan story in its *'Walrus'* column. It is reported that one of the Dylan Internet groups had been discussing the meaning of *'Blowin' In The Wind'* and amongst a variety of high-flown theory and off-the-wall interpretations came a lone voice suggesting that it was just a naïve political plea from a callow youth. This caused another participant to ask how he'd come by this revisionist view. *"Because I'm Bob"* was the somewhat surprising response. Asked to prove it, *"Bob"* said he'd sing *'Highlands'* at his next show. Dylan's next show was the San Diego / Chula Vista concert, at which he performed *'Highlands'*. A great story but do you really believe it?

The Wicked Messenger #4360 Published in issue #87 of *ISIS* November 1999

Dylan Song for Dunblane Campaign (6 October 1996)

Awaking, I turned on the radio earlier today (BBC Radio Scotland, to be precise). The news report said that *'Knockin' On Heaven's Door'* had been chosen for a recording by the surviving children of Dunblane Primary in support of a campaign to ban the private ownership of guns. It was said that this was with the agreement of Dylan himself. A local musician, Ted Christopher, who came up with the idea, was then interviewed. He said that Dylan had originally denied permission to amend the lyrics but permission had now been given.

Immediately switching channels, to BBC Radio 4 this time, I came in part way through the national news, just as there was a reference to the 23rd Psalm and quoting of the following words *"All these guns have caused too much pain/This town will never be the same again"*. Although I missed the intro to this news item, it seemed to be connected to the Radio Scotland piece. And so it was.

When the *Sunday Times* plopped on the doormat, there it was, a front page news story headline read, *"Dunblane parents to record Dylan anthem"*. The same lyric was quoted, slightly longer and a bit different. *"Lord all these guns have caused too much pain/This town will never be the same, so for the bairns* [children] *of Dunblane, we ask, please – never again"*.

There had been initial disappointment when Dylan's manager turned the proposal down. However, it seems that the aforementioned Ted Christopher has now received a fax from Jeff Rosen, at Dylan's publishing office, saying, *"After careful consideration, I have decided in this one instance to allow Mr Dylan's lyrics to be altered for your worthy cause"*.

In addition, tonight's news on Scottish television actually showed the "letter" received from Jeff Rosen.

The Wicked Messenger #3494 Published in issue #69 of *ISIS* November 1996

Addendum:

Youngsters from the Scottish village of Dunblane went on to record the song as a tribute to the 16 children and school teacher slain in the town in March 1996.

The children, some of whom lost brothers and sisters in the massacre, recorded the song at London's Abbey Road studios. They were accompanied on lead guitar by Mark Knopfler of Dire Straits. The project's organizer, Ted Christopher, told Sky Television that he believed this was the first time that Dylan had ever allowed his lyrics to be altered and recorded. The record's sleeve carried a drawing of *"Christmas Time"* by Emma Crozier, one of the children shot dead by loner Thomas Hamilton when he stormed the school gym armed with two pistols, two revolvers and 743 cartridges. In the space of three minutes Hamilton fired 105 rounds. All of the 34 persons present were shot, one adult and sixteen children died. Hamilton then put the gun into his mouth and pulled the trigger. He died instantaneously, leaving behind a ghastly trail of death and devastation.

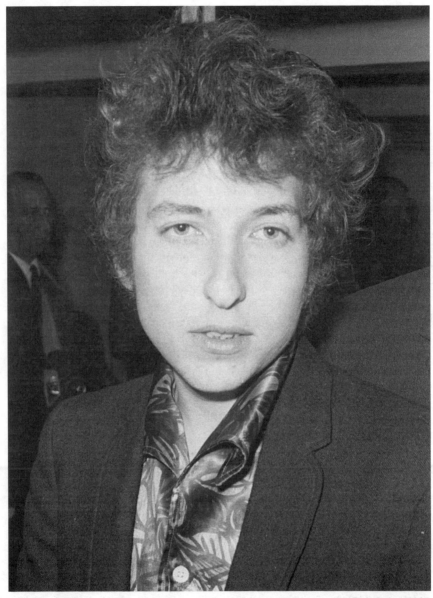

Bob Dylan 1965

Don't Be a Pawn in Somebody's Game:
Kennedy and the Civil Rights Movement

James Dunlap

Dylan's departure from the 'Folk Protest Movement' and his complex musings over the roles that music and politics would play in his life were several years in preparation, but a few short months were critical. Over the course of 1963, Dylan first came to recognize that both the political world and his interior life were a good deal more complex than he had once believed during more innocent and carefree days.

The reasons for Dylan's intellectual evolution can be traced to a few key events in the latter half of the year. In July, he joined Theo Bikel and Pete Seeger for several days at a voter-registration drive in Greenwood, Mississippi in order to, among other things, sing protest songs in front of a strong press contingent and somewhat disbelieving sharecroppers.

Dylan had also gone to Greenwood, his first trip to the South, to establish his credibility among traditional leaders of the Folk Protest Movement. The folklorist Alan Lomax, for instance, contended that a folk singer had to *"experience the feelings that lie behind his art"*, and he discounted the value of many performers who did not have a sufficiently authentic background. A considerable debate on this topic ensued on the pages of *Sing Out!* magazine. According to Lee Hays (a former member of both the Almanac Singers and the Weavers), good topical songs must come from direct personal experience. John Cohen of the Boston-based New Lost City Ramblers was the most articulate opponent of Lomax, Hays, and those insisting on "authenticity" in its narrowest terms. As a member of probably the first Northern urban bluegrass group (bluegrass was originally Appalachian hillbilly music), Cohen may have taken his position out of a kind of necessity.

* * *

The symbolic importance of President Kennedy in representing the potential for positive change, particularly among young members of the 'Folk Protest Movement', cannot be underestimated. As the first of a new generation of leadership, Kennedy was generally felt to represent idealism and reform, moderated only by a political realism (which some resented) that may, however, have been necessary to achieve the goals of the civil rights movement at a time of deep national division. Furthermore, the First Lady, the former society debutante Jacqueline Bouvier, added to the excitement associated with an era of change. Her glamorous image was splashed almost continually on the covers of fashion and news magazines, overshadowing movie stars, professional models and often the President himself.

Richard Fariña once specifically compared a joint appearance of Joan Baez and Bob Dylan with the promise of change that Kennedy represented:

"[Baez and Dylan] claimed to be there not as virtuosos in the field of concretized folk music but as purveyors of an enjoined social consciousness and responsibility. They felt the intolerability of bigoted opposition to Civil Rights. . . When they left the stage to a whirlwind of enthusiastic cheers, it seemed that the previously unspoken word of protest, like the torch of President Kennedy's inaugural address, had most certainly been passed".[1]

The folk singer Eric Andersen described how it felt to be involved with the 'Folk Protest Movement' during the heady days of the Kennedy administration:

"Folk music had a medieval flair to it, and pageantry, it had a feeling of truth and of, yes, we can do it, just freedom, and everybody's going to get it together and it's just going to be won. And Kennedy, he was sort of like the shadow of flight, he sort of protected this kind of thing".[2]

In the spring and summer of 1963, the President had come to favour voter registration drives over more militant and confrontational forms of direct action in giving expression to civil rights protest. Voter registration differed from the earlier use of privately chartered buses by the 'Student Nonviolent Coordinating Committee' ('SNCC', pronounced "snick") to test and require enforcement of a recent Supreme Court decision mandating the integration of interstate bus terminals. Calling on federal agents to protect these integrated 'Freedom Rides' raised serious issues involving the states' superior rights to police their bus stations. Kennedy had hoped to avoid these issues by focusing instead on the enforcement of federal laws regarding voting.

In order to minimize incidents of racial conflict with state authorities, leaders of the civil rights movement made a strategic compromise with President Kennedy and, at his urging, focused on voter registration. By limiting their advocacy to voter registration drives, civil rights leaders chose to rely on conciliation and the political process to achieve positive change. The reformers were led to believe that the Kennedy administration would support registration and protect their efforts from violence and arrest in the South.

In addition to voter registration and the Freedom Ride busses, there were still other approaches to achieve civil rights. Besides 'SNCC', the civil rights movement in the early 1960s also included Martin Luther King's 'Southern Christian Leadership Conference' (the 'SCLC'), which used strong but respectful moral leadership in attempts to affect change through nonviolent action. The 'SCLC' also used its close association with Southern churches to distinguish itself from Communism and its agitators, which was an association still carried by those, like Pete Seeger, who had refused to testify before the 'House Un-American Activities Committee' ('HUAC'). With strong ties in the Northern states, there was also the 'National Association for the Advancement of Colored People' (the 'NAACP'), which was a principal sponsor of the many lawsuits brought before the federal courts based on the civil rights guarantees in the Bill of Rights. Both the 'SCLC' and 'NAACP' were at first viewed as patient with the pace of social change. Both were rewarded with the support of wealthy contributors.

'The Congress on Racial Equality' ('CORE') was an additional civil rights organization, which was eventually absorbed by 'SNCC' in the early 1960s. 'CORE' was associated with the confrontational sit-ins that began in 1960 at a Woolworth's lunch counter in Greensboro, North Carolina. Dylan's girlfriend, Suze Rotolo, came to the civil rights movement through 'CORE', which undoubtedly played a role in shaping Dylan's views toward confrontation and the civil rights movement. Like 'CORE', Dylan would eventually come to favour honest, direct confrontation over conciliation.

* * *

The civil rights leader Jim Forman, the Secretary of 'SNCC', spoke with Dylan at length over several days while they were at Greenwood. Dylan paid rapt attention. Forman would have told Dylan that the solidarity of King's 'SCLC' was beginning to rupture and that King's church-led appeals to the nation's morals would soon be supplemented with more direct action. Using stealth and working at night to avoid being shot, elitist cadres of dedicated black and white students would risk their personal safety to further advance 'SNCC's causes. The defiant use of underground tactics, which developed over the course of the summer of 1963, was necessitated, in part, by the failure of the Kennedy administration to provide the voter registration efforts with the protection that was believed to have been promised.

In the liner notes from *"The Times They Are A-Changin'"* (recorded August to October 1963, released January 1964), Dylan acknowledged the failure of 'SNCC's multi-racial voter registration drives. He addressed Jim Forman with, in part, the following lines, reflecting their conversations that summer: *"Jim, Jim/where is our party?/where is the party that's one/where all members're held equal/an' vow t'infiltrate that thought/among the people it hopes t'serve"*.

With Kennedy's failure to support even his own compromise, the political process increasingly was seen as corrupt. Conciliation as a means of change was becoming suspect, and Forman's direction of the civil rights movement would soon lead to the development of the Black Power movement. That movement would reject conciliation and conventional political alliances in favour of black American's independent self-reliance.

Through 'SNCC' and the nascent 'Black Power Movement', Dylan was given a sense of integrity and of the strong comradeship that stems from commitments forged during dangerous times. In coming years, the 'Black Power Movement', largely initiated by Forman, eventually spawned leaders, such as George Jackson (of the 'Black Panthers') and other heroes, such as Mohammed Ali and Ruben *"Hurricane"* Carter, that Dylan came to admire and praise in his songs.

While at Greenwood, Dylan debuted *'Only A Pawn In Their Game'*, one of his last protest songs. The song is an imagined account of the kind of man that would have killed Medgar Evers, the Mississippi field secretary of the 'NAACP' gunned down only a month before in front of his house by a shot in the back. As in an earlier song, *'Masters Of War'*, the later song's villains are political leaders and members of law enforcement who, in the case of the Evers song, spread bigotry throughout the South for personal gain. To maintain their political positions, Dylan argued, the Southern sheriffs and governors create a culture of racial hatred. Their words, in turn, incite the poor white man, who, together with others like him, don hoods, burn crosses and stage lynchings against the black man with the frenzied madness of an animal pack.

In acting out their racial obsessions, the poor Southern whites don't think about their own meagre conditions. It does not occur to them to challenge authorities on their own behalf. So the killing is not the fault of the impoverished white shooter: *"he's only a pawn in their game"*. Dylan describes Evers' killer as follows: *"He's taught in his school/From the start by the rule/That the laws are with him/To protect his white skin/To keep up his hate/So he never thinks straight/'Bout the shape that he's in/But it ain't him to blame/He's only a pawn in their game"*.[3]

'Only A Pawn In Their Game' belongs among Dylan's more thoughtful finger-pointing songs, songs in which he displays a unique insight into the various characters that he portrays, be they the referee who failed to stop the Moore-Ramos bout, the hypocritical judge who barely sentenced rich William Zanzinger or the kind of man who would shoot Medger Evers. With *'Only A Pawn In Their Game'*, Dylan again shows that he is capable of seeing the world in ways that others do not.

The lyrics of *'Only A Pawn'* contain clues having broad implications about the direction that Dylan's thinking was headed. With *'Only A Pawn In Their Game'*, without saying so directly, Dylan implied that the calls for changed ways of thinking by members of the 'Folk Protest Movement' were likely to be in-effective. In spite of the movement's good words and intentions and its years of activism, elected officials behind closed doors motivated by personal gain still made (or failed to make) the real decisions that set history's direction. And it was they who affected how people really thought, without their even knowing it.

With Greenwood as the background for *'Only A Pawn'*, Dylan may have made the connection between his analysis of the Southern bigotry of poor whites and the failure of the voter registration efforts. Both failures resulted from closed-door betrayals by apparently allied but now seemingly corrupt politicians. In recognition of this, even Martin Luther King and the once-conciliatory 'SCLC' were now changing directions, as Forman predicted, towards increased militancy. In his song, Dylan also suggested that the causes of racial division were broad-based and systemic, much as 'SNCC' and Jim Forman had come to conclude. Deep-rooted social and political problems were not easily to be resolved by the techniques of the 'Folk Protest Movement', one-on-one, by appeals to an individual's conscience.

A final, dark message lurks at the end of *'Only A Pawn'*, largely as a result of the disappointments experienced during the voter registration drives. Leadership is not to be trusted. This message applies regardless of whether one's political sympathies lie with the Left or the Right. Dylan's talent for distinctive insights was leading him to reject the received wisdom of others. Instead of continuing to accept the directions of others, he would soon abandon the 'Folk Protest Movement' and seek instead to obtain first-hand knowledge of all the experiences the world has to offer. Think critically and be independent, Dylan seems to be urging. Do not be a pawn in some larger game.

* * *

Following Dylan's Greenwood appearance, disillusioned by the President's inaction and the results of making political concessions, Jim Forman discouraged attendance at the Kennedy-endorsed, politically expedient March on Washington, scheduled for later that summer. With recent events, Dylan may have begun to suspect that his singing had a somewhat questionable impact on advancing the subjects of the civil rights movement. The black folk singer Taj Mahal made some candid and critical observations about the eventual shortcomings of a form of protest that Dylan, too, undoubtedly began to doubt:

"I did one show with the 'Freedom Caravan' or whatever it was called. It was in a place that was hot as hell. Phil Ochs got up and started singing about how he wasn't marching and he wasn't this and he wasn't that. And these black kids were sitting there in the heat, bored shitless, listening to this guy who had nothing to do with them. They were being used".

"I realized that the folksingers were talking at people . . . Who needed Joan Baez or Phil Ochs or me, for that matter?"[4]

Despite Jim Forman's admonitions not to attend, just six weeks after singing at Greenwood, Bob was at the March on Washington. For a few moments, he sang on stage, entertaining the audience as a crowd of several hundred thousand gathered throughout the day. Joan Baez was the first to sing, at a single microphone in front of the Washington Monument. In addition to *'We Shall Overcome'*, Joan chose an Odetta song, *'Oh Freedom'*. She was followed by Odetta herself and then the entertaining former bluesman, Josh White. Next, Peter, Paul and Mary gathered around one microphone to sing Pete Seeger's song, *'If I Had A Hammer'*, and their then-current hit, *'Blowin' In The Wind'*. Dylan sang *'Only A Pawn In Their Game'*. He then joined Joan and his friend from the Gaslight, the black folk singer Len Chandler, in a rendition of the great Negro spiritual, *'Keep Your Eyes On The Prize'*.[5]

After this display of black and white folk singers performing together and singing each other's songs, the crowd turned from the Washington Monument to the Lincoln Memorial, where two black women singers would rouse the audience. The legendary opera singer Mirian Anderson sang *'He's Got The Whole World In His Hands'*, followed by the genius of gospel, Mahalia Jackson, whose classic number *'How I Got Over'* led directly to the appeals of civil rights leaders. Martin Luther King gave his religiously inspired *"I Have a Dream"* speech. The speeches also included a more critical, potentially divisive speech by John Lewis, chairman of 'SNCC', who predicted that the cause of black Americans would eventually prevail, not religiously through God's intervention, and not through moral righteousness or conciliation, but rather through the social and physical force of the black Americans' being. An early draft of Lewis' speech was written by Dylan's new friend, Jim Forman.

In reaction to the event, some black Americans questioned the prominent role at their demonstrations of figures symbolizing young whites, such as Joan Baez and Dylan. Thereafter, they were welcomed to continue to stand behind, but not necessarily to stand in front of, the leaders of the black civil rights movement.

* * *

In addition to his direct observations of the civil rights movement, Dylan soon came to believe that the continued concerns of Woody Guthrie's original New York backers, the sponsoring founders of the 'Folk Protest Movement', were largely those of a bygone era, shaped by the Great Depression, World War II and McCarthyism. The members of this older guard were inadequate role models as the sixties exploded with calls for new forms of experimentation. Many of the struggles that Woody's old colleagues fought were also understood as incestuous ones; that is, within their own movement about leadership and political theory and about toeing the correct political line (particularly in re-hashing past hearings before the 'HUAC', where Burl Ives, Theo Bikel, Pete Seeger and Irwin Silber of *Sing Out!* magazine had each responded to Congressional questioning with varying degrees of cooperation).

Abstract debates about participation in a political movement were, Dylan came to believe, too removed from contact with the real people–the minorities, labour and the poor–who the movements professed they were trying to help. Detached from the present-day world of actual people, the initial leaders of the 'Folk Protest Movement' were understood as having lapsed in importance, as having committed themselves to being a movement devoted only to being a movement. After leaving the 'Folk Protest Movement' behind, Dylan explained his position in a 1966 interview by noting the differences between being dedicated to a real thing and being dedicated to an artificial or abstract construction:[6]

Hentoff: *"Do you think it's pointless to dedicate yourself to the cause of peace and racial equality?"*

Dylan: *"Not pointless to dedicate yourself to peace and racial equality, but rather, it's pointless to dedicate yourself to the cause; that's really pointless. That's very unknowing. To say "cause of peace" is just like saying "hunk of butter". I mean, how can you listen to anybody who wants you to believe he's dedicated to the hunk and not to the butter?"*

In Greenwood, Dylan had heard first hand of the dark reality of broken promises and the resulting need for underground political action. Within six months, Dylan would speak out, albeit awkwardly, about his growing dissatisfaction with many of the tenets of the non-confrontational, well-to-do wings of the civil rights movement. They imposed beliefs and required behaviour to which Dylan could no longer conform. He also asserted his individualism, seeking the freedom to think for himself. He would not be a pawn in the liberals' game any more than the poor whites should have been pawns in the racist wars taking place in the South.

The Kennedy Assassination

In November 1963, in the midst of Dylan's re-thinking of his relationship to the politics of the 'Folk Protest Movement', President Kennedy was assassinated. The man that Eric Andersen had described as the *"shadow of flight"*, protecting reform and the 'Folk Protest Movement', was shot from the sky. The nation suffered a crippling shock. As a loss, whether to national and global politics or in its impact on his young family, the killing's immensity was almost unthinkable. Immediately, the blue-ribbon Hoover Commission was formed to determine officially whether Lee Harvey Oswald acted alone. The Commission also set out to define what the public should think of the event, explaining it finally as the act of a lone madman. At the time, Kennedy's death was not perceived as heroic or meaningful in the sense that he died in the service of a higher cause. Instead, the death only served to underline the ultimate tragedy of the human condition.

On a personal level, the Kennedy assassination caused Bob to reflect on life's fragility and its sometimes meaninglessness, bringing him to awkward confessions about how he now saw himself in the world. If there were inexplicable, random or even counter-progressive forces shaping history, resulting in irrational acts beyond one's control, then someone taking an active part in that history (as Dylan was rapidly finding himself) might want to re-think his role. In the first of his *"11 Outlined Epitaphs"* (the liner notes from his January 1964 album, *"The Times They Are A-Changin'"*), Dylan alluded to the effect that Kennedy's assassination had had on him. It brought feelings he'd never felt before and left him drained and exhausted, like a wrung-out dishrag:

"The shot has shook/me up . . . for I've never/heard that sound before/bringing wild thoughts at first/ragged wild/numb wild/now though they've leveled out/an'

69

been wrung out/<u>leavin' nothin' but the strangeness</u>/the roots within a washed-out cloth/drippin' from the clothesline pole/strange thoughts/<u>doubtin' thoughts</u> . . ."

Friends around him feared that Dylan might himself be the target of an assassin. With his heightened self-consciousness, themes of nothingness and fatalism crept into his work. Dylan's view toward political reform became cynical and almost selfish. As he said at one point:

"I can't see myself on a platform talking about how to help people. Because I would get myself killed if I really tried to help anybody. I mean, if somebody really had something to say to help somebody out, just bluntly say the truth, well obviously they're gonna be done away with. They're gonna be killed".[7]

Dylan knew immediately that, as a consequence of the Kennedy assassination, the context in which he viewed the music of the 'Folk Protest Movement' had been irreversibly changed. In describing the days following the assassination, Dylan recalled:

"The next night, Saturday, I had a concert upstate, in Ithaca or Buffalo. The song I was opening with was 'The Times They Are A-Changin'' and I thought 'Wow, how can I open with that song? . . . Something had just gone haywire in the country and they were applauding that song. And I couldn't understand why they were clapping or why I wrote that song, even. I couldn't understand anything. For me, it was just insane".[8]

Precisely because the assassination was so inexplicable, it overturned many of the basic assumptions of the 'Folk Protest Movement' and the conciliatory struggle for civil rights. Those movements were based on gradually effecting positive change through rational appeals to peoples' consciences and the political process. Dylan was already moving away from that position, as evidenced by the wider implications of *'Only A Pawn'*. The Kennedy assassination hastened his intellectual movement, challenging Dylan's basic assumptions about the laws that govern existence and how we understand who we are. Dylan was moving away from the progressivism of the 'Folk Protest Movement' towards a form of existentialism that would eventually find a new meaning through music. The reasons for Dylan's intellectual evolution are not hard to describe.

The foundation of most forms of progressive thinking, such as that behind the 'Folk Protest Movement', is the existence of a rational, natural order of being from which wrongful thinking, like prejudice or racism, is viewed as an irrational aberration. Because men and nature are thought to be fundamentally rational, progress away from wrongful thinking can be viewed as inevitable. Further, for progressive thinkers, progress is believed to be hastened by the efficacy of reasoned behaviour undertaken by groups of individuals (like the 'Folk Protest Movement') or through progressive institutions of law, such as the Supreme Court's decisions in the 'NAACP's series of civil rights cases. Kennedy's assassination indicated, by contrast, that the steady forward march of history could be suddenly shattered. A radical interruption in the nation's progress could apparently be affected by a lone gunman and a single, inexplicable act of violence. Oswald's act thus challenged the liberals' prior confidence in the imminent triumph of their reason-based belief in the advance of mankind.

Dylan also had personal reasons for his darker mood in the closing months of 1963. He felt his Midwestern Jewish roots were cruelly and unfairly exposed in Andrea Svedberg's *Newsweek* article of November 1963, which also stirred controversy over whether Dylan or a high school student was the true author of *'Blowin' In The Wind'*. In *'11 Outlined Epitaphs'*, Dylan explained how he had been content with his early celebrity, with all the *"posters an' the like that're painted for me"*, until he was attacked by his critics, whom he characterized as hurlers of garbage, defiling his image. As Dylan described it, *"[T]he nex' time I looked/the gloves of garbage/had clobbered the canvas/leavin' truckloads of trash/clutterin' the colors/with blindin' sting/forcin' me t'once again/slam the shutters of my eyes"*. According to his closest friends at the time, however, the Kennedy assassination, and not the *Newsweek* article, had the greatest effect on Dylan's negative outlook at the end of 1963.[9]

* * *

Less than a month after the Kennedy assassination, Dylan was called upon to speak as the recipient of the 'Tom Paine Award' and guest of honour at an 'Emergency Civil Liberties Committee' ('ECLC') fundraiser in New York City. The previous year, the award had been given to the world-renowned philosopher and mathematician Bertrand Russell for his contribution to civil liberties. At the time, Russell was enjoying particular fame for his resistance to the manufacture of atomic bombs in England. The protest marches that Russell had led included group singing, which had given Pete Seeger the idea for *Broadside* magazine (which, in turn, supported Dylan's early finger-pointing protest songs).

On the surface, Bob Dylan seemed to share the same background and concerns for civil liberties as the great Bertrand Russell. In December 1963, however, the 'ECLC's designation of Dylan as the recipient of its highest honour was ironic and probably hard for him to bear. Bob despised hypocrisy perhaps as much as anything, and the 'Folk Protest Movement' was rapidly becoming a cause in which he no longer believed. Nonetheless, Bob was being honoured for his contributions to it. Making matters worse, the award was handed to him by Clark Foreman, the father of Dylan's reckless, expressive friend from Boston. Geno Foreman strongly rejected his father's beliefs.

When Bob finally reached the podium to deliver an acceptance speech, the depth of his re-thinking was clear, although he spoke with considerable confusion. It was Friday the 13th after all, and he'd had too much to drink. He stumbled over his references to the assassination, saying in effect that he saw something of himself in Oswald. Bob appears to have meant that he, like Oswald, was frustrated and sometimes felt rage at the world, particularly at its political processes. As a loner and self-perceived outcast, he sometimes felt like striking back.

With the Kennedy assassination, Dylan argued, we must recognize that these are violent times, and we all must acknowledge that there is violence, both in and around each of us. As Dylan looked down from the dais at the guests of the Americana Hotel, he saw black and white faces in their formal attire. He questioned aloud their notion of progress and their apparent goal of uplifting the black man to the point where he would wear similar, respectable clothes. You don't serve to improve a black man's condition by having him wear a tie, said Dylan. Each person is who he is. He remembered his friends from Greenwood and their mission, and he couldn't connect them with the banquet attendees. As he further tried to explain his feelings, Dylan said that he also resisted other people's telling him what he can and can't do, and where he can and can't visit. Dylan closed his remarks by praising those who favoured open travel to Castro's Cuba and accepted the *Tom Paine Award* on their behalf, further confusing and alienating the members of his audience:

"And I look down to see the people that are governing me and making my rules–and they haven't got any hair on their head–I get very uptight about it. (Laughter) And they talk about Negroes, and they talk about black and white . . . I don't see any colours at all and if people have taught through the years to look at colours–I've read history books, I've never seen one history book that tells how anybody feels . . . So, I accept this reward–not reward (Laughter) award–on behalf of Phillip Luce who led the group to Cuba which all people should go down to Cuba.[10] *I don't see why anybody can't go to Cuba. I don't see what's going to hurt by going any place. I don't know what's going to hurt anybody's eyes to see anything".*[11]

With his reference to Cuba, Dylan was not so much endorsing Castro as he was criticizing the U.S. government. In late 1963, travel to Cuba was in the news largely on account of the esteemed black journalist, William Worthy, who made four trips to the island nation in defiance of a U.S. ban. Upon his last return, he was tried and jailed, until his conviction was overturned on appeal in 1964. Phil Ochs told the story in his song, *'Ballad Of William Worthy'*, which contains the lines, *"[I]t is strange to hear the State Department say/You are living in the free world, in the free world you must stay".*[12]

Without being as clear as he might have wanted to be, Dylan's position apparently was based on the underlying hypocrisy of a government (the United States) that professed freedom for its citizens and then imposed restrictions upon an individual's exercise of that freedom through the institution of travel bans. His approach to the Cuban travel issue was similar to his use of irony in *'With God On Our Side'*. In exposing hypocrisy in that song, the self-righteous beliefs of modern Americans were shown to be no better than the beliefs of the forbears whom they ridicule.

In many ways, with his 'ECLC' speech, Dylan was re-enacting a scene at the end of *"Bound for Glory"* in which Woody Guthrie reacted to being put on stage before New York City's well-to-do patrons of the arts and charitable causes in the

Rainbow Room, high above Rockefeller Center. Like Woody, Dylan couldn't relate to the moneyed interests represented, nor could he sense the honesty or motivations of the persons in attendance. Like Woody, Dylan felt as though he were being used.

Dylan's appearance at the 'ECLU' dinner might also be analogized to James Dean's last film, *"Giant"* (1956). *"Giant"* was a sprawling epic in which Dean's character, the ranch hand Jett Rink, receives a small inheritance of land that subsequently yields oil, transforming him into a millionaire. For years, Jett is able to live extravagantly, but he finds no happiness in it as others around him attempt to take advantage of his wealth and betray him. Throughout it all, Jett refuses to sell out. The film closes, however, with him collapsing in a drunken stupor at a testimonial dinner given in his honour.

* * *

As revealed in a letter of apology written later that month, December 1963, Dylan's anger and frustration at the 'ECLC' dinner stemmed in part from his impatience with liberal organizations that he regarded as each constituting little more than a kind of mutual admiration society. He was also reacting against the notion, first put forth in *'Who Killed Davy Moore?'*, that liberals can somehow distance themselves from the unpleasant aspects of the events that surround them, setting themselves apart and above others over whom they feel they can pass their judgment.

In his remarks to the 'ECLC', Dylan revealed the same kind of problem that he was coming to have with participating in political or charitable movements of any type – he resented being told what he should think, see or feel. Henceforth, he would think for himself and live for himself. He would refuse, as his earlier song intimated, to find himself playing a pawn in anyone else's game. Like the leaders of 'SNCC', Dylan was shedding associations with others who sought to chart his direction in order instead to strike out on his own.

Dylan's lecturing of well-to-do patrons at a liberal, charitable fundraiser about his misgivings about them and their goals, tentatively announcing his newfound apolitical stance while revealing his personal self-doubts, was an inappropriate and regrettable act. At the same time, however, Dylan's remarks at the 'ECLC' fundraiser provide revealing insights into the direction that his thinking was heading. Dylan later explained his 'ECLU' experience to a friend, as follows:

"They didn't understand me because they got mind-blinders on. They couldn't understand that Oswald was like me, and like you. He was uptight about the times we're livin' in, about all the lies they feed ya, about the history books that tell ya facts not worth a damn, but never once tell you how somebody <u>feels</u>. That's what Oswald was about. That's what I'm about. But those people don't understand. All they can see is a cause, and using people for their cause. They're tryin' to use me for something, want me to carry a picket sign and have my picture taken . . . They're all hung up on games. But the games don't work any more".[13]

Significantly, after the Kennedy assassination, Bob's songwriting career turned away from social and political causes. Instead of exploring the outward meaning of public events, Dylan turned inward. He wanted to explore the realm of people's feelings. This theme stood in contrast to the pursuit of a more rational outlook toward solving social problems. The theme culminated, of course, in his song *'Like A Rolling Stone'*, with its chanted chorus of *"How does it feel?"*

Dylan was beginning to adopt the outlook of a dispossessed person who, because he or she no longer senses a strong foundation of support, must learn to be self-sufficient. Such a person seeks confirmation of self-worth not through widespread social validation, but inwardly, in-and-of-himself. As a budding existentialist, Dylan was losing interest in all "causes" that professed to have neat, packaged answers to who people are and how they should act. Setting himself apart, Dylan would deliberately pursue his own course, steadfast and alone, with both eyes wide open.

Notes:

[1] Farina, Richard. *"Baez and Dylan: A Generation Singing Out"*, *Mademoiselle* (August 1964 issue), reprinted in David A. DeTurk and A. Poulin, Jr. (eds.), *"The American Folk Scene: Dimensions of the Folksong Revival"*. Dell, 1967, p. 251-52 (emphasis added).

[2] Scaduto, Anthony. *"Bob Dylan: An Intimate Biography"*. Grosset, 1971, 161.

[3] Medger Evers' killer was, in fact, Byron de La Beckwith, a white supremacist fertilizer salesman, who was freed by two all-white juries and went free until convicted of murder in a third trial 31 years later. He was a World War II veteran and an avid anti-Communist. Ironically, he considered the South's assertion of states' rights in opposition to integration, as well as the Confederate rebellion in the Civil War, as part of an ongoing worldwide struggle for freedom and self-determination.

[4] Von Schmidt, Eric and Rooney, Jim. *"Baby Let Me Follow You Down"*. 2 ed. *Amherst, MA: U Mass. Press*, 1994, 218.

[5] Crosby, David and Bender, David. *"Stand and Be Counted"*. Harper Collins, 2000, 14-17.

[6] The Nat Hentoff interview originally appeared in *Playboy* magazine (March 1966 issue). It is reprinted in Craig McGregor, ed., *"Bob Dylan, The Early Years: A Retrospective"*. Da Capo Press, 1990, pp. 124-45.

[7] Scaduto, op. cit. at 177.

[8] Id., 160 (emphasis added).

[9] Id., 160-61.

[10] Phillip Abbott Luce was then a radical leader against segregation who identified his own activism, not unlike that advocated by Jim Forman of 'SNCC', with the revolutionary approach of Fidel Castro and Che Guevera, fighting guerrilla warfare from the mountains. He then felt that Castro's government represented the future for the Americas. Luce, an acquaintance of Dylan, is quoted at some length in the 'Report of the Senate Fact-Finding Subcommittee on Un-American Activities in California', no. 13, 1965, available from the Online Archive of California.

[11] *Half-Moon Foundation, Inc.* 'Bob Dylan and the 'NECLC" <http://www.corlisslamont.org/dylan.htm>. (Accessed 11 June 2003).

[12] Bob's girlfriend Suze Rotolo also favoured free travel to Cuba. Two of her acquaintances, Pete Karmen (who later travelled across country with Bob) and Albert Maher, actually defied the ban and visited Cuba. Robert Shelton. *"No Direction Home: The Life and Music of Bob Dylan". Beech Tree*, 1986. 222-25, 271 and 295.

[13] Scaduto, op. cit., 190-91.

Published in *ISIS* issue #116, September 2004

Mississippi 'NAACP' leader Medgar Evers (with placard), being arrested whilst picketing outside the Jackson Mississippi branch of Woolworths, with national president Roy Wilkins & local police (1964)

A Close Encounter of the Third Kind

Meeting Dylan

Tony DeMeur

Now let's get this straight, where Dylan is concerned, I am in no way an 'anorak'. An occasional 'duffel coat' maybe, but never an 'anorak'.

Our paths, Mr Zimmerman's and mine, crossed for the first time in, I believe, 1962. It was a Sunday night and I was preparing for bed following belated completion of my homework and prior to facing a thrilling new week at Enfield Grammar School, when my interest was caught by a television play titled *"Madhouse On Castle Street"*. Apart from a quirkily attractive central performance from a very young David Warner, I can really only remember the sight of this strange, curly-haired geezer sitting at the bottom of the stairs playing guitar and harmonica (on a rack!) and singing this song in a rough but highly memorable voice and the context somehow made it all seem a lot weirder.

Then, a few months later, I remember Marco Pugliesi, the really cool prefect who sneered at us third formers, swanning round the playground brandishing a copy of *"The Freewheelin' Bob Dylan"*. He then sold his collection of 45s by great rock 'n' roll and r&b artistes, including obscure original Chuck Berry and Eddie Cochran sides, for he had 'seen the light' and Dylan was the way forward. We all thought he was crazy to offload these gems – a fact that I feel Mr Zimmerman would readily concur with – but we purchased them hungrily.

Cut to 1969 and I'm wrapping up printing blocks at *Westminster Press* when this ex-Oxbridge bloke, who worked in the office, asks if I have a reel-to-reel tape recorder. I do and spend every available hour that I'm not in that hell-hole running off copies on my mono *Ferrograph* of the *"Great White Wonder"*, later to be legitimately released in the mid-70s as *"The Basement Tapes"*. For all this turgid, time-consuming toil, I received not one silver shilling but my 'bootlegging' credentials were assured.

Next stop The Astoria, Charing Cross Road in London's West End at the tail end of the eighties and I bump into Stan Lynch, Tom Petty's drummer whom I'd got to know through opening for The Heartbreakers across the States in my band "Fabulous Poodles". He's over playing Wembley Arena for several nights with Roger McGuinn and Dylan. He points out this hunched, shadowy figure in the corner wearing shades, seemingly oblivious to everything that's going on around him and another image is burnt into my memory.

In the early nineties Dylan is playing a week of shows at the Hammersmith Odeon and on the Thursday night I'm playing with my band "Ronnie & The Rex" at the brand new Jongleurs club in Camden. During the band break I spot my misanthropic mate, John Dowie, on the prowl for alcoholic placation. A long-term awesomely obsessive Dylanophile, he's purchased tickets for both tonight's show and tomorrow's and just walked out in disgust. *"How was it?"*, I redundantly inquire. *"He was CRAP! I'm bloody well not going back tomorrow or ever again"*. He then goes on to bad-mouth my band whilst necking the beers from our 'rider' and I'm ready to rip his head off. I smoulder with resentment over this for a couple of days and then I get an invite to a post-gig bash on Saturday night – following Dylan's final show – at Dave Stewart's studio in Crouch End in North London. I arrive around 10.30 after performing a stand-up gig in Islington, and amplifiers have been set up alongside a drum kit and microphones, presumably for some late night jam with Bob.

I throw back the free Buds and chat away to Bob Geldof and The Blockheads' Johnny Turnball and get twitchy for the arrival of His Bobness.

When he finally makes his shambling entrance, at around 1.30, I am, as they say, "many sheets to the wind" and it suddenly occurs to me that I should attempt to make amends with Dowie and adopt a Buddhist approach to the situation. I will try to get Dylan's autograph for him on a *"Ronnie & The Rex"* promotional card so that he – Dowie – will see how mean-spirited he'd been to viciously slag off the both of us and he will learn from this situation and find a new spiritual plane. Mmm.

I drunkenly push my way forward to get next to the great man but, being a whole lot more "Bud" than "Buddha", I blow it big-time. When Dylan asks me who I am and what I do, I murmur, something along the lines of: *"Oh, compared to you I am nothing"*. Aaaaaaaaaargh!

Dylan, to his eternal credit says *"Hey, man, we all of us have something to offer"*, or some such placating comment but by this time I'm so eaten up with embarrassment I fall into the background to lick my social bruises. Sean Hughes, a chum of Dave Stewart, asks what's wrong and I spill the whole miserable nine yards of my excruciation and he says he'll ask Dave to get the autograph for me. He performs this task quickly and generously and I stagger out at stupid o'clock with my trophy safely tucked inside my pocket.

The following Thursday I'm playing a stand-up gig in The Concorde in Brighton and I nervously invite Dowie along. Just prior to leaving I hand him the newly-framed and wrapped autograph and I watch him open it with a twinge of expectation.

"What's this?" he asks.
"What do you THINK it is?"
"Well it looks like Bob Dylan's autograph".
"Well maybe that's just what it fucking is!"

"Did he sign it with his left hand or his right hand because the right hand ones are worth a lot more money?"

At this I start to lose it but to save a screaming match I storm out of the door of the club and leg it to the station feeling hurt and disappointed that someone who I'd thought to be a friend could be so callously materialistic. Upon arriving back at my gaff in Tottenham, I play back my ansaphone and there it is: Dowie's voice full of contrition; all: *"I'm REALLY sorry. What a kind and generous thing for you to do and I was rotten and don't deserve it"*, etc. I'm chuffed by this but decide to let him sweat for a bit.

A couple of weeks later and I read this piece in a Sunday paper discussing the individual value of autographs of living legends and there he is at No 1: Bob Dylan worth two hundred and fifty smackers. Ouch! I jokingly phone up Dowie in Brighton and start by saying: *"You know that Dylan autograph I LENT you"* and before I can finish he's in with *"Yeah, two hundred and fifty quid so you can FUCK OFF!"*

Somehow it makes it all worthwhile when your friends appreciate your endeavours.

Published in *ISIS* issue #106, January, 2003

Bob Dylan 1965

Daniel Kramer
Bringing It All Back Home

Interview by Derek Barker

New York based award-winning photographer Daniel Kramer has had his pictures published throughout the world and has been exhibited or collected by such museums as the *National Portrait Gallery*, the *Whitney Museum of American Art*, and the *International Center of Photography*. His 1967 book, *"Bob Dylan"*, was the first major photo-book on the artist and Daniel has been nominated by the "Music Journalism" Awards for his photographs of Bob Dylan. His pictures appear on the album covers of *"Biograph"*, *"Highway 61 Revisited"* and *"Bringing It All Back Home"*, which was nominated for a Grammy Award and selected by *Rolling Stone* magazine as one of the *"100 Greatest Album Covers of All Time"*.

Daniel's posed shot of Dylan (head on hand) has become one of the best known of all the images of Dylan. However, before being able to photograph the man whom he once described as having a *"left out in the rain and rusted"* voice, Daniel had to *"run the gauntlet"* of Dylan's office and manager.

In our time-honoured fashion, *ISIS* has created Daniel Kramer's story about photographing Bob Dylan during 1964 and '65, by editing together his answers given to questions asked by Derek Barker in October 2004.

***

I first saw Bob Dylan on a TV show (*'The Steve Allen Show'*, broadcast on February 25th, 1964). I loved the voice, but what struck me most were the words. The fact that someone was saying what he was saying, and of course the manner in which he was saying it was very strong. The song was *'The Lonesome Death Of Hattie Carroll'*. I didn't know who he was when I saw that performance, but I felt that it was unique to be doing what he was doing at that time. It was startling that such a young person was telling that story. Saying those things and saying them that way. I decided there and then that I wanted to photograph him. Eventually, I found out who his manager was, but when I called the office I was told they didn't give interviews and they didn't set any pictures up, so I was kind of turned away, but since I wanted to photograph him I just kept asking. It took a while and after some letters and calls I eventually called after hours, which was a good thing because I got Albert Grossman on the phone and he realized that I had been trying to do this for a while and that I didn't want much; I just wanted an hour to do a portrait. So he gave me a date and said I should go up to Woodstock to make my portrait. That was August 1964.

Just beyond the town of Woodstock there was an unmarked driveway that went up to the home of Albert Grossman, which is where I first met Bob Dylan. A sign posted on a tree along the driveway read: *"If you have not telephoned, you are trespassing"*.

Dylan didn't like to be pinned down, he didn't like to be told, do this, look in the camera, sit here and so forth; he just wanted to be doing his own thing. I think part of that came from the fact that he was innately shy and private. Maybe some of the privacy simply came from being shy, but in any event, he had this energy and wanted to do things, he was always on the move. I did some portraits of him in a rocking chair but he didn't want to sit and pose, and photographing him was a challenge. I have found this with other subjects; they challenge you to see what you can come up with. One of the ways he challenged me was, he said, *"We're gonna watch some movies"*. They put me in a darkened room and we watched home movies; me, Dylan, and Dylan's road manager and friend Victor Maymudes. We just watched home films in Albert Grossman's old kitchen. There was no light! How was I supposed to photograph him? It was his way of testing me; he did this with journalists, he would ask a question of them. He asked a question of me and I think I surprised him by coming up with a very good photograph of them watching these films. We ended up having lunch at Bernard's Café and we got the chess-playing pictures. The day just went on for four, five, or six hours. We did other things, he climbed a tree; he got very helpful after a while and I thought I had a successful day, including some of those rocking chair portraits. Anyway, ultimately I thanked him for his day and I said that I would show him the pictures. That was all there was to it. The shoot was essentially black and white but I do have colour in a lot of situations. I had several camera bodies, sometimes I would have four or five because you don't want to have to change lenses.

The next time I saw Dylan was at Albert Grossman's New York office. I went up to show Albert and Bob the pictures of the day; I spread out these 11" x 14" prints and Bob got a big kick out of the shots of him sitting up the tree. When we were standing at the table looking at the pictures, Bob turned to me and said, *"Hey, I'm going to play a concert in Philadelphia next week, would you like to come?"* and I said, *"Yeah, that would be really good, only I don't have a car"*, and he said, *"Well, I'm gonna be driving, tell me where you live and I'll come and pick you up"*. So he and Victor Maymudes came by and picked me up and we drove to Philadelphia. That was nice because there was a chance for us to get to know each other.

There were a number of concerts, I can't give you a specific number as we speak, but Philadelphia (Town Hall, late September 1964) was the first time I'd seen him perform live; it was very, very exciting, more than I realized it would be. After that concert he said he had to go elsewhere, but I didn't go with him because I had other commitments. He asked if I could drop him and Victor off at the airport when we got back to New York and if I would keep the station wagon, a late model Ford, and pick them up from the airport the next week. It wasn't planned; it was all just whatever happened. Next, I think there were a couple of concerts in New Jersey, one of which was at Princeton University. Allen Ginsberg was at that show. I then photographed Bob at the Halloween concert. If the concerts were only 100 miles or so from New York City they would drive, but if the shows were any further they would fly.

At that time we started doing a lot of things together; the recording session photos, the cover picture for the album, plus we went to Kingston one night and we played billiards and played on the pinball machines. To be honest, I don't know how I ended up at the *"Bringing It All Back Home"* recording session, Bob might have said, *"Do you wanna take pictures at the session"*, or I said, *"You're having a session, I think I would like to come and take some pictures"*, I don't know, we just ended up doing these things together. There were times that we went out to places together and I didn't take a camera. We would go down to the Village or out to dinner, I didn't take photographs on some of those occasions and maybe I should have.

The music for *"Bringing It All Back Home"* all happened in the studio, it wasn't brought in pre-determined, and my pictures of Dylan were basically made the same way, except for the album cover, which was pre-determined. That picture was made in January 1965, after the recording sessions. I can't remember whether it was Bob or Albert who asked me to do the album cover, but it was frowned upon by the art department at *Columbia Records*. I didn't have the kind of reputation they wanted for the cover picture of their guy, but Bob and Albert insisted, and they insisted rather strongly. They told people up there . . . well they said harsh things, they said, this is how it's going to be; so I got to do this cover and I had to really think about it, to make something special, and I'm pleased to say that I think it is something special.

I wanted to show Bob as someone unique and special, someone at the centre of things with a world turning wildly about him. I explained the concept to Bob; that he was to be stationary in the centre with the rest of the room revolving around him. To accomplish the effect for the cover I built a special rig out of wood and glass that enabled me to turn the camera during the exposure while keeping Bob Dylan sharp, still, and centered. This was 30 years before *Photoshop*, and we did this on one sheet of film. I made a *Polaroid* picture for Bob and then I did a *Polaroid* with him and Sally kind of in place and when he saw that he got very excited.

Of course the *Polaroid* was in black and white, but he understood what we were going to do and he thought it was a really good idea and we all went to work producing the set. There were a lot of props introduced in there, but far fewer than we would have had if I had let Bob have his way! People have written to me over the years asking, *"Who is the mysterious lady in red?"* Not so much now, but at one time I would get requests like, *"Is that Bob in drag?"*

The art designer who was against my doing that cover didn't like what I had done. My friend, Judy Collins, rang me at the studio one day and said, *"You have been nominated for a Grammy for best album cover"*. At first I didn't know what she meant because I hadn't submitted anything. But we got the nomination and I was very pleased to be able to tell the art director he might be getting a plaque with his name on it for the cover that he wasn't too happy about.

I think up until then that wasn't the way people did album covers. They did portraits; strong pictures of the performer either live or in the studio and it was two years later that *"Sgt. Pepper's"* came out. I just question sometimes if my cover didn't stimulate the thinking that you can do posters, you can do showbiz and be entertaining, you can use the cover to make statements; because if you look around historically you don't find that kind of thing before, so I think it gave the feeling of, ha, ha, look what you can do with an album cover! Sell records!

Bob called the studio one day and asked me, *'What are you doing?'* I guess I'm supposed to say I'm working; anyway he asks if he can come by with some friends and make some pictures. So, Bob, Peter Yarrow, and John Hammond Jr, appeared at my studio door and Bob told me that he wanted to make some *'street pictures'*. So, we ran around Fifth Avenue and we made a bunch of pictures; some quite silly and some OK, one of them ended up on the back cover of *"Bringing It All Back Home"*; the one with the two policemen. He liked to be photographed with policemen.

The next thing we did was the *"Tarantula"* cover that never was! That session, up in Woodstock in March '65, was intended to produce the cover for Bob's book. He wanted Sara Lownds in the picture and we started to devise it and I have some shots where they are both sitting in front of an old shack. Then we put Sara in there looking out and we found all these things inside, family things that were stored in there, the framed picture that is on the front of the shack is of Pete Yarrow's cousin. I think we were having too good a time and when we looked at the picture we all agreed that in essence it was too close to the album cover, so it was an agreement on all parts. It was an interesting picture, but not what we needed for the book cover.

I finally got him in to the studio, which I think was very important and significant for both of us, because, as we started out saying, he didn't care to be pinned down, he just liked to jump around. I told him it was very important that we had a serious session, I didn't use the word serious, but I meant one in which we could do portraits where I had more control and I could try to get something more specific. He eventually said OK and I don't know if he had ever really done that before, have a real studio session, and it went fine and as a result of it we got some pictures that are still being used today. There were some really good ones, he lent himself to that. The *"Biograph"* box set cover twenty years later would show that. I'm never happy when designers colour my pictures, but I was pleased that Bob chose that picture for *"Biograph"*. I don't usually let people do that sort of thing to my pictures, but then I usually go along with what Bob would like. I feel that the making of the pictures is not one-sided. The pictures are not good because he posed and I took them, they're good because we did them together and I think he has the right to take certain liberties.

Bob always let me work. To get an understanding of that, at Philharmonic Hall, on October 31, which recently was released as the '64 live concert CD, there's a press box where the photographers were required to photograph from. I was told that I had to go up in that press box and photograph from there. That's not the way I worked and that's not the way you get good pictures. Anyway, Bob was doing a soundcheck or something and I was backstage and he asked me, *"How are things going, are you getting what you need?"* and I said, *"Well, not really, because I have to be up in this press box and I just wanna be where I wanna be"*. So Bob told Albert to tell the house manager that I should get permission to do whatever I wanted to do. Therefore, I was given carte blanche. I walked out on stage took photographs from behind; there were never any restrictions when we were working. The reasons for this freedom could have been because Bob might not have worked with anyone like me before. I was not a photojournalist, I didn't know what the rules were, I was just making them up as I went along and I just did what I had to do to take good pictures.

We didn't have any automatic cameras, no auto-focuses, no auto this and auto that. I sometimes think about being in the dark with three or four cameras and setting the exposures and turning the lens dials and the shutter speeds and remembering, I am two away from an eighth of a second and thinking, oh, I'll click back two. There were no lights on in the halls and I would just do it all by feel. I would make long exposures of a quarter of a second and a half a second. I have a picture in my book that was made at one second and I hand held it. It was madness, the music was like that and the pictures were like that.

Most of these pictures were made with a Nikon SP; a rangefinder camera that is no longer made. It was a popular camera with photojournalists during the late 1950s through the 1960s. W. Gene Smith was very helpful to me. In the 40s, 50s and 60s, Eugene was the great *"Life"* magazine photojournalist; he was a living legend. I guess he was the Bob Dylan of photojournalism and when he saw my pictures of Dylan he was very encouraging and helpful to me. He told me I didn't have enough wide angle shots to tell my story and I said well, *"I don't have a wide angle lens"*, he gave me his camera that had a wide angle lens on and he said, *"Well, now you do"*. That was just before the Forest Hills concert. The shot of the speakers and the band just perched on top of them wouldn't have happened if Gene hadn't given me his camera with what in those days was a holy smokes 28mm wide-angle lens. It was very exciting to have it and I tried to use it to make statements. The whole time photographing Dylan was like that and that was all part of the excitement.

Bob and I had worked together quite a lot on the *"Highway 61"* album cover. He had to leave for Europe so I took all the pictures over to his apartment and we looked at them on a makeshift viewer and Bob choose that picture. He said, *"This is it, this will be the cover"*. By that point, he had reached that position, he had strength and power with the record company and he could just say, *"This is it"*. The mysterious legs on the *"Highway 61"* picture are holding my *Nikon* SP and we will never know who those legs belong to; it's a secret that I'm taking with me to the grave.[1] Right after when Bob Woodward tells us who Deep Throat is, I'll tell you who the legs belong to. I set that because I really felt I needed something to fill that part of the frame and as my subject was standing there I gave him that camera to hold and I think it helps the balance. The Triumph shirt was Bob's idea. He wanted to wear that shirt and it turned out to be a good idea.

I think by the summer of 1965 Bob was beginning to feel some pressures. You are 24 years old and everyone says you're wonderful and your songs are anthems and on and on; who's prepared for that? So, certainly there's pressure. I mean, he must have been thinking will I ever be able to write another *'Blowin' In The Wind'* or whatever; like next week. I guess every creative person feels that way; you write a novel and it's terrific and you think, well, now what am I going to do? At this time new things were happening that were complicating his life. For example, in the summer of '65 you have the Pennebaker film/tour (*"Dont Look Back"*), that's a whole new and tiring experience. You must remember that you have *"Bringing It All Back Home"* and just a few months later he's recording *"Highway 61 Revisited"*, an incredible album. So, there were two major albums and the film/tour and the book (*"Tarantula"*); who can handle all that? You have to feel pressure, and if you don't then there's something wrong with you!

And then we have the electrifying performance at Forest Hills! I shot Dylan way into the '80s at different concerts, but Forest Hills was the last session of great importance to me. I felt that was the conclusion to my story. It was the metamorphosis. He was going from the more naive folk singer to the rock star and the person who changed the music business. That twelve months period (August 1964 – August 1965) was basically the story for my book and so the conclusion is that concert. Newport, which was a month earlier, wasn't a Bob Dylan concert, it was a festival and some of the old timers weren't too happy, but Forest Hills was the real moment of truth. There's a picture from that concert that I like very much. Bob's in profile and his hair is aglow, back lit, and he's got the guitar and I see him as a centurion, as a warrior about to do battle with the audience. This was his moment of truth. This was the matador before the gate opens and out he was gonna go and find out what he was gonna find out. The rest is history. And those pictures took care of that, I felt satisfied.

Note:

[1] Although Daniel isn't telling who the legs on the *"Highway 61 Revisited"* album cover belong to, *ISIS* happen to know the owner is musician, sixties Dylan companion, and member of the Rolling Thunder Revue tour, Bobby Neuwirth.

In addition, since our interview with Daniel, Deep Throat has identified himself as being former FBI agent Mark Felt. So, that's two more of life's mysteries cleared up.

Published in *ISIS* issue #117, November 2004

And Now, That Cover

The photo session for the cover of *"Bringing It All Back Home"* took place in January 1965 at the Bearsville home of Sally and Albert Grossman. *Columbia Records* suggested they would like a cover that illustrated the recent changes in Dylan. This time round there would be no dowdy black and white photograph, no work-shirt, no acoustic guitar and no folksy looking girlfriend. This cover would deliver a new hip Dylan wearing a silk shirt and cufflinks. It would contain bright colours and a glamorous woman. The cover was discussed at Grossman's Manhattan office and at Dylan's suggestion, Sally Grossman was commandeered to join him in the photograph. Daniel Kramer spent several days preparing for the session and designing a "rig" that he would use to create the swirl effect. The session itself lasted for several hours.

* * *

Starting at the bottom left-hand corner of the record sleeve there is a coffee table and leaning against the table is a Nuclear Fallout Shelter sign for an 80 person capacity shelter. The signs were introduced by the US defence department on December 1, 1961. On the table itself (extreme left, grey blur) is a small black and white portable television. Next is a gold carriage clock, one of Bob's harps, and a black and white item that we are unable to identify. The copy of *Time* magazine is the January 1, 1965 issue featuring "Man of the Year" Lyndon B. Johnson on the cover.

At the centre of the picture is a chaise-longue. This was a wedding present to Albert and Sally Grossman from Mary Travers of Peter, Paul and Mary. As already mentioned, the lady reclining on the chaise is Sally Grossman (wife of Dylan's manager, Albert). Sally is wearing a red pantsuit bought from Sheila Jordan's boutique on Saint Mark's Place in Manhattan's East Village. Sally bought the outfit especially for the photo-shoot and never wore it again.

Dylan is wearing a silk shirt (complete with purple cufflinks), blue jeans and a black jacket. The jacket and the cufflinks were gifts to him from Joan Baez – she would make reference to the cufflinks a decade later in her song about Bob Dylan, *'Diamonds And Rust'*. Contrary to popular beliefs, the Persian kitten in Bob's arms was not his; it belonged to the Grossmans. The kitten is usually misidentified as Rolling Stone. Rolling Stone came later, this Persian, probably named by Bob, was actually called Lord Growling.

Open, on Dylan's knee, is a large format magazine that cannot be identified because only the back cover, which features a full-page advert for a magazine biography of Jean Harlow by Louella Parsons, is visible.

Behind Sally Grossman (to her right) are what appears to be two slightly overlapping cream-coloured rectangles. This is actually a fabric lamp-shade that is caught in the swirling camera effect. Just below the lamp-shade, and again very out of focus, is a tambourine.

The record albums positioned between Bob and Sally are: *"Folk Blues Of Eric Von Schmidt"* (1963); *"Lotte Lenya Sings Berlin (Theatre Songs By Kurt Weill)"* (1955); *"King Of The Delta Blues"* (1961) by Robert Johnson, and *"Keep On Pushing"* (1964) by The Impressions. The black and white album cover, which is almost totally obscured between the Lotte Lenya and Robert Johnson records, is almost certainly *"India's Master Musician"* (1963) by Ravi Shankar. Behind Sally Grossman (to her left) is *"Another Side Of Bob Dylan"* (1964).

Moving up to the ornate plaster mantelpiece, at both ends of which stand gold candlesticks with lighted candles, is a hooded monk-like figure, next to which is probably the most interesting item of all, the clown. The wall-mounted clown face was made by Dylan in 1964 by gluing pieces of coloured glass to a clear glass sheet. Dylan gave the clown to his friend, Bernard Paturel, for display in the Café Espresso in the centre of Woodstock. Dylan borrowed the clown from Bernard to use as one of the props for the cover-shoot. The clown survives to this day and is owned by Bernard Paturel's son who lives in France.

Below the clown is a bright purple/pink item. This is a copy of an "underground" magazine called *Gnaoua*. Published in Tangier in spring 1964, *Gnaoua* took its name from a black African-Moroccan sect known for its ecstatic dancing and possessed trances. The magazine was edited by Ira Cohen and only one issue was produced. It contained material mainly by William Burroughs and Allen Ginsberg and the copy on display here was almost certainly given to Dylan by Ginsberg. The front cover drawing for the magazine, previously described in *The Telegraph* as a *"happy pig"*, is actually a Cantharides beetle drawn by an artist by the name of Rosalind.

To the right of *Gnaoua* magazine is a copy of *"The Best Of Lord Buckley"* (1963).

The large portrait (painting) to the right of the Lord Buckley LP is something of a mystery. However, I'm told that when the Grossmans bought the house it contained a number of portraits of the previous owners' forebears and it is possible that one of those portraits is the painting on the mantelpiece.

Was the album-cover a success? Well, besides being nominated for a Grammy Award, Sally Grossman reported that *"Bob thought we looked dynamic, like Elizabeth Taylor and Richard Burton"*.

So You Want To Be a Rock & Roll Star
The Story of *'Like A Rolling Stone'*

D e r e k   B a r k e r

"The first time that I heard Bob Dylan, I was in the car with my mother . . . and on came that snare shot that sounded like somebody kicked open a door to your mind. . ."

Bruce Springsteen.

The Dylan masterpiece, *'Like A Rolling Stone'*, celebrates its 40th Anniversary this summer (June 2005) and in November 2004 it was named as the number one song in *Rolling Stone* magazine's *"500 greatest songs of all time"*. Dylan responded to this pronouncement by saying: *". . . you know the lists change names . . . I don't really pay much attention to that"*.[1] I suppose Bob is right, the lists do change, but this is nevertheless a fantastic accolade that finally places the song in its rightful place at the very top of the pile. In 1989, *Rolling Stone* magazine published a list of its *"best singles of the past 25 years"*, which placed *'Like A Rolling Stone'* at number two, behind the Stones' 1965 hit *'(I Can't Get No) Satisfaction'*. The 2004 pole reversed those positions.

When released as a single in July 1965, the song only reached number two on the *Billboard* chart (though it did make the number one spot on *Cashbox*) and number four in the UK. The album that contained the song, *"Highway 61 Revisited"*, peaked at number three on *Billboard* and only reached number four in the UK, which makes the *Rolling Stone* pronouncement all the sweeter, especially as anecdotal evidence seems to indicate that Dylan almost disregarded it as a song and that *CBS* came close to disregarding it as a single.

By 1965 Dylan had become weary of the limitations imposed on him by the folk medium and by the end of his eight-date English tour he had decided to quit singing. When stories emerged that Dylan had been ready to quit, many people shrugged off the notion as half-baked or maybe nothing more than a characteristic Dylan put-on; the truth, however, was far from that. By late 1964 Dylan had already begun to relieve his increasing boredom by working on his surrealist writings, many of which would eventually be published in *"Tarantula"*. Dylan's book of prose poems, presented as a novel, had become a way for him to unload a head full of ideas that were driving him insane. When asked by interviewer Paul Robbins why he was writing a book instead of song lyrics, Dylan answered:

"I've written some songs, which are kind of far out, a long continuation of verses, stuff like that – but I haven't really gotten into writing a completely free song. Hey, you dig something like cut-ups? I mean, like William Burroughs? . . . I wrote the book because there's a lot of stuff in there that I can't possibly sing".[2]

Very soon, however, Dylan would realise that he could translate some of his stream-of-consciousness writings into songs. At any rate, the realisation came with *'Like A Rolling Stone'* and the seeds of this song can be seen as early as May 1965 in the film *"Dont Look Back"*. Many commentators have cited the Hank Williams' recording *'Lost Highway'*, with its lyric of *"I'm a rolling stone, I'm alone and lost/For a life of sin I've paid the cost"*, as one of the possible inspirations for Dylan's song. If they are correct, that moment in a London hotel room on May 4, 1965 had been captured by The Don(n) in his film. Also caught on film in *"Dont Look Back"* is the moment, backstage, when Dylan seems to stumble across what he would later describe as being a riff from Richie Valens' *'La Bamba'*. I can't hear the connection between *'La Bamba'* and *'Like A Rolling Stone'*, but I can hear the similarity the between the piano chords played backstage in *"Dont Look Back"* and the finished *'Rolling Stone'*.
  Dylan began writing this long prose poem as soon as he arrived back in the USA from England (June 2-3, 1965). He may even have started it on the plane home.

"I'd literally quit singing and playing, and I found myself writing this song, this story, this long piece of vomit about twenty pages long, and out of it I took 'Like A Rolling Stone' and made a single. And I'd never written anything like that before and it suddenly came to me that that was what I should do, you know. I mean, nobody had ever done that before".[3]

"'Rolling Stone' is the best song I wrote. I wrote 'Rolling Stone' after England. I boiled it down, but it's all there. I had to quit after England. I had to stop and when I was writing it, I knew I had to sing it with a band. I always sing when I write, even prose, and I heard it like that".[4]

"It wasn't called anything, just a rhythm thing on paper".[5]

Depending on which of the interviews you read, *"this long piece of vomit"* was either six, ten, or twenty pages long. Probably the most accurate account of its original length was told to Robert Shelton: *"It seemed like twenty pages, but it was really six. I wrote it in six pages"*. At some stage Dylan began extracting lines from the six pages and *"boiling them down"* into a song.

"I never had thought of it as a song, until one day I was at the piano, and on the paper it was singing, 'How does it feel?'"[5a]

"My wife and I lived in a little cabin in Woodstock, which we rented from Peter Yarrow's mother. I wrote the song there . . . We had come up from New York, and I had about three days off up there to get some stuff together. It just came. It started with that 'La Bamba' riff".[6]

"The song was written on an old upright piano in the key of G-sharp, then later at Columbia Recording Studios transferred to the key of C on the guitar. The chorus part came to me first and I'd sorta hum that over and over: then later figured out that the verses would start low and move on up. The first two lines, which rhymed 'kiddin' you' with 'didn't you' just about knocked me out; later on, when I got the jugglers and the chrome horse and the princess on the steeple, it all just about got to be too much".[7]

Dylan had been amazed by the string of hits that The Beatles had achieved in the USA in 1964–'65. *"I knew they were pointing the direction where music had to go"*, said Dylan. Other people were having hit singles with electrified music, even electrified folk music; so when the Animals achieved success with an electric *'House Of The Rising Sun'*, Dylan must have thought that it was about time he had a hit single.

The potential for *"folk-rock"* was not lost on producer Tom Wilson and on the afternoon of December 8, 1964, four months after the Animals had reached number 1 with *'House Of The Rising Sun'*, Wilson attempted to graft electric instruments on to three existing Dylan recordings, *'Mixed Up Confusion'*, *'Rocks And Gravel'* and his début album rendition of *'House Of The Rising Sun'*! I can only think that it was the chart success of the Animals single that seduced Wilson into returning to Dylan's 1962 performance of *'Rising Sun'* because I'm hard-pressed to think of a more unsuitable selection of material.

Interestingly, after his English tour, which had included him admiring electric guitars in a shop window in Newcastle and showing great interest in an English group called the Freewheelers who were attempting to perform his songs with electric backing, Dylan had gone into Levy's Recording Studio (May 12, 1965). This session (in a studio recently acquired by *CBS*) could simply be discounted as nothing more than Dylan wanting to jam with some British R&B musicians. However, the fact that Tom Wilson was flown out from New York to produce the session suggests that this was meant to be something more than a jam session. Perhaps *Columbia* thought that the best way to challenge the "British Invasion" was to record Dylan in Britain with British musicians! In any event, little was achieved and the session was abandoned. However, nine days later in New York, Tom Wilson was back in the studio experimenting and overdubbing a recording of *'If You Gotta Go, Go Now'* from a January '65 *"Bringing It All Back Home"* album session. This second attempt at overdubbing Dylan's recordings would seem to support the notion that *Columbia* was anxious to release an electric Bob Dylan single. Had Wilson been successful in transforming the Jan '65 recording of *'If You Gotta Go, Go Now'* into a single, we may never have seen *'Like A Rolling Stone'* released as a 45rpm.

Tom Wilson: *"We . . . put like a Fats Domino early rock and roll thing on top of what Dylan had done but it never quite worked to our satisfaction. We flirted with putting ('House Of The Rising Sun') out as a cover of the Animals record– but we never put that version out. That's when I first consciously at Columbia started to try to put these two different elements* [folk and rock] *together".*[8]

Undeterred by his failed attempts to electrify Dylan's songs, Wilson would soon set about embellishing (without their knowledge) the Simon and Garfunkel song, *'The Sound Of Silence'*, with electric bass, guitar, and drums and this time his handiwork went to number 1 on the chart.

Confirmation that *Columbia Records* were trying to propel Dylan's career (and combat the "British Invasion") at this time is evident from a statement that ran in the US trade press on May 29, 1965: *"NOW BOB IS BIGGER THAN BIG BEN. Bob has finally turned the tide and reversed the English wave that has captivated the United States. The English trade papers currently list five Dylan LPs and two singles high in their charts. . ."*

Then, just a few days after his arrival home from England, the Byrds began their march up the *Billboard* chart. And they had achieved this, their first chart success, by turning Dylan's own folksy 2/4 time *'Mr Tambourine Man'* into a 4/4 time pop song. This ethereal and catchy adaptation, which in essence combined Bob Dylan's lyrics with the pop harmonies of The Beatles, was released in April 1965. It went to number one on both sides of the Atlantic and became a million seller.

Personnel

No one is quite sure why Dylan was in *Columbia* Studio 'A' on June 15 and 16, 1965. It would have been unusual for our man to go into the studio for the sole purpose of cutting a single, but the lack of songs that he took with him to the sessions would seem to belie any notion that this visit was a serious attempt at recording an album. Maybe it was an experiment just to see what he had in his arsenal. At any rate, by the time the song was recorded everyone seemed to be talking about it as a single. In an interview with *Rolling Stone* magazine Dylan talked about an A & R man from *Columbia Records* visiting Albert Grossman's home directly after the session and stating, *"that is gonna be a hit single"*.

Whatever the reason for the sessions, it's clear that it was always intended that they would feature a backing band. The personnel recruited for the *"Highway 61 Revisited"* sessions, especially the two sessions that produced *'Like A Rolling Stone'*, have for many years been a cause for disagreement amongst Dylan chroniclers. All are agreed that Mike Bloomfield, Al Kooper and Bobby Gregg were present, but Frank Owens and Paul Griffin (piano – organ), Russ Savakus and Joseph Macho Jr. (bass) and Al Gorgini (guitar), have also all been attributed to the *'Rolling Stone'* sessions on June 15 and 16, 1965.

With the notable addition of guitar wizard Mike Bloomfield, who was there at the request of Dylan himself, Tom Wilson's choice of musicians appears to have been based around those who had accompanied Dylan some five months earlier on the *"Bringing It All Back Home"* album. And then there was Al Kooper. Wilson, who had produced all of Dylan's sessions for the previous two years, invited Kooper along to watch the session, but Kooper had other ideas. *"There was no way in hell I was going to visit a Bob Dylan session and just sit there. . ."*

For years, one of the biggest difficulties in chronicling these sessions has been getting past the myths and legends of Al Kooper. In his autobiography, *"Backstage Passes"*, (and in numerous interviews), Kooper has recounted his tangled tale of how *'Like A Rolling Stone'* was captured in just one take. This assertion was proved to be pure fantasy with the release in 1995, of the *Graphix Zone* produced CD-ROM, *"Highway 61 Interactive"*.

Many of Kooper's recollections of these sessions are clearly wrong. For instance, he attributes both *'Tombstone Blues'* and *'Queen Jane'* to his second studio session with Dylan, when in fact *'Tombstone Blues'* was recorded on July 29 and *'Queen Jane'* on August 2. Kooper has, therefore, managed to mix up three different recording sessions that took place nearly seven weeks apart.

While researching this article, I came across an amazing quote by Kooper in the Wolkin and Keenom book about Michael Bloomfield, *"If You Love These Blues"*. In an interview contained in this book, Kooper's seven-week discrepancy (June to August) mentioned above, pales into insignificance as what was actually a rainy June day becomes *". . . the dead of winter in New York . . . it was snowing out"*. I'll have some of whatever Al was on! On that subject, it's interesting to read the "remarks" section on the studio Tape Identification Data sheet for June 15, *"Lots of hash"*.

Unfortunately, the erroneous accounts given by Al Kooper also seem to extend to several more of the songs from the *"Highway 61 Revisited"* sessions and possibly also to some of the personnel. Although bizarrely my research has revealed that, while Kooper's recollections about his own part in these landmark sessions is extremely shaky, his recall of the other musicians present on the *'Like A Rolling Stone'* sessions concurs with my own findings.

Although conventional wisdom (Krogsgaard, Dundas, Bjorner and just about everyone and anyone who has ever documented these sessions) now seems to gravitate toward Frank Owens taking the piano part on *'Like A Rolling Stone'*, Kooper is adamant that Paul Griffin was the piano man. In his book *"Backstage Passes"*, he reports that Griffin, a man Kooper knew well, was the best player in New York City and tells how his own later sound can be traced directly back to Griffin's playing. The piano dilemma hasn't been helped by the fact that over the years both Griffin and Owens have stated that they played on the song. The truth is that, while both men played on the *'Like A Rolling Stone'* session(s), only one of them, Paul Griffin, is on the celebrated recording.

Recent photographic evidence, in the shape of a Don Hunstein photograph printed on page nineteen of the *"Live 1966"* booklet, has been most useful in helping us confirm the personnel on this session. This photograph, which is credited as being from June 15, clearly shows Frank Owens seated at the Hammond and Bob Dylan playing the piano. The fact that Dylan played piano throughout the June 15 session has always been clear to me simply from the audio evidence. Clinton Heylin is absolutely right when he says in his book *"The Recording Sessions 1960 – 1994"*: *"Forget the musician credits in "The Bootleg Series" booklet–that's Dylan on piano"*.

This, however, provides Krogsgaard, Dundas, Bjorner et al with a logistical problem. If Owens is at the Hammond and Dylan is playing piano throughout, where does Al Kooper fit in? The accepted story is that the organ player was moved to the piano (by Tom Wilson) and that Kooper filled the gap. On June 15, however, Dylan was almost certainly at the piano for the entire session so this move would not have been possible. If Kooper was at the June 15 session (and he maintains he wasn't) he must have played guitar and not keyboard. The above scenario of Kooper taking over the vacant seat at the Hammond therefore could only have occurred at the second *'Like A Rolling Stone'* session.

Contrary to popular beliefs, my information is that neither Al Gorgoni nor Frank Owens was at the second *'Like A Rolling Stone'* session on June 16, a fact confirmed to me by both Gorgoni and Kooper. This meant that there was no rhythm guitarist on the second session, a vacancy that was filled by Dylan himself. Now, without Bob's backside on the piano stool, the legendary keyboard hopping could take place. Paul Griffin, who had been invited to play organ at this second session, was now asked to take over the piano from Dylan, leaving the Hammond free for Al Kooper's distinguished debut on the instrument.

Apart from Michael Bloomfield, all of the musicians were New York-based session men and it has never been clear to me why Dylan decided to invite Bloomfield the eight hundred miles down from Chicago rather than simply using Bruce Langhorne as he had done on his previous album. While there is no doubting Bloomfield's prowess as a guitarist, Langhorne says that Bloomfield told him that when he arrived for the sessions, Dylan asked him to *"play like Bruce Langhorne"*. This seems a strange request when the real deal was already on Dylan's doorstep. There has been some conjecture as to whether Langhorne was simply unavailable for these sessions; however, Bruce Langhorne recently told *ISIS* that not only was he *"in town"* at the time of the sessions but that he was in the studio with Dylan on June 16 and that he played tambourine – a regular size one, not the *'Mr Tambourine Man'* Turkish tambourine – at this session.[9] I have to admit that I had previously failed to notice a tambourine on the track and had always heard the metallic sounds as being one of Bobby Gregg's cymbals. However, after cleaning out my ears and listening to the SACD, the jingle-jangle of a tambourine can clearly be heard.

Bloomfield was reluctant to go down to New York to play on the Dylan sessions and he confided to a friend in Chicago that (based on Dylan's first album) he didn't like Bob's voice and that he thought his music was *"terrible"*. Bloomfield eventually agreed to attend the sessions and Dylan collected him from the Port Authority Bus Terminal after his flight from Chicago. Dylan had invited Bloomfield to arrive three days before the recording was due to start and had taken him up to his Woodstock home to talk guitar licks and to sample Sara's toasted tuna fish and peanut salad. Dylan clearly had a 'sound' in his mind that he wanted to capture or to create.

Bloomfield: *"He taught me these songs* [including] *'Like A Rolling Stone'. . . and he said, 'I don't want you to play any of that B. B. King shit, none of that fucking blues'. . . So we fooled around and* [I] *finally played something that he liked. It was very weird, he was playing in weird keys, which he always does, all on the black keys".*[10]

Although it was overcast and raining quite heavily for mid-June, Tuesday June 15 began like any other New York day. The recording session had been set for 2.30 in the afternoon and as the musicians made their way to the HQ of those whores on Seventh Avenue, the rain started to come down even harder. In order to give himself enough time to hatch a plan, Al Kooper had decided to arrive early at Studio A, which was on the top floor of what was then the New York head office of *Columbia Records*, at 799 Seventh Avenue, between West 52nd and West 53rd streets. Kooper calmly walked into the studio sat down and tuned his guitar.

Kooper: *"Tom Wilson hadn't arrived as yet, and he was the only one who could really blow the whistle on my little charade. I was prepared to tell him I had misunderstood him and thought he had asked me to play on the session . . . Suddenly Dylan exploded through the doorway with this bizarre looking guy carrying a Fender Telecaster without a case".*[11]

"He had it on his shoulder like some guy in a platoon or Johnny Appleseed or something".[10a]

"It was weird, because it was storming outside and the guitar was all wet from the rain. But the guy just shuffled over into the corner, wiped it off with a rag, plugged in, and commenced to play some of the most incredible guitar I've ever heard . . . I was in over my head. I embarrassedly unplugged, packed up, and went to the control room".[11a]

According to Kooper, by the time Tom Wilson arrived he had already retreated to the control room and therefore escaped having to explain the subterfuge of a few minutes earlier. However, the photographic evidence mentioned earlier, in the shape of the Don Hunstein picture from the *"Live 1966"* CD, seems to refute this. In this photograph, which purports to be (and the personnel present utterly confirms it to me) from June 15, the studio clock reads five past four, which is one hour and thirty-five minutes after the session started and the guy on the extreme left of the picture, playing a Fender Jazzmaster guitar, sure as hell looks like Al Kooper. For good measure, Tom Wilson (who Kooper maintains arrived late) can clearly be seen watching out of the control room window! An email to Al was all it took to confirm that the Beatle-booted Jazzmaster guitarist was indeed Al Kooper.[12a] However, after explaining to Al that this picture was from the first *'Rolling Stone'* session, at which he has always maintained he did not play guitar, Al could only conclude that the guitarist in the picture might, after all, not be him, but Kenny Rankin![12] (see note 12 for further details)

Nevertheless, at some stage Kooper must have decided that he was *"in over* [his] *head"* and asked Wilson who the hot guitar kid was. Wilson informed Kooper that he was *"some friend of Dylan's from Chicago, named Mike Bloomfield"*. Wilson said he'd never heard him play but that Dylan said he was the best.

Now rated by many as one of the finest white American blues guitar players ever, at the time of the Dylan session Bloomfield was one month shy of his 21st birthday and this would be his first engagement as a professional session-musician. The two men had met in Chicago in April 1963, where Bloomfield had been making a name for himself with the guitar since age sixteen. Dylan had been booked to open Albert Grossman's Bear club and Bloomfield decided to search out Dylan before the show with a view to putting him down – *"cutting him with* [my] *guitar"*. However, when Bloomfield talked to Dylan he found him to be very personable and the two men ended up spending time jamming together.

Bloomfield: *"I went down to see him when he played in Chicago. I wanted to meet him, cut him, get up there and blow him off the stage. He couldn't really sing, y'know. But to my surprise he was enchanting. I don't know what he had, but he got over".*[10b]

Dylan: *"I was playing in a club in Chicago . . . and I was sitting in a restaurant, I think it was probably across the street or maybe it was even a part of the club, I'm not sure, but a guy came down and said that he played guitar. So he had his guitar with him and he began to play. I said, 'Well, what can you play?' And he played all kinds of things. I don't know if you've ever heard of a man, does Big Bill Broonzy ring a bell? Or Sonny Boy Williamson, that type of thing? Anyway, he just played circles around anything I could play and I always remembered that. Anyway, we were back in New York, I think it was 1963 or 1964* (sic), *and I needed a guitar player on a session I was doing, and I called* [him] *up, I even remembered his name, and he came in and recorded an album".*[10c]

On their arrival at Studio A, the reason for Dylan inviting Bloomfield to come to Woodstock a few days before the start of the recording sessions became apparent.

In an article for *Hit Parader* (Vol. 27 #48, June 1968) Bloomfield said this about the first *'Like A Rolling Stone'* session:

"Bob told me 'You talk to the musicians, man, I don't want to tell them anything' . . . All these studio cats are standing round and I come in like a punk with my guitar over my back and start giving orders. These are the heaviest studio musicians in New York. They looked at me as if I was crazy. Al Kooper was there. I didn't know who he was then. It was my first break, too. Dylan remained isolated . . . He just sang his tunes and they fitted the music around him. As far as I can remember, I never saw any communication between Dylan and the band. There are songs like 'It Takes A Lot To Laugh, It Takes A Train To Cry' and 'Like A Rolling Stone' where there seems to be some sort of communication. It happened almost by mistake . . . he's a mysterious cat. It's weird when you're working with a genius. When you're talking to him you just know he's seeing everything. His

little eyes are seeing every bit of truth and every bit of bull, and he's categorizing it, working with it, understanding it. He's a genius and it's very strange to know a cat like that. Dylan exudes this force, this very magnetic thing, he's a beautiful guy".

So, without realising it, Bloomfield had become the band leader. This concept of "teaching" one of the musicians the songs and then asking them to impart that information to the rest of the band seems to be a commonplace approach for Dylan.

Bloomfield: *"You wouldn't believe what those sessions were like. There was no concept . . . No one knew what the music was supposed to sound like—other than Bob, who had the chords and the words and the melody. But as far as saying, 'We're gonna make folk-rock records' or whatever, no one had any idea what to do. None.*

It was never like, 'Here's one of the tunes, and we're gonna learn it and work out the arrangement'. That just wasn't done. The thing just sort of fell together in this haphazard, half-assed way. It was like a jam session. He had a sound in his mind . . . the Byrds' sound was what he wanted to get in his sessions . . . The producer was a non-producer—Tom Wilson. He didn't know what was happening. I think they wanted rock & roll. We did 20 alternate takes of every song, and it got ridiculous".[10d]

The two sessions that spawned *'Rolling Stone'* would be the last time that Tom Wilson would work with Dylan. When recording for the *"Highway 61"* album recommenced on July 29, Wilson had been replaced by another in-house *Columbia* producer, Bob Johnston. But on to June 16 and *'Like A Rolling Stone'.*

Kooper: *"They weren't too far into this long song . . . before it was decided that the organ player's part would be better suited to piano . . . In a flash I was all over Tom Wilson, telling him that I had a great organ part for the song and please could I have a shot at it".[11a]*

Wilson's retort that Kooper didn't even play the organ was apparently met with, *"Yeah, I do, and I got a good part to play in this song".[11b]* Kooper says that Wilson was adept at wading through his bullshit and therefore quickly informed Al that he didn't want to embarrass him by letting him try out. Minutes later, Wilson had to leave the room and in a flash Kooper was in the studio and sitting at the organ.

Kooper: *"It's difficult to power up a Hammond organ. It takes three separate moves, I later learned. If the organist hadn't left the damn thing turned on, my career as an organ player would have ended right then and there".[11c]*

Wilson then returned to the control room and immediately asked Kooper what he was doing sitting at the Hammond. Kooper just laughed and remained at the keyboard. This moment was captured on tape and can be heard on the *"Highway 61 Interactive"* CD-ROM. The musicians begin to play and Kooper felt his way through the changes *"like a little kid fumbling in the dark for the light switch"*.[11d]

Kooper says he couldn't hear the Hammond properly because the speaker was on the opposite side of the studio and was partly covered with a blanket. But as Kooper says: *"The tape is now rolling, and that's Bob-fucking-Dylan over there singing, so this had better be me sitting here playing something"*.[11e]

Kooper: *"If you listen to it today, you can hear how I waited until the chord was played by the rest of the band, before committing myself to play in the verses. I'm always an eighth note behind everyone else.*

After six minutes they'd gotten the first complete take of the day and everyone adjourned to the control room to hear it played back. Thirty seconds into the second verse of the playback, Dylan motioned toward Tom Wilson. 'Turn the organ up', he ordered".[11f]

Tom Wilson then informed Dylan that Kooper was not an organ player to which Dylan replied:

"Hey, now don't tell me who's an organ player and who's not. Just turn the organ up".[11g]

How Many Takes?

The booklet that accompanies *"The Bootleg Series Volumes 1-3"* gives "official" testament to the recording of *'Like A Rolling Stone'*. However, like much of the official material it is clearly erroneous and appears to have been based on anecdotal evidence from planet Kooper, which is supported by a misleading quote given by Dylan to *Rolling Stone* magazine in 1988, both of which state that the released version of *'Like A Rolling Stone'* was the final take on day one (June 15). These two concurring but woefully inaccurate recollections could be seen as being corroborated by the reproduction of a Tape Identification Data sheet for the June 15 session on the back inside cover of the *"Bootleg Series"* booklet. While the June 15 sheet correctly represents the fragmentary outtake that is included on the *"The Bootleg Series Volumes 1-3"*, it could also be seen as supporting the statements made by Kooper and Dylan that there was only ever one complete take of *'Like A Rolling Stone'*. Had the tape sheet for the following day (June 16) also been reproduced, it would have shown that there were a further fifteen takes – five of which were complete – of the song and that far from being captured in a single complete take, *'Like A Rolling Stone'* was in fact one of the most laboured recordings of Dylan's career up to that point.

As well as five unsuccessful stabs at *'Like A Rolling Stone'*, including a 3/4 waltz time rendition of the song, the June 15 session also included two other songs, *'Phantom Engineer Cloudy'*, a possible reference to the inclement June weather, and *'Over The Cliff'*. These two songs might well have been potential b-sides for the single, but if that were the case, Dylan cannot have been happy with either song and he would end up using *'Gates Of Eden'*, a track from his previous album as the flip side. Of the two rejected songs, a reworked *'Phantom Engineer Cloudy'* would eventually make it onto *"Highway 61 Revisited"* as *'It Takes A Lot To Laugh, It Takes A Train To Cry'* while *'Over The Cliff'*, proper title *'Sitting On A Barbed Wire Fence'*, would remain unreleased for more than 25 years until both of these original takes saw official release in 1991 on *"The Bootleg Series Vols. 1-3"*.

Personnel Revisited

As previously stated, exactly who played on the two *'Rolling Stone'* sessions has long been a cause for disagreement. Now, with the *"Live 1966"* booklet photo and after following a number of clues from my detective bag, I think we are there or thereabouts.

Tuesday June 15th, 1965: 2.30pm – 6.30pm

Bob Dylan (piano, harmonica, vocals), Robert *"Bobby"* Gregg (drums), Joseph Macho jr. (bass), Mike Bloomfield (lead guitar), Al Gorgoni (rhythm guitar) Frank Owens (piano) Al Kooper (guitar at the start of the session, but probably not on *'Rolling Stone'*.

The bass player, who can clearly be seen in the *"Live 1966"* booklet photo, is Joseph Macho jr. (not Russ Savakus as previously proposed by Heylin). The rhythm guitarist at the session is Al Gorgoni. Al Kooper did not play organ at this session.

Wednesday June 16th, 1965: 2.30pm – 5.30pm

Bob Dylan (rhythm guitar, harmonica, vocals), Robert *"Bobby"* Gregg (drums), Joseph Macho jr. (bass), Mike Bloomfield (lead guitar), Paul Griffin (piano), Al Kooper (organ), Bruce Langhorne (tambourine).

The Aftermath

Dylan: *"I recorded it last on a session after recording a bunch of other songs* (sic). *We took an acetate of it down to my manager's house on Gramercy Park and different people kept coming and going and we played it on the record player all night. My music publisher just kept listening to it shaking his head saying 'Wow, man. I just don't believe this'"*.[7a]

Record producer Paul Rothchild: *"Dylan just sat in a chair with a smile plastered on his face and his leg going a mile a minute. He was grooving on the knowledge that he'd made a great record . . . What I realized . . . was that . . . one of the so-called Village folksingers – was making music that would compete with all of THEM – the Beatles and the Stones . . . without sacrificing any of the integrity of folk music or the power of rock 'n' roll".*[3a]

Dylan: *"An A & R man from Columbia Records was also there. He kept saying that is gonna be a hit single and it couldn't be cut. He was anticipating people at the record label saying it was going to be too long. I think that was a big thing to overcome at the time, the length of the song".*[7b]

At the time Shaun Considine was coordinator of new releases at *Columbia Records'* New York HQ.

Considine: *"The song had to be presented at Columbia's weekly singles meeting, and that's where the trouble began. Though just about everyone from the A & R and promotion departments loved it, the sales and marketing people had a different opinion.*

Their objection to the song came on two levels. The unstated reason was that they just didn't like raucous rock 'n' roll. The sales and marketing people had made Columbia a winner by selling mainstream American music . . . But rock? No way.

Of course, this was [not] raised at the meeting . . . What did come up was the length of the song. In 1965, three minutes was the average time for singles played on national radio. 'Like A Rolling Stone' clocked in at one second under six minutes. The solution? Cut the baby in half, the wise Solomon of Sales decreed".[14]

Now, at the same time that the sales team was debating the length of the proposed Bob Dylan single, the records division was moving out of 7th Avenue and into the corporation's new building on Sixth Avenue and staff positions were also being shuffled. This would be the perfect time to lose this problematic six-minute *rock 'n' roll* single.

Considine: *"A memo was sent out saying that the single was to be moved from an 'immediate special' to an 'unassigned release'. Translated, it was in limbo,* [probably] *soon to be dropped".*[13a]

However, just prior to the move Considine came across a studio-cut acetate of *'Like A Rolling Stone'*. He took the record home, played it, loved it as much as he had done when he had first heard it and decided to take it along to a new hip Manhattan club called Arthur, on East 54 Street. Considine took the acetate along to the club and asked the DJ if he would play it. *"The effect was seismic. People jumped to their feet and took to the floor, dancing the entire six minutes. Those who were seated stopped talking and began to listen".*[13b]

The next morning *Columbia* received calls from New York radio stations *WABC* and *WMCA* asking where their copies of the new Bob Dylan single were.

99

Considine: *"Staff meetings were hastily called. Goddard Lieberson . . . was brought into the dispute over the length of the song . . . The release memo came shortly thereafter".* [13c]

Once the release memo came through, things started to move very fast and within a month of the recording session the single was shipped to radio stations and record stores across the United States. The single was released on July 15 and on July 17 it was *Cashbox's "Pick of the Week"*. It entered the *Billboard* Top 100 on July 24 and reached the #2 slot where it remained for 2 weeks. It was a similar story in Britain where the single entered the chart on August 19, peaking at #4. The record stayed on both the US and British charts for 12 weeks.

The song, which was so good it made a young Frank Zappa want to quit music altogether, would define the summer of '65.

Studio session June 15, 1965. Personnel from left - Al Kooper, Al Gorgoni, Mike Bloomfield, Frank Owens, Joseph Macho Jr, Tom Wilson, Bob Dylan

Asides and Besides

The original mono album was mixed by the two Bobs, Dylan and Johnston. The single mix of *'Like A Rolling Stone'* was, however, included as mixed by the original producer, Tom Wilson. Johnston says that the first copies of *"Highway 61 Revisited"* arrived from the pressing plant without Tom Wilson's name on the sleeve and that he demanded that the sleeves be remade with Wilson's name included. Bob Johnston would, however, have to remix the entire album for release in stereo, which of course necessitated his remixing *'Like A Rolling Stone'*, and in process Johnston seems to have made some very subtle changes. There is a story that one *Columbia* executive told Johnston that the whole vocal track needed to be rerecorded! The chance of getting Dylan to do that was zero and Johnston appears to have simply ignored the exec's demand. During the stereo remixing, however, Johnston does appear to have brought Dylan's vocal slightly to the fore. Finally, the stereo mix is a few seconds longer than the single/mono album mix. In an interview for *Mix* magazine, Johnston told Dan Daley about the antiquated recording practices that had to be overcome in *Columbia* studios during their time at Seventh Avenue and this, possibly slightly embellished recollection, is I think worth repeating here.

Bob Johnston: "[With Dylan] *you always had to keep the tape rolling. And that wasn't easy at Columbia; we were using 4-track for ["Highway 61 Revisited"] and the machines were way down the hall. We had union engineers, so one would be in the control room at the console with me, and I'd say 'Roll tape', and he'd tell his assistant near the door, 'Roll tape', and he'd yell down the hall to a guy at the other end, 'Roll tape', and then they'd start all over again yelling, 'Is tape rolling?' God, it took 20 minutes to get those damned machines going. It was like a Three Stooges short. So I got in the habit of using several machines with Dylan so as not to lose anything. He would start a song on the piano, and if the musicians dropped out during it, he'd go to the guitar and start playing another one. I lost one song that way and said never again, so I always used multiple machines".* [14]

Notes:

Opening quote: Speech given by Bruce Springsteen for the induction of Bob Dylan into the Rock 'n' Roll Hall of Fame on January 20, 1988, at the New York Waldorf Astoria Hotel.

[1] *"60 Minutes"* interview with Ed Bradley for *CBS Television*. Interview conducted in Northampton, Mass, Friday November 19, 2004 and broadcast December 5, 2004.

[2] Paul Jay Robbins interview for *Los Angeles Free Press* March 27, 1965. Interview conducted in Santa Monica. Published in three parts on September 10, 17 and 24, 1965.

In truth, Dylan didn't used cut-ups to write *"Tarantula"*, but it was one way of describing the end result of this seemingly random piece of work to the interviewer. Later, however, Dylan would adopt a "similar" method of song writing, which for him would entail jotting down phrases, one-liners, and anything else that he thought of or came across. The pieces of paper would then be stored in a box until required for use in song writing. Dylan has used this technique on most of his recent albums. The method, which he calls *"the box"*, is not used by Dylan to string together random phrases, but rather as a simple method of storing interesting lines that might at some point in time be employed in a song. I guess a cardboard box is easier to find than a notebook and there's no chance of a hard drive failure.

[3] Interview with Martin Bronstein for the *Canadian Broadcasting Corporation*. Interview conducted during the interval of Bob Dylan's concert at Place des Arts in

Montreal, Canada, February 20, 1966. Available as part of the *Chrome Dreams* CD *"Bob Dylan – The Classic Interviews 1965 – 1966"* Catalogue number CIS 2004.

[4] Shelton, Robert. *"No Direction Home: The Life and Music of Bob Dylan"*. Quoted by Ralph Gleason, December 1965.

[5] Interview with Jules Siegel March, 1966, published in the *Saturday Evening Post*, July 30, 1966.

[6] *"Biograph"* notes.

[7] *Rolling Stone* interview September 8, 1988. *"The 100 Best Singles of The Last Twenty-five Years"*.

[8] Heylin, Clinton. *"Dylan Behind Closed Doors – The Recording Sessions [1960-1994]"*. *Penguin Books*, 1996. ISBN 0-14-025749-7

[9] Telephone conversation with Ian Woodward for *ISIS* magazine. February 2005

[10] Wolkin, Mark and Keenom, Bill. *"Michael Bloomfield: If You Love These Blues"*. *Backbeat* 2000. ISBN 0-8793-0617-3. This quote is taken from Bob Dylan's introduction to his performance of *'Like A Rolling Stone'* at Fox Warfield November 15, 1980.

[11] Kooper, Al. *"Backstage Passes & Backstabbing Bastards"*. *Billboard* 1998. ISBN 0-8230-8257-1

[12] Numerous email exchanges between Al Kooper and Derek Barker. Note: In the first email exchange with Al Kooper he stated: *"Sure looks like me playin' an old Fender Jazzmaster"*. However, when it was explained to him that the photograph was from June 15, a session at which he has always maintained he did not play guitar, Al suggested, *"It must be my twin brother, Kenny Rankin"*. It seems that Rankin and Kooper were often mistaken for each other at that time. The problem is, Rankin was not at any of the *"Highway 61"* Sessions!

[13, 13a, 13b, 13c] *The New York Times*. Article by *Shaun Considine,* December 12, 2004. Considine is currently writing a book about New York and the creative revolutions of the mid-1960's.

[14] Daley, Dan for *MIX* (Professional Audio and Music Production) magazine, January 1, 2003

Some of the information regarding the variants of the *'Like a Rolling Stone'* single was taken from Alan Fraser's truly amazing website *"Searching for a Gem"*. www.searchingforagem.com

Fantastic Plastic

Thankfully, the *'Like A Rolling Stone'* single that the record buying public got was the full unadulterated six-minute song, the b-side of which was the equally lengthy *'Gates Of Eden'*. The promos that were sent out to US radio stations were, however, a different story. It seems that sales and marketing had got their way on this one and for radio play the baby had indeed been cut in half!

At the time it was common practice for *Columbia* to press their "hot" 45rpm promos on red vinyl and *Columbia* JZSP 110939/110940 was no exception. I guess they thought that the bright red discs would attract attention amongst the piles of radio promos that dropped onto the programmers' desks each week. Side one of the promo label read *'Like A Rolling Stone'* (Part 1). The timing, which was in bold black ink, read 3:02. The flip side of the disc, which was the continuation of the song, also read 3:02. For some reason not all radio promos were on red vinyl and some copies of JZSP 110940 can be found on black vinyl. This was not uncommon with *Columbia* demos and probably applied to later pressings. In the USA radio promos and jukebox records were one and the same, which meant at the time of release you would have had to pay twice to hear the whole song on a US jukebox! (I believe this may also have been the case in a number of European counties, including the UK). However, after the single became a hit, full length promo versions were supplied both to radio stations and for use on jukeboxes.

Over the years I've read on numerous occasions that the split version of *'Like A Rolling Stone'* was not released to the public and although this was true for the USA, it was not the case everywhere. In many European counties at this time EPs were more popular then singles. In fact, *'Like A Rolling Stone'* was only ever released in France as an EP, though it was available there as a jukebox single with a split of 2:58 and 3:01. Although both France and Spain sold *'Like A Rolling Stone'* as an EP, in reality it was the same as most other regular single releases, i.e. *'Like A Rolling Stone'* backed with *'Gates Of Eden'*. The only difference from the regular release (besides a card cover) was therefore the price! At this time *CBS* Holland and several other European countries imported their EPs from France and to combat the price problem they decided to sell *'Like A Rolling Stone'/'Gates Of Eden'* at the extend play price, but also to release a split *'Rolling Stone'* as a single! The catalogue number of this release was CBS 1.952. Later, when the single became a hit, it was released as *'Like A Rolling Stone'/'Gates Of Eden'*, which now meant that again the only difference between the so called EP and the single, was the card cover. Oh, and of course the price!

There were a myriad of different releases world-wide. In Italy and Greece the single was not released until November '65 when *'Like A Rolling Stone'* was released paired with *'Positively 4th Street'*. The most unusual releases, however, probably originated in South America. In Argentina, both the white label promo and the regular orange label release played at 33rpm and carried the title *'Como Un Vagabundo'* (*"Like A Vagabond"*). In Mexico, *'Like A Rolling Stone'* was issued as an EP; the title there was *'Como Una Piedra Que Rueda'* (*"Like A Stone That Rolls"*). For releases world-wide see website www.searchingforagem.com

First published in *ISIS* #120, May 2005

Columbia
acetate with
3:50 edit

US red radio
promo with
3:02 edit

Vocal Performance and Speech Intonation:
Bob Dylan's *"Like A Rolling Stone"*

Michael Daley

During my thesis research, I studied the vocal style of Bob Dylan from 1960 to 1966. In that six-year span, I found that four distinctive sub-styles could be delineated. The last of these, beginning in 1965 and continuing up to Dylan's motorcycle accident in July 1966, is probably his most well-known sub-style. This sub-style seems to lie in a middle ground between song and speech, with a great deal of sliding pitch and rhythmically free text declamation. This is also the time-period when Dylan had his greatest commercial and critical success, peaking with the release in July 1965 of *'Like A Rolling Stone'*. In addition to the song's commercial success, a number of commentators have pointed to it as an artistic peak, many of them citing *'Like A Rolling Stone'* as the most important single performance of Dylan's 44-year (at the time of writing) recording career.

My intention here is to analyze a recorded performance of a single verse of one of Dylan's most popular songs, observing the ways in which intonation details relate to lyrics and performance. The analysis is used as source material for a close reading of the semantic, affective and 'playful' meanings of the performance, and this reading is compared with some published accounts of the song's reception.

For this analysis, I have drawn on the linguistic methodology formulated by Michael Halliday. Halliday has found speech intonation, which includes pitch movement, timbre, syllabic rhythm and loudness, to be an integral part of English grammar and crucial to the transmission of certain kinds of meaning. Intonation patterns are shared by the fluent speakers of a given language, and the understanding of basic intonational gestures precedes words both in infant language acquisition and in evolutionary brain development.

That is, intonation is a lower brain function than word recognition, thus developing as a perceptual tool much earlier. Speech intonation is a deeply-rooted and powerfully meaningful aspect of human communication. It is plausible that a system so powerful in speech might have some bearing on the communication of meaning in sung performance. This is the premise by which I am applying Halliday's methods to this performance.

The musical object in question is the originally released studio recording of *'Like A Rolling Stone'*, a performance that has generated much discussion among

Dylan's commentators and fans. I begin with a short history of the song's reception among critics and fans, as well as the assessments of Dylan himself.

'*Like A Rolling Stone*' was recorded on June 16, 1965 and was released as a single on July 20. The song was somewhat different from the top-ten fare of the time, though. At a length of over six minutes (it was chopped for radio play) it was significantly longer than the two-and-a-half or three minute standard length then dominating pop radio, with a raucous guitar- and organ-based arrangement and four verses of dense, rapid-fire verbiage. It is generally agreed by commentators that the lyrics, at least on the surface, recount the privileged upbringing and subsequent fall into desperate poverty of a second person "*Miss Lonely*". The narrator's accusations and unflattering observations are couched in a series of declarative statements and questions, culminating after each verse in the famous refrain: "*How does it feel. . .to be on your own. . .with no direction home, a complete unknown, like a rolling stone*" (there are slight variations in the refrain from stanza to stanza). Perhaps the most strikingly unique aspect of the record is Dylan's vocal performance, with its use of nasal, sliding pitches and a speech-like, highly rhythmic declamatory style. Dylan later described, in somewhat stylized terms, the genesis of the song:

"*I wrote it as soon as I got back from England . . . It wasn't called anything, just a rhythm thing on paper – all about my steady hatred directed at some point that was honest. In the end it wasn't hatred. Revenge, that's a better word. It was telling someone they didn't know what it was all about, and they were lucky. I had never thought of it as a song, until one day I was at the piano, and on paper it was singing 'How does it feel?' in a slow motion pace, in the utmost of slow motion. It was like swimming in lava. Hanging by their arms from a birch tree. Skipping, kicking the tree, hitting a nail with your foot. Seeing someone in the pain they were bound to meet with. I wrote it. I didn't fail. It was straight*" (to Jules Siegel, quoted in Scaduto 1973:244-5).

Whether or not one chooses to take Dylan's comments at face value, they provide us with a sense of the artist's own perception of his creative process and the degree to which the endeavour succeeded. They also give us a glimpse into the visual and gestural correlatives of Dylan's sonic sense; he refers here to outward movement, directed towards a specific point. These metaphors, I suggest, are not arbitrary. They are in fact strongly indexed to the metaphorical constructs of much of the reception of '*Like A Rolling Stone*', as well as the gestural aspects of Dylan's use of vocal pitch in the performance.

In addition to the popular acclaim accorded to Dylan's recording shortly after its release, a steady procession of commentators on Dylan's life and work have offered their own assessments.

Anthony Scaduto:

"*When you heard 'Rolling Stone' back then it was like a cataclysm, like being taken to the edge of the abyss, drawn to some guillotine of experience . . .* [Dylan was] *biting off a word, spitting out venom, spreading a virulent emotion, infecting the listener"* (Scaduto 1973:245).

Patrick Humphries:

". . . steamrollering all that had gone before and spiralling onwards through outrageous rhymes and meter, lyrics flung like accusations, affronting yet compelling, that age-old fascination which lures unwary travellers right to the heart of darkness" (Humphries and Bauldie 1991:57).

John Herdman:

"Rock bottom intensity of feeling . . . he tells us what he feels himself, he projects himself with eerie immediacy into the feelings of others, and in so doing he shows us what we feel too" (Herdman 1982:14).

Paul Nelson:

"The definitive statement that both personal and artistic fulfilment must come, in the main, by being truly on one's own" (Nelson 1966:107).

Betsy Bowden:

". . . the absence of any personal pronouns (sic) sucks the listener into the song . . .the song's 'you' gets thoroughly conquered in both sense and sound" (Bowden 1982:104).

Wilfred Mellers:

"Although the words are dismissive, the music – with its jaunty repeated notes and eyebrow-arching rising thirds . . . is positive in total effect" (Mellers 1985: 140).

"Hugh Dunnit" writing in *The Telegraph* (a Bob Dylan fan magazine):

". . . his birth cry is the primal demon voice that whoops out the surging refrains of this song . . . each is a searing, vituperative taunt, designed to needle to the bone. But the tone of the words (as sung) and music is unmistakably joyous, celebratory. [Dylan] is exultant, free, on his own, ecstatic that he is as he once was, a complete unknown – unknown because unknowable" (quoted in Williams 1991:153).

While these assessments are rather broadly variant in tone and content, some recurring themes are discernible. I have grouped some salient metaphors and descriptors from the critical history of *'Like A Rolling Stone'* (including Dylan's own commentary) into five main thematic areas:

Thematic area 1:

Strong antagonism
"venom"
"dismissive"
"affronting"

Thematic area 2:

Attractiveness
"sucks the listener in"
"lures unwary travellers"
"compelling"
siren song metaphor
"drawn to some guillotine of experience"

Thematic area 3:

Positive message
"joyous . . . exultant . . . celebratory"
"personal and artistic fulfilment"

Thematic area 4:

Projecting
Thrusting outward
"spitting out venom"
"lyrics flung"
"directed at some point"
"whoops out"
"spiralling onwards"

Thematic area 5:

Sureness/effectiveness
Virtuosity
Intensity of feeling
Expressivity
"I wrote it. I didn't fail. It was straight"

Thematic area 1 parallels the mood and content of the lyrics as they appear on paper – a strong antagonism is conveyed through the constant, invasive questioning and damning judgments of the invisible first person (who may or may not be identified as Dylan himself). I would doubt, though, that the lyrics alone create such a strong mood of condemnation. Dylan's overall vocal timbre here is quite hard and nasal, the kind of vocal sound that might accompany a 'tongue-lashing' by someone who clearly feels that they are in the right, perhaps directed at a child or some other person in a position of lesser power. Such a tone suits this classic monologic text, where the life-history and inner thoughts of the "you" are co-opted by the narrator who is himself invisible, that is, not named, not described: an inviolable, inscrutable disembodied voice.[1]

Much of Dylan's expressive output around the time that *'Like A Rolling Stone'* was recorded displays a similar style of interpersonal communication. [2]

Thematic area 2, groups together references to the 'attractiveness' of the performance, its power to draw the listener towards something which, when it is named at all, is vaguely dangerous or forbidding. Humphries seems to refer to the ancient Greek myth of the Sirens, who lured travellers towards destruction with an irresistible song. Scaduto, perhaps specifying the nature of the destruction, refers to a *"guillotine of experience"*, which might suggest that the listener experiences some irrevocable change in worldview once drawn into *"the abyss"*. These types of metaphors are difficult to reconcile with the sense of the lyrics as written, so it seems that this theme of 'attractiveness' might be connected in some way with thematic area 5, which is concerned with virtuosic control. The *"abyss"* might be the potentiality of the listener herself being targeted for this kind of vitriol, while at the same time she is drawn to the source by the sheer mastery with which the antagonism is delivered.

Thematic area 3, headed by "positive message", primarily comes from Paul Nelson's 1966 essay, which suggests that all of the characters in *'Like A Rolling Stone'* are actually in some way Dylan. This theme was taken up in the *Telegraph*, whose author connects the performance with a projection of Dylan as triumph-antly breaking the chains of his safe, successful 'folksinger' career in favour of some new, uncharted musical terrain in the rock milieu. Thus the 'story' of the verses is just scaffolding upon which to hang the exultant chorus. Rather than chalking up this interpretation to creative critique, though, I would suggest that this, too, is an impression based on performative factors more than lyric sense. The band's performance certainly helps matters along in this regard. There is nothing careful about the way the studio musicians barrel through the song, in spite of Al Kooper's famous story (found in his autobiography, *"Backstage Passes"*) that this song marked his first-ever try at organ. Dylan, too, contributes sloppily transcendent rhythm guitar and harmonica flourishes. The harmonic structure of the song itself can also be seen as a series of affirmations, with the verse consisting primarily of stepwise climbs from the I to the V chord, which is held until a satisfying return is made to the tonic I. The inevitable perfect cadences that begin each line of text are contradicted only once in the form, when a IV chord intervenes at the prechorus. This IV chord then reverses the movement of the previous lines, falling stepwise down to the I until the upward movement is restored with an extended II – IV – V climb. The choruses condense the stepwise climbs of the verses into terse I – IV – V statements that Dylan might have associated with the irony-free rock 'n' roll aesthetics of *'Twist And Shout'* and *'La Bamba'*. I submit, then, that the commentators who associate *'Like A Rolling Stone'* with joy, celebration and liberation might be hearing these values primarily as embodied in the music, despite the fact that their critical faculties might impel them to look to the lyrics first.

Thematic area 4 might be fruitfully compared to thematic area 2 in that they both seem connected to gesture, space, movement and energy. Whereas area 2 contains metaphors of attraction, area 4 refers to outward projection, ostensibly from the same source that attracts. The references to *"spitting out"* and *"lyrics flung"* directs our attention towards the mouth, and indeed Dylan referred to this song on a number of occasions as *"vomitific"*. Could this thematic area, along with area 2, be related to various listeners' connections with the corporeality of the performance? We hear Dylan's mouth as he sings, but we can also envision his facial expression, perhaps his body movements as well. This we deduce from the aural landscape of the recording, which gives us information about Dylan's vocal timbre, the speed of enunciation, and other details, but I believe that it is in the area of pitch that we will find the greatest correlation to gestural metaphors. As we will see, much of Dylan's vocal pitch use in *'Like A Rolling Stone'* finds him taking a syllable and describing a kind of arc, with medium or short rise and a longer fall. This parallels somewhat the spatial path of an object thrown into the air. And since Dylan performs this arc repeatedly, sometimes several times in a single line of text, it follows that a listener might hear the words as *"flung"*, or even *"spiralling outwards"*, as each arc is succeeded by another.

Thematic area 5 contains metaphors of 'sureness' and 'effectiveness', connected with what might be thought of as virtuosic expressive control. Robert Walser has traced the 18th century origins of the term "virtuoso", a word that is popularly thought of as referring to technical mastery. Walser points out that this technical mastery was always in the service of expressive and rhetorical control (see Walser 1993). The ways that this virtuosity is manifested in *'Like A Rolling Stone'* are twofold. As I hope to demonstrate, Dylan uses vocal pitch to emphasize the lyric sense – this may be interpreted as a rhetorical use of performative virtuosity. But his division of phrases does not always serve the 'sense' of the discourse; on the contrary, his re-alignment of points of emphasis in the lyrics, again through pitch use, can be understood as playful. The virtuoso makes meaningful performances, but he also shows off what he can do. By sometimes obscuring meaning, he displays his mastery.

A close reading of Dylan's vocal performance in *'Like A Rolling Stone'* will allow for a better understanding of the metaphorical constructions that followed in its wake, in the form the critical responses recounted above. This close reading will consist in the main of an analysis, based on Michael Halliday's linguistic method, of pitch use in the second verse and chorus. First, a word on Halliday's method.

Through much of the history of linguistic inquiry, the written word has occupied a privileged place as an object of study. Languages are traditionally analyzed primarily in terms of their grammars; this reflects the popular belief that words and sentences constitute the essential part of human verbal communication. As such, spoken language is routinely transcribed to written form for analysis. Of course, popular knowledge also tells us that 'how you say something is often as important as what you say'. Every native speaker of English performs the language in some way that communicates things that the written word cannot. The scientific understanding of this 'sonic sense' of speech, however, has developed slowly and fitfully until recent years.

As early as the 1930s, work began to be undertaken towards the understanding of speech intonation, the universe of sonic details that accompany every utterance. These details include large and small gradations in pitch, timbre, amplitude and rhythm. The British linguist Michael Halliday has formulated a cogent system for understanding speech intonation in the context of a "functional" English grammar in his 1970 monograph *"A Course in Spoken English: Intonation"* and his larger work from 1994, *"An Introduction to Functional Grammar"*. Since Halliday's work on the nature of speech has constituted one of the starting points for my own research, I include here a thumbnail explanation of his theory as it applies to the present work. The following short explanation is a paraphrase of some of the ideas put forth in Halliday's 1970 and 1994 publications.

Tonality

Intonation in English is organized in units Halliday calls *"tone groups"*. Halliday says of the tone group:

The tone group is one unit of information, one 'block' in the message that the speaker is communicating; and so it can be of any length. The particular meaning that the speaker wishes to convey may make it necessary to split a single clause into two or more tone groups, or to combine two or more clauses into one tone group (Halliday 1970:3-4).

The pattern by which tone groups are distributed throughout speech, called 'tonality', is crucial to the sense of an utterance. The speaker divides up the stream of spoken words into groups, and this reveals to the listener how to mentally organize the information. Almost all of the time, tonality follows a predictable course, with tone groups basically corresponding to grammatical clauses. But when it is disrupted, as in Bob Dylan's 1965 studio performance of *'Like A Rolling Stone'*, grammatical sense can be fundamentally altered.

Tonicity

Each tone group has a 'tonic syllable', a place of prominence, which the speaker seeks to mark as most important and which carries the most pronounced pitch change. It often carries the burden of "new information" in the clause and as such the normative place of a tonic syllable is on the last word in a clause. Placement of the tonic syllable in places other than this is understood to be contrastive. The placement of tonic prominence is referred to as 'tonicity'.

Tone

Halliday has identified five basic tones, or pitch contours, in English. Tone interacts with tonality (distribution of tone groups) and tonicity (placement of tonic prominence) to create meaning in English intonation. Following are the tones identified in Halliday's system:

<u>simple tone groups:</u>

tone 1 falling
tone 2 high rising, or falling-rising (pointed)
tone 3 low rising
tone 4 falling-rising (rounded)
tone 5 rising-falling (rounded)

I have transcribed the lyrics of the second verse and chorus of *'Like A Rolling Stone'* using an adaptation of Halliday's notation for speech intonation. The second verse is not dissimilar to the other three verses in style, but I chose it because it seemed to me to contain the widest variety of playful inflections and pitch gestures. The tones themselves (the numerals that begin each tone group) were chosen on the basis of their resemblance to Dylan's use of sung pitch, as shown here. Each tone group is set off in a separate line of text and framed in double slash marks; syllables with tonic prominence are underlined and rhythmic feet are divided by single slash marks.

a) //5 <u>ah</u> you// (rising, then falling, tone)

b) //1 <u>gone</u>// (falling tone)

c) //1 to the/ <u>fin</u>est//

d) //1 <u>school</u>//

e)//1 <u>all</u>//

f) //1 <u>right</u>//

g) //1'^miss/lonely/but you/know you/only/used to/<u>get</u>//

h) //5 juiced in/<u>it</u>//

i) //1 ^no/body's/ever/taught/you/how to/live out/on/the <u>street</u>//

j) //5 ^and/now you're/gonna/have to/get/<u>used</u> to//

k) //5 <u>it</u>//

1) //1 ^you/say you'd/<u>never</u>//

m) //1 compro/<u>mise</u>//

n) //1 with the/mystery/tramp but/now <u>you</u>//

o) //1 real<u>ize</u>//

p) //1 he's not/selling/<u>any</u>//

q) //1 ali<u>bis</u>//

r) //1 as you/stare in/to the/vacuum/of his/<u>eyes</u>//

s) //1 and <u>say</u>//

t) //1 do you/want <u>to</u>//

u) //1 make a/<u>deal</u>//

v) //1 how does it/<u>feel</u>//

w)//1 how does it/<u>feel</u>//

x) //1 to be/on <u>your</u>/own//

y) //1 '^with/no di/<u>rect</u>ion/home//

z) //2 a com/plete un/<u>known</u>//

aa) //2 like a/rolling/stone//

Below I have transcribed the same verse and chorus "grammatically", using line breaks to mark off likely clause divisions:

ah you gone to the finest school all right miss lonely
but you know you only used to get juiced in it
nobody's ever taught you how to live out on the street
and now you're gonna have to get used to it
you say you'd never compromise with the mystery tramp
but now you realize he's not selling any alibis
as you stare into the vacuum of his eyes
and say "Do you want to make a deal?"
How does it feel?
How does it feel to be on your own
with no direction home
a complete unknown
like a rolling stone?

The verse begins with a tone 5 (line a). This being a tone group unto itself, it would be plausible to refer to this speech function as an initiating call; tone 5 in this case has a meaning of "insistence". This <u>is</u> the second verse, after all, which can be thought of as constituting an expansion of the ideas begun in the first. Thus the highly tonicized first pitch gesture of this verse might be interpreted as a kind of fanfare; musicologist Philip Tagg characterizes such strong upward pitch sweeps as *"a call to attention and action, a strong movement upward an outwards . . . energetic and heroic"* (Tagg 1979:14).

What follows is a rapid-fire series of Tone 1s. The use of the Tone 1 pitch fall here is unremarkable in itself, but it is the "tonicity" characteristics that are unusual here. The listener is bombarded with a series of tonicized words (tonic prominence is used in normal speech as a pointer to the <u>new</u> information in an utterance) and Dylan gives tonic prominence to nearly every word in the first part of the first line. This overloading of new information pointers renders the text as forceful and intrusive upon the listener. There is a sense of an intoxicating sensory overload.

Right away a general non-alignment of tone groups as sung with the grammar of the written lyric is evident. This manifests itself in the distribution of tone groups in many different places within the grammatical clause, as well as the placement of tonic prominence on syllables other than the last lexical item in the clause. In tone groups e) and f) this unusual, seemingly indiscriminate use of tonality breaks up the cohesion of the phrase *"all right"*, a phrase that has become fused, or indivisible, through popular use. The phrase is rendered contrastive to its usual meaning and marks the word *"all"* as a piece of new information. This would force the clichéd phrase to be processed in terms of its actual meaning, rather than as a purely 'textual' conjunctive phrase, which it has become in popular usage. Thus the listener hears *"all right"* as an emphatic confirmation of the text immediately preceding. This technique seeks to renew the cliché, something that Dylan has done lexically in other songs by substituting unexpected words in common phrases (see Ricks 1987).

It would be grammatically plausible to segment the first line of this verse into two clauses as follows:

ah you gone to the finest school all right miss lonely
but you know you only used to get juiced in it

The second clause would usually be distributed over one tone group. This does not happen here, though not because of the overloading of tone groups that occurred in the first clause. Instead, the last part of the first clause (*"miss lonely"*) is included in the second clause's tone group, which itself cuts off at *"get"* rather than being completed with *"juiced in it"*. Thus the normative placement of the tone group on the clause is shifted backward by one phrase. This has the effect of presenting a grammatically incoherent group of words as a single package of information. This clouds the meaning of the clause somewhat, but perhaps more importantly it constitutes a poetic strike against grammar, at least as it appears in straight written narrative. Clearly Dylan, like Chuck Berry and others before him, is revelling in his virtuosic master of the medium of sung text here.

The next couple of lines contain relatively little in the way of pitch playfulness, even though symmetry would suggest that the pitch falls should continue at the same rate. Dylan, though, refuses to do the expected. When the chorus begins, tonic syllables seem to be in their proper places. But Dylan throws in a few more curveballs. Curiously, the last two lines are sung in contours similar to tone 2. This would seem to introduce a mood of questioning – tone 2 indicates uncertainty, most often. But this coincides musically with the melodic resolution to the tonic, or home note, so the overall effect is that of closure.

Close reading of the vocal performance of a song, as I have attempted here, can yield a good deal of information about how meaning is handled beyond the lexical and grammatical levels of the lyrics. In the case of the second verse of *'Like A Rolling Stone'*, these prosodic details can be seen in the context of that song's reception; intonational play and emphasis in the performance might be connected to perceptions of virtuosic expressive control, a sense of 'expressivity' or 'intensity of feeling', and gestural metaphors such as *"flung"* and *"spiralling*

113

outwards". On the other hand, certain aspects of reception can be more precisely connected to other facets of the musical object: a sense of strong antagonism might be traced mainly to the lyrics, while a feeling of celebration and joy may be connected to the general raucousness and energy of the band's performance.

Though I am certain that pitch in sung language does <u>mean</u> in a significantly patterned way, I am also aware that singing is not speech, and other factors do enter the semantic and affective landscape of musical expression. Nonetheless, a look at Dylan's use of pitch in this song, through the lens of linguistic speech intonation, goes a long way toward explaining the precise nature of Dylan's communication of meaning in sung performance. One need only observe the many gestural and metaphorical correlations between the linguistic aspects of the performance and the effects of that performance (as recounted in the reception history) on listeners. A certain thoroughgoing nature of Dylan's aesthetic is suggested here, with musical, linguistic, gestural and (perhaps subsuming all of these) metaphorical aspects all articulating a cohesive, deeply embedded system of drives and directions. Postponing any further investigation into this broader inquiry for now, this analysis of vocal performance in the second verse of *'Like A Rolling Stone'* reveals much common ground between speech and song in the transmission and reception of meaning, though the precise nature of this shared sign-system may only be understood through further interdisciplinary inquiry.

[1] Mikhail Bakhtin described, as opposed to dialogism, monologism: *"Monologism, at its extreme, denies the existence outside itself of another consciousness with equal rights . . . Monologue is finalized and deaf to the other's response, does not expect it and does not acknowledge in it any decisive force"* (quoted in Brackett 1995:7). Although I would characterize the lyrics as monologic, the song in performance takes on a dialogic character by virtue of the many layers of sound and the complexities of mass commercial dissemination.

[2] This kind of discursive control and venomous rhetorical skill can be observed in action in the film *"Dont Look Back"*, a documentary about Dylan's 1965 British tour immediately preceding the composition and recording of *'Like A Rolling Stone'*. A sequence in the film captures a conversation between Dylan and "the science student", a young amateur journalist. Dylan immediately takes the student to task, questioning his inner motives, 'turning around' the responses, toying with and effectively crushing his young victim with rhetoric. This seems to have been a favourite game at the time for Dylan and his cronies, a way of weeding out the unhip.

Bibliography:

Bowden, Betsy. *"Performed Literature: Words and Music by Bob Dylan"*. Bloomington: *Indiana University Press*, 1982.

Brackett, David. *"Interpreting Popular Music"*. Cambridge: *Cambridge University Press*, 1995.

Halliday, Michael. *"A Course in Spoken English: Intonation"*. London: *Oxford University Press*, 1970.

Halliday, Michael. *"An Introduction to Functional Grammar"*. London: *Edward Arnold,* 1994.

Herdman, John. *"Voice Without Restraint: A Study of Bob Dylan's Lyrics and their Background"*. New York: *Delilah,* 1981.

Humphries, Patrick and John, Bauldie. *"Absolutely Bob Dylan"*. London: *Viking,* 1991.

Mellers, Wilfrid. *"A Darker Shade of Pale: A Backdrop to Bob Dylan"*. New York: *Oxford University Press,* 1985.

Nelson, Paul. *'Bob Dylan: Another View'*. Reprinted in *"Bob Dylan: A Retrospective"*. Edited by McGregor, Craig. New York: *William Morrow and Co,* 1966.

Ricks, Christopher. *'Clichés That Come To Pass'* in Gray, Michael and Bauldie, John eds. *"All Across the Telegraph: A Bob Dylan Handbook"*. London: *Sidgwick and Jackson,* 1987: 22-29.

Scaduto, Anthony. *"Bob Dylan"*. New York: *Signet,* 1973.

Tagg, Philip. *'Kojak: 50 Seconds of Television Music'*. Goteborg: *Skrifter fran Musikvetenskapliga Institutionen,* 1979.

Walser, Robert. *"Running With The Devil: Power, Gender and Madness in Heavy Metal Music"*. Hanover, NH: *Wesleyan University Press,* 1993.

Williams, Paul. *"Bob Dylan: Performing Artist: The Early Years: 1960-1973"*. Lancaster, PA: *Underwood-Miller,* 1991.

First published in *ISIS* #106, December 2002. Mike's Master's Thesis won the York Thesis prize for 1997. The version published here was revised by Mike for presentation in Caen, France in 2005.

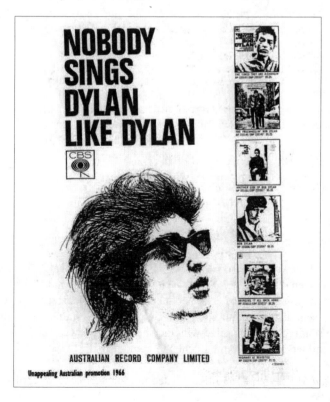

Stories in the Press

When asked in an interview about his recording activities with Dylan, Allen Ginsberg replied:

"I think I invented the chord change in 'In The Garden'. We [Ginsberg and Dylan] *went around trick or treating in Izuma Beach or something . . . in masks and I had my harmonium, and I was playing a funny ascending chord thing where you just move one finger at a time . . . you know, like a C chord, and then you lift that finger.* [it was] *1978. We had masks on . . . We gave* [all the stuff that people gave us] *away to the kids that were trick and treating too. We went to people's doors and sang . . . He had on a puma mask, and I had a clown mask. He had this supreme hippie mother tiny chick who made clothes for him and she made masks for us".*

Taken from issue #26 of *ISIS* September 1989
Extracts from an interview with Allen Ginsberg published in *Goldmine* September 8, 1989

Killer 'Cured' after Concert

"A Man who killed his mother while believing that he was the son of God, and that Bob Dylan was God, has been confirmed cured after going to the musician's Hobart concert".

The man, Richard Dickenson, believed that Dylan was communicating with him through the album *"Desire". "After five years' therapy at Risdon prison* [Australia], *a psychiatrist and two psychologists concluded he no longer believed he was receiving messages from Dylan".* Unfortunately, however, they had no way of testing that, until Dylan came to the locale to play a concert. Dickenson was accompanied to the show by a prison officer and a nurse.

Printed in issue #43 of *ISIS* July 1992

Another Gossipy Thing

A New York newspaper, for February 11, 1988, reported that *"the other night"* Dylan had been dining at R.J. Scotty's on 9th Avenue NYC and ordered the house speciality, linguini with lobster. When it came to the table, it still had its shell on, so Dylan sent it back. The chef, one Sergio Pertot, started screaming about someone sending back his prize-winning speciality. He was only placated when Dylan went personally into the kitchen to apologise.

The Wicked Messenger #1330 first printed in issue #24 of *ISIS* April 1989

Dylan's an Expert when it comes to Fan Support

A recent item plumbing the mystery of why Bob Dylan, at age 62, is suddenly doing ads for *Victoria's Secret* prompted this underwear-related recollection from loyal Dylan fan Patti Carney of Gaithersburg:

"I saw Dylan at the 9:30 club a few years back. I was lucky enough to be right in front of the stage. When Dylan finished his last set, a woman standing behind me threw her bra to him – she acted like it was the most casual thing in the world – and it landed onstage.

The band left; then came back for an encore. At that point the stage crew had cleared the stage of items thrown to Dylan, including the bra. When Dylan came back onstage, he looked down at those of us in front and said, 'Who took my bra?'

Who knows, maybe there are women all over the world who throw him their bras, thus making him eminently qualified to appear in an underwear commercial!"

Printed in issue #114 of *ISIS* April 2004
Originally published in the *Washington Post*

Michael Bolton

Michael Bolton: *"He's not extrovert by any means. It's very difficult to know what goes on in that mind. I don't think it's done purposely, but he can leave you wondering whether he wants to work with you again, or even if he likes you. He's in his own world, his poet's perception. It's not a linear perception. From what I saw, his time is very valuable to him. There was a lot of stuff going on – people coming up the hill and in and out of his house for meetings, a constant flow of activity".*

The Wicked Messenger #2115 printed in issue #38 of *ISIS* August 1991
Originally published in *Q*

Stories in the Press

Boxing is increasingly popular in America, but Gina Gershon (of *Showgirls* fame) was surprised when she jumped into the ring to find her opponent was Bob Dylan. *"I can't hit you, you're Bob Dylan"*, she told him. But then he whacked her so they had a fairly fiery bout. I'm not sure who won but he had an unfair advantage as she kept thinking about him singing *'Leopard Skin Pillbox Hat'* every time she went to thump him.

Over the years, Dylan has been spotted attending many US boxing bouts.

Taken from issue #66 of *ISIS* May 1996

Bob Dylan 1966

Think Twice
Dylan's Poetry

Justin Tremel

In recent years, academics have argued about Bob Dylan's importance in literary studies. Some have heralded Dylan as one of the most important literary poets of the 20th century, while others have dismissed him as an irrelevant, not to mention untalented popular performer. In trying to justify Dylan as a legitimate man of letters, Dylan advocates have focused mainly on the lyrics of his songs. My endeavour here is to examine two of Dylan's non-musical poems from an academic standpoint, to provide a textual basis that supports my resolve that not only is Dylan a poet, but he is a very talented, relevant, and enjoyable poet. Dylan's untitled free verse poem found in the liner notes of his 1965 album, *"Highway 61 Revisited"*, and his 1963 poem, *'Last Thoughts On Woody Guthrie'*, when examined prove to be successful examples of poetic form, folk tradition, and paradox used to critique social environment.

What is essential to grasp from the free verse poem of the liner notes of *"Highway 61 Revisited"* is the emergence of an individual sane voice from the stranglehold of a world gone mad. In this poem Dylan offers glimpses of absurd characters arguing over inconsequential dilemmas and enacting bizarre happenings. The artistic strength of the work is the manner in which Dylan conveys his voice to the reader. In the liner notes of Dylan's previous album, *"Bringing It All Back Home"*, he sheds light on what lies at the heart of his unique poetic approach.

> *my poems are written in a rhythm of unpoetic distortion/*
> *divided by pierced ears. false eyelashes/*
> *subtracted by people constantly torturing each other.*
> *with a melodic purring line of descriptive hollowness–seen at times thru dark*
> *sunglasses an other forms of psychic explosion.*[1]

"Psychic explosion" is perhaps the best way of describing the distinctive emotion that the poem conveys. While Dylan employs a number of literary devices to produce this *"explosion"*, the main vehicle that he relies on is his innovative and dexterous control of imagery.

Dylan's various images display, to use his term, a certain, undeniable *"descriptive hollowness"* – an expressive paradox. Consider this image from the poem –

> . . . *Autumn, with two zeros over her nose arguing over the sun being dark.*

Those instruments meant for perception and observation are replaced with *"two zeros"* – manifestations of nothingness, blindness. The relation of the two contradictory images produces a *"descriptive hollowness"*, a paradox that despite its conflict and duality produces a very singular emotive understanding. One sees paradox working throughout the poem. Dylan writes, *"the doll house where Savage Rose & Fixable live simply in their wild animal luxury. . ."*. Dylan again sets up an opposition, namely the opposition of living simultaneously simply and luxuriously. This contradiction suggests the pettiness of materialism. This sentiment is then reinforced with the image of the "doll house", suggesting a lack of depth, hollowness.

Dylan's puzzling and, at times, directly contradictory images can easily confuse the reader when examined individually, but as one sorts through these dashed phrases and loosely-connected occurrences, the scattered images combine to form a brilliant yet horrific pastiche. As Dylan has said about his work, *"I write in chains of flashing images"*. These picturesque images and bizarre goings-on coalesce into a hellish carnival, a twisted yet at the same time truthful portrayal of society with all of its foolishness and absurdity. In the poem, characters like Paul Sargent who *"busts everybody for being incredible"* and the Cream Judge who is *"writing a book on the true meaning of a pear"* personify the absurd, the senselessness of society. All of the characters taken together form what Dylan labels the *"WIPE-OUT GANG"*. As Dylan writes, *"the WIPE-OUT GANG buys, owns & operates the Insanity Factory"*. That is to say 20th century American society (as Dylan perceives it, with all of its petty values, its hollow morals, and its absurd conventions) creates and perpetuates madness which he is able to reproduce through the use of the unreal, through "twisted" grammar, and his paradoxical images.

The madhouse, carnival-like atmosphere is not confined just to this poem, but seen throughout *"Highway 61"*; such a circus-like world emerges from several of the songs on the album as well.

From *'Desolation Row'* –
> *They're selling postcards of the hanging,*
> *They're painting the passports brown.*
> *The beauty parlor is filled with sailors,*
> *The circus is in town.*

From *'Like A Rolling Stone'* –
> *You never turned around to see the frowns*
> *On the jugglers and the clowns,*
> *When they all come down and did tricks for you.*

From *'Ballad Of A Thin Man'* –
You hand in your ticket,
And you go watch the geek.
Who immediately walks up to you,
When he hears you speak.

From *'Queen Jane Approximately'* –
Now when all the clowns that you have commissioned,
Have died in battle or in vain.

Dylan is always a member of this absurd carnival, playing the character of the fool. Most critics cite Dylan as the clown in this masquerade. In relation to the album's songs, the prominent journalist and music critic Ralph Gleason places Dylan as the jester: *"He is the clown, the Napoleon in rags, a Don Quixote of today"*.[2] Likewise, Dylan is also the Clown in the liner notes. The Clown of the poem derides Autumn and all of her phoniness. *"What do you mean you're Autumn and without you there'd be no spring! you fool! without spring, there'd be no you!"* In a world of such absurdity Dylan argues that one cannot deal with absolutes; one cannot be truly objective.

Even though this outlook on the universe seems dismal, it is not the complete view of *'Highway 61'*. It would be a mistake to confine Dylan to a philosophy that culminates into nothing more than a vacuous and meaningless existence. In his analysis of the album, journalist and folk critic Irwin Silber does exactly that; he summarizes Dylan's philosophy too narrowly. He claims that the album boils down to *"the same basic statement: Life is an absurd conglomeration of mean-ingless events . . . we are all living under a perpetual sentence of death and to seek meaning or purpose in life is as unrewarding as it is pointless"*.[3] Silber portrays Dylan as a resolute nihilist; however, such a concrete view does not truly describe Dylan's outlook. As Dylan said in a 1966 interview, *"I'm really not the right person to tramp around the country saving souls . . . I'm not a shepherd. And I'm not about to save anybody from fate, which I know nothing about"*. Dylan denies again and again that he has any universal message, any key to living, yet that is not the sum of his entire philosophy.

Had Silber not limited his analysis of the album solely to its songs, but also included the album's liner notes in his examination, he might have taken Dylan's philosophy of this period to its logical conclusion. While Dylan rejects any set values for every individual to live by, he embraces fully the individual experience. As he writes –

You are right john cohen – quazimodo was right – mozart was right . . . I cannot say the word eye any more . . . when I speak this word eye, it is as if I am speaking of somebody's eye that I faintly remember . . . there is no eye – there is only a series of mouths – long live the mouths –

Dylan's main message emerges, in the carnival of society, no one can live by any singular vision of the world, including Dylan's own vision – *"there is no eye"*.

A consummate mode of living or a universal outlook on life simply does not allow for the existence of a true individual. While *"there is no eye"*, there are individuals striving to express their personal view of the world. Dylan celebrates the individual and his expression, as he writes, *"long live the mouths"*. Thus, Dylan's wide genius lies not in any set rationalization, but rather in his compelling, honest, and individual expression of the irrational and absurd that he views around him. Paul Nelson sums up well this focus on the individual. As he writes –

"To put it as simply as possible, the tradition that Dylan represents is that of all great artists: that of projecting, with the highest possible degree of honesty and craftsmanship, a unique personal vision of the world we live in, knowing full well that unless the personal is achieved, the universal cannot follow". [4]

The free-verse poem of the liner notes of *"Highway 61"* reveals a talented poet craftily and compellingly presenting a sane, individual voice crying out against the madcap world he finds himself in. Likewise, Dylan's 'Last Thoughts On Woody Guthrie' reveals the plight of an individual to find sanity and self in a hostile, senseless society, although 'Last Thoughts' operates in a very different mode of expression than the free-verse of the *"Highway 61"* poem.

In order to fully understand 'Last Thoughts', one must view the poem as deeply rooted in a traditional American folk heritage. The workshirt-clad Dylan of 1963 was very different from the hipster Dylan of 1965 not only in appearance, but also in ideology and in artistic expression. In 1963, at the time of the poem's composition, Dylan still presented a very conscious folk mentality, and this mentality finds expression in Dylan's artistic output. As pre-eminent Dylan critic, Michael Gray writes –

"Dylan is the great white folk singer. He has drawn on this tradition in two ways: he has used its established characteristics for some of his song structures and he has used its very lively inventiveness as a source of strength for his own". [5]

Just as Dylan adopts structures of the folk tradition in his songs, he also employs the tradition heavily in 'Last Thoughts'. Dylan's imagery in this poem recalls material of folk narratives and songs. In 'Last Thoughts' one finds railroads, wagons, ponies, card games, firewood, and sundown. Dylan also employs *"the hillbilly grammar construction"*[6] of multiple negatives not only in his songs of this period but also in the poem: *"And it ain't on no rich kid's road map/And it ain't in no fat kid's fraternity house"*. The deliberately corrupted grammatical structure lends the lines a certain horse-sense, a sense of obviousness and truth devoid of all literary pretension.

Though imagery and grammatical construction reveal the presence of folk influence in *"Last Thoughts"*, the most important and present folk tradition that he employs is repetition and anaphora (the same expression is repeated at the beginning of two or more lines). Throughout the poem Dylan will state a certain idea and then restate it a number of times. For example –

You need something to make it known
That it's you and no one else that owns
That spot that yer standing, that space that you're sitting
That the world ain't got you beat
That it ain't got you licked
It can't get you crazy no matter how many
Times you might get kicked

While at first glance such lines appear simply redundant, that is not the case. Taking from the American folk tradition, Dylan consciously constructs the poem with a number of these instances of repeated motifs or ideas. Compare the above lines to an example of Woody Guthrie's speech.

"I hate a song that makes you think that you're not any good. I hate a song that makes you think that you're just born to lose, no good to nobody, no good for nothin' because you're either too old, or too young, or too fat, or too slim, or too ugly, or too this or too that. Songs that run you down, or songs that poke fun at you on account of your bad luck or hard travelin'.

I'm out to fight those kinds of songs to my very last breath of air and my last drop of blood. I'm out to sing songs that'll prove to you that this is your world. That it has hit you pretty hard, knocked you down for a dozen loops. And no matter how hard it's run you down and rolled over you. No matter what color, what size you are, how you're built".[7]

Dylan consciously and skilfully constructs a tribute to his then-idol Guthrie, in the language and setting that Guthrie himself was steeped in.

The use of repetition cited in the paragraph above relates also to Dylan's carefully crafted structure of the poem. The bulk of the poem is written in rhyming couplets occasionally interrupted by unrhymed lines and brief changes in rhyme scheme to abab or abba. The changes in rhyme-scheme correspond to shifts in the narrative flow of the poem. For example, the poem opens with eleven rhymed couplets all dealing with the images of idle despair and disillusion, and then Dylan shifts rhyme scheme.

And yer minutes of sun turn to hours of storm
And to yourself you sometimes say
'I never knew it was gonna be this way
Why didn't they tell me the day I was born'

This shift interrupts the flowing cadence of despair in the previous 22 lines. Owing to the shift in rhyme scheme, Dylan forces the reader to pause on these lines and take special note of these lines. Throughout the poem Dylan returns to the cadence of the rhyming couplets and then interrupts the cadence for emphasis. Consider the following lines –

And you say to yourself just what am I doin'
On this road I'm walkin', on this trail I'm turnin'
On this curve I'm hanging
On this pathway I'm strolling, in the space I'm taking
In this air I'm inhaling
Am I mixed up too much, am I mixed up too hard
Why am I walking, where am I running
What am I saying, what am I knowing
On this guitar I'm playing, on this banjo I'm frailin'
On this mandolin I'm strummin', in the song I'm singin'
In the tune I'm hummin', in the words that I'm writin'
In the words that I'm thinkin'

Notice how the word *"hard"* sounds boldly out of sync with the surrounding lines, as it has no corresponding rhyme. It is as if Dylan forces the reader out of the poetic world of the poem to briefly question *"am I mixed up too hard?"* and then plunges him back into the dominant cadence of the poem.

While deliberate attention to structure and folk tradition contributes to the poem's effectiveness, the poem's thematic elements and the manner in which they are expressed ultimately create the beauty of the poem. As in the *'Highway 61'* poem, *'Last Thoughts'* deals with the struggle of the individual against a society that he finds no place in. Dylan writes –

The ones who jump on the wagon
Just for a while 'cause they know it's in style
To get their kicks, get out of it quick
And make all kinds of money and chicks
And you yell to yourself and you throw down yer hat
Sayin', "Christ do I gotta be like that
Ain't there no one here that knows where I'm at
Ain't there no one here that knows how I feel
Good God Almighty
            THAT STUFF AIN'T REAL"

The entire poem traces the progress of an individual going from despair to confusion, and ultimately to hope. The plain language and folk conventions harmonize with the thematic focus on the individual.

Dylan is able to advance effectively his philosophy into very different poetic modes. Thus Dylan proves to be a talented and diversified poet. His poetic vision transcends the restraints of a single poetic form. Dylan very adeptly crafts the language and images of his poetry to reflect its various meanings. Talking generally about Dylan's poetry is difficult as he operates in such a wide variety of media and explores such a variegated assortment of themes. As critical heavy-weight Christopher Ricks has stated, *"Any general praises of his art are sure to miss what matters most about it, that it is not general but highly and deeply individual, particular".*[8] Considering the analysis of the two Dylan poems presented here, however, I would echo a general description of Dylan's poetic achievements that I believe holds true for all of his work. *"But one thing that hasn't changed, unlike the times, is Dylan's three qualities – the three that for T.S. Eliot characterize Tennyson: abundance, variety, and complete competence".*[9]

[1] Dylan, Bob. *"Bringing It All Back Home"* Liner Notes, New York: *Columbia Records*, 1965.

[2] Gleason, Ralph. *'The Children's Crusade'. "Bob Dylan The Early Years"*. Ed Craig McGregor. New York: *Da Capo Press*, 1990 p.178.

[3] Silber, Irwin. *'Topical Songs: Polarization Sets In', "Bob Dylan The Early Years"* Ed Craig McGregor. New York: *Da Capo Press*, 1990 p.103.

[4] Nelson , Paul. *'Bob Dylan: Another View', "Bob Dylan The Early Years"*. Ed Craig McGregor. New York: *Da Capo Press*, 1990.

[5] Gray, Michael. *'Song And Dance Man III: The Art Of Bob Dylan'*. New York: *Continuum*, 2000.

[6] Ibid.

[7] Transcribed from *'Will Geer reading Guthrie', Folkways. "The Original Vision". Folkways* CD SF40001, 1989.

[8] Ricks, Christopher. *"Dylan Among the Poets"*. BBC Radio, Nov 11, 2001.

[9] Ibid.

Published in *ISIS* issue #100, January 2002

You Can Call Me Al

Derek Barker

During the spring and summer of 1961, Bob Dylan had a succession of career helpers, promoters and amateur managers. Izzy Young, owner of the Folklore Center in New York, helped most of the Village folksingers, including Dylan (at Albert Grossman's suggestion Izzy would arrange Dylan's first proper concert, at the Carnegie Recital Hall in November 1961). Carla Rotolo, then personal assistant to Alan Lomax and sister of Bob's girlfriend Suze, and Sybil Weinberger touted around a demo tape of his songs and Dylan worked informally with Terri Thal (soon to become the wife of Dave Van Ronk). Ultimately, though, it was with Roy Silver that Dylan signed a contract. Silver, who with Bob Gibson had begun a college talent-booking agency called *Campus Concepts*, was now managing up-and-coming comedian Bill Cosby, Tiny Tim and others. Although Dylan signed a five-year management agreement with Silver, he saw him more as a booking agent than a manager and he was soon spending more time talking to, and confiding in, a larger than life figure from the West Coast. Enter The Bear.

Born on Chicago's West Side in 1926 to Russian-Jewish immigrant parents, Albert Grossman received an MSc in economics from Roosevelt University before going on to work for the Chicago Housing Authority, from which he was dismissed, some say for misconduct. He turned his attention to music and in 1957 opened the Gate of Horn, which within months of opening became Chicago's premier folk club, creating audiences for Odetta, Bob Gibson (with whom Grossman shared an apartment for two years on Chicago's North Side) and Big Bill Broonzy. Although the club was small and undercapitalized, it became renowned, not only in Chicago, but across the United States. Grossman would go on to operate a second Chicago club, the Bear.

Albert Grossman was an imposing man who looked a decade older than his real age. He wore a suit and tie and metal-framed tinted spectacles, over which sat large the black bushy eyebrows that crowned his empty, unblinking gaze. Described by Robert Shelton as having a face that suggested an *"owl forced into the light"*, he was known as both "The Bear" and "The Floating Buddha". After co-directing the first Newport Folk Festival (1959), Grossman began looking for opportunities on the East Coast and following numerous visits opened an office in New York, basing himself there. He was already managing the likes of Odetta and Bob Gibson and in 1960, soon after arriving in New York, he began representing Peter Yarrow, whom he'd met in the Café Wha? At the time, Yarrow was a solo performer, but after a year as Peter's manager, Grossman approached him with the idea of putting together a group, which Grossman said would be a *"sure-fire success"*. The group, a trio, would consist of Peter Yarrow, Noel Paul Stookey and the flaxen-haired Mary Travers – The Kingston Trio with sex appeal. Grossman was always prospecting for further talent; his involvement with Dylan, however, was to be a slow burn affair. Grossman had seen and heard Dylan many times in the Greenwich Village clubs but initially had only shown faint interest in the fledgling folk singer. The two men became closer after Roy Silver began operating from Grossman's office and closer still after Grossman heard acetates of Dylan's first album. Then, in April 1962, Grossman heard Dylan play his latest composition, *'Blowin' In The Wind'*, and his mild interest turned into a fervent desire to own a part of the author of the song.

It seems that Dylan was already looking to part company with Silver and for a short while there was the possibility that one-time "song-plugger" Harold Leventhal, who had been representing Pete Seeger and The Weavers since 1950 and was also Woody Guthrie's manager, might take up the baton. Dylan made an approach to Leventhal, but then his interest cooled, probably because he was now being courted by The Bear. Silver knew nothing of Dylan's approach to Leventhal; he was, however, acutely aware that Grossman was moving in on his boy and quickly decided that a battle with his "landlord" would be a futile exercise. Therefore, when in May 1962, Grossman offered Silver $10,000 and continuing use of the space in his office to surrender his agreement with Dylan, Silver quickly agreed. Although Grossman would later sign, amongst others, Janis Joplin, The Band, and Todd Rundgren, it was the deal with Silver for Dylan that would make him a multimillionaire. Before jumping into bed with Grossman, however, Dylan took advice from several people, including his record producer at *Columbia*, the legendary John Hammond snr. All seemed well, but Dylan was warned against signing the usual seven-year contract. He chose to ignore this advice and signed for the full term. He would live to regret his decision.

Regardless of later differences, Grossman was unquestionably the right man for the job and both parties benefited greatly from their liaison. There is no doubting that Grossman was a hard-nosed businessman – witness his dealings with the hapless Tito Burns in *"Dont Look Back"* – and that he was not liked by everyone. Todd Rundgren once said that Grossman was the person he would most like to hit in the nuts with a baseball bat, or words to that effect. On the other hand, Bob Gibson, one time partner of Roy Silver, called Grossman *"One of the most honourable men I've ever known"*. Liam Clancy stated in an interview that, in his opinion, Grossman simply *"thought he was God"*. In his book *"The Mayor of MacDougal Street"*, bluesman and folk revivalist Dave Van Ronk says: *"He [Grossman] could be a wonderful companion . . . it wouldn't be until two days after you saw him that you would realize your underwear had been stolen. 'Shit, man, my shoes are on – what happened to my socks?'"* There is no doubting that Grossman was one of the true heavy-weights (no pun intended) of music management and that he was ruthless in his dealings, but in most cases, his ruthlessness was employed to secure the best possible deal for his artists and he certainly made a better friend than enemy.

Sally Anne Buehler was studying seventeenth-century English literature at Hunter College until the excitement generated around Greenwich Village in the late fifties/early sixties seduced her into leaving Hunter and taking a job as a waitress at the Café Wha?. Sally cites Kerouac's Beat film *"Pull My Daisy"* as the catalyst for her dropping out. Just as the Village folk scene was beginning to percolate, Grossman began buying property near Woodstock, a countrified arts and crafts colony about a hundred miles north of New York. After finally noticing her at The Bitter End, Albert, who was thirteen years her senior, began dating Sally Anne; they married in November 1964. Sally earned her own slice of immortality when, draped in a little red number, she was captured by photographer Daniel Kramer as she reclined on her chaise-longue in the living room of the Grossmans' Bearsville home.

By the time *"Bringing It All Back Home"* was in the shops, Dylan's career was moving along at quite a pace. It would seem that Grossman originally signed Dylan for his skills as a songwriter but by now he had recognized his artist's prowess as a performer. By 1966, however, the strain from the workload, especially the touring, was becoming too much for Dylan. The ever-worsening relationship between artist and manager became even more strained after Dylan's decision to stop touring.

In the summer of 1968 (on what appears to be a whim), Dylan decided that he would change the name of his music publishing company, *Dwarf Music*, to celebrate the birth of his son Samuel. Administrator Naomi Saltzman, however, informed Bob that would not be possible because 50% of *Dwarf Music* was owned by Albert Grossman. Two years earlier, while on tour in Sweden, Dylan had signed a ten-year contract with Grossman. It appears, however, that Dylan had never read the documents, which his attorney David Braun, who also represented Grossman, had delivered to him.

Almost immediately after discovering this, Dylan formed a new publishing company, *Big Sky Music*, but there was no way out of the May 1966 contract. While *Big Sky* might have given Dylan a little more control over his music publishing – his new office at Gramercy Park now carried out all of the administration – Grossman continued to receive his 50% from the new company. In reality, therefore, Grossman was now getting 50% of Dylan's publishing rights for doing virtually nothing. In his biography *"Down The Highway"*, author Howard Sounes opines that Dylan might have recorded *"Self Portrait"* (a double album of <u>non</u>-Dylan compositions) partly to prevent Grossman from earning from the publishing rights!

Much to his manager's annoyance, Dylan began to tempt key players away from the Grossman empire. Naomi Saltzman immediately joined Dylan from *Trio Concerts*, a promotions company owned by Grossman, which was originally set up to book concerts for Peter, Paul and Mary – hence the company name. Next, Bob informed attorney David Braun that he would only be able to continue to act for him if he desisted from acting for Grossman. Braun chose Dylan.

On August 19, 1969, the week of the Woodstock festival, Dylan's management contract with Grossman came up for renewal. Dylan refused to participate in both endeavours and it would be a year before the artist and his now "ex-manager" could agree on anything. The end of the sixties brought with it the end of the Grossman management era. Dylan had refused to resign in '69, Peter, Paul and Mary split in 1970 and in October of that year, the world and Albert Grossman lost Janis Joplin. Grossman's only compensation was that the year before Janis' death, he had taken out a $200,000 accidental death insurance policy on her. After the insurance company argued that Joplin's drug overdose was a suicide and not an accident, Grossman received $112,000 through the courts.

Feudal lord Grossman then began spending more time on his 100-acre estate near Woodstock where he tended his array of plants (he had a diploma in horticulture) and added to his collection of antiques. His great love of good food, which almost certainly contributed greatly to his premature death, was realized with the opening in 1971 of his haute cuisine restaurant The Bear.

The Bear, which struggled at first, had its heyday from 1973 to 1980 when Dylan's friends Bernard and Mary Lou Paturel, who formally ran the Café Espresso on Tinker Street in Woodstock, operated it. In recent years, The Bear Cafe has seen a resurgence as one of the finest eating-houses in the area and for the past five consecutive years has been honoured by *Wine Spectator* for having one of the most outstanding wine lists in the world. A bottle of 1989 Pomerol, Chateau Petrus, will however set you back $1900.

1970 also saw the beginnings of Bearsville Studios, and the Bearsville record label, for which Todd Rundgren became an engineer, an in-house producer and later a recording artist. Grossman's Bearsville Complex, which nestled in the heart of the Catskill Mountains, five minutes from Woodstock, also included the Little Bear Chinese restaurant and a long-time unfinished theatre. All was not cosy, however, and the summer of 1970 also saw further arguments between Dylan and Grossman.

Dylan might have been free of Grossman as his manager, but the extremely lucrative (for Grossman) 1966 publishing agreement still had seven years to run. Eventually, both parties signed what became known as the "July 1970 Agreement", in which Dylan reaffirmed that 50% of his publishing receipts would continue to be paid to Grossman, who in turn yielded that the publishing deal could be modified to end three years early – 1973 as opposed to 1976.[1]

While this amendment meant that Dylan would regain early control of his publishing, Grossman would continue indefinitely to receive a half share of Dylan's works prior to that date (1973). In 1979 – possibly motivated by his divorce settlement and the losses made by the film *"Renaldo and Clara"* – Dylan appears to have reneged on the "July 1970 Agreement" and on May 18, 1981, Grossman filed suit against Dylan in the state of New York for unpaid commissions, claiming Dylan owed him circa $51,000 in back royalties.[1] Considering Dylan was continuing to pay Grossman $250,000 per annum[1] this claim would seem a little petty. Grossman, however, was also requesting $400,000 in punitive damages. Dylan would later counterclaim on eighteen different points, including allegations of mismanagement and overcharges of more than $7.1 million in commissions.[1] Delaying tactics by Dylan and his two sets of lawyers would keep court proceedings at bay until April 1985 and the suit would not be settled until May 1987, by which time Albert Grossman had already been dead for almost two years. The final settlement with the "Grossman Estate" meant that the Estate would continue to retain a 50% share of his *Witmark* publishing rights, but that all rights to revenue from *Dwarf* and *Big Sky* would belong to Dylan. The *Witmark* rights were valued at one million dollars and Dylan agreed to pay a further two million dollars to settle all other of the plaintiff's claims, past and future. Just three years after the settlement, the 28-year renewal rule – US Copyright Act of 1909 – kicked in and Dylan was able to regain the rights to all of his work lodged with *Witmark*. At last, Dylan had full ownership of his entire back catalogue.

Notes:

Albert B. Grossman died from a massive heart attack on the morning of Sunday January 25, 1986; he was on a transatlantic flight bound for London where he was to stop off on his way to the MIDEM music fair in Cannes, France. He was aged 59. He left no will and his business empire was tied up in the courts for some time until his widow, Sally, eventually won control. Dylan attended neither the funeral nor the memorial service.

"Pull My Daisy" is a short (28 minutes) film made in 1958, which typifies the Beat Generation. Directed by Robert Fran and Alfred Leslie, *"Daisy"* was adapted by Jack Kerouac from a stage play he never finished titled *"The Beat Generation"*. Based on an incident in the lives of Neal Cassady and his wife Carolyn, *"Pull My Daisy"* tells the story of a railway brakeman whose painter wife invites a bishop over for dinner. However, the brakeman's bohemian friends crash the party with comic results. *"Pull My Daisy"* has been deemed *"culturally significant"* by the United States <u>Library of Congress</u> and selected for preservation in the <u>National Film Registry</u>.

[1]Sounes, Howard. *"Down The Highway: The Life Of Bob Dylan"*, Doubleday, 2001

Based around an article by Rory O'Connor published in *ISIS* issue #14, May 1987

Paul Butterfield, Albert Grossman & Mike Bloomfield at the 1965 Newport Festival

Bob Dylan 1969

Some Thoughts on *"John Wesley Harding"*:
How the "Old" Dylan was Killed
(And Nothing Was Revealed)

James Dunlap

The 1968 album, *"John Wesley Harding"* (*"JWH"*), represents a major turning point in Bob Dylan's career. By the fall of 1967 (when it was recorded), he had, of course, already made several major career changes. In the first, in emulating James Dean and then becoming "Bob Dylan" (initially a Woody Guthrie clone), he had abandoned Bobby Zimmerman, the son of a small-town Jewish merchant. Within five years, he would abandon, not only his subsequent topical protest song career, but folk music altogether in favour of surreal lyrics and an electrified sound.

By the time of his 1966 World Tour, Dylan was performing with increasingly risk-taking defiance, showing little regard for his mind, body or his fans' expectations. The dramatic denouement of this phase in his career was the motorcycle accident of July 29, 1966. Dylan finally went "over the edge" and disappeared, seemingly snuffed out in his prime. When Bob re-emerged to public view eighteen months later, he had returned to a more traditional sound: his prior existential angst had become modest understatement instead. A two-piece Nashville band now accompanied Bob's guitar.

Different Approaches

Critics over the years have tried to describe the meaning and importance of *"John Wesley Harding"* from a variety of different perspectives. In general, they fall into three categories, which may overlap: (a) a broad cultural perspective, where Dylan's songs are seen as providing commentary on American myths and legends and/or then-popular trends; (b) a religious perspective, focusing on the meaning of the songs' Biblical allusions; and (c) a non-religious biographical perspective, which attempts to relate the song's various fables to real events in Dylan's life.

* * *

Among the more commonplace observations about *"JWH"* is that its simplicity ran counter to then-popular trends. The album seemed to represent an implicit critique of the production values that informed such other recent recordings as *"Sergeant Pepper's Lonely Hearts Club Band"* and the Rolling Stones' *"Their Satanic Majesty's Request"*. For that reason, the critic Jon Landau called Dylan's isolated contrarianism *"egotistical"* (52) (even though he recognized that the "new" Dylan was self-consciously a *"modest man"*) (43).

Landau also detected a new kind of seriousness in Bob's latest songs, playing fewer games than before. He thought that such seriousness reflected the influence of the Vietnam War (52), as though the singer were adopting the stance of a religious or conscientious objector. Intentional references to the events of the day appear, however, rather unlikely. In *"Chronicles"*, Dylan confessed that, at the time, he couldn't relate to protest or the news (114-15). Instead, he was concerned about being a good family man.

Nonetheless, broad underlying themes about the condition of America in the second half of the 1960s doubtlessly run throughout *"JWH"*. Greil Marcus has described Dylan's songs of the immediately preceding period, the Basement Tapes, as reflecting the inevitable betrayal that stems from the infinite idealism of American democracy (89). This, of course, is reflected in Dylan's decision to retreat from the world and suspend his career. Steven Scobie, similarly, sees Dylan's newer songs as being about the betrayal of trust. This can be argued quite literally in that some of the lyrics include pleas for forgiveness, such as Tom Paine's request in *'As I Walked Out One Morning'*. The lyrics also feature weeping, such as the singer's reaction to the death of a saint in *'I Dreamed I Saw St. Augustine'*. Many of the characters in *"JWH"*'s songs are portrayed as suffering or in misery.

Michael Gray begins his analysis of *"JWH"* with the observation that Dylan's characters–an outlaw, a wayward immigrant, a lonesome hobo, and even a covetous simpleton–are all drawn from American legends. The brevity of the songs and their somewhat vague descriptions then require the listener to fill in the gaps. Gray suggests that Dylan's point (or, in any event, the result of his method) is to call into question many of our most cherished myths (33-35).

* * *

A second major context in which *"JWH"* has been seen is religion. Two writers in particular, Robin Witting and the late Bert Cartwright, traced countless Biblical allusions, finding references in almost each line. Dylan himself once supported this approach, calling *"JWH"* the *"first biblical rock album"* (Cott 60). In addition, guests to Dylan's home at the time observed a Bible on a lectern for easy consultation (along with a volume of Hank Williams lyrics). Finally, at about the same time, Dylan claimed familiarity with Biblical parables. In response to a friend's comment that he didn't seem like the type of person who, in a hotel, would pick up and read from a Gideon's Bible. Bob answered, *"Well, you never know"* (Cohen and Traum 273-74).

One of the difficulties in using the Bible to interpret *"JWH"* is understanding what Dylan intended with all his allusions. Cartwright concludes simply that, with the album, the singer describes *"his experience of himself and America in the context of the living God"* (37). Dylan biographer Anthony Scaduto proclaimed confidently that *"JWH"* was *"Dylan's version of the Bible"*, containing *"songs written as parables describing the fall and rebirth of one man—Bob Dylan"* (249). While his general assessment seems apt, it led Scaduto to some unusual results, such as his conclusion that the *"fairest damsel"* in *'As I Went Out One Morning'* was a symbol of institutionalized religion and was therefore perverted (251).

In one of the most important early essays on Dylan, Steven Goldberg declared Dylan to be a mystic and went on to praise *"JWH"* as Dylan's masterpiece. According to Goldberg, Dylan's renunciation of topical songwriting in 1964 was followed by a period of attempting to achieve spiritual transcendence, which only resulted in misery and existentialist isolation. With *"JWH"*, Dylan returned among men, seeking salvation through a new kind of simplicity and compassion.

The critic John Herdman made interesting use of religious themes when he described Bob's whole album as about *"not knowing"*, in a spiritual sense. Thus, Bob can be seen searching throughout *"JWH"* for a religious solution to life's meaning, but he doesn't find it. In the end, many of the songs are not about faith, but, in Herdman's words, they have an atmosphere of *"hollowness, emptiness, vagueness, insubstantiality"* like the onset of a sickness (101). As a consequence, Dylan turns away from religion towards more traditional certainties: his family and the countryside. Indeed, the album ends with two light-hearted songs that point in that direction: *'Down Along The Cove'* and *'I'll Be Your Baby Tonight'*.

* * *

As with the presence of religious themes, Dylan has given direct clues that there are non-religious personal components to many of his songs. In an interview with Scaduto, Dylan said:

"Before I wrote "John Wesley Harding", I discovered something about all those earlier songs I had written. I discovered that when I used words like 'he' and 'it' and 'they' and talking about other people, I was really talking about nobody but me. I went into "John Wesley Harding" with that knowledge in my head" (249).

"JWH" can be seen to represent Dylan's self-conscious adoption of a new kind of solipsism, finding meaning in himself and his family alone. Understanding the personal components of *"JWH"* thus requires some understanding of the issues with which Bob was then dealing.

By the summer of 1966, the hectic pace of Bob's concert touring had visibly taken its toll, physically and emotionally. Nonetheless, his manager, Albert Grossman, had already scheduled another 60 concert dates on tours that seemed to extend indefinitely. Dylan's book *"Tarantula"* was overdue and pressures for its completion were building. Dylan's fame and the adulation of his fans (and the condemnation by others) all continued to grow, seemingly exponentially. His motorcycle accident was a chance for Bob to recuperate. As Dylan has repeatedly said, it was then time for a change.

The months subsequently spent in Woodstock recording informally with The Band may seem idyllic in retrospect, but the many pressures hadn't let up. At the time, Grossman was involved in negotiating a new record contract, and three companies (principally *Columbia* and *MGM*) were bidding for his services. With negotiations over a new contract stalled (in part from concerns about Dylan's health and drug use), tensions about the artist's future earnings potential began to arise. Bob was beginning to learn of Grossman's excessive compensation arrangements. For instance, his manager had long been receiving a hidden percentage of Bob's royalty earnings, and he was caught billing Dylan's company for large personal expenses. Bob's conflicts with Grossman were growing on other issues, as well. His manager was not pleased with the changing directions that Dylan's musical styles had been taking.

In this pressure-filled context, *"JWH"* conveys a surprising sense of musical, psychological, and spiritual calm, an antidote for what had ailed him. It can be understood as setting forth the singer-songwriter's reflections on the "old Bob Dylan" and his quest to invent a "new Bob Dylan" who, among other things, would be independent from the pressures of the recording business and of answering to the needs of his fans. On the album, the evolving new Dylan is especially coy, as if wanting to hide from an intrusive public and thus avoid past mistakes.

The Liner Notes

The liner notes to *"JWH"* make Dylan's position clear at the outset. Cast as a humorous fable and using characters with fanciful names, Dylan tells a story that may well have been set in upstate New York. Three record producers and business managers, cast as three kings, come to Woodstock to visit and do homage to Bob ("Frank"), who is accompanied by his wife Sara ("Vera" or the *"better half"*).[1] Dylan is also accompanied by Grossman ("Terry Shute"), who is sketched roughly as an insatiable philanderer. Vera, for instance, catches him *"prying open a hairdresser"*. He then drops *"his drawer"* and then *"rubbed the eye"*. Frank, however, simply refers to Shute as the *"arrogant man"*.

After the three kings arrive (like the three record companies), they initially debate the relative values of faith and froth[2] (meaning frivolity), and the third king concludes, *"The key is Frank"* (who, in the story, represents the "new" Dylan). The Grossman character then gives a little speech, elevating the limitless prospects of Dylan's ultimate destiny, if he is allowed to do as he pleases. This could easily be a parody of Grossman's notorious obstinacy and negotiating techniques. Dylan relates that Terry Shute, *"[g]etting to the source of things . . . proudly boasted"* as follows:

"There is a creeping consumption in the land. It begins with these three fellas and it travels outward. Never in my life have I seen such a motley crew. . . . They scorn the widow and abuse the child but I am afraid that they shall not prevail over the young man's destiny, not even them!"

Dylan (as Frank) did not, however, care to have Grossman, with his questionable business practices, as his representative. In fact, Dylan had no interest in leaving *Columbia Records*, nor did he then seek to cultivate such high expectations about his future records. So, in the liner notes, he turned with a blast and said to his manager, *"Get out of here, you ragged man! Come ye no more!"*

The first king then addresses the Frank character, stating, *"Mr. Dylan has come out with a new record. This record of course features none but his own songs and we understand that you're the key"*. Frank replies that he is. He then proceeds to confound and mystify his guests by, among other things, ripping off his shirt and punching his fist through a plate-glass window. In addition, a light bulb fell from his pocket, reminiscent of the ubiquitous oversized industrial bulb that he had carried to a London interview in 1965, as shown in the film *"Dont Look Back"*. In that film, a reporter then asked, *"What is your real message?"* Dylan replied, *"My real message? Keep a good head and always carry a lightbulb"*, indicating perhaps that he claimed to have some form of secret and superior knowledge.

In the liner notes' fable, by contrast, Dylan took the bulb and *"stamped it out"*, crushing it with his foot. Dylan seems to indicate he once was reputed to be a bearer of certain ideas or visions, and he's now prepared to crush that notion, surrendering his prophetic voice.[3] Despite Dylan's efforts to (in Tim Riley's words) *"deflate his demigod status"* (176), the foolish kings are nonetheless convinced that they have been given special access to something miraculous. They leave.

At the end of the fable, Frank's wife Vera asks, *"Why didn't you just tell them you were a moderate man and leave it at that . . . ?"* Frank counsels patience instead. Nonetheless, as the liner notes say, Frank (i.e. the "new" Dylan) is the key.

The Songs

Clinton Heylin has provided detailed information on the three recording sessions for *"JWH"*, which took place in Nashville in October and November of 1967. With a few exceptions that are themselves significant, the songs were generally recorded (and probably composed) in the order they appear on the album. Significantly, they tell a rational story that corresponds roughly to Dylan's spiritual odyssey in the fifteen months following his motorcycle accident.

Biographer Robert Shelton was perhaps the first to note that there was logic in the album's presentation of themes, suggesting that the songs on the first side conveyed a sense of guilt, while those on the second side suggested atonement. The closing two light country songs bring a sense of attaining grace (445). If the songs were indeed written in the order recorded, it may also be helpful to note that Dylan's early idol, Woody Guthrie, had died on October 3, 1967, just two weeks before Bob started recording *"JWH"*. Woody's presence, and Bob's thoughts about his own early career, both seem to lurk behind many of the album's songs. In particular, Bob's thoughts about Woody seem to inform the earlier songs that Shelton most associated with guilt.

The October 17-18 Sessions

'Drifter's Escape'

The first song recorded was *'Drifter's Escape'*, a seemingly simple tale of the conviction of a man who has suffered emotionally (*"My trip hasn't been a pleasant one"*). Even after the jury's verdict is read, as in a tale by Franz Kafka, the song's narrator still doesn't know what he has done wrong. The judge, in a God-like role, explains there's no point in trying to understand, leaving the drifter without an answer. The jury *"cried for more"*, which was *"ten times worse"* than the trial itself. Then lightning strikes and the drifter escapes.

Without much imagination, the drifter appears to be a Dylan-like figure from 1965-66. Bob was then under pressure and unhappy with aspects of his career. Many of his songs from those days–ranging from *'It's All Right Ma'* and *'Stuck Inside Of Mobile'* to *'Sad-Eyed Lady Of The Lowlands'*–seemed to evoke existential angst or spiritual longing. Dylan had not been fulfilled and saw himself as a helpless sinner: *"Oh, help me in my weakness"*, he cried. The God-like judge does not respond. Meanwhile, the jury's cries (like those of his fans) are relentless. Then, an external force intervenes (like a motorcycle crash), and Bob escapes from both the courtroom and jury. One can imagine that the drifter escaped to his house in Woodstock where he read the Bible and Hank Williams' lyrics. *"Luke The Drifter"* was a pseudonym used by Williams and it was the title of one of his albums of sung parables. In *"Chronicles"*, Dylan said that he loved it (96).

'I Dreamed I Saw St. Augustine'

The next song recorded was *'I Dreamed I Saw St. Augustine'*. Most critics attempt to address the possible significance, if any, of Dylan's invocation of a particular historical figure, a bishop and philosopher from Roman North Africa who died in the fifth century. Paul Williams and Mike Marqusee feel there is no significance; Bob Shelton (449), Andy Gill (129-30), and Tim Riley (178) each note that St. Augustine spent his youth as a carouser and that his book, *"Confessions"*, recounts his years of debauchery in a way that might have appealed to Dylan. Following his misspent youth, St. Augustine became the author of books of redemption that might also have been analogous to Dylan's "conversion" from the life of a rock star to that of a modest family man.[4]

It may be, however, that a key to understanding the personal aspects of this song is its first line (and its title), as well as the song's melody, all of which evoke a 1936 song, *'Joe Hill'*, about a labour organizer and songwriter who, in 1915, was executed in Utah on a phoney murder charge. The first line of the earlier song, *"I dreamed I saw Joe Hill last night, alive as you or me"*, is, except for the proper name, identical to Dylan's in *'St. Augustine'*. This provides clues to Dylan's intent. In the earlier song, Joe Hill appears after his death to explain that he's present (at least in spirit) wherever workers organize. In that regard, *'Joe*

Hill' is very similar to the ending of John Steinbeck's novel, *"The Grapes Of Wrath"*, and Woody's song derived from it, *'Tom Joad'*.

Woody Guthrie, like Joe Hill, was an active labour union supporter, and his followers remained the leading participants in the protest song tradition when Dylan first arrived in New York. Indeed, Dylan's first original songs were published in two magazines, *Sing Out!* and *Broadside*, which were sponsored by close associates of Woody. Dylan, however, had abandoned writing topical songs sometime in 1964. On the occasion of Guthrie's death, Bob seems to be reflecting on his past. As the rest of the song indicates, he seems to regret his role in the death of the Joe Hill tradition, as well as the loss of fellowship and positive values that once adhered to that tradition. It's a mood that Dylan would often evoke, beginning perhaps with 1963's *'Bob Dylan's Dream'* (like *'St. Augustine'*, another dream reference). Recalling his first friends and the days of his youth, Dylan concluded, *"Ten thousand dollars at the drop of a hat,/I'd give it all gladly if our lives could be like that"*.

Like the liner notes, *'St. Augustine'* can be understood as being about an "old" Bob Dylan, cast loosely in the role of a Guthrie-esque saint, and the "new" Bob Dylan who has the dream. In the song, Bob imagines his old self, successful and wealthy (*"with a coat of solid gold"*), but still searching for values and life's meaning, presumably with integrity (like a vagabond, with a *"blanket underneath his arm"*). This "old" and originally prophetic Bob Dylan was *"[a]live with fiery breath"*. While he now seems almost wistful, the new Dylan recalls nonetheless that his former self was, like the drifter in the song recorded earlier that same day, *"in the utmost misery"*.

In the dream, St. Augustine would like to address his former colleagues, probably other singer-songwriters (*"gifted kings and queens"*). He could, however, be looking for anyone who once turned to him for inspiration and guidance: *"'Arise, arise,' he cried so loud,/In a voice without restraint"*.[5] Dylan may want to warn his friends about selling out and the evils of materialism. It's probably too late though: he's *"searching for the very souls/Whom already have been sold"*.

The key lines of the song, St. Augustine's core message to his fans and former colleagues, are as follows:

No martyr is among ye now
Whom you can call your own,
So go on your way accordingly
But know you're not alone.

Dylan has thus dreamt of a prior version of himself who then withdrew from public life and the discomfort it brought him. He wants to make it clear to those that he addresses, the *"gifted kings and queens"*, that they should not follow him: he says *"go on your way accordingly"*. At the same time, Dylan wants to encourage his listeners and let them know that, at some level, he still shares their concerns. Like both Tom Joad and Joe Hill, Dylan's dream thus brings forth an image of a spiritual participation in the lives of others (*"know you're not alone"*).

Probably prompted by Guthrie's death, Dylan seems nostalgic about his earlier days as a leader and part of a movement.

The song's final verse tells us that the "old" Dylan (the St. Augustine character) no longer exists. The "new" Dylan, the author of the song, admits that he *"was among the ones/That put him out to death"*. This makes the new Dylan, upon waking, *"alone and terrified"*. He is isolated in Woodstock and about to change the direction of his musical career. In the concluding lines of the song, Dylan puts his fingers on a glass, most likely a mirror, and considers the alternatives that he has faced in his life. He weeps. Having already described himself as a martyr, there is considerable conceit in this closing. *"Jesus wept"* is among the most famous lines in all of the New Testament (John 11:35).

'The Ballad Of Frankie Lee And Judas Priest'

A more detailed narrative of recent events in Bob's life is hidden in the lengthy song, *'The Ballad Of Frankie Lee And Judas Priest'*. Significantly, the song, like *'St. Augustine'*, also features the death of its leading character who, again, stands for the "old" Dylan. The song can also be understood as a parable about the relationship and growing distance between Dylan ("Frankie Lee") and his manager, Albert Grossman ("Judas Priest"). The song relates how Albert had taken Dylan, the young Woody Guthrie protégé, and helped mold him into an epicurean artist, sharing the older man's taste for fine drugs and fine women.

The ballad begins with the manager, Judas Priest, inviting Frankie Lee to take the money he needs. Judas, of course, was an infamous traitor and would have been an apt name for Grossman, who had recently been discovered stealing. And, as noted by Wilfred Mellers (156-57), the pronunciation of Frankie Lee could as easily have been rendered "Frank E. Lee", linking the name to "Frank" on the album's liner notes as well as to Dylan's Civil War interests and one of his self-confessed heroes, Robert E. Lee (38).

Feeling sheepishly embarrassed to take money with Priest looking on, Judas says he will wait in a place down the road, a place he calls Eternity. Frankie might know it as Paradise. Next, a passing stranger sent by Judas seeks to identify the Dylan character with the question, *"Are you Frankie Lee, the gambler,/Whose father is deceased?"* While the heart-attack death of Dylan's own father did not occur until the following year, Bob may be thinking again of his mentor-like father figure, Woody Guthrie, who had died just two weeks before.

The *"place down the road"* where Judas awaits could easily be Albert's Bearsville estate, where Dylan stayed so much of the time before he bought his own Woodstock home. Bearsville, just outside of Woodstock proper, became a kind of playground, as the growing retinue surrounding Grossman and Dylan would use it as a regular crash pad. Albert was a man of large appetites, and he liked to display his possessions for others to see. He had shed his business suits and let his hair grow, coming to resemble something of a modern-day Benjamin Franklin. In Bearsville, Grossman was widely known to provide the best drugs and feature the most gorgeous women (Goodman 97).

139

In Dylan's song, Frankie Lee arrives at a house of many pleasures, with 24 windows and *"a woman's face in ev'ry one"*. Dylan, or Frankie Lee in the song, trembles at the sight. He then goes wild (*"foaming at the mouth"*) and finally succumbs to his erotic temptations for sixteen days and nights. Dylan may even allude to the growing dispute with his manager over the royalty rights to his songs, when he sings, *"Well, Frankie Lee . . ./He soon lost all control/Over ev'rything which he had made"*. On the seventeenth day, in the arms of Judas Priest, Frankie Lee died of thirst, as though he had neglected his basic needs in the pursuit of many pleasures from Judas.

What happened next? The penultimate verse describes how the "old" Dylan is removed from the scene to make room for the new one. Without a damaging word or leak to the press, the removal appears to take place *"in jest"* (as though it were a mere ruse).[6] The only person who does not take it lightly is the little neighbour boy. Dylan, of course, had become Grossman's neighbour.

The complete verse is as follows:

No one tried to say a thing
When they took him out in jest,
Except, of course, the little neighbor boy
Who carried him to rest.
And he just walked along, alone,
With his guilt so well concealed,
And muttered underneath he breath,
"Nothing is revealed".

The song concludes with a series of morals: that one should not be where one does not belong and that you should help your neighbour carry his load. These are probably red herrings, deflecting the listener's attention from the sly reference to the guilt of the little neighbour boy. However, Dylan does admonish himself, really, not to mistake Paradise for Grossman's world, *"that home across the road"*.

* * *

In the end, Frankie Lee died in order that a "new" Dylan could be born. On prior occasions, Dylan had used a similar technique to describe symbolically the evolution of his different "selves" and the replacement of one by another. One example is, *'It's All Over Now, Baby Blue'*, written in January 1965 when Dylan had just begun to record with electric instruments. Like *'Frankie Lee And Judas Priest'*, it is also about the end of an era and the need for a new beginning. It should not be too hard to imagine that, at least in part, Bob could be talking to himself when he addresses the *"Baby Blue"* figure. A key line describes an armed orphan: *"Yonder stands your orphan with his gun/Cryin' like a fire in the sun"*. Like the St. Augustine figure, the orphan spoke with fiery breath. His need to express himself was intense, like a fire on the sun. He's not a protest singer anymore; he's going to be born again as a kind of hip existentialist.

Dylan was aware that, whenever he invented himself anew, he "killed" the old Dylan (originally Robert Allen Zimmerman). The old Dylan (initially, Zimmerman) had, however, given his new identity birth. In creating a new identity, he was playing a role somewhat like the father to a newborn son. In replacing the old Dylan, the "new" Bob Dylan then became like Oedipus, killing his father and becoming an orphan. In *'Baby Blue'*, wielding a gun, Dylan was the instrument of his own orphaned status. In *'Frankie Lee'*, a little boy carried out the "old" Dylan.

While the notion of using metaphors from Greek myth to explain the evolution of Dylan's successive identities may seem somewhat far-fetched, there is no doubt that Dylan thought of himself in that way. In *"Tarantula"*, he said as much. In that book, he even intimated that one or more of his previous incarnations still lingered on, like a ghost. In a fictional epitaph for one of his old selves (he's in at least his third incarnation), Dylan wrote:

Here lies bob dylan/. . . killed by a discarded Oedipus/who turned/around/to investigate a ghost/& discovered that/the ghost too/was more than one person.

The meaning is clear if one understands that only an "old" bob dylan was killed, and the "new" Bob Dylan who killed him is referred to here as Oedipus.

The November 6 Sessions

After having recorded three songs dominated by reflections on, and images of, his personal circumstances prior to his Woodstock retreat, Dylan returned to Nashville on November 6 and recorded five songs that generally asked the questions "Where am I now?" and "What next?" The next set of songs suggests somewhat fearfully that birth pangs may accompany the full emergence of the "new" Bob Dylan. Other songs lay out in parables the new rules that the singer should follow (or the mistakes that he should avoid).

'All Along The Watchtower'

The first song recorded in early November was *'All Along The Watchtower'*. It begins with a dialogue between two characters, the Joker and Thief who, as Stephen Scobie has argued at length, can be taken as symbolic aspects of Dylan's character (as well as myths emanating, in Scobie's view, from the universal "trickster") (189). The scholar Aidan Day, like Scobie, sees the joker and the thief as different aspects of a single person, engaged in "self-dialogue" about issues of creativity and business (132-33). He's probably right. It's time for a change, time for Dylan to escape a bad situation and replace it with another: *"'There must be some way out of here,' said the joker to the thief"*. The thief tries to calm the joker, reminding him that many among them *"feel that life is but a joke"* and then adding hopefully: *"But you and I, we've been through that and this is not our fate"*.

Scobie and Day, and many other modern literary critics working in the tradition of modern structuralism, studiously avoid issues of historical authorship and artistic intent in their interpretation of lyrics (or at least they purport to do so). It's the words alone, they say, that should inform the song's meaning. But it's also easy to see the historical Dylan in the figures of the joker and thief. He began his career as a kind of a thief, copying the styles of Woody Guthrie and raw Southern bluesmen. He "borrowed" melodies freely for his own compositions. He may even have referred to himself as a thief in *'Sad-Eyed Lady Of The Lowlands'* when he addressed his muse with the following line: *"Now you stand with your thief, you're on his parole"*. Of course, Dylan was a joker as well, particularly in his interviews and prose writings. That aspect of his character is also associated with drugs, cynical put-downs, and his conspiratorial band of friends originally from Boston, particularly Bobby Neuwirth.

Issues regarding the music business seem to have prompted Dylan's crisis: *"Businessmen, they drink my wine, plowmen dig my earth"*. Obviously, music executives fill themselves with the fruits of Dylan's labour–his blood and tears, transubstantiated Christ-like into wine. *"Plowmen"* (who could be other recording artists covering Dylan's songs or even the publishing houses holding his copyrights) sift through his work for their own advantage. From the watchtower, *"princes"* patrol the fortress. They may be analogous to the *"kings and queens"* that Dylan (as St. Augustine) would like to have addressed and warn. It was too late for them (their souls had already been sold). In *'All Along The Watchtower'*, the princes also seem to have been already co-opted by the industry.[7]

Much has been made, and justifiably so, of the close parallel of the song's imagery to that of the Old Testament's Book of Isaiah (21:8-9), including Bob's use of the watchtower and two horsemen. It is then tempting to cast Dylan, like Isaiah, as an American prophet who is foretelling destruction of a society for its sinful ways, not unlike Dylan's role as the author of *'A Hard Rain's A-Gonna Fall'*. It is equally likely, however, that Dylan is just talking to himself about the need to change his life and career. The allusion to prophecy serves to underline the inevitability of a radical change and perhaps associate radical change, like the prophet Isaiah, with the sinful or corrupt behaviour of others.

'John Wesley Harding'

If *'All Along The Watchtower'* says that things in Dylan's life have to change, the next song recorded in order, *'John Wesley Harding'*, provides a partial statement of where Dylan stands now.[8] It purports to be about the Western outlaw, John Wesley Hardin, whose name Dylan seems to have misspelled intentionally. As a consequence, Anthony Gill suggests that Dylan is not really singing about a specific historical character, but rather about the "outlaw myth" in general (127-28). In an interview with Jann Wenner, Dylan all but confirmed this when he said he chose the name simply because it *"fit the tempo"* (354).

Unlike the real Hardin, Dylan's outlaw *"was a friend to the poor"* and was *"never known to hurt an honest man"*. This makes the figure an obvious successor to Woody Guthrie's version of Pretty Boy Floyd, who committed robberies but saved the poor from mortgage foreclosure by pen-wielding bankers. (Guthrie's description of Floyd was alluded to in one of Dylan's earliest songs, *'Hard Times In New York Town'*: *"[A] very great man* [i.e. Woody] *once said/That some people rob you with a fountain pen"*.) A second outlaw then of interest to Dylan was John Hardy, obviously similar to the *"JWH"* name. At the time Dylan's album was being completed, the record producer Milt Okum was preparing an anthology of sheet music consisting of the favourite songs of famous folk singers. Dylan was asked to participate. He picked the traditional song *'John Hardy'*, which, incidentally, utilizes the same tune that Woody Guthrie used for his composition *'Tom Joad'* (based on *"The Grapes Of Wrath"*).

Dylan saw himself as a kind of an outlaw. Tim Riley wrote that Dylan's Harding, like the singer, was a *"gunslinger-in-exile who suddenly shows up back in town, downs psychedelia's show-biz camp with understated aplomb, and rides into the sunset with his woman at his side"* (172). One can find closer parallels between Dylan and his mythical outlaw hero by looking at the lyrics directly. While many of the specific attributes of Dylan's Harding probably have no counterpart in the singer's own biography, there are lines that suggest Dylan does want to make a few strong points about himself. They include:

All along this countryside,
He opened many a door . . .
With his lady by his side
He took a stand.
. . . And there was no man around
Who could track or chain him down,
He was never known
To make a foolish move.

This describes the Dylan who had "opened doors" in revolutionizing topical songwriting, who had invented folk-rock, and who had pioneered the use of both personal and surreal lyrics. He acknowledges this, but then he describes his self-imposed retreat with his wife. He took a stand, and no one could find him. He had escaped scrutiny for over a year, and he had become an elusive recluse. Using Harding as his surrogate, he now tells his critics, don't sell Dylan short. He never made a foolish move.

'As I Went Out One Morning'

The next song recorded was *'As I Went Out One Morning'*. It presents biographical issues that, when recorded, seem out of Dylan's narrative sequence. Like *'St. Augustine'*, the song can be taken to be a reflection on aspects of Dylan's career before his retreat to Woodstock. Not coincidentally, it was placed next to *'St. Augustine'* on the album.

In *'As I Went Out One Morning'*, Dylan is first described as going out *"[t]o breathe the air around Tom Paine's"*. This is likely an allusion to Dylan's association with the protest song movement, most heavily in 1962 and 1963. Specifically, the line may allude to Joan Baez and her circle of friends and supporters. In 1963, Dylan and Baez started a series of organized tours together, buoyed by the success of *'Blowin' In The Wind'* and *'With God On Our Side'*. Dylan's new fame was on the rise, and, in December 1963, he was awarded the Tom Paine award by Emergency Civil Liberties Union (ECLU). Clark Foreman (formerly with the Roosevelt administration) was then the head of the ECLU and a close friend of Baez and her family. Bob gave a speech at a fundraising and award dinner that was thrown in his honour.

Dylan's ECLU speech was a disaster (as, among other things, he said he saw something of himself in President Kennedy's assassin, Lee Harvey Oswald). Biographers generally dismiss the speech as the result of Dylan's nerves and having been influenced by over-indulgence in alcohol. At the same time, the speech also included a number of signs that Dylan would no longer follow the leaders of the civil rights and protest song movements. He would strike out on his own instead and follow his own muse. Despite his newly declared independence, Dylan's muse would, however, continue to be associated with Joan; their romance and touring together continued throughout 1964.

Dylan's early muse (from his days around Tom Paine) is described as the *"fairest damsel/That ever did walk in chains"*. Besides being chained, revealing lines about the fair damsel include, *"I offer'd her my hand/She took me by the arm"*, thus describing a relationship that appears imperfectly matched. The damsel is likely, on some level, to be a reference to Joan, whose commitment to civil rights and social reform was pure and impeccable, but whose imagination and willingness to experiment in search of spiritual truths was limited, in Dylan's view. Freedom obtained through the political process is, in the end, not the same as opening the doors of perception and experiencing freedom as a state of mind.

The fair damsel who took firm hold of Dylan could also represent other aspects of the muse-like figures who dominated Dylan's songs before his retreat. Like the mythical Queen of Spades in *'I Want You'* or the Sad-Eyed Lady of the Lowlands herself, she seems to take firm hold of Dylan and makes promises to secretly accept him, if he agrees to serve her. Before his motorcycle accident, Dylan seemed to find himself often enslaved by his muse, like the French poet Charles Baudelaire was with his mistresses. In *'She Belongs To Me'*, for instance, Bob described how one might start out standing, but end up *"peeking through a keyhole down upon your knees"*. In the same song, the spellbinding enchantress is described accumulating souls like the owner of a second-hand store (*"She's a hypnotist collector/You are a walking antique"*).

In the final verse of *'As I Went Out'*, the real Tom Paine appears, and he causes the muse-like character to loosen her grip. The real Tom Paine, symbolizing true freedom, understands that Dylan's freedom is important. In the closing lines of the song, the real Tom Paine apologizes: *"I'm sorry, sir,' he said to me,/"I'm sorry for what she's done"*. Dylan has embarked on a new path; he's no longer serving his former mistress or muse.

'I Pity The Poor Immigrant'

The final two songs recorded during these sessions were *'I Pity The Poor Immigrant'* and *'I Am A Lonesome Hobo'*. They're equally simple parables, warnings really about how not to live. Both mention corruption and reliance on material things as representing false values. As a consequence, the listener is tempted to view both the songs in the context of Dylan's dispute with his manager, but they can be read on other levels as well. Cartwright, for instance, sees the narrative voice of *'I Pity The Poor Immigrant'* as belonging to God. This is based in part on Dylan's apparent use of a series of quotes from Leviticus 26 referring to the fate of each of the wayward Jews when, as a wandering immigrant, he *"turns his back on me"* (i.e. God). (39). Referring to the same song, Scaduto thinks Dylan is painting a picture of a corrupt business world, a vainglorious battlefield fought by one who doesn't "see"; then, the glass shatters and the immigrant sees that his life had been wasted (255-56). The song may be, in part, Dylan's warning to himself not to be like the immigrant. Much of *"JWH"*, from *'St. Augustine'* through *'Dear Landlord'*, is about the dangers of serving material wealth.

'I Am A Lonesome Hobo'

Most critics also see something of Dylan's life in *'I Am A Lonesome Hobo'*. In that song, the narrator appears to have violated moral codes in exchange for his prosperity: *"I have tried my hand at bribery,/Blackmail and deceit"*. As a result, he has lost all family and friends, and he's forced to wonder off in shame. But in the end, the lonesome hobo appears to gain wisdom, and he provides a warning to others: stay free from petty jealousies, live by *"no man's rules"* and don't pass judgment on others. In the last year before his accident, Dylan did appear to violate at least some of the precepts that he set forth. In interviews, for instance, he was an aggressive existentialist who would not easily tolerate fools.

While *'I Am A Lonesome Hobo'* seems to exude melancholy, suggesting for instance that the singer's life may be ending (*"soon I will be gone"*), it is at least plausible that the reference to death is, as in *'Frankie Lee'*, merely about the loss of an identity. Much like *'St. Augustine'*, these short parables are sad and wistful because they include recognition of past mistakes and missed opportunities. And they're perhaps fearful tales about having to be reborn as the "new" Bob Dylan in a radical and irreversible change, like jumping off a cliff. In 1967, at the age of 26, the "old" Dylan must die: *"Where another man's life might begin,/That's exactly where mine ends"*. Where the old Dylan's life ends, the new Dylan's begins.

The November 21 Session

'The Wicked Messenger'

The final recording session for *"JWH"* occurred on November 21, also in Nashville. The first song, *'The Wicked Messenger'*, continued in the form of the simple parables that closed the last session, with the Wicked Messenger representing (again, on one level) the "old Bob". The song is confusing, and it may not be as profound as some critics make it. Several Biblical references are important. Proverbs 13:17 states that a wicked (or, in some translations, simply "bad") messenger falls into mischief (and a good messenger brings healing). In general, if Bob's message was bad, he'd get into trouble.

With "old" Bob's existentialist or punk attitude, his message was often that *"life has no meaning"*, as in *'It's Alright Ma (I'm Only Bleeding)'*. In that song, Dylan described life's meaninglessness as an immense *"darkness"* that *"even at the break of noon"* eclipses both the sun and the moon. There is really nothing to be understood: *"To understand you know too soon/There is no sense in trying"*. That kind of message made Bob a wicked messenger.

In Dylan's song, the Wicked Messenger's tongue doesn't speak, it only *"flatters"*. While these lines might suggest that Dylan's old songs were somehow obsequious or deceitful, they also may evoke Dylan's notorious propensity to engage in seductions: a bad messenger falls into mischief. This possibility is supported by some of the lyrics that follow. When the Wicked Messenger produces a note reading *"The soles of my feet, I swear they're burning"*, he's probably alluding to Proverbs 6:28, which is part of an admonition against adultery (i.e., you can't get away with it; if you walk on coals, you'll burn your feet). The image of the "old" Dylan that emerges thus seems to be a mischievous philanderer who feels that life has no meaning. On a more symbolic level, as a bad messenger, he once "seduced" the public into thinking that he was some kind of prophet.

In the final verse, the song opens up. Dylan submits to the judgment of the *"people that confronted him"*, perhaps alluding to his angry fans during his last world tour. They admonish him to bring good news, or don't bring any. This comes as a liberating revelation to Bob: it *"opened up his heart"*. Paul Williams thinks this last line is sarcastic and bitter, as Dylan the poet was seldom inclined to take heed of the general public's advice (246). The poet's duty, says Williams, is to tell the truth. But the next two songs that Dylan recorded (and the next few years of Dylan's career, including *"Nashville Skyline"* and *"Self-Portrait"*), say exactly what happened. *'Down Along The Cove'* and *'I'll Be Your Baby Tonight'* are the happy songs of a modest man. Instead of seeking transcendence and the meaning of life, at the most he seeks wholeness, which he finds with his wife.

'Dear Landlord'

'Dear Landlord' was the last song recorded for *"JWH"*, which is fitting. At the end, Dylan seems to be saying, "Here's my completed record; don't judge it too

harshly". At one level, it's as though Dylan is asking to be given some slack by his advisors, particularly his manager (who literally had been Dylan's landlord, providing him with free use of Grossman's Gramercy Park apartment and a cottage on his Bearsville estate): *"Please don't put a price on my soul./My burden is heavy,/My dreams are beyond control"*. Dylan continues with a promise to work hard: *"When that steamboat whistle blows,/I'm gonna give you all I got to give"*.

Dylan also reproaches his manager for his pursuit of material advantage, perhaps alluding to the recent record negotiations, contrasting Grossman with his own conscious decision not to maximize his wealth at the expense of other aspects of his life. After explaining he may have worked too hard to get too much too fast, Dylan continues, *"anyone can fill his life up/With things he can see but he just cannot touch"*. In justifying his new direction, he concludes modestly that *"each of us has his own special gift/ . . . And if you don't underestimate me,/I won't underestimate you"*. These were the last words of the last recording session.

* * *

Reviewing the songs recorded for *"JWH"* in the order that they were recorded, and probably written, helps tell the story of an important transitional period. They were re-sequenced for the final album, and the new sequence also made sense. Each side began with a "Here-I-am" song. Dylan appears favourably in *'John Wesley Harding'* (he never made a foolish move) and in *'Dear Landlord'* (he has a special gift and works hard). Side One otherwise features reflections on the early – and mid – 1960s, ending with his motorcycle accident (*'Drifter's Escape'*). Side Two has parables about imminent change and provides guidance with new rules to live by. The album ends with two songs by the fully realized "new" Dylan, *'Down Along The Cove'* and *'I'll Be Your Baby Tonight'*. The last two songs set the tone for the next several years. In this regard, understanding "Frank" (the "new" Dylan) is indeed the key.

Notes:

[1] The name *"Vera"* that Dylan used in his story may have been derived from "veracity" (meaning truth) in much the same way that Sara's character, Clara, in Dylan's film *"Renaldo and Clara"* could have been derived from "clarity". In many ways, Sara seemed to represent the kind of calm and clear vision that Dylan sought to emulate in these years.

[2] In a review entitled simply 'Bob Dylan' from *Sing Out!* magazine, Vol. 14, No. 1 (Feb-Mar 1964), Irwin Silber wrote disparagingly of most young folk singers, and he made use of the rather unusual word *"froth"*. Dylan may have remembered it. Excepting Bob, Silber wrote: *"Other folk singers purport to deal with words and images that grow out of people's experiences, like Trouble, Poverty, Lonesomeness, Hard Times, but its froth when you examine it"*. Dylan, by contrast, wrote songs about *"the world as it really is, or at least as it seems to him"*.

3 In *"Chronicles"*, Dylan recently described his attempts to undermine his standing as the *"spokesman of his generation"*. He said he wanted to *"send out deviating signals" and create "some different impressions"*: *"At first I was only able to do little things, local things. Tactics really. Unexpected things like pouring a bottle of whiskey over my head and walking into a department store and act pie-eyed"* (120).

4 If Dylan did want to suggest something about the career of the saint, it is possible that he encountered the name from an allusion in T.S. Eliot's *"The Waste Land"*, which places a line from *"Confessions"* in the midst of his poem about the possible salvation of a wasted society.

5 Noting the similarity of Dylan to his description of the saint, one scholar, John Herdman, used a line describing St. Augustine from this song as the title of his general overview of the singer, *"Voice Without Restraint"*.

6 When Grossman was negotiating new royalty contracts from competing record companies, some expressed reluctance to sign Dylan if he were suffering, as some speculated, from a drug addiction. Marc Eliot makes an unusual, matter-of-fact assumption that the accident was a mere ruse for Dylan's heroin detoxification (116-17).

7 In addition to the Bible, Dylan may have been reading T.S. Eliot while recuperating in Woodstock, including Eliot's *"Love Song of J. Alfred Prufock"*. In that poem, Eliot wrote *"In the room the women come and go/Talking of Michelangelo"*. Dylan's comparable line, following his reference to *"princes"* who kept the view, is *"While all the women came and went"*.

8 Dylan recognized that *'John Wesley Harding'* sounded incomplete and that it didn't fit well within the "suite" that comprises the rest of the album. Because it didn't seem to belong anywhere else (and perhaps because of the affirmative stance of its lead character), it became the album's opening song by default and incidentally gave the album its title (Wenner 353).

List of Works Cited:

Cartwright, Bert. *"The Bible in the Lyrics of Bob Dylan"*. 1992. Fort Worth, TX: priv. pub., 1985.

Cohen, John and Happy Traum. *'Conversations with Bob Dylan' Sing Out!* (October-November 1968) rep. in Craig McGregor, ed. *"Bob Dylan: The Early Years"*. 1972. New York: DaCapo, 1990, 265-292.

Cott, Jonathan. *'Bob Dylan: The Rolling Stone Interview, Part II'. Rolling Stone.* November 17, 1978.

Day, Aidan. *"Jokerman: Reading the Lyrics of Bob Dylan"*. Oxford: *Basil Blackwood*, 1988.

Dylan, Bob. *"Chronicles Volume One"*. New York: *Simon & Schuster*, 2004.

Eliot, Marc L. *"Rockonomics"*. New York: *Citadel*, 1993.

Gill, Andy. *"Don't Think Twice It's All Right/Bob Dylan: The Early Years"*. New York: *Thunder's Mouth*, 1998.

Goldberg, Steven. *'Bob Dylan and the Poetry of Salvation'. Saturday Review* (1970) rep. in McGregor, ed. 364-72.

Goodman, Fred. *"The Mansion on the Hill"*. New York: *Times/Random House*, 1997.

Gray, Michael. *"Song and Dance Man III"*. New York: *Cassell*, 2000.

Herdman, John. *"Voice Without Restraint"*. New York: *Delilah*, 1982.

Heylin, Clinton. *"Bob Dylan: The Recording Sessions"*. New York: *St. Martin's*, 1995.

Landau, Jon. *"It's Too Late to Stop Now: A Rock and Roll Journal"*. San Francisco: *Straight Arrow*, 1972.

Marcus, Greil. *"Invisible Republic"*. New York: *Henry Holt*, 1997.

Marqusee, Mike. *"Chimes of Freedom: The Politics of Bob Dylan's Art"*. New York: *The New Press*, 2003.

Mellers, Wilfred. *"A Darker Shade of Pale: A Backdrop to Bob Dylan"*. New York: *Oxford U.*, 1985.

Riley, Tim. *"Hard Rain: A Dylan Commentary"*. New York: *Knopf*, 1992.

Scaduto, Anthony. *"Bob Dylan: An Intimate Biography"*. New York: *Grosset*, 1971.

Scobie, Stephen. *"Alias Bob Dylan Revisited"*. Calgary, Alberta: *Red Deer*, 2004.

Shelton, Robert. *"No Direction Home: The Life and Music of Bob Dylan"*. New York: *Beech Tree*, 1986.

Wenner, Jann. 'The Rolling Stone Interview: Dylan'. *Rolling Stone.* Nov. 29, 1969 rep. in McGregor, ed., 317-56.

Williams, Paul. *"Performing Artist: The Music of Bob Dylan/Volume One"*. Novato, CA.: *Underwood-Miller*, 1990.

Witting, Robin. *"Isaiah on Guitar: A Guide to John Wesley Harding"*. London: *VALIS*, 1991.

First published in *ISIS* #120, May 2005

A Close Encounter of the Fourth Kind
I Left Home And Landed In Brussels

Adrian Richardson

On our arrival in Brussels, some 36 hours before Dylan's concert there, speculation about our hotel was rife; surely we hadn't been booked into the Sheraton, with as many stars as the universe? It turned out that was exactly what had happened. I made my way up the eight floors to a single room slightly longer than a football pitch. Ecstasy!

The Statenhal (The Hague, Netherlands, June 10, 1989) was strangely laid out, free standing at the front, seats behind. There was a far exit that led to the toilets via some white-painted steps, which overlooked the backstage outside door! I made my way there. Then, as 8pm struck and the support band began their set, the Globejogger (Dylan's tour bus), rolled up to the stage door and Dylan got out to be met by three minders, two girls, and a tall guy wearing a leather hat (who I later found out was a songwriter). Dylan appeared friendly; he gave the red-headed girl a kiss on the cheek, shook hands with the hat man and then entered through the side door to the hall. My 40th concert lived up to my expectations – SUPERB!

I returned to the Sheraton with the thought in the back of my mind that if Dylan was not going to stay here in Holland, but travel direct to Brussels, then the Sheraton was surely the place he would stay. Bingo! The Globejogger was parked outside the hotel! Whoever booked Bob in here is gonna be really pleased to see us turning up. Heads will roll!

I headed for the bar where the heavies were hanging out. After about twenty minutes there was some kind of incident around the main lobby. The story later related to me was that a local guy had been robbed of his wallet earlier that evening and was now accusing Dylan of the crime! The Police were called and the guy took a lunge at Dylan who apparently remained very cool throughout. He readily agreed to be searched and when nothing was found he went back to his room.

At 2.00am the hotel bar closed. This seemed a little suspicious to me, after all we were residents, and we had also heard that Dylan's only demand of his hotel while staying in Dublin was that the bar remained open all night. Was this an attempt to remove us from the bar prior to Bob's arrival?

I went to my room and ordered a drink through room service but was told that the bar always closed at 2.00am. Unconvinced, or perhaps just plain bloody- minded, I went back down to the bar. The heavies were still there though they didn't have drinks and the bar was closed. I settled down for a long vigil. At 3.00am the heavies suddenly left for their rooms. Lots of "goodnights" and "see you in the mornings". It all seemed a little too contrived. I stayed my ground.

At 3.15 a lift door opened and a minder got out. Seeing me still there he walked over and said, *"Look, Bob's coming down now, and he doesn't want any hassle, OK"*. I agreed, the lift doors opened and out walked Dylan. Ignoring us both he left by the front door. I hung around until 4.30am and then decided to call it a day.

I woke at 10.30am and went down to the lobby. Dylan and the band were checking out around mid-day so we decided to hang around. After a while guitarist G.E. Smith appeared and was quite chatty. No, he didn't know where Bob was, or when he was leaving. Yes, he was enjoying the tour and he was interested to read the London press reviews we had with us. Chief of security Jim Callaghan was very amiable. He told us that Bob wasn't in the hotel and that we should go out and enjoy the city. We took the chance and went for a meal. On our return Jim borrowed the press cuttings to show Dylan, (the last we saw of them!), but still insisted that Dylan was not in the hotel.

At around 3.30pm the Globejogger arrived and luggage was wheeled onto it. There were no other signs of activity. Our own coach to the venue was leaving at 5.00pm and a dilemma set in. Should we hang around in the hope of catching a glimpse of Bob and make our own way to the concert? The courier made one final request for everyone to get on the coach and suddenly everyone was leaving – except me! As the bus disappeared from sight it suddenly felt like a very bad decision.

During the next 30 minutes Bob's American minder joined the Globejogger, as did the two girls from The Hague and the songwriter in the leather hat. Jim Callaghan came and went several times through the lobby. He asked how I was getting to the venue and when I told him by taxi he said that I could go on the Globejogger . . . WOW! Then he thought about it a little more and said it would cause too much trouble. I did my level best to look understanding.

Suddenly, without warning, Dylan came round the corner clad in his infamous grey tracksuit top, hood tightly drawn up. He walked straight past me and started talking to Callaghan who caught my eye and, as they finished he turned and said, *"Bob, I'd like you to meet your biggest fan"*, (a pun on my physical size). Dylan looked and nodded. *"That's his expression, Bob, not mine"*, said Callaghan. I chipped in to the conversation to salvage a little dignity. Dylan asked me if I was going to the show that night and had I been to the British shows? I told him that I was and that I had, and he said he hoped that I'd enjoy that evening's performance too. Then he turned and walked away.

Shell-shocked is, I believe, the expression. I just stood there. A few minutes later Jim Callaghan walked out, looked at me and said *"Oh, come on"* and waved me towards the Globejogger! Once on board we were all told that if we saw Bob not to acknowledge him and to look away. Then he told me that Bob had been out cycling around Brussels all day and that he had been telling me the truth when he said, *"Go and enjoy the city"*. He also said that that Dylan would be cycling to the venue tonight. When we arrived at the venue Callaghan went into the hall and then came back and said: *"I've left your pass at the box office, OK"*. I thanked him and went for a drink.

Recalling the previous concert sequence, I returned to the Globejogger just before 8.00pm. There were plenty of heavies in attendance and a crowd of onlookers, maybe thirty in all. Bang on 8.00pm the support started up and Bob came biking up the hill towards us! He looked a little apprehensive of the crowd waiting for him, but happily everyone played it cool. Bob stepped off his bike and disappeared inside. Another magic moment!

I picked up my ticket from our courier and was reminded about the pass that Jim had left for me. I said I wasn't going to bother with it because I had my original ticket now, but on second thoughts, I thought it might look a bit ungrateful if I didn't pick it up. I gave my name at the box office and received a red pass – *"ACCESS ALL AREAS!"* I couldn't believe it!

The only way to get back-stage was to use the entrance Bob had used. Two doormen ushered me through and as I walked around I saw Bob and Jim in a small dressing room. Bob was towelling himself down after his bike ride and was wearing only tracksuit bottoms. He looked very fit indeed; muscular shoulders and arms and a flat solid stomach. He definitely looks after himself these days. I walked on, still unsure about my position, but Jim called me back. I walked into the small room and Jim asked if my ticket was alright. I thanked him and said I was looking forward to the show. Bob asked if I had gone home happy from Glasgow. I said no, I went very happy to Birmingham! *"Great"*, he said, *"Make sure he gets a good view of the show, Jim"*.

I had a fabulous view from the side of the stage where I spotted several different kinds of passes, mostly green in colour, giving varying degrees of access including an after show party badge. Where this party took place I do not know. Bob left very fast, directly from the stage to the Globejogger. The party seemed to be taking place back-stage, maybe he just forgot, I don't know. I picked up a song-sheet and made my way back to the Sheraton. An unforgettable seven days.

Published in *ISIS* issue #26, September, 1989

Bob Dylan 1969

The Gang That Couldn't Shoot Straight
Joey Thirty Years On

D e r e k   B a r k e r

April 2002 was the 30th anniversary of the Mafioso murder of Joey Gallo. This anniversary, coupled with Dylan's recent comment about the Mafia, has prompted me to take another look at the Gallo story.

* * *

The song's opening line, *"Born in Red Hook, Brooklyn, in the year of who knows when"*, immediately creates a feeling of mystery and intrigue, which sets a romantic scene that helps to place Joey as a Billy the Kid or Robin Hood type of outlaw.

Joey Gallo was in fact born into the rough-and-tumble streets of Red Hook, Brooklyn on April 6, 1929. His father Albert, an illegal immigrant, had married Mary Nunziata and they had five children, Carmela, Larry, Joey, Albert and Jacqueline. It was easy to become a petty criminal in Red Hook, it came with the turf, and Joey and his two brothers joined local street-gangs as soon as they were old enough to fight. In 1950 Joey Gallo, then twenty-one, was arrested for burglary. His attitude in court was so bizarre he was sent to King's County Hospital for psychiatric tests. Gallo was diagnosed as a paranoid schizophrenic, but he later convinced the court that this was due to a misunderstanding! From that time on, however, Gallo was known as "Crazy Joe".

On his own patch Joey was a well-liked and respected individual who tried to help the people of his community. The area controlled by his gang was allegedly one of the safest and cleanest neighbourhoods in New York. He did not tolerate drug-pushing or theft and even built a swimming-pool for the local kids. There is, however, no doubt that Joey wanted more power and a bigger slice of the cake – or should that be pizza?

The Gallo gang's first move to gain prominence came when they acted on a contract put up by the Profaci family for the life of one Albert "The Mad Hatter" Anastasia. Unfortunately for Anastasia – head of what had formerly been the Mangano family, but now christened "Murder, Inc." by the press – he had a well-documented routine. He started most days with a haircut, shave and a shoeshine. Around ten in the morning on October 25, 1957 Anastasia walked into the barbershop of New York's Park Sheraton Hotel, at 870 Seventh Avenue, in Manhattan. He sat down in chair four, closed his eyes and as he reclined the seat his face was covered with a hot towel. As the barber began to clip his hair, two men wearing fedoras, sunglasses and overcoats, walked in and drew revolvers. The gunmen motioned the barber away from the chair and proceeded to pump bullets into Anastasia who eventually succumbed to the barrage. Shortly after their successful hit on Anastasia, both Larry and Joey were given their "badges" and "made" into the Profaci family. Joey in particular soon caught the attention of the law-enforcement agency. The special team, affectionately known as "The Pizza Squad", had been set up by the NYPD to deal with organised crime.

Most of his own family members considered Joe Profaci a tyrant and many of his rivals for power came from within his own organization. Long after the other bosses had ceased the "approved" Sicilian practice of collecting tributes from their men, Profaci continued to demand $25 a month from each of his men as a tithe.

Like many of Profaci's soldiers, the Gallo brothers became tired of Joe Profaci's greed; the final straw came with the murder of Frank "Frankie Shots" Abbatemarco. One of the biggest loan-sharks and gamblers in New York, "Frankie Shots" also ran a numbers racket that grossed almost one million dollars a year. He had, however, committed the cardinal sin of holding back on his dues to Profaci. In exchange for their part in his murder, the Gallos and their top gunner, Joe Kelly, expected a slice of Frankie Shots' racket. However, after the Gallos dispatched Shots no such reward was forthcoming.

The Gallos then began to recruit other members who were disenchanted with their crime boss and by early 1960 over 100 men, almost half of the Profaci "family", had formed a new gang headed by Carmine Persico and Joe's elder brother Larry. Finally, on February 27, 1961 the new faction kidnapped four of Profaci's closest advisers, including family under-boss, Joseph Magliocco, and Joe Profaci's brother, Frank. It is believed the Gallos had also intended to take Joe Profaci but he escaped and went into hiding at his holiday home in Florida. On the promise that their demands would be met the Gallos eventually released their hostages. However, Joe Profaci reneged on the deal, so all that was left was for the two gangs to take stock and wait for the right time to act.

On a hot August day in 1961, Profaci made his move. One of the Gallo gang, Joseph "Joe Jelly" Giorelli, went out on a fishing trip in Sheepshead Bay and never returned. His wife received a parcel containing his shirt, wrapped around a flounder. This was a Mafia message that meant Joe Jelly was "sleeping with the fishes". Two days later, on August 20th, Larry Gallo was attacked and almost garroted to death in the Sahara bar on Utica Avenue, Brooklyn. His life was saved by the timely arrival of two cops who were checking out an open door. The first the Gallo gang knew of this was when they heard about the attempted murder on the six o'clock news. The Profaci-Gallo war lasted until 1962 when Joe Profaci died of cancer. However, even after the death of the Mafia boss, the Gallos remained adversaries of the Profaci family.

On May 12, 1961, Joey was arrested for conspiring to extort. He was sentenced on December 21, 1961. Judge Sarafite handed him the maximum sentence of seven years and three months to fourteen years and six months – Dylan obviously had difficulty in rhyming that one. Gallo served a total of nine years and two months of his sentence in six different prisons. He began his term in Attica and was eventually released on parole from Sing Sing on March 10, 1971. He lost some weight during his time in prison but after his release continued to buy suits in his old size.

Shortly after his release from prison the film version of Jimmy Breslin's mob farce, *"The Gang that Couldn't Shoot Straight"*, was premiered in New York and Gallo was so impressed by Jerry Orbach's portrayal of him that he invited the actor and his wife to join him for a meal at an Italian diner in Brooklyn. It was during that meal that Gallo revealed his interest in literature (he'd read extensively while in the pen), announcing that he preferred Sartre[1] to Camus.[2] Gallo's literary knowledge astounded Orbach and he began to think of this man – who would rather read than rob – as a "noble savage". Shortly after this night he started to introduce the mobster to his society friends from stage and screen. One of these friends was theatre director Jacques Levy, who at the time had just begun working with Bob Dylan on what would later become the album *"Desire"*.

Before long Gallo's new circle of friends produced many surprises. The racketeer was not only immortalised in song by Bob Dylan, but he also secured an advance from *Viking Press* to write his prison memoirs. Gallo appeared to enjoy the company of Hollywood stars and New York actors and now seemed to consider himself as some sort of celebrity. Indeed, in one press interview he said that he was now clean and that he was a writer.

On March 16, 1972 at the Orbachs' West 22nd brownstone home, Gallo married his second wife, Sina Essary. Allan Jones sang *'The Lord's Prayer'*, the assistant conductor of the New York Metropolitan Opera played piano and the same minister that had wed Tiny Tim and Miss Vicki on Johnny Carson's *'Tonight Show'* performed the ceremony.

Three weeks after his wedding, Gallo was celebrating his 43rd birthday and 'holding court' at an uptown Manhattan nightclub – the Copacabana – when, in the early hours, he decided he wanted food, Chinese food. Chinatown bordered Little Italy, which at the time was the territory of Gallo's arch-enemy, the new boss of the Profaci family, Joe Columbo. Even so, and against the wishes of his new wife, their daughter, his sister Carmela, and his close friend Pete the Greek, the party headed down to Chinatown, only to find the restaurants had closed for the night.

Whether through bravado, or pure stupidity, Joey decided they would drive the few blocks from Chinatown to Umbertos on Mulberry Street, in the heart of Little Italy. This was despite the fact that Joe Columbo, who had been shot within a couple of months of Joey's release from a prison, had put a contract out on him. In any event, Joey was seen entering the Clam House, a telephone call was made, and at five in the morning on April 8, 1972, as he was finishing up his birthday meal of scungilli and clams at a rear table, Sonny Pinto and two brothers, Benny and Cisco, gunned Gallo down. Despite having been hit twice, Joey did indeed manage to push the butcher-block table over to protect his family. And as the song says, he then staggered out into the streets of Little Italy where he died from a .38

calibre bullet that cut through his carotid artery. It was a stark ending for such a colourful New York legend, famed for such antics as bringing a lion cub into an East Side nightclub. Legend has it that "Crazy Joe" was known to saunter around the streets of Brooklyn with his lion on a leash. Gallo is said to have kept the lion in his Brooklyn basement to scare loan-shark victims into paying up.

"He made a mistake, Crazy Joe did", Deputy Police Commissioner Robert Daley said as he shivered in the freezing rain at the murder scene; *"He should have gone to bed last night".*[3]

At his funeral, at Green-Wood Cemetery, Brooklyn, his sister Carmela allegedly stood in front of his casket and cried out, *"The streets are going to run red with blood, Joey"*. Later that day, one of Joe Columbo's men, Gennaro Ciprio, had his head blown off by a shotgun blast as he stood outside a restaurant in Bath Beach, Brooklyn. Over the next few weeks many other men were killed or wounded on the streets of Brooklyn in what became an extended period of mob assassinations.

"Bob Dylan's Dalliance with Mafia Chic"

At the time of its release, the song *'Joey'* caused a great deal of controversy both in the Dylan world and in the press. *"Bob Dylan's Dalliance with Mafia Chic"*, was the title of a piece written by Lester Bangs and published in *Creem* in April 1976. The piece was highly critical of Dylan's apparent championing of a proven gangster and alleged murderer.

It was, however, argued by Nigel Hinton in *'The Telegraph'* #14, November 1983, that Dylan was not the narrator of the song. Hinton –

"Bob Dylan is the poet who created a narrator who tells the Joey Gallo story as he (or maybe in this case she. ed) *saw it. Just a brief glance at the lyrics shows that the whole narrative is told from close in – by someone who knew and loved the entire family and who was actually present at some of the events, including the funeral –*

I heard his best friend Frankie say 'he ain't dead, he's just asleep.'
Then I saw the old man's limousine head back towards the grave. . .

"It is obvious that Dylan himself was not present, nor is he even imaginatively reconstructing it as though he were, but that he is telling the story from the point of view of someone who was".

The person, or persons in question, we must assume to be Marty and Jerry Orbach (ed.)

Dylan – *"I was with Jacques. I was leaving town and Jacques says he was going up to some place to have supper and I was invited to come up if I felt like it and I was hungry. So I went with him and it was up to Marty and Jerry Orbach's place, and as soon as I walked in the door Marty was talking about Joey. She was a good friend of Joey's. They were real tight. I just listened for a few hours. At the time, I wasn't involved in anything that he was involved in, but he left a certain impression on me. I never considered him a gangster. I always thought of him as some kind of hero in some kind of way. An underdog fighting against the elements. He retained a certain amount of his freedom and he went out the way he had to. But she laid all these facts out and it was like listening to a story about Billy the Kid. So we went ahead and wrote that up one night".*

From the above it would seem clear that Dylan is, as Nigel Hinton asserts, telling the Gallo story from someone else's 'first hand' point of view. The question remains, however, did Dylan tell the story simply because it was interesting and cinematic, or did he tell the story because he was sympathetic towards Gallo, and because he believed the "noble Savage" view of Gallo adopted by Marty and Jerry Orbach?

In any event, if we are to believe the statement made by Dylan at his Press Conference in Rome in July 2001, then there can be no real justification for the song. Dylan –

"Let's take "Godfather", a movie about the scum of the earth. Human dirt like the Mafia, to glorify [them] *horrifies me very much. Those criminals are no heroes – they're dirt".*

Strong words, indeed. The *"Godfather"* movie was premiered in April 1972, some three years before Dylan wrote *'Joey'*, so has he changed his opinion of Mafia portrayals since 1975, and if so, why is he still performing the song in concert? Dylan has performed *'Joey'* as recently as the 1999 USA fall tour. It's just a pity that one of the journalists present at the Rome Press Conference wasn't sharp enough to ask the question.

[1] Sartre, Jean-Paul, 1905 - 1980. French author and philosopher, a leading proponent of existentialism.

[2] Camus, Albert, 1913 - 1960. French existentialist novelist, essayist, and dramatist, born in Algiers.

[3] Al Guart for *New York Post.*

Based on an article by Keith Charles Marsh that first appeared in issue #14 of *ISIS,* in July 1987. Reworked as *"The Gang That Couldn't Shoot Straight"* by Derek Barker and published in *ISIS,* #101 in March 2002.

Blood on the Tracks 30 Years On

Derek Barker

Thirty years ago, at a time when his nine-year marriage to Sara Lownds seemed to be irreparably failing, Bob Dylan was continually writing and rewriting the songs that would eventually become, what is considered by many music critics to be one of the finest record albums of all time and certainly the best album of the 1970s, *"Blood On The Tracks"*.

Sacrifice was the Code of the Road

Friends in Woodstock had said that Bob and Sara seemed blissfully happy while living there and that it was only after the move from New York to California that things began to take a turn for the worst.

First, there was the reconstruction of the new Dylan home at Point Dume. The fairy-tale house, or as some would later come to call it, "Sara's folly", had become a burden on Bob, not so much financially, but in the monumental amount of time taken to complete the ever changing project. Bob began drinking quite heavily and he was smoking again after having quit for a while. In themselves, none of these things was serious, but together they were pointers that after eight years of happy family life he was ready and willing to leave behind the mundane routine and go back to the rock 'n' roll lifestyle.

The 1974 tour was promoted by Bob's new-found friend David Geffen in association with impresario Bill Graham, who handled the logistics. Geffen, who in 1970 had founded *Asylum Records* at the age of 27 and had sold it within two years for $7 million, only to take control again a year later, wasn't short on hype for what was billed in the press as Dylan's *"Comeback Tour"*.

In terms of ticket applications, the tour was boasted as being the biggest in US rock history. The applications, supposedly five million requesting an average of four tickets per letter, came at a time when the Postal Service was already under pressure with seasonal mail and there were rumours that the deluge of ticket applications almost brought the US Postal Service to a halt.

Along with the likes of the 1973 Led Zeppelin tour, which also played the 18,500 capacity Chicago Stadium, this tour heralded a new, some would say extremely unfavorable, direction in rock music. The venues were massive, the largest that Geffen and Graham could find. The concertgoers in the upper tiers were in danger of nosebleeds, yet the average ticket price was $8, high for 1974.

159

The musicians travelled between shows in a private jet, Starship 1. The excesses of the mid-seventies rock era had arrived. On the whole, Dylan didn't enjoy the experience and he would choose not to tour with The Band again. This was in no way a reflection on The Band; the more likely scenario being, "I did this in 1966, why did I need to do it over again".

With the tour behind him, Bob would spend spring in New York City. The reason for his visit to the Big Apple is unclear, but he flew in from Los Angeles on April 24th and after a few days in town he went to find a man he'd heard a lot about from friends.

Dylan had learned about the 73-year old painter and art teacher Norman Raeben from friends of Sara's.

Dylan: *"They were talking about truth and love and beauty and all these words I had heard for years, and they had 'em all defined. I couldn't believe it . . . I asked them, 'Where do you come up with all those definitions?' and they told me about this teacher".*

Dylan: *"He looked into you and told you what you were . . . I had a lot of fantasy dreams. He doesn't respect fantasy".*

Bob later described Raeben as being *"More powerful than any magician".*

Dylan: "[Raeben] *taught me how to see . . . in a way that allowed me to do consciously what I unconsciously felt".*

The best explanation of this statement is given by Paul Williams in his book *"Bob Dylan – Performing Artist The Middle Years".*

Williams: *"There's a point . . . in a creator's life, where one can no longer pretend not to know certain things; and this knowledge or awareness becomes an insurmountable burden to new creation unless one learns methods of completely accepting and assimilating it (Going through self-consciousness back to un-consciousness) and thereby regaining freedom".*

Dylan: "[My time with Raeben] *locked me into the present time more than anything else I ever did . . .* [there were] *all these different selves that were in there, until this one left, then that one left, and I finally got down to the one that I was familiar with".*

Whilst Norman Raeben might have helped Dylan to find himself, some, including Bob, might also say that Raeben's teachings were a decisive factors in the break up of his marriage.

Dylan: *". . .Needless to say it* [his time with Raeben] *changed me. I went home after that and my wife never did understand me ever since that day. That's when our marriage started breaking up".*

With a new focus and a redirected psyche, Bob Dylan spent much of the summer of 1974 on the eighty-acre farm that he had recently brought on the banks of the Crow River, northeast of Minneapolis. Sara did not accompany Bob to the farm and only made the occasional visit there. Instead, Bob was joined by Ellen Bernstein, a twenty-four-year-old *Columbia Records* executive who was in charge of A&R at the company's office in San Francisco.

It was during that summer on the farm that Bob began writing new songs into a red notebook, and having now returned to the *Columbia* fold, he decided to return to his old stomping ground to record his next album. *Columbia* Studio A, at 799 Seventh Avenue, where he had recorded all his early successes up to *"Blonde On Blonde"*, was now renamed A&R Studio and was operated by Phil Ramone and Don Frey.

Recording in Studio A1 at A&R began on September 16, 1974 and barring overdubs and mixing the album was finished in four days straight. To begin with, Dylan seemed pleased with the results, but as time passed, he began doubting the merits of certain songs. The final straw appears to have been when his younger brother David told Bob that the album wouldn't sell. David's reasoning for this bold statement was that he thought the songs were too dark and too similar. As an album it would be a depressing listening experience.

Dylan's decision to re-record five of the ten songs sparked a heated and contentious debate that still rages today.

Kevin Odegard: The ISIS Interview

Kevin Odegard: "The story starts in January 1974 when Bob Dylan went back on the road. The tour contained great excess and much partying and we believe it led to one of the rifts that contributed to his divorce. The first question is, why didn't Dylan enjoy this huge mega hall tour that he'd just come off of with The Band? Well, he'd been gone for seven or eight years, out of the scene, out of the spotlight and he came back to a different business. Rock 'n' Roll in the United States, because of Bill Graham, had become a huge mega hall business. You weren't playing to three and four thousand people anymore you were playing to 17,000, 20,000, 30,000, 40,000 people. It was very well packaged and very well organised. Dylan's next tour, Rolling Thunder (1975), was a righteous rebellion Bob didn't pay attention to what the mainstream was doing, he just did his own thing.

Anyway, in the summer of 1974, he began writing and although much of it will later change, originally, he wrote everything in the key of E. As it came out, piece by piece, he would play much of it for various friends and he got mostly negative reactions. He spent some time in the Bay Area where he visited Mike Bloomfield at his house in Marin County. Mike wanted to play along, but the whole thing went so poorly that Mike very nearly kicked him out of his house! Bob wouldn't slow down, would stop between songs, wouldn't give him keys, no lead sheets, no chords, nothing. He just played it top to bottom, the entire *"Blood On The*

161

Tracks", if you can imagine that! And in open tuning, which is a very difficult thing for any guitarist to follow. Also, Bob is a far better guitarist than many of us give him credit for. He's far ahead of most of us, both in and out of the studio. He never used a capo to go up and down keys and that amazed the musicians in New York and in Minneapolis. He then went down the hill to Sausalito and played it for Pete Rowan, he played for Shel Silverstein on his houseboat, and all along the line he got mixed reactions.

He had already played about eight of the songs for Stephen Stills and Tim Drummond. This was at the St Paul Hilton on July 22, 1974. Dave Crosby didn't get into the room and Graham Nash was left outside with his ear to the door! He was dying to listen to Bob play these songs but no, he didn't get in the room. Bob sat down cross-legged on the floor with these two friends and again he played the songs without stopping and he's very excited about the whole thing. After the session broke up, they walked out of the room and Stills shook his head and said, *"Well, he's an OK songwriter, but he's not much of a musician"*. That was a direct quote to Graham Nash, who just couldn't believe his ears.

Anyway, *Columbia* wanted what they considered as one of their lead icons back. John Hammond Sr brought him back to the label, they met with Goddard Lieberson, the president, and signed a three record deal.

On the morning of the 16th (September 1974), Eric Weissberg was up at A&R Studios working on an advertising jingle when he bumped into Phil Ramone in the hallway. Eric was assigned the job of finding the musicians to play on the Dylan session. The bass player was Tony Brown, the piano player was Tom McFaul, Richard Crooks was on drums and Charlie Brown III and Barry Kornfeld on guitars. Later, at the next session, Paul Griffin and Tony Brown were called in to do some live stuff, one of which was the beautifully haunting New York version of *'Idiot Wind'*. So, the first session was the full band and the only thing that came out of the full band session, that made it onto the final album, was *'Meet Me In The Morning'*.

The second session, with just Tony Brown and Paul Griffin, was the next day. Tony Brown described Dylan as saying absolutely nothing in a seven-hour session. Not a word was exchanged between the two of them. Dylan was so focused and so obsessed with getting this material together, they didn't speak about anything. But Tony Brown is aware just how truly magnificent this batch of songs was and he just got on with it. *'Shelter From The Storm'* and *'You're Gonna Make Me Lonesome When You Go'* from this session made it onto the final album.

For the next session, Dylan asked Ellen Bernstein to bring in Buddy Cage from the New Riders of the Purple Sage. Bernstein had played Bob some of the New Riders' new album and Bob asked her to get a steel guitar player. Buddy was the victim of a practical joke or two in the studio as Bob relaxed more and Mick Jagger arrived in the control room and begged to play on a track. Bob got Cage all fired up and after the take Cage cursed Bob. He soon realised, however, that Dylan's attitude was a ruse designed to bring the best out of him and with that first take out of the way, Cage quickly did overdubs for *'Call Letter Blues'*,

'You're A Big Girl Now', and he believes, 'Tangled Up In Blue'. Ultimately, though, none of these tracks made it onto the final album. After the session, they all went out partying together.

The thing was mastered at that point and it's circulated and it's a wonderful piece of work, but as Phil Ramone likes to say, "if artists are left to ruminate on their work, they will very often throw a horn section in whether it's appropriate or not". And Bob was left for three months to wonder lyrically and musically whether he'd achieved what he wanted to do and by the time he got home to Minnesota to celebrate the holidays he was racked with doubt. In fact, he had serious enough doubts to play it for his younger brother (David Zimmerman), with whom he wasn't very close. Anyway, what David told Bob was that the songs were fine, but it was not a commercial record. It wasn't radio friendly; "It's just not going to sell". So, Bob asked David if he could set something up. David was a record producer; he was the jinglemeister of Minneapolis, another Eric Weissberg, and Bob asked him to line up some musicians. David Zimmerman was managing me, and had been for seven years up to that point. He also managed a couple of other artists and he was working a lot at Sound 80, producing all these jingles. Billy (Peterson) and Bill (Berg) worked on all of the jingles at the studio and they were set-up there, which was an advantage that Paul Martinson had over his mentor, which was Phil Ramone.

Bob was particularly interested in working more on 'Lily, Rosemary And The Jack Of Hearts'. He hadn't gotten quite the right feel on that one in New York and that song was a problem for him. The first call David made was to Paul Martinson to line up Sound 80. Martinson was the engineer there. Of course, this was over the Christmas holiday; Paul couldn't get hold of any musicians but he did book the studio time. We got called on the 26th of December and we put the whole thing together that night, literally.

I campaigned for a couple of friends of mine for the rhythm section, the late great fretless bass player out of Minneapolis, Doug Nelson and for percussionist Stanley Kipper, but that decision had already been made. David's first choice was the 'house' rhythm section at Sound 80, Billy Peterson and Bill Berg, with whom he was familiar and comfortable. They were certainly an inspired choice. Berg had just finished coming off a Cat Steven's album ["Buddha And The Chocolate Box"] and they had both worked on a great Leo Kottke album, "Dreams And All That Stuff". Now, if you can follow Leo Kottke through a song then that's great, but the next time it's going to be completely different. So the best practice they could possibly have gotten for "Blood On The Tracks" was to have just finished an entire album with him. The only questions from there were, where do we find the guitar (Bob wanted a certain sound and had asked David to find him a small 1930s Martin) and who would we use on keyboards?

Dave and I called up keyboard player Gregg Inhofer. Gregg was the new whiz kid in town. He was a kind of fusion jazz bandleader and had just come off the road from touring with Olivia Newton-John. With that done, I called my friend Chris Weber at Podium musical instrument shop in Dinkytown and told him I had a client for a guitar".

163

For Chris Weber, the Minnesota *"Blood On The Tracks"* recording sessions were a surreal experience that started with a simple request to supply an acoustic guitar. Weber, who had recently taken over ownership of the *Podium* music store, had just brought in a pristine condition 1934 double-0 size Martin from someone who had inherited the instrument from his or her grandfather. Only three days after getting the Martin, Weber got a telephone call from Kevin Odegard asking: *"Do you have any old Martins?"* Weber reasoned that Odegard must have seen the guitar in the shop and was trying it on. Odegard informed Weber that he hadn't been to the store and that he didn't know what he was talking about, but that he wanted the guitar for a client.

Kevin Odegard: "Chris wouldn't agree to bring this guitar, which was on consignment to him, unless number one, he knew who the client was, and number two, he could accompany his instrument to the session. We exchanged several phone calls but there was nothing doing. Finally, I got David Zimmerman to agree that I could tell Chris that the client was Bob Dylan. But I had to swear him to secrecy.

The guitar is widely known in folk music circles as the Joan Baez guitar. It has a very small body and it doesn't overpower a microphone in the studio. It also has a very mellow sound. If you listen to Joan's *Vanguard* recording of *'Farewell Angelina'* you'll hear the exact guitar tone that you hear on *'Lily, Rosemary And The Jack Of Hearts'*.

The Minneapolis sessions began with Chris Weber in the vocal booth, because we were banging around, making too much noise in the main studio and Bob wanted to hear the tone of this guitar and to make sure it was the right thing".

Chris Weber takes up the story:

"When Dylan came into the studio I introduced myself and said that he may remember the *Podium* from the days when he lived above Gray's Campus Drug down the street. We chatted a little, then he said, *'Oh, you've got the guitar. Let's look at it'*. . . The guitar was a rare 1934 *Martin* 0042G. The 'G' means gut-string set-up. It wasn't exactly the guitar that Bob was looking for, but it was close. The neck was a little bit wider and of course, it wasn't really designed for steel strings, although it was certainly strong enough to support them. . .

He took me into a little glassed-in area used for vocal recording and he says, *'Do you play?'* I said, *'Yes'*, assuming that he wanted to hear something played on it from the other side so he could check out the sound, something I'd done for hundreds of customers. So I played a rag for him and he said, *'You play well'*. Then, he said, *'Listen, do me a favour. I'm going to teach you a song in here. Learn it and then teach it to the band, OK?'* And then he started teaching me *'Idiot Wind'*. So, then he goes for a cup of coffee with his son Jakob in the vending machine area, and I go out and teach it to the guys, who are wizards, so it takes all of five minutes.

Bob walks back into the recording booth, and I, feeling like a fifth wheel, go back and start putting the guitar away. He gave me a look from the booth, and so

I walked around to the door and said, *'It looks like you're all set. Would it be OK if I stuck around and listened to you guys record?'* And he said, *'No, man, I want you to play guitar'.* I was stunned, totally stunned.

[After that first night] I thought that would be it. But then, the booking agency called me and asked if I could come down for another session and bring a 12-string guitar, as well as an A, D and a G harmonica and the old Martin, too. So, I showed up that Monday night, and that's when we did *'Tangled Up In Blue'"*.

Kevin Odegard: "[Before that first session started], Bob picked up his guitar and showed Chris Weber a very odd C-minor chord. From out in the studio, this song (*'Idiot Wind'*), was rather dissonant, but once you got the progression down you understood there was a pattern to the thing; it was verse, verse, chorus; verse, verse chorus; verse, verse, chorus; but it was an odd song. Chris changed one chord in there to I believe an A-Minor 7th, which allowed Bob to elongate *"slowly into autumn"*. It made it fit a little bit better to the vocal delivery in the lyric. It was just a little bit more graceful. If you hear the New York version, it starts with Bob strumming two chords and going into the song. With our Minneapolis version, we're there from the first note. *"Someone's got it in for me"*; it's like a shotgun. This was the one that took the longest. There were quite a few takes of *'Idiot Wind'*. Bob maybe wasn't warmed up and was having trouble punching in the lyrics.

After a number of takes, he came back and sat down at the organ and in a very retro manner (and it was very obvious to me what he was doing) Bob turned on the Lesley speaker on the B3 Hammond organ, and says, *"Roll it Paul"*, and that's the organ you hear on *'Idiot Wind'*. And it sounds very much like a throwback to *'Like A Rolling Stone'*. Gregg is on there as well, but Bob is the one you hear turned up and he sticks out the most and has the most retro sound.

We thought we were done for the night. Certainly, Billy Peterson was done, because he had his gig down at the Longhorn nightclub. His sax player, Bob Rockwell, wouldn't put up with anybody being late. Can you imagine saying goodbye to Bob Dylan when Bob wasn't quite ready to go yet? But he knew we'd got the take. It was the song he worked the hardest on and there were an awful lot of overdubs and there was also further mixing down the line. You can hear a lot of overdubbing on the Minneapolis sessions. Dylan overdubbed on every song. Paul played it back over the speakers and about 30 seconds into it, Bob put his finger across his throat and said *"Ok that's good"*. He knew we had it.

Bob wanted to do another song and went straight into *'You're A Big Girl Now'*. The band played it without the benefit of a bass player. I don't think Gregg Inhofer could get the Hammond sound that Bob wanted so Bob asked him to go play piano and Bob played the organ himself. We just did two takes and that was it for the night. Before we finished though, Bob played that flamenco flourish, which was dubbed on after. That was Bob Dylan himself playing that guitar flourish. We floated out of there and thought, well, that's it, we've all played with Bob Dylan. That's something to tell our grandchildren! But the next day we all got 'phone calls asking us to come back on Monday. Chris Weber, who still thought he was dreaming, was especially pleased to be coming back because at that time he still hadn't sold Bob the Martin guitar.

We arrive at the second session and Bob was much more relaxed, much more upbeat and talkative. He'd gotten over the cold that he had at the first session and he was very pleased with what he'd got at that session. As I recall, I was sitting on a ledge next to Bob and he was playing *'Tangled Up In Blue'* in G. He was teaching us the songs himself now. He was more comfortable with us at this second session and he didn't feel the need to teach us the songs through Chris. Also, he'd found that Bill Berg was such a fine musician, that all he had to do was open his mouth and Bill had got it. Bill Berg was, and still is, the most fantastic, on target, killer drummer, and a very creative individual, and Bob had figured that out very quickly.

Now, the song wasn't going anywhere and he turned to me and asked what did I think. I let my guard down. I forgot who I was with, and I told him it was *"passable"*. He stood up and he was indignant; he was righteously offended. He stood up and he said, *"passable!"*. Well, I felt like Donovan in *"Dont Look Back"*. He gave me the look and I sweated right through my clothing! Well, in a very short space of time I found myself back-pedalling with the suggestion that we move it up a key to give it more energy. At first, he looked disgusted, but he looked around the room and my fellow musicians supported me with little nods for whatever political or musical reasons I don't know, but everyone kinda shook their heads in agreement, and Bob turned to me and said *"OK"*.

He gave one of the finest live first take performances I've ever heard any artist give in my life. I can't think of an exception; possibly early Spirit in the late sixties. There was nothing I'd ever heard in my life that was as good as that first take of *'Tangled Up In Blue'*. When he went into the harmonica solo he was dipping and weaving and Paul was trying to follow the harmonica around with the mike. I came up with a lick that I had taken directly from a Joy of Cooking record. They were a group out of the Bay Area and it was from a song called *'Midnight Blues'*. It worked well as the opening to *'Tangled Up In Blue'* and as a repeating figure on the front of each verse. When we'd finished the song we all turned and looked at each other. We knew that we'd had a divine moment. We got it in that one take. Bob didn't even listen to it back. He knew it was that good.

Now, for the first time Dylan picked up the old Martin 0042G to start the next song. To begin with, it sounded like a hoedown and then he began telling the story of *'Lily, Rosemary And The Jack Of Hearts'*. He rehearsed this for about two or three minutes and then David came out and said to Billy and Bill, *"When you think this song is finished, it's not. Just keep playing, this is a long song"*. And again we got a first take!

Vanessa Weber, Chris's wife, had been dispatched to the *Podium* to bring back the correct key harmonica, because we didn't have a D harmonica there and *'Lily, Rosemary And The Jack Of Hearts'* was in D. So Bob picked up an A harmonica and started searching for notes at the beginning of the song. If you listen to the beginning of *'Lily, Rosemary And The Jack Of Hearts'* he's searching everywhere and not finding too many notes, but the odd thing about it was that it worked. It acts as a perfect counterpoint to the story. It gives the song a quizzical feeling.

Now, at that stage in the session Billy (bass) had to go to work again! Chris had been thinking ahead and had mentioned to Bob that there were a couple of players that he could have close at hand if they were needed. One was a mandolin player named Peter Ostroushko. So, as Billy was packing away his bass, Chris quickly got on the 'phone to Peter Ostroushko who was at his hang-out, the 400 Bar, playing pinball, and called him in. Unfortunately, Peter was unwell and he couldn't give Bob exactly what he wanted. Bob then asked Peter very politely if he could borrow the mandolin. So, the mandolin you hear on 'If You See Her Say Hello' is Bob. So that's it, another first take. All the songs were first takes apart from 'Idiot Wind' at the first session. I mean, Bob might have done a little rehearsal, like the couple of minutes of 'Lily, Rosemary And The Jack Of Hearts', but that wasn't an attempt at a take; the tape wasn't rolling. There was a rumour, in Clinton Heylin's "Recording Sessions", that we might have attempted 'Meet Me In The Morning' at the end of the sessions. The answer is no.

David Zimmerman, Bob Dylan and Paul Martinson returned to the studio on New Year's Day for what was scheduled to be an all day mixing session. After about ten minutes Bob stopped Paul and said, "I don't like what we're doing here. I don't want it to sound all polished and clean and steely". Bob held up one of the seven-inch reels, which Paul Martinson had given him to take home and listen to, and Bob said "I want it to sound like this. I want it to sound exactly like this". Paul said well, OK, but there are some highs and lows that need to be ironed out. Also, there are areas of 'Idiot Wind' that are out of control. So Bob said "OK, make 'Idiot Wind' sound like the rest of these". So with the exception of 'Idiot Wind', there was EQing or processing done to the live takes that were on the two-track safety tapes. The two-track "Revox" safety mix became those four songs that made it onto "Blood On The Tracks". 'Idiot Wind' was processed. It needed work and it got that work before it was mastered. The other four tracks, 'Tangled Up In Blue', 'If You See Her Say Hello', 'You're A Big Girl Now', and 'Lily, Rosemary And The Jack Of Hearts' were virgin one take performances. They were left untouched except for overdubs".

***

Kevin Odegard and the other musicians who played on the Minneapolis sessions have never been credited on any of the incarnations of "Blood On The Tracks", including the new SA-CD release. Nor have any of the musicians received RIAA awards for the album's multi platinum status. The only release to list the correct musicians came with the inclusion of 'Tangled Up In Blue' on "Bob Dylan's Greatest Hits Volume 3".

Kevin Odegard and Andy Gill are authors of the book "A Simple Twist of Fate: Bob Dylan and the Making of Blood On The Tracks". Da Capo Press, 2004. ISBN 0-306-81231-2

Derek Barker interviewed Kevin Odegard for *ISIS* Magazine on March 25, 2004.

Notes:

The information contained in this interview was gathered by Kevin Odegard and Andy Gill for their book *"A Simple Twist of Fate – Bob Dylan and the Making of Blood On The Tracks"*.

Information regarding the sessions that produced the masterwork that is *"Blood On The Tracks"* has always been a little vague. Thanks, however, to the research carried out by Odegard and Gill much more is now known about the sessions, especially those in Minneapolis.

The fact that Bob Dylan played the flamenco style guitar figures and mandolin on *'If You See Her, Say Hello'* and that he was responsible for the Hammond organ parts on both *'Idiot Wind'* and *'You're A Big Girl Now'*, or which instruments were overdubbed onto the live tracks, is all new and valuable information. Therefore, a more complete listing of who played on which tracks is attempted below.

The Songs:

Tangled Up In Blue
(Recorded December 30, 1974 - Minneapolis)

Bob Dylan: (vocal, guitar, harmonica)
Bill Preston: (electric bass)
Kevin Odegard: (guitar)
Chris Weber: (Guild 512 twelve-string guitar)
Greg Inhofer: (keyboards).
Bill Berg: (drums)

Simple Twist Of Fate
(Recorded September 19, 1974 New York City)

Bob Dylan: (vocal, guitar, harmonica)
Tony Brown: (bass)

You're A Big Girl Now
(Recorded December 27, 1974 - Minneapolis)

Bob Dylan: (vocal, guitar, harmonica, Hammond B-3 organ & flamenco [overdub])
Kevin Odegard: (guitar)
Chris Weber: (Martin 0042 guitar)
Greg Inhofer: (piano)
Bill Berg: (drums)

Idiot Wind
(Recorded December 27, 1974 - Minneapolis)

Bob Dylan: (vocal, guitar, harmonica & Hammond B-3 organ [overdub])
Bill Preston: (electric bass)
Kevin Odegard: (guitar)
Chris Weber: (Martin 0042 guitar)
Greg Inhofer: (keyboards)
Bill Berg: (drums)

You're Gonna Make Me Lonesome When You Go
(Recorded September 17, 1974 - New York City)

Bob Dylan: (vocal, guitar, harmonica)
Tony Brown: (bass)
Paul Griffin: (organ)

Meet Me In The Morning
(Recorded September 16, 1974 - New York City)

Bob Dylan: (vocal, six-string guitar, harmonica)
Charles Brown III: (guitar)
Eric Weissberg: (guitar)
Barry Kornfeld: (probably guitar)
Thomas McFaul: (Hammond B-3 organ)
Tony Brown: (bass)
Richard Crooks: (drums)
Buddy Cage: (pedal steel guitar [overdubs])

Lily, Rosemary And The Jack Of Hearts
(Recorded December 30, 1974 - Minneapolis)

Bob Dylan: (vocal, Martin 0042 guitar, harmonica)
Bill Preston: (upright bass)
Kevin Odegard: (guitar)
Chris Weber: (Guild 512 twelve-string guitar)
Greg Inhofer: (keyboards)
Bill Berg: (drums)

If You See Her, Say Hello
(Recorded December 30, 1974 - Minneapolis)

Bob Dylan: (vocal, Martin 0042 guitar, mandolin [overdub], flamenco style guitar
[overdub])
Kevin Odegard: (guitar)
Chris Weber: (guitar & Guild 512 twelve-string [overdub])
Greg Inhofer: (Hammond B-3 organ)
Bill Berg: (drums)
Peter Ostroushko: (second mandolin. Very low in mix)

Shelter From The Storm
(Recorded September 17, 1974 - New York City)

Bob Dylan: (vocal, guitar, harmonica)
Tony Brown: (bass)
Paul Griffin: (Hammond B-3 organ)

Buckets Of Rain
(Recorded September 19, 1974 - New York City)

Bob Dylan: (vocal, guitar)
Tony Brown: (bass)

***

In all, 21 tracks are available from the New York and Minneapolis *"Blood On The Tracks"* recording sessions. Sixteen of these tracks are to be found on officially released albums. Ten of the tracks comprise the standard *"Blood On The Tracks"* album, while the remaining six tracks can be located on either *"The Bootleg Series Volume 1-3"*, *"Biograph"*, or in the case of the alternate *'Shelter From The Storm'*, on either the *"Jerry Maguire"* soundtrack, or *"The Best of Bob Dylan"*, (SONYTV28CD).

None of the five New York tracks scrapped from the original test pressing and replaced on the final album has been released in its <u>original form</u>. The versions of *'Idiot Wind'*, *'If You See Her, Say Hello'* and *'Tangled Up In Blue'* released in 1991 on *"The Bootleg Series Vols. 1-3"* were previously unreleased <u>alternate takes</u>. Reportedly, this is because the original scrapped tracks had been widely bootlegged and complier/producer Jeff Rosen wanted to include versions that were new to fans. The version of *'Big Girl'* featured on *"Biograph"* and the *"Blood On The Tracks"* New York track are the same take from the recording session on September 17. This recording was, however, remixed (albeit only slightly) for inclusion on *"Biograph"*.

Therefore the five New York tracks that were replaced on the final album can only "officially" be found on the rare original New York A&R test pressing circulated in November 1974, which means that most collectors will need to resort to bootlegs to obtain these takes.

Amazingly, *TAKRL* released all five tracks on their vinyl bootleg album, *"Joaquin Antique"* within six weeks of the *Columbia Records* version. Subsequently, these tracks have appeared on other bootleg albums including several CD releases.

The original *"Blood On The Tracks"* album, as recorded at A&R Studio, New York was released in 1998 on a bootleg CD as *"Blood On The Tracks – New York Sessions"*, *Scorpio* S-19322. It was also released in 2001 as a CD-r on *OMR* (*Original Masters Revisited*).

***

The following is a complete listing of the available takes:

Tangled Up In Blue
(Recorded September 16, 1974 – New York City)
(*"The Bootleg Series Volume 1-3"* Columbia 468086 2)

Tangled Up In Blue
(Recorded September 19, 1974 – New York City)
Unreleased take with different lyrics.
(*"Blood On The Tracks"* test pressing PC-33235 / acetate)

Tangled Up In Blue
(Recorded December 30, 1974 – Minneapolis)
(*"Blood On The Tracks"* Columbia PC-33235)

Simple Twist Of Fate
(Recorded September 19, 1974 – New York City)
(*"Blood On The Tracks" Columbia* PC-33235)

You're A Big Girl Now
(Recorded September 17, 1974 – New York City)
Alternate take (a remixed version appears on *"Biograph"*)
(*"Blood On The Tracks"* test pressing PC-33235 / acetate)

You're A Big Girl Now
(Recorded December 27, 1974 – Minneapolis)
(*"Blood On The Tracks" Columbia* PC-33235)

Idiot Wind
(Recorded September 16, 1974 – New York City)
Unreleased take with different lyrics
(*"Blood On The Tracks"* test pressing PC-33235 / acetate)

Idiot Wind
(Recorded September 19, 1974 – New York City)
(*"The Bootleg Series Volume 1-3" Columbia* 468086 2)

Idiot Wind
(Recorded December 27, 1974 – Minneapolis)
(*"Blood On The Tracks" Columbia* PC-33235)

You're Gonna Make Me Lonesome When You Go
(Recorded September 17, 1974 – New York City)
(*"Blood On The Tracks" Columbia* PC-33235)

Meet Me In The Morning
(Recorded September 16, 1974 – New York City)
(*"Blood On The Tracks" Columbia* PC-33235)

Lily, Rosemary And The Jack Of Hearts
(Recorded September 16, 1974 – New York City)
Unreleased take with extra verse.
(*"Blood On The Tracks"* test pressing PC-33235 / acetate)

Lily, Rosemary And The Jack Of Hearts
(Recorded December 30, 1974 – Minneapolis)
(*"Blood On The Tracks" Columbia PC-33235*)

If You See Her, Say Hello
(Recorded September 16, 1974 – New York City)
(*"The Bootleg Series Volume 1-3" Columbia* 468086 2)

If You See Her, Say Hello
(Recorded September 19, 1974 – New York City)
Unreleased take with different lyrics.
(*"Blood On The Tracks"* test pressing PC-33235 / acetate)

If You See Her, Say Hello
(Recorded December 30, 1974 – Minneapolis)
("Blood On The Tracks" Columbia PC-33235)

Shelter From The Storm
(Recorded September 17, 1974 – New York City)
("Blood On The Tracks" Columbia PC-33235)

Shelter From The Storm (alternate take from Sept 17)
(Recorded September 17, 1974 – New York City)
(this version has an extra verse)
("Jerry Maguire", Film Soundtrack *Epic* EK 67910
"The Best of Bob Dylan" SONYTV28CD)

Buckets Of Rain
(Recorded September 19, 1974 – New York City)
("Blood On The Tracks" Columbia PC-33235)

Call Letter Blues
(Recorded September 16, 1974 – New York City)
("The Bootleg Series Volumes 1-3" Columbia 468086 2)

Up To Me
(Recorded September 19, 1974 – New York City)
("Biograph" Columbia C5X and C3K 38830)

Addendum Notes by Alan Fraser (edited by Derek Barker)

In his book, *"The Recording Sessions [1960-1994]"*, Clinton Heylin lists September 23-25, 1974 as the dates for the overdub sessions that included Paul Griffin adding organ to *'Idiot Wind'*. However, Michael Krogsgaard's 1996 article *'Bob Dylan: The Recording Sessions, Part 3'* doesn't list recording sessions for those dates, but instead, gives a date of October 8, 1974 for the Griffin overdub session. This is the date of the test pressing label shown in Heylin's book *"Day by Day"*). Krogsgaard's dating of the Griffin overdub session as October 8th has caused speculation that the first test pressing, from September 25, 1974, must contain a currently uncirculated version of *'Idiot Wind'*, without the Griffin overdub. However, Tony Brown, the bassist for the *"Blood On The Tracks"* sessions, says the organ is indeed present on *'Idiot Wind'* on the "9/25/74" acetate. Brown says that he and Paul Griffin played with Dylan on all takes of *'Idiot Wind'*, and that he does not remember Griffin recording overdubs. He does, however, remember steel guitarist Buddy Cage recording overdubs – these are noted in the Krogsgaard article.

The position is confusing, in that Krogsgaard lists the basic track for *'Idiot Wind'* as being take six from September 16, 1974, when Paul Griffin is not listed as being present (Tony Brown confirms Griffin wasn't there on the first day). The only other complete take of *'Idiot Wind'* listed by Krogsgaard is take four from

September 19, 1974, when again Paul Griffin is not listed. Krogsgaard's research gave him access to the session records and tape box labels, but he was not able to listen to the tapes themselves. Until the tapes are listened to and catalogued completely, no one can say if such a take exists.

However, while the issue of the October 8, 1974 overdub session remains unresolved, Clinton Heylin has told Derek Barker that although record exec. Ellen Bernstein was in possession of several different test pressings, containing different track sequences, they all contained the same musical material, and as far as he is aware, there was never a pre-overdub pressing and therefore none of the different test pressings contain a version of *'Idiot Wind'* minus organ.

Other songs rumoured to have been written for the album but which are not listed in the Krogsgaard sessions and have never come to light are:

'Don't Want No Married Woman'
'There Ain't Gonna Be Any Next Time'
'Bell Tower Blues/Climbed Up The Bell Tower'
'Where Do You Turn?/Turning Point'
'It's Breaking Me Up'
'Ain't It Funny?'
'Little Bit Of Rain'

* * *

Thanks to: Jonathan P. Foulkes for the information about the two different circulating versions of this test pressing. Also thanks to Derek Barker, Bob Stacey, Peter Stone Brown, Larry Weaver and Rod MacBeath for material included in this entry.

First published in *ISIS* #114 & 115, May & September 2004

Stories in the Press

"Apocryphal Now", which back in 1991 came free with *NME*, was a collection of *"fascinating facts and astonishing anecdotes"* that except for the bits of myth, were all true!

Bob Dylan and Van Morrison share, amongst other things, an accountant, and when the said gentleman discovered that Van The Man and Bob were both in town he invited them for a meal. The evening arrived, so did Bob and Van, but not a word was uttered by either. Throughout the meal's several courses they remained as impassive as the Easter Island statues. Not only did they not exchange conversation, neither of them said a word to their, understandably, ill-at-ease host. It got late and eventually Bob left. Upon which Van leant across the table with a twinkle in his eye and said to his host: *'I thought he was on pretty good form tonight, didn't you?'"*

In the same issue of *"Apocryphal Now"* was the tale about Dylan and Dave the plumber. For those lucky ones who don't have access to the British press, or were perhaps living on another planet in 1991, here it is again with a twist.

Finding himself in Crouch End [London] and looking for Dave Stewart's 'Church' recording studio, Dylan knocked on the door of a house that was next door to the first church he came across. *'Is Dave here?'*, Dylan asked when the lady of the house appeared. *'No'* said she, *'but you can come in and wait if you like, he won't be long'*. So, Dylan popped himself down at the kitchen table and waited. Dave's wife became increasingly agitated as to where she had seen this rather mournful looking face before. Eventually, she checked a few album sleeves in the next room and just as realisation was beginning to dawn (hubbie Dave came home). *'Don't panic'* [she said] *but I think Bob Dylan's in the kitchen'*. After what must have been several delicious minutes of confusion, all became clear, and Dave and his wife were able to direct Bob to Dave Stewart's studio down the road.

Taken from issue #39 of *ISIS* October 1991

Bob's Bid for Home of a Fan

Continuing on from the Dave Stewart tale; when Sandra Pavilou, 40, opened her front door to greet a prospective house buyer she couldn't believe her eyes. *"There was this big man, a woman and a little guy. When I saw the little one was Bob Dylan I was speechless"*.

It seems that Dylan was interested in buying the £300,000 house so he could have somewhere in London that was close to the Dave Stewart's studio.

Sandra, who is a fan and owns *"Lots of his albums"* said, *"It would be great if he moved here"*. *Sun* journalist, John Kay, also informs readers that Dylan is a fan of the local Indian restaurant.

The Wicked Messenger #2631 printed in issue #50 of *ISIS* September 1993

The *Daily Express* expanded this piece informing that the Indian restaurant in question was the Shamrat of India. The owner, who said Dylan, who he recognised from the film *Pat Garrett and Billy the Kid* (he must have been carrying a knife and wearing a cowboy hat; or perhaps he arrive by horse), had visited the restaurant several times with Dave Stewart and amazingly he remembered what they ordered! Here goes then:

Samosas to start, followed by chicken Madras, *"Medium hot"*, he recalls, pilau rice and nan bread. The meal was washed down with (and this is where the owner, Mr Ali struggles with total recall) either *Kingfisher* or *Carlsberg* lager; probably the latter.

Printed in issue #50 of *ISIS* September 1993

Andy Kershaw and his gift of Hedgerow Jam

Even more on Dylan in Crouch End, this time concerning a BBC radio DJ and a jar of jam! Andy Kershaw: *"Dylan was sitting on the edge of a drum riser in Dave Stewart's recording studio in Crouch End . . . It's hedgerow jam, Bob, I explained . . . hedgerow jam, I persisted. Bob turned the jar in his hand and squinted at the label. I might as well have handed a mobile phone to a chimpanzee. I coughed, made with, er, real hedgerows, Bob . . . Without a word, Dylan set it down on the drum riser. I dare say it's there to this day"*.

Kershaw goes on to describe the ensuing TV interview as an event so humiliating that, *"I tried my hardest to get the BBC to have the video sealed in concrete and dropped in the nearest Pacific Trench"*. Kershaw then fast-forwards to the summer of 1993 when Dylan is house-hunting in Crouch End.

"Bob went to view the house of a friend of mine and murmured approval only of the ghastly bathroom – equipped with burgundy suite and gold taps – that was, in part, forcing my chum to sell up. The Bob . . . went and settled on a place in Hampstead".

Finally, Kershaw tells of a visit that Dylan and Victor Maimudes (described as, his, er, *"chess roadie"*) made that summer to Banners, a Crouch End restaurant. They wanted a drink but the place only had a restaurant licence and they didn't want anything to eat. Donna, the waitress, tried to explain but to no avail. Eventually . . . Bob's chess partner blew it with the most uncool remark he could have uttered. *"Don't you know how this is?"* he demanded of Donna. *"I'm afraid not, she said"*.

The Wicked Messenger #3477 printed in issue #69 of *ISIS* November 1996

Addendum

I'm told that Banners, at 21, Park Road, Crouch End, now displays a plaque informing, I guess, *"Bob Dylan Woz Here"*. I wonder if it also informs customers that he didn't actually get served?

"Blood On The Tracks": A Review

Derek Barker

"Blood On The Tracks" is arguably the finest album that Bob Dylan has ever made. Furthermore, the opening track, *'Tangled Up In Blue'*, which deals with the complexities of relationships, is considered by many as Dylan's best ever song. Dylan once said of *'Tangled Up In Blue'*, *"It took* [him] *ten years to live and two years to write"*.

With *'Tangled Up In Blue'*, Dylan says that he was trying to defy time:

"So that the story took place in the present and the past at the same time. When you look at a painting, you can see any part of it, or you see it altogether. I wanted that song to be like a painting".

With this statement Dylan makes it clear just what a profound effect art teacher Norman Raeben had on his writing at this time. According to Dylan, he was again *"doing consciously what* [he] *used to do unconsciously"*. He doesn't say in what respect, but he might be referring to his shifting use of pronouns. Aidan Day argues that the way in which the song divides its *"I"* into *"I"* and *"he"*, and its *"she"* into a succession of *"shes"*, can leave the reader wondering whether we are in the presence of one or more stories.

As Paul Williams points out this "conscious" use of movable pronouns was not new to Dylan. And although the original version is sung mainly in the first person, *"the potential for identity switching is constantly present right under the surface of the song's structure"*. Williams goes on to say:

". . . The breakthrough is not Dylan being aware of his use of such techniques (he was talking about this sort of thing at least as far back as 1968) but rather his ability to be conscious of what he's doing and still have it come out as magical and mysterious and pregnant as it did when he was an unconscious arrogant whiz kid who never even thought about looking back".

This newly regained spontaneity is immediately evident from the opening song and regardless of how many different stories are to be found within this song there is no doubting that the main protagonist is Dylan's then wife Sara.

Dylan told Interviewer Craig McGregor:

"Joni Mitchell had an album out called "Blue" and it affected me, I couldn't get it out of my head. And it just stayed in my head and when I wrote that song I

wondered, what's that mean? And then I figured that it was just there, and I guess that's what happened, y'know".

When asked if the *"Blue"* in *'Tangled Up In Blue'* was the same *"Blue"* as in *'It's All Over Now, Baby Blue'* Dylan replied:

"No, no. That's a different blue. That's a character right off the hay-wagon. That Baby Blue is from right upstairs at the barber shop, y'know off the street . . . a different baby blue, I haven't run into her in a long time . . ."

Dylan also told McGregor, *"That's the first* [song] *I ever wrote that I felt free enough to change all the . . . what is it, the tenses around. . .*
    The he and the she and the I and the you, and the we and the us – I figured it was all the same anyway – I could throw them all in where they floated right – and it works on that level.

Much has been written about the identity of Dylan's poet from the 13th century and while Dante immediately springs to mind (Dylan would later sing about the theatre of Divine Comedy in the song *'Caribbean Wind'*.) another more plausible candidate would seem to me to be Francesco Petrarch.

In his March 12, 1978 interview with Craig McGregor Dylan said *". . . Yeah that poet from the 13th century . . . Plutarch. Is that his name?"*

Well, no, Plutarch, real name Mestrius Plutarchus, was not an Italian poet, but a Greek historian, essayist and biographer. Also, he lived (circa 45 – 125 A.D.), which is a mere twelve centuries before the Dylan character. Dylan was clearly confusing two people's names here, but would he really confuse the names Plutarch and Dante! They don't sound too similar do they? More likely the name Dylan was searching for was that of the Italian poet Petrarch.
    Petrarch lived from 1304 to 1374, which puts him right in the frame (well, almost). More importantly though, his primary poetic theme was his passion for unattainable love. His work *"Trionfi"* contains six allegorical figures: Love, Chastity, Death, Fame, Time, and Divinity. Chastity triumphs over its predecessor, and finally Divinity triumphs over them all and remains supreme, as the symbol of peace, eternal life, and the everlasting union of the poet with his beloved Laura.
    Although *'Simple Twist of Fate'* is a much less complex song, it still manages to maintain the standard of writing set by the opening track, and while there is no doubt that at least part of *'Tangled Up In Blue'* is the story of Bob and Sara (*"She was married when they first met/Soon to be divorced"*, which certainly seems to refer to Sara), those who think that the entire album is about Dylan's failing relationship with his wife could not be further from the mark.
    According to Heylin, who has seen the little red notebook in which Dylan wrote his close to final drafts of the songs that were destined to become *"Blood*

On The Tracks", *'Simple Twist of Fate'* was originally subtitled *'Fourth Street Affair'* and is almost certainly about Suze Rotolo.

Certainly, if we are to take the song's closing lines as a literal statement, *"She was born in spring, but I was born too late"*, the main character can not be Sara who was born on October 28, 1939, but then again, Suze was born in November (1943), so that doesn't fit either! Bob's second significant love, Bonnie Jane Beecher, was born a month before Dylan, in April 1941, but *'Fourth Street Affair'* wouldn't work for this North Country girl.

Also, the word "affair" doesn't seem quite right for Bob's relationship with Suze Rotolo. Though waiting for her by the *"waterfront docks"* certainly does fit. This notion is very much reinforced by the final verse of the Rolling Thunder Revue and 1978 tour renditions of the song:

"She would have stayed with me, 'Stead of goin' back off to sea/And leavin' me to meditate, Upon a simple twist of fate".

'You're A Big Girl Now', on the other hand, would seem to fit Sara perfectly. The line, *"Oh, but what a shame if all we've shared can't last"* would seem to indicate the possible break up of a long-standing relationship. Dylan, however, begs to differ, and in the notes to *"Biograph"* he complains about the *"stupid and misleading jerks"* who have written suggesting the song is about his wife.

Bob's son, Wallflower, Jakob Dylan, once told his manager, Andrew Slater: *"When I'm listening to 'Subterranean Homesick Blues', I'm grooving along just like you, but when I'm listening to "Blood On The Tracks", that's about my parents"*. Regardless of the subject matter, the song is extraordinary and the closing, oh so short harmonica phrases are to die for.

The *"idiot"* of *'Idiot Wind'* was borrowed from art teacher Norman Raeben. It seems that *"Idiot"* was one of Raeben's most used words. Raeben's widow apparently informed the late Bert Cartwright: *"According to Raeben's observation of life, there was an idiot wind blowing and blinding all human existence"*. According to one of Raeben's ex-students (on a *WBAI* special radio 'phone-in, 1986) the painter *"used to call everybody an idiot because they couldn't see the nose on their face . . . He called Dylan an idiot all the time"*.

Pete Hamill's at times rather overblown but more often beautiful liner notes, describe the song thus:

"The idiot wind trivializes lives into gossip, celebrates fad and fashion, glorifies the dismal glitter of celebrity. Its products live on the covers of magazines, in all of television, in the poisoned air and dead grey lakes. But most of all, it blows through the human heart".

The song's eight verses, reinforced by four differing "choruses", (this album doesn't contain any true choruses) outline the various "idiot winds" that have touched Dylan's life. Robert Shelton said the song, *"Has some of the sting of 'Rolling Stone'* [and] *much of the anguish of Ginsberg's 'Howl'"*. He went on to say:

"It could be a ranting truth attack, an expression of the narrator's personal disorder, ruefulness, and suspicion in an equally disturbed society in which people's spoken words are in apposition to their real emotions . . . a portrayal of a milieu where gossiping and backstabbing have replaced caring and believing".

While all of this is probably true, as early as the second verse, the song's focus fall's on Sara:

"Even you, yesterday/You had to ask me where it was at/I couldn't believe after all these years/You didn't know me any better than that/Sweet lady".

As is the case with most of the rejected New York songs, *'Idiot Wind'* is more direct and confessional than its Minneapolis replacement.

Also, by the time the song has been rewritten Dylan's focus seems to have changed slightly. On the New York version, recorded three months earlier, the singer is willing to shoulder much of the blame for the failing relationship.

"We pushed each other a little too far/And one day it just jumped into a raging storm".

By Minneapolis, however, the blame has shifted away from the singer and squarely onto the other party. Only in the last chorus of this version does the *"you"* become *"we"* as Dylan relents and re-shoulders some of the responsibility for the breakdown:

"We're idiots, babe/It's a wonder we can even feed ourselves".

Not only does the final version direct the blame away from the singer, it also tends to concentrate the singer's rage toward the women and away from other sundry targets, such as the host of Dylan copycat artists. Therefore, the line *"Lady killers load dice on me/Behind my back, while imitators steal me blind"*, gives way to the, *"I kissed goodbye the howling beast. . ."*

The opening verse, which fires a salvo at the press, however, remains steadfastly unchanged. Dylan had never been in love with the press and the recent (July 1974) syndicated reports that Dylan was breaking up with his wife and might also be conducting an affair with Lorey Sebastian, the ex wife of singer John Sebastian, certainly did not help to enamour them to him .

Dylan: *"With that particular set-up in the front* [of the song] *I thought I could say anything after that. If it did seem personal, I probably made it overly so – because I said too much in the front and still made it come out like, 'Well, so what?' I didn't really think it was too personal. I've never really said anything where I thought I was giving away too much. I mean, I give it all away, but I'm not really giving away any secrets. I don't have that many secrets. I don't find myself in that position".*

183

In other sections of the song, lines and verses seem to have been changed for no other reason than they maybe work slightly better. One example would be the change from:

"I threw the I Ching yesterday, it said there might be some thunder at the well/Peace and quiet's been avoiding me for so long, it seems like livin' hell".

To:

"I ran into the fortune-teller, who said beware of lightning that might strike/I haven't known peace and quite for so long I can't remember what it's like".

There is no doubting that the lyrics to the later released version of *'Idiot Wind'* are more spiteful and pointed (if that is possible!), but as noted by Paul Williams, the later released version also has *"[a] really striking change . . . in the tone of the performance. The earlier 'Idiot Wind' is folk rather than rock in its overall sound".*

Despite previous comments, in a 1985 interview with Bill Flanagan, Dylan admitted that he came very close to giving too much information away about his personal life with *'Idiot Wind'*.

"I came pretty close with that song 'Idiot Wind', a lot of people thought that song, that album "Blood On The Tracks", pertained to me. Because it seemed to at the time. It didn't pertain to me . . . I've read that that album had to do with my divorce. Well, I didn't get divorced till four years after that. I thought I might have gone a little bit too far with 'Idiot Wind'. I might have changed some of it. I didn't really think I was giving away too much; I thought that it seemed so personal that people would think it was about so-and-so who was close to me. It wasn't".

In truth, *'Idiot Wind'* is only one of many songs on *"Blood On The Tracks"* that delves deeply into Dylan's personal life. Paul Williams concurs with me that the *"dealing with slaves"* line in *'Tangled Up In Blue'* might well be the closest the singer has ever come to *"acknowledging that he had some substance abuse problems"*.

In a deeper, and slightly more subjective analyse of *'Idiot Wind'*, Paul Williams offers up Dylan's former manager, Albert Grossman, as being a good candidate for the *"your corrupt ways have finally made you blind"* line. Williams goes on to say that, *"at times the 'you' is, as much as anyone else, himself"*, and suggests that it is perhaps some *"destructive alter-ego that wishes he was dead ('flies buzzing around your eyes'). That verse, surely, couldn't be addressed to the woman he loves. Or could it? The gloves are off in this song."*

Whatever the interpretation, this monumental song with its rolling Hammond organ is yet another classic song from a truly classic album.

In total contrast, the next song, which closes side one of the vinyl record, and begins with a jaunty little harp solo, is a gentle love song.

'You're Gonna Make Me Lonesome When You Go' completely changes the tempo of the album, and whilst on first hearing you might be excused for thinking that this is a throwaway or filler song, a closer examination will reveal that this is in fact a quite wonderful ditty with some very clever lyrics. The way in which Dylan changes the pronunciation of Honolulu to Honolula to make the word rhyme flawlessly with Ashtabula is just one example.

Thanks to Clinton Heylin, we know that at least one of the songs on *"Blood On The Tracks"* is addressed to Ellen Bernstein. Bernstein informed Heylin:

". . .We were out walking out in the fields somewhere and I found a Queen Anne's lace (a wild carrot with lace like white flowers)*, and he didn't know that that's what it was called . . . this was in Minnesota . . . I did say I was planning a trip to Hawaii, and I lived in San Francisco. Honololu, San Francisco, Ashtabula".*

So, this time the crimson hair (across your face) belongs to Ellen Bernstein, but is this the same crimson hair as in *"wond'rin' if she'd changed at all if her hair was still red"*. Assumedly not.

The second side of the vinyl album opens with another change of pace in the shape of a straightforward blues number. Heylin informs us in *"The Recording Sessions [1960 – 1994]"* that *'Meet Me In The Morning'* is one of only two songs absent from the red Minnesota notebook (the other being *'Buckets Of Rain'*). He also reveals that there is no information that Eric Weissberg and the band Deliverance was in attendance at any recording session other than the first session, which took place on September 16, 1974 and that *'Meet Me In The Morning'* was not recorded at that session. Heylin's conclusion, therefore, is that Dylan must have dubbed his newly scribed *'Meet Me In The Morning'* lyrics onto a basic take of *'Call Letter Blues'*, which was recorded with Deliverance at the September 16th session. If indeed this is the case, it was a rather impressive and wholly uncharacteristic piece of studio trickery on Dylan's part. It's clear to me that the take of *'Call Letter Blues'*, recorded on the 16th and released on the *"Bootlegs Vol 1-3"*, could not be the track in question, and Heylin himself suggests that Dylan must have found another basic track on which to dub his new lyrics.

Guitarist Buddy Cage says that he added pedal steel embellishment to both *'Meet Me In The Morning'* and *'Call Letter Blues'* (probably on September 23). And although the audio evidence confirms this, it seems a little strange to me that at this late stage Dylan still hasn't made a decision as to which of the two songs would make the album. Presumably, Dylan chose *'Meet Me In The Morning'* over *'Call Letter'* because the lyrics to the latter were too personal.

Paul Williams describes the wonderfully cinematic *'Lily, Rosemary And The Jack Of Hearts'* as the *"Minnesota miracle"* and the difference in performance between the only New York take of the song and the released Minnesota version is indeed staggering.

At close to nine minutes, this three chord fifteen-verse (sixteen in New York) song could so easily become tiresome, and despite comments by Andy Gill in the book *"A Simple Twist Of Fate"*, it doesn't. Gill opines that *'Lily, Rosemary'* is the weakest song on the album. I've never analysed the album that way and in my opinion *"Blood On The Tracks"* is a complete masterwork that doesn't require breaking down in to its component parts. Admittedly, this song lives or dies on the performance, but as Williams says the performance is a miracle. All the musicians are to be congratulated, but the two Bill's, Berg and Peterson, drums and upright bass, lay down a groove that carries along a saga that contains some of Dylan's best narrative work. Dylan's panache for cinematic songs would continue on his next album, *"Desire"*, when his collaboration with theatre director and writer Jacques Levy created the island drama *'Black Diamond Bay'*. Later still, *'Brownsville Girl'* and the rather less successful *'Highlands'*, would periodically rekindle the latent playwright in Dylan.

Taken at face value, *'Lily, Rosemary And The Jack Of Hearts'* is a tangled tale of love set in the Wild West, in which Rosemary eventually finds the courage to break away from Big Jim and in doing so kills him with a penknife.

Are the characters purely fictional or do they have any basis in fact? Is the Jack of Hearts just another romantic Dylan outlaw, or is Jack perhaps a Dylan persona? According to Clinton Heylin, Dylan told *CBS* A&R executive Ellen Bernstein; *"Everyone's gonna wonder who the Jack of Hearts is. I have no idea who it is"*.

However, as Heylin goes on to point out; *"Presumably, Dylan would insist it was a mere coincidence that the Jack of Hearts tallies so well with the attributes attached to the magician, the Magus, in A. E. Waite's tarot pack, and that this particular tarot pack – featured on the inner sleeve of Dylan's next album – paints the Magus surrounded by two flowers, the lily and the rose"*.

The real beauty of this song is that it is Dylan's gift to us and each listener can make of it what they will. Peter Hamill says, *"It should not be reduced to notes, or taken out of context; it should be experienced in full"*.

By this stage the reviewer begins to run short of superlatives, but the songs just keep a-coming! *'If You See Her, Say Hello'* is one of the best vocal tracks on the album. Incidentally, the best vocal not on the album belongs to the wonderful outtake *'Up To Me'*.

Peter Hamill describes the opening lines to *'If You See Her'* as being, *"As light as a slide on ice, and as dangerous"*.

As with *'You're A Big Girl Now'*, the song has five verses and no choruses, and regardless of the different players (mostly lovers) in this "Passion Play" of an album, clearly Sara Dylan is the focus of this particular song. Bob informs the listener that the woman in question is no longer around. In reality, however, it is he who has left the marital home and he confirms this in the penultimate verse:

"I see a lot of people as I make the rounds/And I hear her name here and there as I go from town to town".

During the next four years both the lyrics and their sentiment would change drastically.

In the spring of 1976 in Tallahassee and Lakeland, Florida, Bob began the song with the verse:

"If you see her say hello, she might be in North Saigon/She left here in a hurry; I don't know what she was on/You might say that I'm in disarray and for me time's standing still,/Oh I've never gotten over her, I don't think I ever will".

In this version Bob has gone from being all right (*"Say for me that I'm all right".*) in the released version, to being in disarray. Disarray, however, turns to anger and possible jealousy, as the singer informs anyone that might be making love to her to watch their backs.

"If you're making love to her, watch it from the rear/You'll never know when I'll be back, or liable to appear/For it's natural to dream of peace as it is for rules to break/And right now I've not got much to lose, so you'd better stay awake".

In the closing lines to the released version Dylan sang:

"If she's passin' back this way, I'm not that hard to find/Tell her she can look me up if she's got the time".

It's clear from this that the singer would like to see her again and we know that there was, for a time, a strong possibility of reconciliation. Sara accompanied Bob to the SNACK benefit, in San Francisco and was to have gone with him to visit David Oppenheim who had just had a house built in the Savoie region of France. Oppenheim says that Dylan called Sara every day of his six weeks stay. However, by the spring of 1976 Dylan is asking the Lord for the strength to say no.

"Well I know she'll be back someday, of that there is no doubt/And when that moment comes, Lord, give me the strength to keep her out".

By the time of the rehearsals for the 1978 tour there's even a slightly quirky organ driven version (that actually works quite well), in which Dylan draws back from the warning that he had issued to would-be suitors and relents that, *"She's better off with someone else and I'm better off alone".*

However, he still sticks to the notion that seeing her again would be a mistake. The problem seems not to be that he doesn't want to see her again, but he has worries that maybe if he did meet with her he might weaken and allow what now seems to be a doomed relationship to resume.

"If she's passin' back this way, most likely I will be gone/But if I'm not just let her go, it's best that she stays gone".

And so to *'Shelter From The Strom'.* Rich in imagery, in this the penultimate song from *"Blood On The Tracks"*, Ellen Bernstein appears to provide the singer with the shelter he needs from the emotional storm that is troubling him greatly at this time.

The theme of empathy with Christ's suffering, which Dylan adopted in *'Shelter From The Storm'*, would become a familiar trait in his writing, but it would never be as direct as in this song:

"Suddenly I turned around and she was standing there/With silver bracelets on her wrists and flowers in her hair/She walked up to me so gracefully and took my crown of thorns/'Come in', she said, I'll give you shelter from the storm".

And

"In a little hilltop village, they gambled for my clothes/I bargained for salvation an' they gave me a lethal dose/I offered up my innocence and got repaid with scorn/Come in', she said, I'll give you shelter from the storm".

Musically, *"Blood On The Tracks"* is a very simple album, yet the lyrics are both mysterious and awe inspiring. It is also one of those very rare albums that is instantly pleasing, but which continues to grow with repeated listening.

The album's closer, *'Buckets Of Rain'*, is a wonderfully understated song and the line, *"Life is sad/Life is a bust/All you can do is do what you must"*, not only sums up Dylan's feelings at this juncture, but it also echoes the sentiments of the album's opening song, *"The only thing I knew how to do was to keep on keepin' on"*.

I'll leave you with the words of Peter Hamill:

"[The real] wonder is in the spaces, in what the artist's left out of his painting. To me, that has always been the key to Dylan's art. To state things plainly is the function of journalism; but Dylan sings a more fugitive song: allusive, symbolic, full of imagery and ellipses, and by leaving things out, he allows us the grand privilege of creating along with him. His song becomes our song because we live in those spaces".

Notes:

Major sources used in the preparation of this text:

Heylin, Clinton. *"Bob Dylan – Behind The Shades: Take Two"*. *Viking*, 2000.

Heylin, Clinton. *"Bob Dylan Behind Closed Doors: The Recording Sessions [1960 – 1994]"*. *Penguin Books*, 1995.

Williams, Paul. *"Bob Dylan Performing Artist The Middle Years: 1974 – 1986"*. *Underwood-Miller*, 1992.

Various Interviews with Bob Dylan.

Lyrics quoted in this text: *"Bob Dylan Lyrics 1962 – 1985"*. *Jonathan Cape*, 1987.

Live performance lyrics are taken from circulating audience tapes.

A previously unpublished article from the *ISIS* Archive.

Tangled Up to Me:
Reflections on Two Mid-career Muse Songs

James Dunlap

'Tangled Up In Blue' surely belongs at or very near the pinnacle of Bob Dylan's greatest songwriting achievements. It's the lead song on 1974's "Blood On The Tracks", announcing his return to greatness after a considerable decline. Dylan has enhanced the song's reputation by drawing attention to the album's importance: the song's strength, like the album's, consists in achieving what Dylan called a "triumph over time", a kind of visionary achievement attained after months of therapy with the artist Norman Raeben. Through mental exercises, including painting, Dylan was trying to learn to write songs again and "to do consciously what [he] used to do unconsciously".[1]

Critics love 'Tangled Up In Blue' because it exemplifies some of Dylan's best qualities: subtlety and nuance, emotional complexity, and an openness to varied interpretations primarily due to its ambiguous use of pronouns.[2] In addition, the fact that the events it describes seem to be chosen almost at random. Both tenses and pronouns are horribly mixed, suggesting a narrator with a memory that consists only of tragic fragments and loss, allowing free speculation about the songwriter's psyche. In all of these respects, 'Tangled Up In Blue' is similar to a second song, 'Up To Me', recorded at the same time but not released until 1984 as part of the "Biograph" retrospective. Besides their contemporaneity and similar narrative techniques, the two songs should be considered together for one other reason: plausible insights into the subject matter and meaning of one song can, perhaps, be validated if the same approach can be shown to help in understanding the other.

* * *

The seven verses of 'Tangled Up In Blue' describe a series of memories (not from Dylan's life exactly, but from a fiction that might have felt to have been like his life). The events, like a sequence of snapshots, all involve women, or maybe one particular woman. In fact, a superficial example of the critical debate about the song's meaning involves whether Dylan's memories are focused on only one woman or whether there is more than one.[3] The repeated use of the single pronoun "she" in each episode may lull the listener into assuming there's only one; however, the internal evidence may suggest otherwise. For instance, the parents of the first girl in the song are described as not approving of Bob or his family because of their lack of material things (suggesting that Dylan is a potential suitor and the girl's not yet independent or married). The second image is of a woman who clearly <u>was</u> married when she first met Bob. The images seem inconsistent if they're both meant to be the same person; the issues of parental disapproval in connection with the first girl presumably would not have arisen if he'd first met her when she was married.

Even without resolving such issues, the listener can get a good sense of the meaning of *'Tangled Up In Blue'* simply by its structure and sound. In the first eleven out of the thirteen lines of each of seven verses, Dylan sings jauntily in a deliberate cadence as though reciting from rote memory. He develops an image with a tension that builds until it finally breaks in the next-to-last line. Following the last regular rhyme, Dylan appends an added phrase, in each case ending with a rhyme for "blue". For example, the somewhat hurried but emphatic last regular rhyme of the promise, *"We'll-meet-again-<u>some</u>-<u>day</u>"* is followed by the enigmatic drawn-out image, *"on the av-ve-nuuuue . . ."* Dylan stretches each syllable of this added phrase slowly, as if contemplating it with extra care or deliberately creating suspense. Each verse then snaps back, like waking suddenly from a dream, forcefully stating the songwriter's condition: *"<u>Tan</u>-gled <u>up</u> in <u>blue</u>"*. A short instrumental break follows so the listener can reflect on the singer's condition. Like some kind of personal mantra, the song's title refrain is then repeated at key points in the narrative until we suspect it to be somehow linked with the songwriter's ultimate destiny.

And what is it to be *"tangled up in blue"*? It's not the plural "blues", identifying a musical idiom; rather, it's the singular "blue", perhaps the state of mind that gave the musical genre its name, as in "Bob's feeling blue". But "blue" is also a colour that runs throughout Dylan's songwriting career: the *"blue-eyed son"* of *'A Hard Rain's A-Gonna Fall'*, *"Baby Blue"*, and *"Little Boy Blue"* are all probably aspects of Dylan himself–with eyes strikingly coloured light blue, as Joan Baez once noted, like robins' eggs.[4] *"It's all over now"*, for instance, was the message sung to *"Baby Blue"* in the song that marked one of Dylan's major transitions, as he struggled to escape protest songwriting. In *'Visions Of Johanna'*, Dylan delivered some healthy self-criticism to the *"Little Boy Blue"* (who, for instance, took himself too seriously). Still later, in *'Never Gonna Say Goodbye'*, the songwriter exchanged words with a *"Baby, Baby Blue"* (who, like Dylan, underwent a name change). So perhaps Dylan is tangled up with aspects of himself; significantly, the aspects of himself all involve relations with women.

Dylan has on occasion immersed himself in a world of mystical correspondences and symbolism (he's also disclaimed doing any such thing). His enthusiasm has apparently included astrology and tarot, whose images would appear in the artwork or lyrics for his next two albums. It's a fair guess that he may have considered the symbolism of colours as well, in which case he would have discovered that, in the Western occult tradition, blue is identified with spiritual qualities, the unconscious mind and inspiration.[5] Somewhat similarly, one of Rimbaud's better known shorter poems, *'Vowels'*, postulated correspondences between colours, letters of the alphabet, and abstract ideas. In that poem, "blue" was the letter "O", which was then linked to images of infinity and god-like pronouncements of ultimate things (associated, as well, with the sustained calling sound of a medieval trumpet–a "clarion"–which could almost be the *"futile horn"* remembered from an earlier lifetime in *'Shelter From The Storm'*). Rimbaud wrote: *"O, supreme Clarion full of strange stridor,/Silences crossed by worlds and angels:/–O, the Omega, violet beam from His Eyes!"*

"Blue" is also a phase in Picasso's career, the Blue Period, with which Dylan was clearly familiar. In a recently recovered recording from April 1966, during a concert in Sydney, Australia (a few weeks before the so-called "Royal Albert Hall Concert" that is now *"Live 1966"*), Bob can be heard introducing *'Just Like Tom Thumb's Blues'* with the story of a famous older painter (whom, he said, we call "Tom Thumb"). The painter now sells *"many, many paintings"*. Ostensibly alluding to Picasso (but probably referring to himself, as well), Dylan explained that the song was about the painter's *"Blue Period"* (a *"very important period"*, Bob added knowingly). The story was told in a highly suggestive and dreamy manner, seemingly linking Dylan's use of the word in his song's title with his "blue" mood on the stage. Picasso's use of blue gave his paintings a kind of melancholy and somewhat surreal atmosphere that could also be likened to Dylan's attitude during his 1966 tour. In 1974's *'Tangled Up In Blue'*, the singer may find himself trapped by some or all of these qualities.

***

Initially, *'Tangled Up In Blue'* can be approached as a straight narrative. It begins with a recollection of waking up on a sunny morning ("sunlight" seems to mean inspiration, in the sense that it allows one to see clearly), thinking about an unnamed woman, *"wondr'in' if she'd changed at all"* and *"if her hair was still red"*. The relationship was a long time ago; it might have become serious, but her parents didn't approve. Having said that, the image shifts, like a jump-cut in the movies, to Dylan hitchhiking out to the East Coast (without his inspiration, and thus in the rain), leaving the redheaded woman and especially her parent's values behind. The girl and her parents could almost allude to Judy Rubin, an early summer camp friend from a well-respected Jewish household. By the time Bob reached college, her parents had dismissed him as unworthy.

The first verse is reminiscent of Dylan's mythologized runaway image, his early romanticized (and sometimes imaginary) loves and his departure from Hibbing and then from the University of Minnesota. As Dylan looks back on his past, he starts to lament: *"Lord knows I've paid some dues"*, but the listener senses that Dylan would have had it no other way. Although freedom comes at a cost, it's a value to be treasured and won.

The next image is of a brief affair with an unhappily married woman. The tale is told with obvious irony (*"She was married when we first met/Soon to be divorced"*); the singer's wordplay combined with his omissions of detail invite the listener to fill in the gaps. Some gaps, of course, could be filled from Dylan's biography: Sara was married to the fashion-photographer Hans Lownds when

Dylan first met her. Their relationship started before her divorce. In his song (as in life), the songwriter implies that he helped cause the change in her marital status; looking back, the freedom gained was perhaps a mixed blessing: *"I helped her out of a jam, I guess"*. By not explaining further, Dylan teases his listeners, drawing them in as they wait for more clues.

As a result of some unspecified confrontation, the couple then heads West as if in flight, taking *"that car"*. A specific vehicle is thus identified as a significant character in the story. However, as in Dylan's use of the phrase *"I guess"* and his vagueness generally, part of the story is left untold. We don't know the car's significance, and we're left in suspense. With this storytelling technique–like Alfred Hitchcock's holding a camera shot an instant too long on, say, a doorknob or a sharp kitchen utensil–Dylan suggests that some ultimate "significance" looms just beneath the surface, waiting to be revealed. In the song, the couple then take *"that car"* as far as it could go (and not, as the cliché would have it, "as fast"), soon abandoning it as though it were a symbol of their short-lived and broken affair. As the two head off in separate directions, however, Dylan and his accomplice know they're linked in some important way, perhaps through the special freedoms they've shared. He was on the road when he met her; she has since left her husband behind, abandoning security (one can imagine) to live more like the singer. As newly forged kindred spirits, the two are likely to have further encounters: *"We'll meet again someday . . . on the av-e-nue . . ."* because both of them, it seems, are now *"tangled up in blue"*.

In the third verse, the songwriter finds himself working as a cook in the great north woods until he loses his job (*"the ax just fell"*), then he drifts to New Orleans where he's passively employed again. Things just happen to him. Although it seems as though nothing is planned, destiny is quietly at work. All the while, for instance, one special woman never *"escapes"* (i.e., can't "get her out of") his mind: he can't forget her. A likely candidate, *"she"* could be the once-married accomplice from the car flight West. But she could be anyone, even someone completely new, not previously introduced.

In the fourth verse, Dylan finds himself in a topless bar, looking hard at the side of his waitress's face (in a clear spotlight, hardly a subtle clue that she will prove "significant"). She, in turn, studies the lines on his face like words that have a tale to tell, as if they were the keys to understanding his past and what makes him unique. Bob and the waitress both sense that the other holds an important secret (but we as listeners don't know what yet, and the singer doesn't know either). Eventually, the waitress comes right out and asks if she knows him. At one level, the lyric works like a pick-up line (*"Don't I know your name?"*), but in the context of the song, the question suggests that there is something much more important at stake: issues of identity. The question posed by the waitress points to a moment of recognition. Someone "knows" Dylan, not superficially but in a more profound sense. He has lost his anonymity. His secret is out, and, embarrassed, he can only answer by muttering.

The next verse is a continuation of his encounter with the waitress, as *"she"* admonishes him for his faulty introduction (*"'I thought you'd never say hello', she said/'You look like the silent type'"*). The narrative, such as it is, now moves quickly from recognition towards self-realization. The waitress introduces Dylan to an Italian poet from the thirteenth century, who (although not specifically identified) is almost surely Dante Aligheri.

Dante (1265-c.1321) is Italy's most celebrated poet and perhaps the most famous poet of the late Middle Ages. His three-volume epic, *"The Divine Comedy"*, successfully combined the philosophy of Aristotle with the theology of St. Thomas Aquinas in a guided tour through hell, purgatory and several levels of heaven, replete with lessons about how one should and should not live. Most importantly, Dante's writing is linked to a real-life woman whom he met as a child and thereafter worshipped largely only from afar. The woman was Beatrice, married early to a Florentine banker. Dying at the age of only twenty-four, she continued to preoccupy Dante as he dedicated himself to preserving her memory. She became the poet's muse and the inspiration that guided him literally, as a character, in his spiritual tour through Paradise in *"The Divine Comedy"*. In a second book, *"La Vita Nuova"*, Dante was more specific, writing a series of sonnets surrounded by prose commentary that explained how his experience of Beatrice was transmuted into poetry, becoming a treatise on the art of a kind of poetry inspired by a woman. Like Beatrice, the *"she"* of *'Tangled Up In Blue'* has similarly given inspiration to Dylan:

> *And every one of them words rang true*
> *And glowed like burnin' coal*
> *Pourin' off of every page*
> *Like it was written in my soul . . . from me to you,*
> *Tangled up in blue.*

Stepping out of the pages of Dante, the "she" of the fifth verse has become the physical embodiment of artistic inspiration, accompanying Dylan and allowing him to communicate.

The single appearance in the song of the pronoun *"you"* occurs here in the fifth verse. As the suspended lyric that forms the rhyme for "blue", it hangs in the air for a moment as it is sung, suggesting further significance. Superficially, the reference to the soulful words written *"from me to you"* can be taken as though Dylan were simply addressing the waitress. But the "you" is surely also "us" (those who constitute the audience for Dylan's songs); this makes the subject of the verse all the clearer: What came pouring off the page that "she" provided was like it was written in "his soul" for "us" to hear.

The object of Dylan's search in the song (the "she" that he couldn't *"get out of* [his] *mind"*) is revealed as the once-known, now-elusive source of his creative expression. As in his real-life studies with Norman Raeben, Dylan's trying to find through his use of symbolism in song what he once was able to do without thinking: compose his songs effortlessly and get them out of his mind by singing. Dylan's encounters with women could be understood as a quest for an archetypical lost love, or, as the critic Aiden Day wrote, for an *"ideal pattern of the speaker's own deepest identity"*.[6] Building upon Day's observation, it may be that, in his encounters with different women, Dylan sees opportunities to be united with an aspect of his own creative self, personified as a female. *"She"* is the missing half of the singer, the element that would make his creativity whole, regardless of whose body she might inhabit. At the right time and with the right person, this aspect of his inner self would indeed *"escape"* from his mind and be apprehended as a real person, standing physically outside the realm of his imagination.

In the course of the song, the snapshot images of women, real or imagined, become multi-faceted aspects of a single muse that exists, dream-like, as a continuous thread throughout Dylan's life, like Dante's Beatrice. From this point of view, the missing linear narrative to Dylan's lyrics becomes irrelevant, because the mystical female figure is timeless.

The sixth verse brings to mind something closer to a real time and place from Dylan's past, like the first verse's evocation of small-town Minnesota. It is Greenwich Village. *"Montague Street"* could stand for where Bob and Sara lived (they actually purchased a townhouse on MacDougal Street in September 1969). In the song, the time could well have been the end of the decade when *"There was music in the cafes at night/And revolution in the air"*. These were the months of the fiercest fighting in Vietnam, as well as the fiercest war resistance at home and increasing racial unrest. At the time, Dylan was past the first crest of his creative outburst, just back from the Isle of Wight concert, preparing for work on his *"Self-Portrait"* album. In his recent memoir, *"Chronicles, Volume One"*, Dylan has written about moving back to New York at this time to *"demolish* [his] *identity"* and renounce his fan's high expectations of him.

In the sixth verse, the pronouns begin to shift wildly again. In a 1985 interview, Dylan acknowledged this aspect of his work and tried to explain it:

"Sometimes the 'you' in my songs is me talking to me. Other times I can be talking to somebody else. . . . It's up to you to figure out who's who".[7]

In the liner notes to *"Biograph"*, Bob said much the same thing about *'Tangled Up In Blue'*. He acknowledged *"the way the characters change from the first person to the third person, and you're never quite sure if the third person is talking or the first person is talking"*. He then added, *"But as you look at the whole thing it really doesn't matter"*. Nonetheless, one still may be tempted to try and sort it all out.

In *'Tangled Up In Blue'*, with some effort, the listener must conclude that the "I" of the sixth and penultimate verse is the singular creative muse that lies behind all the other "she's" in the song. This "I" (the muse) is the creative self that lived with Bob and a Sara-like figure, packed away as though forgotten *"in a basement down the stairs"*. In this verse, the new *"she"* is Sara, *"he"* is Bob and *"they"* (or *"them"*) are Bob and Sara together: *"I lived with them on Montague Street/In a basement down the stairs,/ . . . Then he started into dealing with slaves/And something inside of him died./She had to sell everything she owned/And froze up inside"*.

In the late sixties, then, "inspiration" (personified as an undoubtedly female "I") lived with Bob and Sara, neglected. Then Bob *"started into dealing with slaves"*, perhaps meaning slaves to drugs, from the word *"dealing"*, or perhaps those contracting with, and thus binding themselves to, the music industry (Dylan was especially challenged by his manager Albert Grossman and by record companies regarding contract obligations from the time of his 1966 accident up until *"Blood On The Tracks"*). In this increasingly unhappy time, Sara *"had to sell everything she owned/And froze up inside"*, thus losing whatever made Sara herself and sounding as though she'd become infertile or cold in her relationships (which, as a metaphor, would be consistent with the singer's loss of creativity). And what then became of Bob's inspiration, his female creative self? In an act of self-preservation, his inspiration (speaking in the first person as *"I"*) withdrew and finally escaped:[8]

And when finally the bottom fell out
I became withdrawn.
The only thing I knew how to do
Was to keep on keepin' on like a bird that flew . . .
Tangled up in blue.

The *"bird that flew"* could be an allusion to the subject of John Keats' poem, 'Ode to a Nightingale', in which the bird symbolizes the fleeting nature of inspiration and recollections of timeless beauty. The same bird made an appearance in an early version of 'Visions Of Johanna' and, of course, is featured in 'Jokerman' (*"Jokerman dance to the nightingale tune/Bird fly high by the light of the moon"*).

In the last verse, the pronouns return to their prior usage, and the songwriter talks again about his inspiration as *"she"*. The songwriter is *"goin' back again"* (perhaps *"back"* in the sense of drawing on his memories, beginning with the red-haired girl). He's *"got to get to her somehow"*. Despite the difficulties the song describes, it ends with a satisfying element of self-recognition. Traveling in search of inspiration is what Dylan does (and what makes him different from others): *"But me, I'm still on the road/Headin' for another joint"*. He understands his hot-and-cold relationship with his creative self and that there are two sides to his nature: *"We always did feel the same./We just saw it from a different point of view/Tangled up in blue"*.

In the end, it seems that Dylan's muse, like the subject of 'Sad-Eyed Lady Of The Lowlands', has a mind of her own, she comes and goes when she pleases and can't be contained or controlled. Although they always will come from different points of view, Bob's search for her, or the memories she invokes, appears to allow for the creative process of at least making the song that he's singing now: 'Tangled Up In Blue'. The inspiration is back, if only viewed from afar and just for a moment.

'Up To Me' is in many ways the mirror image of 'Tangled Up In Blue'. It appears to have much the same background story, telling of an inspiring muse who flew away to escape a deteriorating relationship. When *'Up To Me'* opens, the muse has been long gone, and Dylan, who's been on the road for an indeterminate time, decides it's now time to seek her out. The song then recounts their brief reunion, with shifting points of view that has Dylan singing both his part and hers, the same technique as used in *'Tangled Up In Blue'*. And the same tone of nostalgic acceptance runs through both songs, just as the melodies somewhat resemble each other. Finally, while both songs are outstanding, it is easy to see why, to avoid redundancy, only one was selected for *"Blood On The Tracks"*.

'Up To Me' begins with Dylan remembering the bad times, when *"everything went from bad to worse"* despite increased material wealth. In his pre-accident days, Dylan may have been at death's door, and close friends lost their lives to drugs or bad luck (Paul Clayton, Richard Farina, Geno Foreman). Although the muse is long gone, Dylan recalls, *"at least I heard your bluebird sing"*, thus acknowledging the gift of music that was his in those days. Now, he concludes, it's time to stop playing games (*"somebody's got to show their hand"*), because time's running out: *"I guess it must be up to me"*.

The next verse is her voice. As in *'Tangled Up In Blue'*, the muse-figure explains why she left. It wasn't a conscious decision, and it wasn't based on what others were thinking. In fact, if she weren't stubborn, she'd have let the situation slide, although *"the heart inside* [her] *would've died"*. Just as with the Sara-like figure of *'Tangled Up In Blue'*, this second figure was being *"froze up inside"*. And like the muse, she flew, here reaching *"for the risin' star"*. That was her role, her destiny: that, she says, *"was up to me"*.

The identity of the speaker in each subsequent verse seems generally to alternate, so the next would be Bob's. With his trademark railroad and flower images, he sings in celebration of new beginnings, like spring, and the onset of an almost Arthurian quest: *"Oh, the Union Central is pullin' out and the orchids are in bloom"*. In part, Dylan is the chrysalis emerging as a new butterfly (along with the orchids), and in part he's the reforming sinner near the end of his rope (unsmiling, with only one good shirt left). He confesses his renewed need for his muse: somebody's got to find her trail, Dylan says offhandedly. Of course, it must be up to him.

The line, *"In fourteen months, I've only smiled once and I didn't do it consciously"*, is a tempting allusion to fourteen years of recording or the fourteen albums (more or less, depending on how or whether you count two *"Greatest Hits"* collections and a film soundtrack) up to and including *"Blood On The Tracks"*. He did smile obviously on only one album cover, *"Nashville Skyline"*, in a photograph by Elliott Landy, and that smile wasn't planned. Landy has since explained how the picture was taken with little thought, almost jokingly while the singer and photographer were tramping about Dylan's muddy Woodstock yard in search of ideas for the album's back cover.[9] The picture, of course, became the front cover, not the back.

In the fourth verse, Dylan's muse has clearly assumed a woman's physical body, and Dylan is reunited with her. She says somewhat cryptically:

It was like a revelation when you betrayed me with your touch
I'd just about convinced myself that nothing had changed that much.

Their encounter might recall Judas' identification of Jesus to the Roman authorities (betrayed by a kiss). But Dylan's language also allows for the better inference that she was unwittingly led astray by Dylan (the word *"betray"* has a dictionary meaning of, among others, *"to seduce someone trustful"*). So Dylan seduced her, and the couple got back together again.

The following lines suggest that things had changed for the better, that the constant descent from bad to worse may have since reversed itself, at least temporarily. Their respite is symbolized by his delivery of a master key. It clearly appears to be the woman's voice speaking: *"The old Rounder in the iron mask slipped me the master key"*. According to the dictionary, a *"rounder"* is someone who literally *"makes the rounds"*, ranging from checking prisoners periodically in their cells to going from one drinking establishment to another (or *"heading for another joint"*, as at the end of *'Tangled Up In Blue'*). The *"iron mask"* introduces a prison image, suggesting a locked-up or unknowable self, at least without the aid of a muse. His inspiration is captive, like the *"she"* in the prior song that he couldn't get to escape from his mind.

There follows a highly ambiguous couplet, without quotation marks, as it appears in *"Lyrics"*:

Somebody had to unlock your heart
He said it was up to me.

Because of Dylan's imprecise use of pronouns and the lack of punctuation, determining who is *"me"*, *"you"*, and *"he"* is almost impossible. However, because *"he"*, the Rounder, was locked up and gave her the key, it seems likely that the words are still the woman's, speaking now to Bob's creative self, the *"you"* of the line, *"Somebody had to unlock your heart"*. This would be consistent with Dylan's treatment of the muse-figure: Bob's the one who needs a woman to release his inspiration; she has the key (here, willingly given to her, in particular) to set his inspiration free (here, Dylan's muse-inspired creativity would be associated with the phrase *"your heart"*).

The following five verses are especially obscure, involving (among others) an officers' club, a post office and an incident at the Thunderbird Cafe. They contain simple units of memory or emotion clothed in images, not unlike those of *'Tangled Up In Blue'*. The images each relate generally to being trapped or separated, to being imprisoned or seeking escape. For instance, Dylan refers to a Sara-figure's disappearance into an *"officers' club"*, a place to which he does not have admittance. The couple is thus separated, with Bob waiting in vain for circumstances to change (*"hopin' one of us could get free"*). When things don't change (and, it's implied, Sara's at fault), Dylan knew it was time for him to break free from his dependency, getting *"free"* in a second sense of the word.

Another verse refers to working as a postal clerk (probably in the woman's voice). It appears to allude to a nurturing female's role in effecting Dylan's privacy and lengthy career hiatus following his motorcycle accident. Here, a Sara-like figure hauls his *"picture down off the wall"*, which otherwise would have identified Dylan as the subject of a "Wanted Man" poster, commonly on display in post offices (*"near the cage"* where she *"used to work"*). But she hides him away, thinking it best:

> *Was I a fool or not to try to protect your i-dent-ti-ty?*
> *You looked a little burned out, my friend, I thought it might be up to me.*

In the last half of the song, there appears to be a number of unresolved conflicts that involve temptation and infidelity. First, Dylan meets someone new who can satisfy all his needs but who, at the same time, makes his life awful and complicated. This would not be unlike Bob's short-lived relationship with *Columbia Records* executive Ellen Bernstein, with whom Bob was intensely involved at the time:

> *She's everything I need and love but I can't be swayed by that*
> *It frightens me, the awful truth of how sweet life can be.*

In an unusual twist for the songs of this period, Bob declares, somewhat ambiguously, that it's time to do something different and let someone go: *"[S]he ain't a-gonna make me move,/I guess it must be up to me"*.

Dylan next acknowledges the complexity of the Sermon on the Mount, which contains Jesus' strictures against adultery and giving free reign to lustful thoughts. Fidelity, Dylan observes, is implicit in the taking of marriage vows (from the stomped *"broken glass"*, a ceremonial performed at Jewish weddings):

> *We heard the Sermon on the Mount and I knew it was too complex*
> *It didn't amount to anything more than what the broken glass reflects.*

If you take more than your share in having extramarital affairs (or *"bite off more than you can chew"*), then *"you pay the penalty"*.

The song concludes with Dylan's agony and the reaffirmation of his ruptured relationship. One night in the Thunderbird Cafe, a real location off L.A.'s Sunset Boulevard, Bob forces himself to look away from Dupree, a familiar pimp, and from Crystal, a willing prostitute, avoiding eye contact so as not to look interested. He fights temptation and wants to seek reconciliation with his now-stubborn muse. But the muse-figure (almost synonymous now with Sara), she won't cross the line; her line of principle is drawn in the sand. She's unwilling to take the wandering singer back (or, if she's at fault, she won't change her mind or behaviour). In any case, Bob is now free to *"cross the line"* in another sense (the song is full of such puns). Frustrated, he can now break the rules and get out of line. Maybe he'll take up with Crystal after all and accept an offer from pimpin' Dupree.

In the song's final verses, Bob seems to explain to his jealous muse-figure that Estelle was her rival with whom he strayed (again, temptingly similar to his affair with the real Ellen Bernstein): *"She's the one you been wond'rin' about, but there's really nothin' much to tell"*. Ironically, as with Sara, so with Estelle: *"We both heard voices for a while, now the rest is his-tor-y"*. Life is short, and time passes quickly: *"The ringleaders from the county seat say you don't have all that much time"*. And now it's time to move on: *"One of us has got to hit the road. I guess it must be up to me"*.

* * *

'Tangled Up In Blue' and *'Up To Me'* both belong to a period of very self-conscious writing in which Dylan explored his own creative identity, often in terms of his relationships with women (both real and imagined). In these works, the images of women are seemingly inseparable from Dylan's internal creative process; at times, Dylan's explorations of women, the creative process and his own identity lead him to talk about female characters figuratively almost as though, like memory, they were aspects of himself. One line of *'Up To Me'*, in particular, may suggest that Bob knows he's portraying an internalized muse, that his female inspiration both lives within him and has an independent existence. Picturing Dylan with sunglasses on, he confesses (as though he shared the same set of eyes with another): *[T]he girl with me behind the shades, she ain't my property/One of us has got to hit the road,/I guess it must be up to me"*.

Leaving romance behind, Dylan appears destined to be a solitary wanderer, but the figure of the wanderer is also that of a storyteller. Dylan, like the wanderer, is compelled to transmit the knowledge gathered from experience in the form of his songs: *"Somebody's got to tell the tale,/I guess it must be up to me"*. From his wanderings, Dylan would emerge periodically–like the Ancient Mariner, Faust or even Cain–to explain what compelled him to be as he is. Destiny would always play a role in Bob's relationship with his muse, and he knew it. He thus concluded *'Up To Me'* with the following lines:

No one else could play that tune, You <u>know</u> it was up to me.

Notes:

[1] Williams, Chris. *"In His Own Words: Bob Dylan"*. London: *Omnibus*, 1993, 49.

[2] For an assessment of structuralist critiques of the song, <u>see</u> Gray, Michael. *"Song & Dance Man III: The Art of Bob Dylan"*. London: *Cassell*, 2000, 261. Gray especially notes the opportunities for critical interpretation that Dylan provides whenever he revises his lyrics, an issue that I will not address here.

[3] Alexander, Robert *"Bob Dylan: An Illustrated History"*, Rinzler, Alan *"Bob Dylan: The Illustrated Story"* and Scobie, Steven *"Alias Bob Dylan Revisited"* all opt for one woman. Herdman, John *"Voice Without Restraint: Bob Dylan's Lyrics and Their Background"* and Day, Aiden *"Jokerman: Reading the Lyrics of Bob Dylan"* each hold out for more than one.

[4] From her composition, *'Diamonds & Rust'*, released as a single *A&M* 1737-S in 1975.

[5] Biederman, Hans. Trans. Hulbert, James. *"Dictionary of Symbolism"*. New York: *Meridian*, 1989, 44-45.

[6] Day, Aiden. *"Jokerman: Reading the Lyrics of Bob Dylan"*. Oxford, Eng.: *Basil Blackwell*, 1988, 61.

7 Cohen, Scott. *'Not Like A Rolling Stone Interview' Spin*. Vol. One, No. 8, December 1985.

8 Interestingly, in Chapter XXV of *"La Vita Nuova"*, Dante justifies his use of personification and allegory. In a digression from his main themes, the Italian poet explains why, for linguistic reasons, it was appropriate for poets, both ancient and modern, to treat inanimate things or concepts (he mentions *"Love"* specifically) *"as if they had sense and reason . . . making things which do not exist speak"*. Alighieri, Dante. Trans. Reynolds, Barbara. *"La Vita Nouva"*. Middlesex, Eng.: *Penguin*, 1969, 74. Dylan's inanimate inspiration, packed in the basement, also speaks out, much in the way that Dante suggested.

9 Landy, Elliott. *"Woodstock Vision: The Spirit of a Generation"*. New York: *Continuum*, 1994, 81-82.

Published in *ISIS* issue #117, November 2004

Understanding Bob and Renaldo

James Dunlap

The Allerton Building in downtown Chicago (about 500 miles southeast of Hibbing, Minnesota) has housed the Art Institute's celebrated collection of European paintings since the turn of the last century. For over 75 years, one of the most popular canvases in that collection has been a depiction of an amorous episode from Torquato Tasso's *"Jerusalem Delivered"*, an epic poem from the Italian Renaissance that recounts the story of the First Crusade.

The 18th century painting, by the Venetian artist Giovanni Tiepolo, portrays a brave knight, Rinaldo, who lies daydreaming under a spell cast by a majestic sorceress. Hovering on a cloud overhead and draped in flowing regalia, the sorceress (Armida) sits astride her magic chariot with a long white scarf soaring into the sky behind her. Spellbound by love herself, she intends to keep Rinaldo diverted from battle. Later, through acts of willpower, Rinaldo will escape from Armida and lead the Crusaders to victory.

I. Introduction

"Renaldo And Clara", Dylan's agonizingly long, self-referential film epic, has been largely neglected by critics and biographers. One reason, of course, is that it's been generally unavailable since its limited and short-term release in January of 1978. However, many feel the movie is best left disregarded. They see a somewhat promising concert film that, unfortunately, was spoiled by Dylan's bewildering pseudo-documentary filler and the failed attempts at surrealistic fiction by members of his entourage. Others see only a record of Dylan's morbid self-absorption during his brief final reconciliation with his wife Sara.

The audience for *"Renaldo And Clara"* faced numerous obstacles at the outset. The character "Bob Dylan" was played by the legendary 300-pound Canadian rockabilly singer, Ronnie Hawkins, and the role of Dylan's wife Sara was played by Ronee Blakely. Bob Dylan played "Renaldo" (the film ultimately would appear to be his dream), and the real Sara Dylan played Renaldo's wife Clara (as well as, somewhat cruelly, a Mexican prostitute). As the film's editor and director, Bob did little to aid the viewer in understanding whatever it was he meant to say.

An abundance of Christ-images throughout the film added further to the barriers for audience acceptance. These images seemed to reveal that the film's creator thought of himself as a misunderstood or suffering prophet. The *New Yorker* movie critic, Pauline Kael, titled her review *'The Calvary Gig'* and felt that, by 1978, there was no public left that would see Bob Dylan as a messiah. She was not sure, however, how to assess the loyalties of the carefully selected concert troupe, the Rolling Thunder Revue, who followed Bob on his musical pilgrimage and participated with him in its filming (225).

The film's looming difficulties could probably have been discerned early. Initially, there were plans for a script, and Sam Shepard, the playwright, was retained to accompany the concert tour and provide it with words. It soon became apparent, however, that the chaotic assembly hurtling through the Eastern U.S. and Canada could not be restrained to learn lines or rehearse. As a consequence, the film began to resemble an unscripted home movie. As Dylan described it later, about one third of the scenes were planned, one third were spontaneous and a final third were the result of blind luck (Cott I 189).

Despite the movie's obvious shortcomings, *"Renaldo And Clara"* provides a valuable and unique illustration of how Dylan's mind worked. Filmed in late 1975, he subsequently spent a full year editing it; rarely has Bob spent so much time on a single project. The film is important for that reason alone. In addition, in the months surrounding its premiere, Dylan probably spoke more about his film and its meaning than he ever has about any of his other projects.

II. What Kind of Film Is This?

Because much of *"Renaldo And Clara"* appears to be spontaneous, one might conclude that it should not be thought of as the result of Dylan's conscious design. However, Bob took a decisive role in shaping the film at three principal points. First, as Shepard recalled (13), Dylan had a conception from the outset of the film's overall subject matter and genre, which (amazingly) survived through the movie's completion. Second, during the location filming, Bob often instructed his actors about the character "types" and generalized scenes they were being asked to play, making sure that specific points were covered (Cott I 189). In other cases, particularly if he was onscreen, he led other actors through their improvisations (e.g., Sloman 143-45). Because the film was meant to be built around broad archetypes rather than narrowly crafted words, the spontaneous dialogue that often resulted still worked within a pre-established design.

Finally, during the editing process, Bob brought out themes and made associations that were critical to the film's meaning. The selection, cutting, and arrangement of four hours of film from the hundreds that were shot was like shaping clay or assembling a statue from random found objects.

* * *

During the first meeting about his screenplay assignment, Shepard recalled that Dylan identified two French films as precedents: Francois Truffaut's *"Shoot The Piano Player"* and Marcel Carne's *"Children Of The Paradise"*. With the benefit of hindsight, one can look back on those models and get a good sense of what Dylan intended.

"Shoot The Piano Player" (1960) is the story of a has-been concert pianist who has been forced to perform in a fetid Parisian bar. The lead, Charlie, is played by Charles Aznavour with the deadpan elegance of Buster Keaton. In a spoof of Hollywood crime dramas, the small piano player's gangster brother arrives unexpectedly in flight from a double-cross with the mob. There follows a hodgepodge of scenes mixing irreverent nonsense with serious flashbacks. Charlie considers, among other things, the suicide of his wife, the career he might have had, and the allure of a young barmaid who tries to both help and seduce him. The film's title is apt: it comes from the aphorism, *"Don't shoot the piano player; he's trying as hard as he can"*. Disjointed vignettes about love, success, and the meaning of life constitute the bulk of the movie, which is at once a comedy, a psychological drama and a crime mystery. It jumps from one thread to another seemingly without any transition. With his own film, Dylan would follow a similar path.

"Children Of The Paradise" (1943-45) is even more complex (like Dylan's film, it is over three hours). It also works on many levels at once. Set in the realm of acrobats, dancing girls, and theatres in pre-1840 Paris, the film is an epic of infatuation, jealousy, deception, grief, murder and true love lost forever. The lead character, the white-faced mime Baptiste, is in love with a tragically unattainable woman, Garance.

Like Dylan's film (in which Bob also appeared in whiteface), *"Children Of The Paradise"* is filled with rich concepts about the different types of primal relations between men and women, and Dylan appears to have borrowed very specific ideas from it. For instance, Baptiste's simple wife Nathalie expresses her hope that someday Baptiste will love her just as she loves him. *"Children Of The Paradise"* then ends, exactly like Dylan's film, with the male lead character facing two women. They represent different kinds of love, and the characters are forced to address how they care for each other. In the corresponding climactic scene from *"Renaldo And Clara"*, Sara and Joan Baez together confront the Dylan character, asking him in turn, *"Renaldo, do you love her?"* In the end, he gives his reply to each, echoing a major theme of the French film: *"Do I love her like I love you? No. Do I love you like I love her? No"*.

Several other key moments in *"Children Of The Paradise"* seem to have specific counterparts in Dylan's work. As just one example, after a long and complex separation, Baptiste meets Garance by chance in a sordid dance hall and volunteers to escort her home. When they kiss, Garance proposes (to coin a phrase), *"Love is so simple"*. Much later, when the couple is briefly reunited again, the heartfelt line is repeated, becoming an unforgettable moment. It reappears, of course, at the centre of *'You're A Big Girl Now'*, from 1974.

Bob was incensed when commentary about his songs from this period asserted they were about his wife Sara, and he was ridiculed for his sanctimony. Bob may have been simply thinking about how he included universal ideas that he'd seen and borrowed from other sources, including *"Children Of The Paradise"*.

Allen Ginsberg described the editing techniques that he witnessed during the completion of *"Renaldo And Clara"* as the linking of images that hooked into each other on many levels (105-6), not unlike Dylan's songwriting techniques. Dylan and his friend Howard Alk identified each scene with themes (e.g., Love, God, Rock 'n' Roll, Death) and placed them on index cards, which were then spread on the floor and scrambled about to create relationships. As a result, numerous scenes – such as David Blue's recollections of different aspects of Greenwich Village in the early 1960s (while playing pinball) – were cut up and appeared out of sequence at different points in the film.

A number of scholars and critics, including Steven Scobie and C.P. Lee, have provided useful summaries of various "threads" that weave in and out of *"Renaldo And Clara"*. In addition to Blue's pinball-playing recollections, these threads include poetry readings, prison images, a bordello scene, and conversations relating to travel. One enthusiast, Marc Stein, has even provided a scene-by-scene synopsis that has been posted on a number of Web sites, including rec.music.dylan.

The film's many scenes can be further grouped, not just by episodic threads, but by type (e.g., documentary, dramatic or surreal). Although the categories aren't always distinct, this additional type of grouping can help distinguish among the levels of meaning that Dylan was trying to link. Far from being arbitrary, the editing of mixed types of footage was meant to suggest that different kinds of experiences are related and connect on some level. In ascending order of abstraction, the film types are as follows:

1. Concert footage, generally filmed through a blue filter with a white-faced Dylan. Dylan's songs are particularly intense, with the camera focused so tightly on his face that we feel almost as though we're inside of his mind (which is undoubtedly the point). The film leaps in and out of performances, as though everything in Bob's mind is intertwined and never-ending, as though all things are happening at once.

2. Newsreel or documentary-type footage that may or may not include members of the "cast" (i.e., the Rolling Thunder Revue). The largest block of this type features the imprisoned boxer, Rubin "Hurricane" Carter, who is interviewed in connection with the potential appeal of his murder conviction. Wrongly imprisoned, Carter had become, in Dylan's words, a *"philosopher in chains"*, which was meant to be understood as symbolic of the larger themes in Bob's movie (G 119). Dylan apparently saw something of himself in the boxer's life and writings.

3. Home-movie styled episodes involving members of the Rolling Thunder Revue, arising fairly directly from their road experiences. These, too, are of different types:

a. Scenes where people interact normally as themselves, just as they might in real life. Thus, we view Allen Ginsberg and Dylan at a cemetery in Lowell,

Massachusetts where they visit Jack Kerouac's grave. Later, the entire retinue descends on "Mama", an older but sprightly gypsy landlady at her inn, where Joan Baez tries on a white wedding gown. Although there is a quality of cinéma vérité to these scenes, there is often something deliberately artificial and unsettling about them as well.

b. Short scenes or "glimpses" from the road, subtly transformed so as to make them unreal, like a slightly altered reality. Thus, Ronnie Hawkins enters a hotel lobby, and a reporter is shown to mistake him for Bob Dylan (although he is, in fact, playing the role of "Bob Dylan"). In another scene, Joan Baez is filmed in her hotel room with her wet hair wrapped in a white towel, talking aloud about her need for companionship. These scenes seem innocuous, but they also provide links to the film's broader motifs. For instance, the movie asks on many levels, "Who is Bob Dylan?" and seems to suggest that we're all acting roles. Joan Baez will later be transformed into the love-starved "Woman in White".

c. Lightly scripted or improvised scenes from the road, generally longer, where the players appear to be acting in a somewhat conventional drama. In a darkened restaurant, for instance, Sara and Helena Kallianiotes talk about their each needing a ride, and a truck-driving stranger who volunteers to help them. The women wonder aloud about trust, disappointment, coincidence, and how to reach their different destinations (whether "in life" or on the road is deliberately left ambiguous). Seemingly innocent dialogue with implications about larger themes, while often amateurishly performed, indicate Dylan's serious intent.

4. Heavily scripted scenes – often with costumes and "found" sets – that are frequently confusing but intended to be symbolic in their role in the film. Thus, Sara (as Clara) delivers a rope to Harry Dean Stanton ("Lafkezio"), who uses it to escape over a prison-like wall, achieving "freedom". In a Wild West bordello, the founding Beat poet Allen Ginsberg (as "the Father") prepares to have the very young David Mansfield, "the Son" (an innocent lamb or Christ image), initiated in some undefined way. A turbaned Woman in White (played by Joan Baez) is ridden around a snowy city on an elegant, open horse-drawn carriage, eventually confronting Bob and Sara (as Renaldo and Clara) as a part of the movie's awkward conclusion. The more heavily symbolic scenes dominate the last half of the film.

* * *

By shuffling index cards that represent scenes, Dylan's editing techniques could be analogized to the "cut-up" methods of William Burroughs' surrealistic novels, such as *"Naked Lunch"*. The cut-up method, at least in theory, involves scrambling pieces of paper to produce the sequence of words that would later be used in creating a book. The analogy to Dylan's film would be incorrect; the scenes in *"Renaldo And Clara"* do not follow each other in a random order. The episodes are deliberately linked by overlapping symbols and melodic themes. However, apart from recognizing the unifying effect of overlapping songs (which, softly playing in the background, can sound like a distant memory), critics have not paid much attention to the significance of the associational edits. A consideration of the logic behind the jump-cuts can help further reveal Dylan's themes and underlying concerns.

Based on the logic of its jump-cuts, one series of seemingly disparate scenes can be understood as loosely involving the meaning of life in the face of death, as well as the importance of maintaining a right relationship with both God and women. These are the kind of broad themes that were used on index cards to assist in the editing process. In this particular series, the Girlfriend character first complains to "Bob Dylan" (played by Ronnie Hawkins) that there's *"no security out there on a rock 'n roll stage"*. The Dylan character replies, *"There's just no security anywhere"* and adds, *"Honey, the world, the world is ready to explode, it may go tomorrow . . . Let's go out having fun"*. The Girlfriend, who wants to live on a farm, responds, *"I want to go in God's country when I go"*.

The scene then cuts to an evangelical preacher haranguing a New York City street crowd about sins and their consequences. The edit links three ideas about human behaviour in response to the possible end of the world: one can (i) live for the moment, (ii) seek out God's country, or (iii) prepare for the Day of Judgment. The next scene, also related, may involve a small group of the concert tour's road crew (it appears to include Larry Sloman–the journalist and author of *"On The Road With Bob Dylan"*). They are talking in a diner late at night about the meaning of God's work. *"Pepper Steak"*, offers one facetiously. Another explains that God's work is potentially everything, and it can be especially found in the way that one does things.

Here, Dylan has taken several ideas about God and related them to the way that men and women act in the world. There is the rock star's credo of "live for today", the preacher's call for repentance, the first diner's facetious dismissal of God, and the last diner's reverent attitude toward performing God's works. By inference, Dylan (the film's author) seems to be questioning the "Bob Dylan" character's live-fast, love-hard and die-young approach. This questioning is further underlined by the implied messages of the scenes that immediately follow.

Following the diner scene, there's a long shot of the moon, a feminine symbol for most of recorded time, and then the film cuts to a shot of Dylan trudging alone through the snow on his way to a tavern. An aching, soulful version of *'Ballad In Plain D'* plays idly in the background (which, unlike the original song, is now performed like a tender reminiscence). This song naturally evokes Dylan's memory of his relationship and break-up with Suze Rotolo. That memory and the image of Dylan alone in the snow resonates with the prior competing rock-star approach to the conquest and collection of women. The emotions resonating from this sequence of mixed scenes and genres cumulate to create an unusual poignancy, very much like the effect of similar juxtapositioning in *"Shoot The Piano Player"*.

lll. What Else to Watch For

In addition to large themes and associational edits, certain discrete images (notably Dylan's wide-brimmed hat and a red rose) reappear in different scenes. Through editing, these images, like a musical leitmotif, are intended to unite the scenes and give the film added continuity. By calling attention to themselves, Dylan has also suggested that these images signal that something happening on the screen is particularly important (G 118, G 122-23, Cott I 178). However, Dylan's success with this device depends on the ability of his audience to discern the meaning of the connecting images. To appreciate what Dylan is trying to say, it may not be enough to recognize that there is a recurring "hat" image: one also wants to know what that hat means. While Dylan was not very helpful in this regard, he did not leave us clueless.

An early relevant sequence in the film includes David Blue's memories of passing a hat for money in the Greenwich Village cafes. This is followed, first, by a disfigured black poet asking for money; second, by an isolated shot of Dylan's broad-brimmed hat (a particularly weird effect); and next, by a record executive talking about the commercial difficulties involved in releasing Dylan's song 'Hurricane' with its hard-to-sell social commentary. The sequence ends with an almost disbelieving deejay announcing the imminent arrival in town of the Rolling Thunder Revue. Mixed in with all this, wearing his hat and idly strumming his guitar (with a woman at his side), Dylan states boldly, "I am the Law" to a garage mechanic with whom he is trading a luxury car for a motorcycle.

In this sequence, Dylan equates the hat with money ("passing the hat") and then with Dylan's power, reminding us that he is different from record executives. His use of money isn't limited to commercial success: he's helping a black man (not just the disfigured poet, but Hurricane Carter, as well). He's also financing this throw-back, small-venue Rolling Thunder Revue and its filming with his own funds (to the deejay's amazement). Dylan can metaphorically trade his big car for the freedom of a motorcycle. In making his movie, he is the law (unlike Sam Peckinpah, whom Dylan had witnessed having such a hard time with the producers of "Pat Garrett And Billy The Kid"). When a gullible female reporter later asks who is Bob Dylan, she's told that he is the one with a hat.

Besides the hat, a second ubiquitous symbol is the red rose that passes from hand to hand throughout the film. The possible meaning of this image are several: On many occasions, Dylan has used flowers as a shorthand for "song" in close association with natural creativity and the fecundity of his muse. In 'Love Minus Zero/No Limit', for instance, he would boast of his muse, "My love she laughs like the flowers". In his prose liner notes "Eleven Outlined Epitaphs" (1964), Bob gave a direct indication of his early symbolic use of the flower: "[M]y road is blessed/with many flowers/an' the sounds of flowers/liftin' lost voices of the ground's people/up up/ . . . an' that, then, shall/remain my song". At the time, Dylan seemed to feel that his songs, like the traditional songs that he'd always admired, grew naturally (like flowers) from the common ground of "the people" and could therefore be shared.

In an important interview with Allen Ginsberg, Bob also likened the rose in *"Renaldo And Clara"* to female sexual organs (G 118). As the interview continued, Dylan made a further association between the red flower and inadequate or desperate women who, using female guile, flaunt their femininity for selfish ends. In the film's climactic closing scenes, when the Woman in White (Joan Baez) arrives to confront Sara and Bob, she cradles a rose in her hands like a votive candle. She is a negative character, representing Death's ghost, and, according to Dylan, Renaldo rids himself of death when she leaves (G 113). By contrast, Dylan described one of his film's strong characters, the Girlfriend, as pure and giving; as a consequence, he says, she never has to use the rose (G 116).

With his rose symbolism, one can discern the possible influence of the 20th Century French novelist, philosopher, and dramatist, Jean Genet. In such early works as *"The Miracle Of The Rose"* and *"Our Lady Of The Flowers"*, Genet found the beauty of nature to have powerful, almost satanic qualities that profoundly affected his mental state. Because Genet, a homosexual orphan and thief, was psychologically paralyzed by insecurities about his identity, he often felt threatened by the unselfconscious beauty that flowers symbolically represented to him. Because of their inhuman lack of self-consciousness, flowers simply had an ability to manifest an absolute existence that Genet lacked. In accordance with the Frenchman's somewhat perverse logic, a flower's beauty became miraculous, powerful, satanic and evil – something to be overcome (Coe 17). Only a rare human being could pass beyond the furthest boundaries of human experience and share in the miraculous of the inanimate world.

Dylan clearly knew of Jean Genet and his work. He cited him favourably as early as 1964 when, in the last of four letters to his friend Tami Dean, he wrote, *"dont be afraid of gene genet"*. In a March 1966 interview with Robert Shelton, he said he liked all of Jean Genet's "old books" (which would include those with the flower motifs), but not his newer scholastic lectures (400).

Besides Dylan's use of the rose in his film, he made statements in his interviews about *"Renaldo And Clara"* that sounded very much like Genet. For example, when asked what a *"conscious artist"* practices, Bob replied *"Actuality"*, handed Allen Ginsberg a flower and, like a Zen koan, challenged Ginsberg to improve it (G 109). Because Dylan said the flower was God-given, the implication was that it could not be improved. In a second interview, he announced that he was no longer writing songs about goddesses placed on pedestals: *"The flower is what we are really concerned about here. The opening and the closing, the growth, the bafflement. You don't lust after flowers"* (Rosenbaum 147). Dylan's association of the words *"bafflement"* and *"lust"* with his flower symbolism could easily relate, as in Genet's case, to the bewildering *"otherness"* of their God-given, unselfconscious beauty.

Dylan's view of the rose, like Genet's, was also somewhat ambivalent: positive aspects of the rose were apparently associated with fertility as nature intended (Cott I 179) and unselfish earthly women, like the Girlfriend. When Bob then portrayed other women negatively as demanding and self-centred, they were denigrated for their misuse of the rose (G 118). Dylan's ambivalence occurred because he encountered women who used their natural femininity for destructive purposes, but he felt a fatal attraction to them. He thus suffered from their abuse of the rose. As an example from his film, Dylan wore the rose conspicuously when he performed *'Isis'*, which ends with the line: *"What drives me to you is what drives me insane"*. Referring specifically to the rose in that scene, Dylan remarked, *"By that time it's* [i.e., the rose] *all shattered and fallen apart"* (Cott I 178-79).

Dylan appears to have overcome his emotional weakness for destructive women only at the end of *"Renaldo And Clara"*, resolving them on a higher level. He explained the process of his transcendence as follows:

"You can't be a slave to your emotions. If you're a slave to your emotions you're dependent on your conscious mind. But the film is about the fact that you have to be faithful to your subconscious, unconscious, superconscious – as well as to your conscious mind" (Cott I 175).

Dylan wants to lose his base emotions, his past, and his identity in order to be united with a kind of Jungian timeless spirit. In discussing his film, he once said, *"[D]eep in our soul we have no past . . . any more than we have a name"* (Cott I 191). Indeed, one is tempted to see in each of the characters of *"Renaldo And Clara"* some aspect of Dylan's life, transmuted into archetype and myth.

In *"Dylan – What Happened?"*, Paul Williams wrote that his favourite parts of Dylan's film had this mythical component, seeming to represent a *"kaleidoscopic dynamic between a man and a woman, wearing all different masks and never quite getting to or away from each other"* (68). Williams also took away from the movie the sense that Dylan has or had *"another way of looking at reality"*. He concluded that Dylan believed that life is an illusion and that only willpower holds it together (68-70).

Williams' conclusions echoed Dylan's own comments. In his Ginsberg interview, when asked *"Did you make this film as a representation of yourself psychically?"* Bob answered simply, *"Yes"* (G 113). In discussing the film's broader themes, he went on to reveal (albeit enigmatically) a number of specific details about the unusual ways that he looked at himself and the world.

IV. More About How Dylan Thinks

Dylan's explorations of his own identity had been a long-standing concern, originating perhaps when he first felt himself out of place in the small town of Hibbing. When he changed his name, his sense of himself became more complex. Thereafter, Dylan frequently exhibited alienation and a heightened degree of self-consciousness, which he sometimes attempted to resolve through his art. That's how he described *"Renaldo And Clara"*:

"It's about naked alienation of the inner self against the outer self . . . taken to the extreme" (Cott I 175).

Norman Raeben's teaching directly addressed Dylan's alienation and inner conflicts. Based on what Dylan himself has revealed, Raeben's work seemed to involve, first, a recognition of the different "prisons" in which each of us is contained. These prisons exist because of our egos and our past memories, and they obscure our perception of our true selves and the present. In discussing his painting lessons with Raeben, Dylan specifically mentioned having to discard all of his many selves in order to deal with that one self that he recognized as his own:

"I was constantly being intermingled with myself and all the different selves that were in there, until this one left, then that one left, and finally I got down to the one that I was familiar with" (Hughes).

Dylan's "therapy" with Norman Raeben also helped him achieve what he called a *"triumph over time"*, which he has since linked to both *"Blood On The Tracks"* and *"Renaldo And Clara"*. In describing his goals to Allen Ginsberg, he said at the outset:

"You wanna stop time, that's what you wanna do. You want to live forever, right Allen? Huh? In order to live forever you have to stop time. In order to stop time you have to exist in the moment" (108).

The sense of "no-time" can exist when one is fully engaged in the making or apprehension of art. As Dylan said:

"It's like if you look at a painting by Cezanne, you're lost in that painting for that period of time . . . yet time is going by and you wouldn't know it, you're spellbound" (Cott I 190).

But the concept of "no-time" is more complex than simple absorption in a work of art.

According to Dylan, Raeben conceived of time as though the past, present, and future existed all at once in a single room (Cott II 359). From this point of view, one's life path would then exist at all moments, looming ahead as well as behind. This outlook on life seems well-represented by the subject matter and presentation of songs like 'Tangled Up In Blue', 'Shelter From The Storm', and 'Isis'. In them, one's destiny, like time itself, seems as inescapable as the set of train tracks over which a railroad must pass.

A railroad, like a river, is a favoured metaphor for the course of one's life. Interestingly, the first challenge that Dylan delivered to the A-Unit camera crew of *"Renaldo And Clara"* when they began shooting was: *"Did you get any rivers? We're gonna need lots of rivers. And trains. Did you get any trains?"* (Shepard 23).

* * *

In his studies with Raeben, Dylan apparently sought to escape a kind of psychic confinement resulting from an acute awareness of the passage of time and a loss of control over the events in his life. In order to do that, to escape the oppressive feeling of having the course of one's life set in advance like railroad tracks, it would be necessary to rise above his then-present mental condition. To continue the railroad metaphor, only with a new perspective could one properly experience both the immediate passing view (as if from the railroad car window) and the outlined path of whole journey (as if viewing the tracks from high up in space).

The enlightened viewpoint urged by Raeben seemed to involve the transfiguration of the individual into a kind of archetype, seeing aspects of oneself like the anthropologist Joseph Campbell or the poet Robert Graves might, in terms of universal myths. The result of this kind of quasi-aesthetic, archetypical perception of one's own life is, apparently, to experience life in its immediacy <u>and</u> in its significance. Such an experience would be (i) without deleterious ego, (ii) unmediated by trivial distractions, and (iii) without unproductive and irrelevant memories that are "dead". Dylan's communication of this experience is what *"Renaldo And Clara"* was trying to achieve.

In his film, Dylan criticized those characters who are weighted down by "death" (a word he seemed to use metaphorically to include burdensome memories and attitudes that are "anti-life"). For instance, the character *"Sara Dylan"* (played by Ronee Blakely) is undone by her bickering with Ramon (played by the guitarist Steven Soles), whom the director later identified as her dead lover (G 120). Similarly, the Woman in White (played by Joan Baez) is, in Dylan's words, a *"ghost of Death"*, a clinging sign of lifelessness (G 114). As Renaldo achieves spiritual progress, she becomes a part of Renaldo's past.

Dylan spoke of the superior experience of life as being one of *"Actuality"* (G 109). The role of Clara (played by Bob's wife) represented the capacity to experience that Actuality. A key to understanding Bob's meaning may be found in the word "clarity". It comes from the Latin root "clarus", meaning bright or clear, which is also the origin of the name "Clara". Dylan once made the connection almost explicit: *"Clara"*, he said, *"is supposedly the clear understanding of the future which doesn't exist"* (Hughes). With the entire phrase, Dylan may have meant that, in a world of archetypes, our normal concept of "the future" doesn't apply. All time simply exists all at once. Dylan used the clarity concept again when he said that his film was about Renaldo (who began as mere "actuality" with a small "a") and then transcended himself *"to a higher Actuality and Clarity"* (G 110). With Clarity/Clara, Renaldo can reach a higher plane.

* * *

According to Dylan, the superior level of reality is like a dream. *"I live in my dreams"*, he once said. *"I don't really live in the actual world"*. His film, he then added, *"concerns itself with the depth of the dream – the dream as seen in the mirror"* (Cott I 181). This quality of being dream-like is not intended to mean "dreamy" (e.g., vague or fantastic); it is, rather, to be understood as the conscious product of the wilful dreamer. Dylan's description of his lessons with Raeben

211

make particular sense in this context: At the time, he was learning *"to do consciously what* [he] *used to be able to do unconsciously"* (Cott II 358).

Ordinarily, we view dreams as an inferior mode of perception, the last resort of the powerless and deprived. But Dylan views the dream-exercise as a kind of discipline, like meditation, that allows for the distillation of experience and for self-realization. It is an exercise that conjures up an individual's life almost like God creating the universe. When Dylan analogized his "dreaming" to the use of mirrors, he meant it as a way of discovering selfhood. In this way, the dreamer exists before the person: Renaldo the dreamer, said Dylan, *"may not even have a soul. He may in actuality be Time itself"* (G 111). Time itself is the precondition for all creation and that which exists all at once everywhere.

Dylan has constantly drawn a distinction between a "dream", which is genuine, and a "fantasy", which is simply made up. Anyone, said Dylan, can make things up or fantasize. Dylan views himself instead as a privileged dreamer and a medium through whom visions that are real are transmitted:

"A dream has more substance than a fantasy . . . You have to have seen something or have heard something for you to dream it . . . It's happened, it's been said, I've heard it: I have proof of it. I'm a messenger. I get it. It comes to me so I give it back in my particular style" (Flanagan 94).

In the end, Dylan's dreaming provides for an escape from chains; like flowers, "chains" is used frequently in his lyrics. In a literal sense, chains result in confinement for those who wear them, like a criminal or a slave. In direct opposition to a chained figure, Clara, said Dylan, represents freedom; to her, the entire world is in chains, *"bondage to themselves, slaves to their ego"* (G 115). In *"Renaldo And Clara"*, Dylan conceived of chains in this universal sense and hoped others could relate to his story. As he explained to Ginsberg, *"Renaldo is you, struggling within yourself, with the knowledge that you're locked within the chains of your own being"* (110).

* * *

In a dense summation of Renaldo and his spiritual odyssey, Dylan explained, *"You can almost say that he dies in order to look at time and by strength of will can return to the same body"* (Rosenbaum 132). Dylan also said that the whole film was a dream, Bob Dylan's dream, and that the exhausted performer who appears in the next-to-last scene lying spread-eagled on his dressing room floor is the person who is dreaming the dream (G 110). In this regard, Dylan's lead character is much like the medieval knight Rinaldo, the dreamer whose story of enchantment and escape is told in a painting that hangs in Chicago.

The final scene of *"Renaldo And Clara"* is of a night-club performer, jauntily singing *"In a world that no one understands/'Tis the morning of my life"*. In a sense, the last song is also a beginning (the *"morning"*), the beginning of the dream. By completing the film and returning to its beginning, Dylan realized his dream, which was meant to be his "triumph over time".

V. Where *"Renaldo And Clara"* Fits

"Renaldo And Clara" occupies a critical point in Dylan's biography, standing as it does at a crossroads between his marriage and his conversion to Christianity. It is largely about Dylan seeking to escape from a chain of events that recently had been dragging him down. Dylan's friend and collaborator, Howard Alk, gave as revealing a description of Dylan's condition as anyone, although of course he attributes the state of mind to Renaldo:

"Renaldo's caught in a period of alienation from himself – caught up in the mess of not being able to compete with his other self, the man he is working to become in order to survive the hellhole he's found himself in . . . He's trying to make it into the future, but he can't do that unless he leaves the unimaginable past behind" (G 117-18).

"Renaldo And Clara" also represents a kind of crossroads in cultural history, standing astride the free-form "Beat" prose of the 1950s and 60s and the "post-modernist" movement of the 1970s and beyond. On the one hand, the filming was spontaneous, improvisational and thus Beat-like. The Beat movement's founder, Jack Kerouac, specifically extolled the virtues of "spontaneous prose", and Dylan and Ginsberg visited Kerouac's grave in the film. In another lengthy scene, Ginsberg read from his poem *'Kaddish'*, and he also was cast in the role of "the Father".

Besides its Beat components, the film also reflects more recent trends; Dylan himself called it a *"post-existentialist movie"* (Cott I 172). The movie clearly contains elements of the so-called post-modernist movement, as initially defined by Susan Sontag in her book *"Against Interpretation"* (1966). That movement consisted largely of exploding categories of genre and thus defying the audience's expectations, eliminating narrative structure and forcing the critics to focus on the self-conscious acts of the artwork's creator. *"Renaldo And Clara"* is certainly all of that, and more. It is an important but often forgotten chapter in Dylan's evolution that deserves more thoughtful consideration than it has been given.

List of Works Cited

Coe, Richard N. *"The Vision of Jean Genet"*. New York: *Grove*, 1968.

Cott, Jonathan. *'Bob Dylan'*, *Rolling Stone* interview 26 Jan. 1978, reptd. in Cott, Jonathan *"Visions and Voices"*. New York: *Doubleday*, 1987, 167-96 (Cott I).

Cott, Jonathan. *'Bob Dylan'*, *Rolling Stone* interview 17 Sept. 1978, reptd. in Herbst, Peter, ed. *"The Rolling Stone Interviews: Talking with the Legends of Rock and Roll"* (1967-1980). New York: *St. Martins*, 1981, 354-63 (Cott II).

Flanagan, Bill. *"Written in My Soul: Rock's Great Songwriters Talk About Creating Their Music"*. New York: *Contemporary*, 1986.

Ginsberg, Allen. *'Bob Dylan & Renaldo & Clara'* in John Bauldie ed. *"Wanted Man: In Search of Bob Dylan"*. New York: *Carol-Citadel*, 1990, 104-24 (G).

213

Hughes, Karen. *'The Karen Hughes Interview'* 1 Apr. 1978, reptd. in *"What Was It You Wanted No. 3"*. , n.d., n.p.

Kael, Pauline. *'The Calgary Gig'*. *The New Yorker* 13 Feb. 1978, reptd. Thomson, Elizabeth and Gutman, David eds. *"The Dylan Companion"*. New York: *Bantam-Delta*, 1990, 224-230.

Shelton, Robert. *"No Direction Home: The Life and Music of Bob Dylan"*. New York: *Random House-Ballantine*, 1986.

Shepard, Sam. *"Rolling Thunder Logbook"*. New York: *Penguin*, 1978.

Sloman, Larry. *"On the Road with Bob Dylan: Rolling with the Thunder"*. New York: *Bantam*, 1978.

Rosenbaum, Ron. *'The Playboy Interview'* Playboy Mar. 1978, reptd. in *"Younger Than That Now"*. New York: *Avalon-Thunder's Mouth*, 2004, 109-60.

Williams, Paul. *"What Happened?"*. Glen Ellen, CA: *Entwhistle*, 1979.

Published in *ISIS* issue #118, December 2004

Bob Dylan 1975

Bob Dylan 1978

Stories in the Press

On Sunday April 9, 1995, Alan Rimmer of the *Sunday Mirror* reported of Bob Dylan's plight to find a bed after his concert at Manchester's Apollo Theatre. The anecdotal evidence was that Dylan declined to sleep in the hotel that had been booked for him and demanded to be taken elsewhere. An eyewitness, who had followed him from his concert, said, *"It was about 2am and he was obviously very tired. He was being bundled about wrapped in a blanket by his bodyguards"*. Dylan was taken to the Crown Plaza Holiday Inn, but was informed by the desk clerk that the Presidential Suite was already occupied by British television show host Michael Barrymore. The story is that Dylan then asked if Barrymore would vacate the suite, which lead to a confrontation and Dylan and his people were eventually asked to leave. The eye witness reported, *"He looked a sad figure standing outside in his blanket waiting for his tour bus"*. Dylan then demanded that the bus leave the town so that a hotel could be found elsewhere. After a fruitless journey to Preston the bus returned to Manchester and parked outside the original hotel. Dylan, however, still refused to go in to the hotel and food was brought out for him to eat on the bus. The following day, the *Sunday Mirror* journalist tried to talk about the incident with Dylan but was told by one of his entourage, *"Mr Dylan never talks to anyone . . . not even me"*.

This item seems a little strange to me, especially as the *Sunday Mirror's* *"eyewitness"* was able to report about two Manchester hotels, a trip to Preston, and still managed to be with Dylan and co when they arrived back at the starting point.

Ian Woodward remarked on this story in *The Wicked Messenger* #3108 in *ISIS* and followed-up with this amusing item from the same tour.

"When . . . someone telephoned the North West Castle Hotel in Stranraer to seek confirmation of Dylan staying there on April 10, 1995; there was a delay while the hotel staff member checked, the reply was, 'I'm sorry but I can't comment on that'". I guess we'll take that as a "yes".

Printed in issue #60 of *ISIS* May 1995
Originally published in *Sunday Mirror*

The P–problem with *"John Wesley Harding"* (part one)

When the series of fifteen SACDs were released last year (2003), *ICE* magazine received a number of queries about the mix on *"John Wesley Harding"*. *ICE* asked SACD producer, Steve Berkowitz, to comment:

"That album was so hard to do, the toughest one. You have no idea. They can complain all they like about the mix but we didn't remix it. It's the original two-track mix but we mastered it about six different ways . . . it's a very troublesome

tape. I'm not criticising Bob Johnston in any way but it's not like there was a lot of production on the recording of "John Wesley Harding". It was not recorded optimally. It has some real technical problems, so they compensated in the final mastering by compressing the top and the bottom tremendously. They completely rolled the bass out of the mix. There's almost no bass on it! And they squashed the whole top of it too, to get rid of the p's and the ticks and the pops at the front of his mouth. The reason why the record is so mellow is because it's squashed! So we un-squashed it, tried to open it up into what the musicians actually played. The original bass is big and growly . . . it sounds like John Entwhistle! It's like a real rock band . . . it's not quite 'Boris The Spider' but it's very aggressive. It's nothing like what the mellow record sounds like. That's because they put a huge filter on the bottom. They notched out a whole bunch of it. And what the record sounds like, through history, feels appropriate. However, there's a lot of nuance of the playing, and the ensemble playing and Bob's delivery, that has never been heard as clearly as it is now".

Berkowitz also described *"John Wesley Harding"* as the most *"revelatory"* of the fifteen SACDs so far, compared with its LP version. Because the LP master tape was doctored so much and because the SACD presents the master tape without the original doctoring, the difference is more noticeable.

The P–problem with *"John Wesley Harding"* (part two)

Getting back to those popping P's on *"John Wesley Harding"*, an *ICE* reader cited *'The Ballad Of Frankie Lee And Judas Priest'*:

"At 0:16, the p-pop on the first "priest" distorts the track and makes my speakers jump. Two other p-pops are really noticeable in the first minute of the song. My vinyl version does not have the same concern".

Legacy's Berkowitz responded: *"If you go back to your original album, you'll hear that they cut the beginning of the letter off! Listen to the record – they literally sliced a whole bunch of those P's off with a razor blade. The original tape is . . . up and down in levels and all those P's . . . it's so bad. So Mark Wilder* (who engineered the SACD reissue) *worked for days on those P's . . . I think he had to deal with and de-pop about 120 times on that album.*

It's as if they recorded the whole thing without a windscreen – at all. It was brutal!" Asked why the track wasn't recorded again, Berkowitz added, *"I'm not sure, in those days, how much Dylan had to do with the mix and the mastering. One of the philosophies of the '60s was – artists would come in and play. And record production was done by other people".*

The Wicked Messenger #s 5467 and 5488 printed in issue #114 of *ISIS* April 2004 Originally published in *ICE*

1978 And All That

Derek Barker

Like many other Dylan enthusiasts living outside of America, my first chance to see Bob Dylan live in concert did not arrive until June 1978. At the time, I liked the man's music and even owned a few of his albums, but in reality, Bob Dylan ranked as little more than a top class artist that I dearly wanted to see perform live. I reasoned that the last night would probably be the best performance of his Earls Court residency, so I decided I would try to get tickets for June 20. A friend spent the night outside the designated Birmingham box office (*Cyclops Sounds*) and managed to get front row seats! Since that June evening 25 years (or for me half a lifetime) ago, the man and his music have consumed much of my life, and it is fitting therefore, that a quarter-century on, we should be devoting a considerable chunk of this book to a behind the scenes look at that momentous tour; a tour that on Tuesday, June 20, 1978 changed my life, and by the close of 1978 changed the life of Bob Dylan also.

It's amazing how little has been written about the 1978 world tour. Excluding the Isle of Wight Festival, this was the first time Dylan had played concerts outside of the USA for twelve years and this tour would therefore have been the first chance anyone now under the age of 45 (and not able to travel to the USA) would have had to see Dylan perform live. Maybe it was due to the fact that Europe had been starved of Dylan for so long, but while the European audiences and press lapped up the '78 shows, our American counterparts, who had been graced with a nationwide tour in 1974 and further regional shows in '75 and '76, were decidedly less enthusiastic for Dylan. A fact that resulted in seats remaining unsold for some of the fall/winter US shows.

Although *"Street Legal"* reached a respectable number eleven on the US album chart, it nevertheless ended a run of three successive number ones, and while the two previous albums, *"Desire"* and *"Blood On The Tracks"*, have since gone on to achieve Multi Platinum status, after more than 25 years, sales of *"Street Legal"* remain below the one million mark. We must therefore conclude that the lukewarm reception afforded to the album at the time of its release continues to this day. The album's songs, are in fact, quite wonderful; only the recording method and production techniques are abysmal. The single from the album, *'Baby Stop Crying'*, which entered into the Top Ten in most European counties, failed even to break into the US *Billboard* Hot 100. It appears that Dylan was no longer the artist that the public and press expected or wanted him to be, least ways in the USA.

218

Background to 1978 World Tour

Dylan had considered continuing to tour after the 1976 Rolling Thunder Revue ended. It transpired, however, that after a few months respite he would spend much of the next year editing the 100 hours of film footage shot on the 1975 leg of that tour into the three-hour-and-fifty-two minute movie *'Renaldo and Clara'*.

Dylan would end up investing in the region of $1.25 million of his own money into the movie, while at the same time the remodelling (a better word would probably be rebuilding) of his Point Dume house, was totally out of control.

What had started out as an extension to add just one extra bedroom to what was to become the new Dylan family home (which was located on the Point Dume Peninsula, overlooking the Pacific Ocean about ten miles north of Malibu Beach, California), began to take on a life of its own in which only one wall of the original house was left standing, and that only remained to satisfy Californian building regulations.[1]

The work on the 'new' house, which had started in 1973, had taken three years to complete and according to friends had put a great deal of strain on the couple's already deteriorating relationship. The finished house, which Bob called his *"own fantasy"*, contained around twenty rooms including a Great Room. This room, with its spectacular vaulted ceiling, was apparently the bane of architect David Towbin's life, because plans for the room, which Dylan had informed Towbin should be large enough to *"ride a horse through"*, were constantly being changed by Dylan. So-much-so, the building contractor resigned on more than one occasion and had to be persuaded by Towbin to return to work. In the end, the cost of remodelling the Dylans' new home, complete with its copper onion dome (a homage to his Russian lineage?) was said to be in the region of $2.25 million.[1a]

Dylan said of the house; *"It's just a place to live for now. The copper dome is just so I can recognize it when I come home"*.

It seemed that the Point Dume property was scarcely finished when Bob and Sara split up. Sara now wanted a divorce, and to that end, she contacted top Californian divorce lawyer Marvin M. Mitchelson.

Mitchelson, who had made his name representing Lee Marvin's girlfriend in her groundbreaking palimony lawsuit, (It was Mitchelson who coined the term *'palimony'*) met with Sara and agreed to represent her.

Under Californian State law, Sara was entitled to half the Dylan "community property" acquired during their marriage (November 22, 1965 – June 29, 1977). This included houses and land in five US states, cash, and most valuable of all, half of Bob Dylan's music rights; rights that spanned the albums from *"Blonde On Blonde"* through to *"Desire"*.

Mitchelson: *"Those musical rights were enormous. That was the real value"*.[2a] Mitchelson's biggest task was to compile a list of the songs Dylan had written and recorded between 1965 and 1977. *"It went on for pages and pages"*, he says, *"I became sort of a fan* [because] *I realized how good Bob was"*. Music rights boosted Bob's notional wealth to approximately $60 million. Because Bob wanted to keep the Point Dume mansion, real estate was traded against cash and share rose to $36 million. If Bob ever sold his music catalogue, Sara would be entitled to a further payout. All the time he retained ownership, she would share in the royalties. *"They keep coming in, year after year"*, says Mitchelson, *"We're talking about millions"*.[2b]

During his time in Woodstock, Dylan had become a staunch family man and there is little doubt that separation from Sara and the children meant far more to him than just money. A viably shaken Dylan told Robert Shelton: *"No one in my family gets divorced"*, and that he *"figured it would last forever"*.[3&4]

Quite soon after the divorce, and probably as some sort of release, Dylan began writing a batch of new songs. (this was before he started work on the songs that became *"Street Legal"*). In May 1978, he told Robert Hilburn about those the songs:

"I had some songs last year I didn't record. They dealt with that period as I was going through it. For relief, I wrote the tunes. I thought they were great. Some people around town heard them. I played them for some friends".

Dylan band member Steven Soles says Dylan came to his apartment one afternoon in 1977 and played him and T-Bone Burnett ten or twelve *". . . Very dark, very intense"* songs. Soles could only recall one title, *'I'm Cold'*.

Writing those songs was clearly an outlet for Dylan's frustration. However, he soon decided that his best release would be to go and play music.

"I was being thrown out of my house. I was under a lot of pressure, so I figured I better get busy working".[5]

He told Jonathan Cott: *"I have to get back to playing music because unless I do, I don't really feel alive . . . I have to play in front of the people in order just to keep going"*.[8]

But first, he would need a manager. Enter Jerry Weintraub.

Sometime in late April or early May 1977 Dylan signed up Jerry Weintraub as his business manager. He had been without proper management since the unofficial parting of the ways with Albert Grossman some seven years earlier. Dylan, who had long since decided that he would never again be 'part-owned' by anyone, used Weintraub as his personal manager and tour promoter. Weintraub's sphere of activity therefore, did not cover Dylan's music publishing companies; those affairs were handled by Dylan's own office, which he had set up during the summer of 1968. Naomi Saltzman (formerly of *Trio Concerts*, a Grossman-owned company) ran the office, which operated out of Manhattan. In early May 1977 Weintraub made an 'official' statement that said Bob Dylan had signed with his company for *"personal legal representation"*.

Dylan later said of his involvement with Weintraub:

"At the time I got Jerry to manage me, I almost didn't have a friend in the world".

By the mid-seventies, Weintraub, who had founded *Management III* in 1965 with two partners and just three clients, was well established both as a manager and as a leading concert promoter. His landmark successes had been the staging of Elvis Presley's comeback concert, since which time his reputation had grown and led to the formation of *Concerts West*, a company that handled shows for such artists as Presley, Sinatra, Judy Garland, Led Zeppelin, Jimi Hendrix, Beach Boys and Neil Diamond, whom Weintraub also managed.

According to Robert Shelton, Weintraub, who once boasted that he worked the 'phones the way Jimmy Page worked the guitar, was known for non-interference with his clients and while he was very much involved in the staging of Dylan's mammoth 1978 world tour (and even accompanied the troupe on the Japanese leg), he was becoming more involved in producing movies. He had apparently smoked a joint with Robert Altman who persuaded him he could be a film producer. The movie *"Nashville"* (1975) followed and Weintraub never looked back. Much of the day-to-day work at the management company was therefore handled by ex-rock-station radio DJ Dick Curtis who Weintraub had employed to oversee operations at his new Beverly Hills office.

Rundown

In September 1977 Dylan took a five-year lease on rehearsal space at 2219 Main Street, Santa Monica. The facility, which later became known as Rundown Studio, would play an important role for Dylan for rehearsals and, to a lesser extent, recording. This studio was of course used to record the album *"Street Legal"*. Rather than return every night to an empty house, and for the sake of convenience, Dylan had one of the building's offices converted into a bedroom and regularly slept and eat at Rundown, much of his time there was spent on the final editing of *"Renaldo and Clara"*, working on songs for his new album and interviewing and rehearsing what would become his 1978 world tour band.

My Head tells me it's Time to make a Change

One of the reasons Dylan decided not to continue with touring after the Rolling Thunder Revue was probably that he had realised that the Revue had run its course. In direct contrast to the relaxed atmosphere of 1975, the second leg of that tour had been somewhat strained. It was time to make a change. Once again, Bob Dylan must reinvent himself, but how?

Bob Dylan: *"When your environment changes, you change. You've got to go on, and you find new friends. Turn around one day and you're on a different stage, with a new set of characters"*.

Weintraub confirmed that Dylan was looking for *"something different . . . A different direction"*, and that he had been to see Neil Diamond in concert and that some of his '78 "stage show" was based around what he had seen at that concert.

Weintraub said: *"I think Bob felt that he was in danger of being stuck inside the sixties".*[9]

Paul Williams: *"This idea – Bob Dylan marketing himself like a Las Vegas crooner, packaged music and showmanship for the mentally middle-aged – is so repellent to the average Dylan fan that the public backlash that resulted is not surprising".*[10]

By the time the tour reached the US, the American press, now tired of the *"Alimony Tour"* tag, were calling this the *"Vegas Tour"*. Even *Rolling Stone* magazine, usually an avid champion of Dylan's work, ran the headline *"Dylan Going Vegas"* and noted his debt to Neil Diamond. At the time, much of the responsibility (or should that be *'blame'*?) for the change in Dylan's approach to touring was heaped at Weintraub's door, but are we to believe that Dylan's new management was the sole instigator of this change in style and direction?

Diamond and Rust

Many Dylan enthusiasts may find it difficult to accept as true the premise that Dylan was 'borrowing' from Diamond's live show. However, the first thing that doubters need to understand is just how big Neil Diamond was at that time. During the eighteen months from June 1976 to the end of '77 he had three 'hit' albums: *"Beautiful Noise"*, which went gold on the week of its release and quickly gained platinum status; *"Love At The Greek"*, which went gold after just two weeks and qualified as platinum within six months, and *"I'm Glad You're Here With Me Tonight"*, which went gold on its release and platinum within a month. Also in January 1978, *Columbia* awarded Diamond a *"Crystal Globe"* for world sales in excess of 5,000,000 albums.

Concert promoter Robert Paterson described Diamond's 1976 Australasian tour as: *"The biggest ever, in box-office terms, outside the United States . . . It is strange that, when we present Diamond in Australia, we have to put him on in the big open-air arenas. Yet if we were to present Dylan there, it would have to be indoors!"* The article, which appeared in the December 13, issue of *New Musical Express*, went on to say that Diamond had now outsold the Beatles in Australia and that in a recent survey, conducted to discover which artist the Australian public would most like to see perform, a staggering 98% opted for Neil Diamond! Closer to home (Bob's home that is) Neil Diamond's face was everywhere:

"They [Columbia] *treated him like royalty, they even put up billboards* [of Diamond] *on Sunset Boulevard that Bob had to look at every time he drove out to see friends in the Hills . . . He decided he should investigate".*[11]

As stated previously, Bob went to see Diamond in concert (possibly in August 1976). In his biography of Bob Dylan, Bob Spitz speculated on what might have gone through Dylan's mind as he watched that concert:

"As Bob Dylan sat in the stylishly dressed audience, it became apparent that Neil Diamond and he had more than a record company in common. They were around the same age (both artists were born in 1941) *and build. Both men had started out among New York's tune vendors, working with acoustic guitars and writing songs that became famous in the hands of more commercial groups . . . A couple of Jewish boys who rose to conquer the stage".*[11a]

By the time Dylan's 1978 tour went on the road, the comparison with Neil Diamond's 'shows' was quite startling. Dylan's big band set-up very much echoed the configuration of musicians that Diamond had used on his transitional album *"Beautiful Noise"*, which featured tenor sax and trumpet, keyboard, a separate percussionist (as well as a drummer) and three female backing vocalists.

Released in July 1976, the songs that made up *"Beautiful Noise"* fit together as a semi-autobiographical concept album of the singers rise to fame, and its personal cost, as well as a memoir of New York's Tin Pan Alley. The track *'Signs'* is evidence of Neil Diamond's interest in all things cosmic, while the album's central theme is best captured in a song titled *'Street Life'*. Would it be pushing coincidence too far to suggest that this track might have influenced Dylan in the choice of the title for his next album, *"Street Legal"*?

A further possible connection is that *"Beautiful Noise"* and Diamond's 1977 live double album, *"Love At The Greek"*, were produced by Robbie Robertson who had recently taken up residence not too far from the Dylan home and who was a regular visitor there.

As preparations for the Dylan tour began to take shape, Patrick Stansfield, who had previously worked with Neil Diamond, was appointed as the head of production. Dylan's people even used the same company that supplied the sound system that Diamond was then using, and the same designer was now dressing both men!

Rob Stoner: *"He had in mind to do something like Elvis Presley, I think. The size band and the uniforms. [But] he wasn't very sure about it, which is why he opened way out of town. I mean, we didn't go any place close to Europe or England or America [for] forever, man . . . and I don't blame him. I think he knew, subconsciously, he was making a big mistake".*[12]

Dylan, and all of his tour musicians, wore "costumes" that were designed for the Dylan tour by *"Spoony"* Bill Whitten out of his LA based *Workroom 27* studio. Whitten had begun designing stage wear for Neil Diamond in 1970 and he continues to do so to this day.

Clearly, some of the above comparisons would come about simply because both artists were now from the same management stable. (In the same way that factions of the press had compared Dylan's '78 tour to Elvis' comeback because the two artists had Jerry Weintraub as a common denominator.) It does seem, however, that Dylan himself was the instigator of many of these parallels with Diamond. If so, he was going against his own intuition. Dylan told Ron Rosenbaum in a 1978 interview:

". . . If you try to be anyone but yourself, you will fail; if you are not true to your own heart, you will fail".[13]

Other factors might have had an influence on Dylan around that time. In 1976/'77, reggae-mania boomed in the States and Bob Marley and The Wailers were named by *Rolling Stone* Magazine as *"Band of the Year"*) Dylan had become a big fan both of reggae music and of its primary force, Bob Marley. Marley had been using female backing singers in the shape of *"I–Three"* since 1973.

If, however, (as he had told Rosenbaum) Dylan was so aware that he had to be true to himself, then why was he following in the footsteps of Diamond, Presley, Marley or anyone?

The probable answer is that with Sara and the children, lawyers, hassles with *"Renaldo and Clara"*, and some concerns over money all strangling his mind, a rather hapless Dylan just wanted to get back to the one thing that had always remained constant in his life, playing music, and one thing he knew for sure was that he couldn't do another Rolling Thunder.

What we can deduce from all of this, is that here we have a man frantically searching for a new direction, both in his music and in his personal life. Those changes would of course take a giant leap forward when Dylan began to find Jesus during the final leg of this tour.

Press accusations that Dylan had embarked on this mammoth tour purely for the money is nothing short of farcical.

"I've got a few debts to pay off", Dylan told *Los Angeles Times* candidly: *"I had a couple of bad years. I put a lot of money into the movie, built a big house . . . and there's the divorce. It costs a lot to get divorced in California".*[2c]

When asked by Philippe Adler if he was touring for the money, Dylan replied:

"No. Of course I need the money and I know how to spend it, but basically it's because I wanted to do the only thing I've ever known how to do, sing and play. I'm a musician that's all".[5a]

Dylan told British music paper *Melody Maker*:

"I earn everything I make. I'm not getting nothing for nothing".[6]

Sure, Dylan may have needed to recoup some of his recent losses, but as was the case in 1966, if the only motive for playing live was money, then he certainly could have put a far more cost effective tour on the road!

The 115-date world tour played in front of almost two million people and grossed in excess of $20 million (about half the amount that Dylan had recently lost), but expenses were also high. Sky high.

The band that departed Los Angeles for Japan consisted of:

Bob Dylan – rhythm guitar, harmonica, vocals
Billy Cross – lead guitar
Ian Wallace – drums
Alan Pasqua – keyboards
Rob Stones – bass, vocals
Steven Soles – acoustic rhythm guitar, vocals
David Mansfield – pedal steel, violin, mandolin, guitar, dobro
Steve Douglas – saxophone, flute, recorder
Bobbye Hall – percussion

Helena Springs – vocals
Jo Ann Harris – vocals
Debi Dye – vocals

Eight players and three female backing singers was, and still is, the biggest band that Bob Dylan has ever put together. The tour, which flew into Tokyo on February 16th in a leased BAC-III jet that had two suites, a bedroom for Dylan and a fully stocked bar for the large entourage, was incredibly lavish. A number of the musicians had very good pedigrees; Steve Douglas had been a key member of the *'Wrecking Crew'*, a group of session musicians who worked with producer Phil Spector at *Goldstar Studios* in Los Angeles. He had played on countless sessions, which saw him working with the likes of John Lennon, the Beach Boys and Elvis Presley. Douglas had also been a member of Elvis Presley's road band in the early seventies.[7]

Dylan is said to have paid percussionist Bobbye Hall $2,500 a week to compensate her for session work she would have to forego while on tour with him. A *Motown* veteran, Hall had worked on sessions for Marvin Gaye, Stevie Wonder, The Temptations and Diana Ross, but having worked also with the Doobie Brothers, Doors, Jefferson Airplane, Janis Joplin, Carole King, Lynyrd Skynyrd and Joni Mitchell, she was no slouch in the rock genre either.

The musicians and their 44-strong back-up travelled in style, stayed in the best hotels, and until the tour arrived back in the USA for the final leg, which began on September 15th in Augusta, Maine, no expense was spared. If this tour had been devised by Dylan as a money-making scheme, he had got it very wrong!

Harvey Goldsmith

Although Harvey Goldsmith helped in promoting Bob Dylan's 1981 and 1984 tours of Britain, he is perhaps better known for arranging more auspicious one-off extravaganzas like the 1996 star studded *'Masters of Music Concert'* for the Prince's Trust (the first rock event to be staged at Hyde Park for twenty years), or for helping to turn Bob Geldof's pipedream into the fundraising miracle that was *'Live Aid'*.

Goldsmith, who is credited as one of the producers of *"The Bob Dylan 30th Anniversary Concert"* held in 1992 at Madison Square Garden, is, however, probably best known by British Dylan fans as the man who brought Bob Dylan back to Britain in 1978 after a twelve-year absence – nine years if you count Dylan's festival appearance on the Isle of Wight.

Harvey Goldsmith had told Robert Shelton that Dylan had only wanted to play *"three or four big outdoor stadiums . . . in England, France, Germany and maybe something in Scandinavia"*.

Shelton: *"It was Harvey who talked [Dylan] into six nights at Earls Court and then advance ticket sales were so good that he got Dylan to agree to the festival thing at Blackbushe, for which Harvey paid all the conversion money. But the Earls Court audience's were real good and Dylan was obviously pleased that he went along with Harvey's suggestions"*.[14]

If, however, we are to believe the brief story that was printed in the British newspaper the *Sunday Mirror* in June 1978, it was not Harvey Goldsmith that we should thank for Dylan's visit to Britain, but a lady by the name of Tamara Rand!

The Fortune-Telling Lady

Although she is not mentioned in any of the biographies about Bob Dylan, the name Tamara Rand does appear in the November 1977 Ron Rosenbaum Interview with Dylan, and also in the aforementioned British 'red top', the *Mirror*.

This is what Ron Rosenbaum had to say about Rand in the introduction to his original interview (this preamble is cut from all of the reprints that I have seen of this interview and is therefore not widely circulated.

"Late one afternoon, Dylan began telling me about Tamara Rand, an L.A. psychic reader he'd been seeing, because 'when the world falls on your head', he said, 'you need someone who can tell you how to crawl out, which way to take'. I presumed he was referring obliquely to the collapse of his 12-year marriage to Sara Dylan. (Since the child-custody battle was in progress as we talked, Dylan's lawyer refused to permit him to address that subject directly.) Dylan seemed concerned that I understand that Tamara was no con artist, that she had genuine psychic abilities".[13a]

In the interview itself, Dylan had this to say about Rand:

"There's this lady in L.A. I respect a lot who reads palms. Her name's Tamara Rand. She's for real; she's not a gypsy fortune-teller. But she's accurate! She'll take a look at your hand and tell you things you feel but don't really understand about where you're heading, what the future looks like. She's a surprisingly hopeful person".[13b]

According to the *Mirror*, *"Many top stars go to the beautiful Tamara for around £75 an hour".*[15]

In the same piece, Rand is quoted as saying: *"I have a kind of doctor-patient relationship with Dylan"*, and that, *"Bob sees me as a solid, stable person with solid values of right and wrong"*.

"I hear things when I touch his hand. He has the hand of an inventor, but his vehicle is words. He is a graphic artist with words. He has the hands of a healer, so his words – his message – are healing in sprit".

Rand said that Dylan came to her when he knew a divorce was inevitable and that he would marry again, *"but not yet"*. She also said that Dylan, *"Will be with us for a very long time"*. The *Mirror* also stated that Dylan kept in constant contact with Rand by phone *"if he's out of town or abroad"*, and that *"he consulted her before he signed his contract to appear at Earls Court"*! Dylan is quoted as saying: *"You need someone who can tell you which way to take".*[15a]

It's not entirely clear when Dylan started consulting with Rand, but a comment she made to the *Mirror* in the June '78 piece stated that she had met him *"just over a year ago"*. This dating would therefore coincide with Dylan's split from his wife Sara (February 1977) and his divorce (June '77). His estrangement from Sara would have presented him with another problem, because Sara was not only his wife and a mother to his children, but according to those close to the couple, she was also Bob's astrologer and psychic guide. Al Aronowitz (a confidant of Dylan's from the sixties) had told me on several occasions that Bob depended greatly on Sara's advice; *"advice that often came through the cards"*.

Aronowitz: *"In the years following his motorcycle accident . . . More and more, he depended on her* [Sara's] *advice as if she were his astrologer, his oracle, his seer, psychic guide. He would rely on her to tell him the best hour and the best day to travel".*[16]

It is impossible to say for sure exactly when Dylan's fascination with fortune-telling and the cards began, but as far back as early 1963 he was singing:

Well, I've spent my time with the fortune-telling kind
Following them fairgrounds a-callin'.

'Dusty Old Fairgrounds' 1963.

Earlier still, while performing in the clubs around Greenwich Village, Dylan would sing a song called *'West Texas'* that contained the lines:

Get me a fortune-telling woman,
One that's gonna read my mind.

'West Texas' (trad).

It seems that a couple of years later Dylan found his *"fortune-telling woman"* in the shape of Sara Lownds.

Dylan had met Sara, who was gifted in psychic reading, at the end of 1964, and there is little doubt that she reinforced beliefs that were already deeply held by him. Dylan would later use playing card imagery, in the form of an incomplete deck of cards, to illustrate that Sara had some imperfections.

> *With your sheets like metal and your belt like lace*
> *And your deck of cards missing the jack and the ace.*
> 'Sad-eyed Lady Of The Lowlands' 1966.

Dylan's use of playing cards (Tarot cards were originally designed to be used for playing games) can be found throughout his work.[17]

Often used as a symbol of death, or of great change, Dylan's first usage of the cards came as early as the writing of *'Ramblin' Gamblin' Willie'* (December 1961 or January '62), a song which, because of Willie's fate, was also known as *'Gamblin' Willie's Dead Man's Hand'*. The fatality in Dylan's song mirrored the death, in 1876, of gambler, sheriff and gunfighter James Butler Hickok, also known as *"Wild Bill"*. Hickok was shot through the back of the head by saloon bum, Jack McCall, at the Number Ten Saloon in Deadwood, South Dakota, while paying poker. Legend has it that Hickok was holding two pair: black aces and eights, a hand known ever since as the *"dead man's hand"*.

When Dylan performed this song for Cynthia Gooding in early spring 1962, he said:

"I can't read cards. I really believe in palm reading, but for a bunch of personal things . . . personal experiences. I don't believe too much in the cards. I like to think I don't believe too much in the cards, anyhow".[18]

It was during the middle to late 1970s that Tarot card imagery came to the fore in Dylan's work and a number of examples are to be found on Dylan's album *"Blood On The Tracks"* (January 1975). The subsequent album, *"Desire"*, released in January 1976, even had Tarot cards in evidence on the sleeve. The most explicit use of Tarot card imagery, however, is to be found on Dylan's 1978 album *"Street Legal"*, which is littered with references to the Tarot. Exactly how much of this album was influenced by his dealings with Tamara Rand, or indeed the woman he was now living with, Faridi Mcfree, will probably never be known. What we do know, however, is that just prior to the writing of those songs Dylan was in regular contact with Rand. Dylan either talked on the telephone with Tamara, or visited her in person at the *Rand Institute*, an office on upmarket Sienega Boulevard in Los Angeles, from the spring of 1977 through most of 1978, but he may well have stopped consulting her when Christ entered his life in late '78 early '79. Rand's reputation took a bashing when she was persuaded to make a fake prediction on US television. On January 6, 1981, on *'The Dick Maurice Show'*, Tamara Rand predicted that a young fair-haired man with the initials "JH" would shoot President Reagan sometime in late March. Her powers to see into the future were apparently confirmed when John Hinckley shot the President. *NBC*, *ABC*, and *CNN* all replayed the footage that showed her making the prediction and Rand soon began appearing on TV shows across the USA. However, when sceptical *AP* reporter, Paul Simon, began to analyse the footage, he was of the opinion that the segment showing the prediction might have been spliced into the tape. Simon confronted Dick Maurice with his suspicions and Maurice confessed that the prediction had indeed been a hoax. He admitted that the so-called "perdition" had been filmed on the day after Hinckley had shot Reagan. Rand insisted that she had predicted the assassination attempt but admitted that she taped a *"dramatisation"* of her prediction on March 31st at Dick Maurice's request. Rand then filed a $10 million slander suit against Maurice claiming that he had defamed her by his accusation that the prediction was a hoax. It didn't take a psychic to predict that her suit went nowhere.

Dylan, however, was about to go everywhere. After a twenty-one-month break from touring and an enormous amount of preparation and rehearsal, February 1978 saw Dylan embark on a 115-date world tour that began in Tokyo, Japan and went on to Australia, followed by seven concerts in Los Angeles, six concerts in London, dates in northern Europe, including five shows in Paris, and a mammoth festival at Blackbushe, England. Then, after a two-month break (during which time he worked on his movie) he embarked on a massive US tour that ran from the middle of September through until Christmas, but our focus here is on his time spent in England.

Coming in (from) Los Angeles

Expectations were running high, both in the media and with Dylan fans. When tickets had gone on sale at selected locations around the country, queues had started forming at least 48 hours before the box offices opened. All six dates at London's 15,700-seat Earls Court sold out immediately.

Dylan arrived at London's Heathrow Airport from Los Angeles on Monday June 12, three days before his first concert and three days before the release of his new album, *"Street Legal"*. Travelling with an entourage that supposedly totalled 44, he was wearing a black leather jacket and dark glasses.

After routinely clearing customs he was greeted by a posse of over-excited record company executives and an assemblage of hired muscle who attempted to hold back a scrum of anxious photographers and a hoard of reporters. A slightly bemused Dylan commented, *"Hey man, it's like a circus here"*.

When asked why it had been so long since he had visited Britain, he joked that it was the English weather that had kept him away. Then, having been in the country for all of ten minutes, one reporter asked if another British tour was planned. (I assume this was in reference to the fact that Dylan was only playing concerts in the capital on this visit).

"I don't know, I might do", said Dylan; *"So far all I've done is thoroughly enjoy myself. I just sort of stand around and watch while everyone else gets upset"*.[19]

229

With that, Dylan slid outside and into a waiting coach that whisked him away to the Royal Garden Hotel on Kensington High Street, where he and the band occupied the 8th floor of the hotel.

The band that accompanied Dylan to Europe was still eight plus three, but changes had occurred since the tour had left for Japan three months earlier. At the close of the first leg of the tour, a clearly unhappy Rob Stoner told Dylan that he was going to quit, though others in the party have since commented that he was asked to leave. In any event, there was clearly tension between the bandleader and the band and Jerry Scheff took over the role as bass player and the bandleader. Scheff, like horn player Steve Douglas, had made his reputation playing in Presley's road band in the early seventies, but had spent most of his musical life working as a hot session player, contributing to more albums than he would probably care to remember. The other change to Dylan's tour personnel was, for want of a better word, a little more 'complicated'. The tour had started in Japan with Helena Springs, Debi (Debbie) Dye-Gibson and Jo Ann Harris on backing vocals. Debi Dye and Jo Ann Harris had worked together for a number of years in stage shows including *Hair,* but it seems that neither girl rated Helena Springs. Dye has been quoted as saying that Springs was chosen more for her looks than any musical ability, and commented that *"As a singer, she was a hell of a dancer"*. Stoner had also felt that Springs was below par and had talked with her about the situation on a number of occasions. It soon became apparent, however, that Dylan was having an affair with Springs, which might explain her inclusion in the band. At any rate, as the first leg of the tour progressed, tensions grew, and Dye left the tour after Australia, partly because she was pregnant, but mainly because she could not get along with Springs. Carolyn Yvonne Dennis, daughter of singer Madelyn Quebec, was brought in to replace Dye on backing vocals but it also seems that she replaced Springs as Dylan's lover.

Dylan dated Dennis off and on after the 1978 tour had finished. After a time, however, their liaison cooled and Dennis eventually married. The marriage failed and after her divorce she re-established her relationship with Dylan and on January 31, 1986, Dennis, then 31, bore him a daughter at the Humana Hospital, in Canoga Park, California. The child was named Desiree Gabrielle Dennis-Dylan. The name of the father listed on the birth certificate was Robert Dylan. The couple married six months later, on June 4. Three days after the marriage Dennis was on stage with her new husband in San Diego as a member of Dylan's backing group, The Queens of Rhythm. Also included in the "Queens" was Dennis' mother, Dylan's new mum-in-law, Madelyn Quebec. Almost no one was aware of Dylan's second marriage. Dylan's friend, guitarist Ted Perlman, said of the wedding:

"We were all sworn to secrecy never to mention it".

The couple went to extraordinary lengths to keep their marriage out of the public-eye and as one might expect, the secrecy, coupled with Dylan's time spent on the road, meant that the marriage was a little unconventional. Dennis did not live at Dylan's house at Point Dume, instead, the couple set up home in a bungalow in the Los Angeles suburb of Tarzana. On August 7, 1990, after four years of marriage, Dennis filed for divorce; the marriage was dissolved in October 1992. Dylan is believed to have made a multi-million dollar settlement. To keep the divorce quiet, court records listed Dylan under the name, R Zimmerman and the judge made an order to seal the file.[1b]

Back in London, Dylan was enjoying being on the road. He was "hanging" with the band and, for the most part, appeared to be pushing his many troubles to the far reaches of his mind.

David Mansfield:

"He generally fraternized with the help quite a bit. He was part of the band – he'd hang out, he'd drink, he'd talk his head off, he'd play, total reverse of '76. He was having a ball. He had all kinds of stuff booked. He just wanted to get on an airplane or bus, and keep playing forever".[12a]

From the various reports, Dylan certainly made the most of his free time in London. By day, he spent much of his time shopping and managed to relax most mornings by swimming. According to Robert Shelton, "[Dylan] *churned up several laps at a north London public pool, where few of the other swimmers recognised him"*. The pool in question was the council owned public swimming pool at Swiss Cottage. He spent his first afternoon in the capital shopping, buying mainly records and clothes for his children. He then went on to see *"The American Friend"*, a mystery-thriller written by Wim Wenders and Patricia Highsmith. Presumably, Dylan was attracted to the film because it featured two of his American friends, Dennis Hopper and David Blue. The next two nights he made the rounds of London music clubs with *CBS Records* press manager, Brooklyn-born Elly Smith.

On Tuesday they went to the *100 Club* on Oxford Street (the adopted home of The Sex Pistols during 1976 & '77). Dylan and co also visited *Dingwalls* at Camden Lock, where they saw a set by the blues band George Thorogood and the Destroyers. While in town, Dylan also attended a performance of Evita and was a guest at a celebrity party.

On the afternoon of Wednesday June 14th, there was a soundcheck at Earls Court, after which, Bob endured a small *CBS* party in his honour at Covent Gardens' latest nightspot, *The Club Next Door*. At the earliest opportunity Dylan and Elly Smith slipped away from the party and made an aborted trip to the *Cloud Club* in Brixton, which was closed. The two then made their way to the *Four Aces* club in Dalston, which according to Robert Shelton was *"open, but not swinging"*. From there they went to the *Music Machine* in Finchley to catch Robert Gordon, whose band then featured Link Wray and Bob's recently departed bandleader Rob Stoner. Dylan met Stoner backstage and while they talked Sex Pistol Sid Vicious lived up to his assumed name by launching an attack on Dylan with a knife. (Four months later Vicious allegedly stabbed and killed his girlfriend Nancy Spungen in Manhattan's Chelsea Hotel). Dylan's evening ended with his second visit in two nights to the *100 Club* to hear another, now long forgotten reggae band. Dylan's eclectic taste in music had grown to encompass reggae, a fact strongly reflected in some of his own new arrangements. During his previous night's visit to the *100 Club* he had heard the reggae band Merger and invited them to appear with him on the bill at the Blackbushe festival.

Robert Shelton: *"Dylan was very open to meeting people during his stay. He saw a lot of people backstage on that tour. George Harrison and Ringo were there* [at Earls Court], *as were the Rolling Stones, Bianca Jagger and her daughter. Jack Nicholson and Shelley Duvall were in London filming; Jack's a big fan. He* [Dylan] *saw quite a few old friends. Happy Traum was there. Mine wasn't the only interview; he also spoke to Philippe Adler of L'Express. He also met Max Jones and Ray Coleman and Michael Gray. Harvey* [Goldsmith] *had organised a thank you dinner after the final concert. All his staff and the crew were invited, as was Dylan. Dylan said that he was going to be there and that I should meet him there so that we could talk and he could give me an interview"*.[14a]

Shusha Guppy accompanied Dylan to the restaurant. The Persian born singer performed a number of Dylan songs in her own concerts, which usually ended with *'Forever Young'*. Dylan, who was fan, had apparently telephoned Shusha and asked her to attend his final Earls Court concert. Also with Dylan that night were Carolyn Dennis, Helena Springs, and Jo Ann Harris.[20]

Robert Shelton: *"San Lorenzo is a very smart restaurant in Knightsbridge, just down the road from where Dylan was staying.*
    I arrived just a few minutes before Bob and managed to get a good table (in the corner) *that I knew would suit him. Bob came in the door and headed straight for me, he was very talkative.*
    There's always that something when he's around, a tension, a feel of excitement and anticipation that he generates wherever he is".[14b]

Shelton had previously written in *Melody Maker*:

"Although I've known and studied him for seventeen years, it is always exciting to be around him. The air still crackles a bit when he walks into a room".[5b]

Bob nibbled at his food and kept working on a bottle of Courvoisier that was near him. He told Shelton:

". . . I'm just the postman. I deliver the songs. That's all I have in this world are those songs. That's what all the legend, all the myth is about – my songs.
    I earn everything I make! . . . Reggie Jackson of the New York Yankees gets three million dollars a year, for striking out! For every dollar I make, there's a pool of sweat on the floor . . . I put in an eight-hour day in two hours onstage".[5c]

Finally, Shelton asked Dylan if he could put his finger on the *"enemy within"*. Dylan laughed at the question and pointed his index finger toward his heart . . .

Sources and Acknowledgments

[1, 1a, 1b] From information contained in *"Down The Highway The Life Of Bob Dylan"* by Howard Sounes, published in London by *Doubleday*, 2001.

[2, 2a, 2b, 2c] Sounes, Howard. *"Down The Highway The Life Of Bob Dylan"*. London: *Doubleday*, 2001.

[3] While Dylan is factually correct in saying that no one in his family had ever been devoiced, Bob's grandparents on his father's side, Anna (Greenstein) and Zigman Zimmerman, did separate.

[4] Shelton, Robert. *"No Direction Home: The Life And Music Of Bob Dylan"*. London: *New English Library*, 1986.

[5, 5a, 5b, 5c] Adler, Philippe. Interview with Bob Dylan for *L'Express*, July 3, 1978.

[6] Interview with Robert Shelton for *Melody Maker*, June 29, 1978.

[7] Steve Douglas died in 1993 at age 55.

[8] Cott, Jonathon. Interview with Bob Dylan for *Rolling Stone* magazine, December 1977, published January 26, 1978.

[9] Barker, Derek. Interview with Jerry Weintraub for *ISIS* magazine.

[10] Williams, Paul. *"Performing Artist – The Middle Years"*. California: *Underwood-Miller*, 1992.

[11, 11a] Spitz, Bob. *"Dylan A Biography"*. New York: *McGraw-Hill*, 1989.

[12, 12a] Heylin, Clinton. *"Behind The Shades: Take Two"*. London: *Viking*, 2000.

[13, 13a, 13b] Rosenbaum, Ron. Interview with Bob Dylan for *Playboy* magazine, conducted November 1977, published March 1978.

[14, 14a, 14b] de Souza, Chris. Interview with Robert Shelton for *ISIS* Magazine, published July 1999.

[15, 15a] *Daily Mirror*, June 11, 1978.

[16] Barker, Derek (editor). *"ISIS A Bob Dylan Anthology"*. London: *Helter Skelter Publishing*, 2001.

[17] The Tarot deck of 78-cards, now used mostly for *fortune-telling*, is an early version of the 52-card deck that is now in common use in Europe, North America and many other counties.

[18] Gooding, Cynthia. Radio show for *WBAI*. Possible broadcast date March 11, 1962.

[19] *Guardian*, June 13, 1978.

[20] Shusha Guppy: Female vocalist born in Iran, moved to Paris at age sixteen to study oriental languages and Philosophy; she married an Englishman and relocated to London in the mid-sixties. Her first album was released in 1972.

Published in *ISIS* issue #108, May, 2003

Bob Dylan 1978

A Picnic Surprise

Derek Barker

After a dozen concerts in mainland Europe, Dylan returned to England on July 13th for a one-off open-air concert at Blackbushe Aerodrome. This concert was not part of the original tour plan and only came about because of exceptional ticket sales for the six concerts in Earls Court. The 94,000 plus tickets for the London residency sold out within hours of going on sale and promoter, Harvey Goldsmith, was extremely keen for more of the same. He had paid Dylan £350,000 for the six Earls Court shows and is reputed to have talked about Dylan earning in the region of £300,000 for "The Picnic". In any event, he persuaded Dylan to return to England after he had finished his mini tour of continental Europe. Consequently, just three-and-half weeks after completing his highly successful Earls Court residency Bob was back for a grand finale. This final performance on the European leg of his tour would eclipse everything else that had gone before (and anything still to come) on the 1978 world tour.

Situated two miles west of Camberley beside the A30 on the Hampshire/ Surrey border (contrary to every other text you will have read Blackbushe is actually in Hampshire and not Surrey) Blackbushe Aerodrome was opened in late 1942 as RAF Hartfordbridge. The airfield was active throughout the Second World War, providing a base for Squadrons of Spitfires and Mosquitos and was home to the Free French Squadron "Lorraine". The current owners have redeveloped the facility into a thriving centre for business that houses many executive aircraft including one of the Royal Household helicopters, a Sikorsky S-76. The concert held at Blackbushe on Saturday July 15, 1978 was the first, and interestingly the last, music event ever to be staged there.

So many People there I never saw in m'life

Promoter Harvey Goldsmith expected the "Picnic" to attract a crowd of between 100,000 and 120,000; the truth is that no one really knows exactly how many people saw Dylan's show that day. So many people turned up with forged tickets that the organisers decided to let all the forgeries in for free. *"Oh well, it's a pretty big airfield. Besides, anyway, the more the merrier"*. Final estimates ranged from 167,000 to a quarter-of-a-million attendees. The most common figure quoted (the one given out by the police) was 200,000. The crowd was later classified as being the *"largest ever assembled to see one artist"*, which is perhaps a little derogatory toward Eric Clapton who was also on the bill. British music paper *Melody Maker* said it was the largest peacetime gathering in British history.

Jugglers and Clowns

Other often quoted statistics stated that the 23-acre site was fenced with 12,000 feet of corrugated fencing, which was painted by local school children with picnic murals and was manned by some 6,000 police and private security men. Also in attendance were about 100 members of the St John Ambulance, five full-time doctors and a number of nurses from the University College Hospital. 500 portable toilet blocks provided the sanitation. Goldsmith apparently wanted more but had problems in locating them. The promoter also hired street theatre groups, clowns on stilts and a Punch and Judy show! (Similar entertainment had been provided around the outer concourse for the Earls Court shows.) There was also a crèche with free jelly and cake. Even the cake was a monster, measuring eight feet in length. Before you could enjoy all of this, however, you had to get to the site. British Rail ran 66 additional trains that left London's Waterloo Station every fifteen minutes. Even so, an estimated 60,000 vehicles turned up at the site and many more were simply abandoned on route. Prior to the event, the M3 motorway was completely blocked, and in an attempt to get past the gridlock, many people drove down the hard shoulder until that also became blocked. Some people then attempted to drive along the grass verges while others simply abandoned their vehicles and walked the remaining six or seven miles to the site.

The rig for Dylan's world tour was supplied by *Stanal Sound* of Kearney, Nebraska. *Stanal*, who had provided Neil Diamond with his sound system for the previous eight years, knew all about big outdoor events. The company had provided Diamond with the first ever four-channel quadraphonic PA system for his 1972 *"Hot August Night"* concert tour. The previous year they had provided Diamond with a stereo PA system; also a first.

For the Dylan shows, *Stanal's* sound chief Tim Charles handled the house mixing, while Chris Coffin mixed the stage monitors. A new type of power-amp called an *"incremental power system"* powered the monitor speakers. These power-amps were so new the accompanying literature carried the words *"temporary operating instructions"*.

Dylan took a personal interest in the Blackbushe bill making several suggestions, some of which Harvey Goldsmith acted on.

Martin Carthy: *"Apparently he [Dylan] wanted me to be on [at Blackbushe], so he told Harvey Goldsmith, and Harvey tried to get hold of me. Not very hard. . . but I got the invitation to come down . . . It took me four hours to get backstage. There were at least three levels of security, and then his caravan. And he had no idea. So I went in and he said: 'Oh, how are you?' and then he said: 'How's Anthea?'"* [Joseph] *And I said: 'She's fine. She's out in hospitality'. And he said: 'Why doesn't she come and see me?' I looked at him and said: 'Do you have any idea what the security is like here?' He turned to one of the blokes and said: 'Can you go and find Anthea Joseph? She's in hospitality'. They came back in five minutes and there she was, festooned in all the passes. You know, there's a level of innocence about him that's really endearing. He didn't have a clue. . ."*

Dylan's set began with an instrumental rendition of *'My Back Pages'*. The crowd instantly erupted; those more than half way back were probably not even aware that Dylan had not yet arrived on stage! During the last few bars of the song, Dylan emerged with a stunning black custom *Strat*, and this time the crowd's roar rolled from the front to the back of the site like a not yet thought of Mexican Wave. After only three weeks away, Bob was back! He took the stage wearing black trousers, a black leather jacket and a white collarless shirt under a black waistcoat. He wore a heavy bead necklace and a magnificent top hat. Although he had previously worn similar headgear in Auckland in March, this specimen was apparently 'borrowed' from a doorman at London's Dorchester Hotel. Other fashion accessories included dark glasses (for part of the show) and no less than five rings. The rings, which were not in evidence at the beginning of the tour (see photos of Dylan in Japan, Australia and New Zealand), were an interesting addition. The content of Dylan's show was something of a surprise (leastways to those that had not read the news regarding the setlist from Nuremberg, Zeppelinfield), in that he played eight songs that had not been previously performed at the Earls Court concerts. The 32-song set was also slightly longer than the rest of the tour and lasted for about two-and-a-half hours.

Blackbushe Set July 15, 1978

'My Back Pages' (*Instrumental. no Dylan participation*)
'Love Her With A Feeling' (Tampa Red)
'Baby Stop Crying'
'Just Like Tom Thumb's Blues'
'Shelter From The Storm'
'It's All Over Now, Baby Blue'
'Girl From The North Country'
'Ballad Of A Thin Man'
'Maggie's Farm'
'Simple Twist Of Fate'
'Like A Rolling Stone'
'I Shall Be Released'
'Is Your Love In Vain?'
'Where Are You Tonight? (Journey Through Dark Heat)'
'A Change Is Gonna Come' (Sam Cooke)(*Sung by Carolyn Dennis*)
'Mr. Tambourine Man' (*Sung by Helena Springs*)
'The Long And Winding Road' (*Sung by Jo Ann Harris*)
'Laissez-faire' (Soles) (*Sung by Steven Soles*)
'Gates of Eden' (*acoustic*)
'True Love Tends To Forget'
'One More Cup Of Coffee (Valley Below)'
'Blowin' In The Wind'
'I Want You'
'Senor (Tales Of Yankee Power)'

'Masters Of War'
'Just Like A Woman'
'To Ramona'
'Don't Think Twice, It's Alright'
'All Along The Watchtower'
'All I Really Want To Do'
'It's Alright Ma (I'm Only Bleeding)'
'Forever Young' (With Eric Clapton on guitar)

Encores
'Changing Of The Guards' (With Eric Clapton on guitar)
'The Times They Are A-Changin'' (With Eric Clapton on guitar)

The Festival Was Over

After the show Dylan raced to Camberley railway station to pick up a special train that was to take him to Waterloo Station. No definite departure time had been fixed so the train simply stood by for the appropriate moment. Dylan was then whisked away and took a two months break before embarking on a further 65 dates in the USA.

The 1978 world tour contained many "firsts": Dylan's largest ever band, his only ever use of brass, the first use of female backing singers, his first ever concerts in Japan, New Zealand, Holland and Germany, and the first electric performances of a rake of songs including *'Love Minus Zero/No Limit'*, *'Girl Of The North Country'*, *'Don't Think Twice, It's All Right'*, *'To Ramona'*, *'Tomorrow Is A Long Time'*, *'All I Really Want To Do'*, *'It's Alright, Ma'*, *'The Times They Are A-Changin''*, and *'Masters Of War'*. Ground breaking stuff, indeed! Dylan had enjoyed the first half of the year on the road, but with the American dates still to come, he was facing perhaps his greatest challenges. I'll leave the last words to Robert Shelton (London June 20, 1978).

Robert Shelton: *"For all the rapport he has with millions around the world, I still feel a sense of foreboding loneliness about him. That maybe the curse of knowing and feeling too much within. . .*

To show my appreciation for his survival as a great artist who is always busy being reborn, I wanted to give him some token . . . I handed him a Judgement card from my [Tarot] deck. It shows a winged angel blowing a trumpet, raising the dead from their graves, and they are reborn again as little children. The Judgement card is like 'Forever Young', telling us that music can revitalize and renew us.

Dylan thanked me warmly for the token gift. 'But you shouldn't break up your pack of cards', he said.

Dylan accepted the card. What else can you give a man who has given us all so much?"

Part of this text is from *ISIS* issue #31, June, 1990. Full text *ISIS* #109, July, 2003

Bob Dylan 1981

Stories in the Press

"Vintage Bob Dylan" has taken on a new meaning . . . [he has] teamed up with Italian winemaker Antonio Terni to produce a blended red wine.

Terni, who owns Fattoria Le Terrazze in Italy's Marche region, is also a partner in an Argentina winery whose Malbec Viña Hormigas Reserva was among wine spectator's "Top 100 Wines" of 2003. A lifelong Dylan fanatic, he spends his free time trailing [Dylan's] European tours and has already produced wine in homage to his hero, a Montepulciano named *Visions of J*, after *'Visions Of Johanna'*.

When the troubadour performed in Milan last year, Terni brought along a few bottles of *Visions of J* and passed them on to Dylan's drummer with a note asking if Dylan would be interested in a joint venture. When his manager called a few days later, Terni thought it was a prank. *"Bob tried it backstage and liked it, and his manager wanted to know more about my wine"*, Terni said. The two agreed to a trial joint venture. Terni would create the wine and Dylan would offer his endorsement, in exchange for a few hundred bottles.

The result is *Planet Waves* 2002, a blend of 75 percent Montepulciano and 25 percent Merlot. Terni says the blend expresses two sides of Dylan's personality. Even the inscription on the back of the bottle, which bears the signatures of both partners, contains a Dylanesque soliloquy: *"Countless waves of causes and effects/have been rolling all along this planet/since it emerged from darkness. When they cross and overlap each other, things happen/What pushed two guys from opposite corners of the world to put their names/on a bottle of Italian red wine?/Destiny? Fate? Coincidence?"*

Terni has produced about 415 cases of *Planet Waves*, 125 of which will be exported to the United States . . . The price tag is $65 per bottle (about £35).

Printed in issue #114 of *ISIS* April 2004
Originally published on www.winespectator.com

Those Japanese Bankers

Dylan played a private gig in Phoenix on February 2, 1996. The sponsors were *Nomura Securities inc.*, who underwrote the *Sony/Columbia* deal some years back. Dylan, along with Crosby, Stills & Nash played the Friday night and Rod Stewart played the Saturday, February 3, concert. *Nomura* have said Dylan had a contractual stipulation such that he was not required to speak to the audience between songs or, indeed, at all.

The gig, which took place at The Pavilion at the Arizona Biltmore in Phoenix, was part of a conference hosted by *Nomura*, with an audience of 800 clients. Dylan's fee was a cool $250,000.

The Wicked Messenger #s3323 & 3393 first printed in issues #66 & #67 of *ISIS* April / July 1996

Top Dollar for Dylan's School Essay

"Aside from the Beatles, he is the single most valued signature in rock and roll". A school essay written by Bob Dylan is getting top marks from collectors as it went on sale for $25,000, despite only netting young Bob a B-minus. The document, written by a teenage Dylan, then Robert Zimmerman, is about Steinbeck's classic tale of social injustice and poverty, *"The Grapes Of Wrath".* As the musician celebrates his 60th birthday interest in his work is growing again, with memorabilia on sale at a New York store including a high school yearbook from 1959 at £5,593.

The yearbook features a picture of Dylan at school in the small-town of Hibbing in Minnesota, and shows that he had a crush on a teacher.

In the book Dylan wrote it was too bad that he and his fellow pupils would have to leave a teacher called Miss Barron behind. *"Don't you wish she'd guide us through the rest of our lives?"* he wrote. He also revealed his rock'n'roll ambition – *"To join Little Richard".* Meanwhile the mouth organ he played at school is being offered for £5,243.

Printed in issue #97 of *ISIS* July 2001

The Chessman Cometh

Actress Sylvia Miles was interviewed by *Scotland on Sunday*. It seems that she is a chess player of a very high standard, having for example, beaten the Russian female champion in 1968. In the aforementioned interview, she was asked about playing chess with Sean Connery and replied as follows:

"I played him but I didn't win. I could have but I let him checkmate me. I suddenly remembered that I once played chess with Bob Dylan . . . and I beat him. I didn't see him for two years, although we had an on-going affair that lasted for 26 years. You have a bad sex life if you win chess games against guys. My advice is, always let them beat you. They don't like it when women win".

Another chess story: In 1975, world chess champion, Bobby Fischer, resigned his title. For a while, he lived on the royalties from his book *"My 60 Memorable Games"* and the fees he charged for meetings. According to an article in *Esquire*, Yasser Seirawan, the highest ranked American grandmaster after Fischer, has reported that at least 20 fans paid for meetings and one of those was *"a rabid chess player and religious recluse named Bob Dylan, whose tour manager is said to have bought him the meeting as a birthday present".*

The Wicked Messenger # 4816, printed in issue #99 of *ISIS* November 2001

Only One Road
The use of the image of the hill in Bob Dylan's songs

Introduction

Over the years numerous writers have commented upon Bob Dylan's persistent use of particular poetic images and metaphors in his song lyrics. Many of these images have been shown to reoccur repeatedly in the artist's work, a kind of sustained revisiting of favourite ideas and themes. The most popular example of this is the image of the "train", a theme that has been widely discussed (but perhaps with most clarity by Michael Gray[1]) – other common Dylan-themes include "(corrupt) judges", "walking (as a metaphor for life)" and the "apocalypse".[2] On looking closer at these regular images, one finds that they are often linked strongly to at least one of the following two factors (and often by both): firstly 'the bible', and secondly 'traditional American music and literature'. To illustrate the above, the train was a symbol of hope and salvation for early Negro gospel-blues singers and features in the music and literature that represents those communities (it also becomes important later to Beat generation writers such as Jack Kerouac). The oppression of people by corrupt rulers and judges is a common point of reference for certain American "depression era" writers (culminating with the works of John Steinbeck) and is also a stock subject for the Old Testament prophets. Walking is used as a metaphor for life in both the Old and New Testaments (for example, Psalm 1:1; 23:4; Colossians 2:6 [AV]; 1 John 1:6-7) and is a common literary device; and apocalyptic literature is legion in biblical writings. It is also worth noting that while it is obvious to point out that Dylan's biblical influences give his songs a somewhat "theological" message, so too does Dylan's knowledge of American culture add to this religious tone. David Lyle Jeffrey has written of *"the deep-rootedness of biblical narrative in the American popular imagination"* and notes that *"from the beginning the Bible was so central to the idiom of American literature that classic American writers . . . are not quite intelligible without some knowledge of the foundational text"*[3] – I would suggest that Dylan falls neatly into this bracket of *"classic American writer"* as he is an artist whose work may be theologically significant not merely due to the influence of the bible but also by the fact that traditional American culture has left its mark upon his writings.

When conducting a thematic study of any artist's output, it is important to note that while certain images may be used regularly over a long period in a seemingly uniform way, it may actually be the case that the artist uses one image to point to a number of different concepts. That is to say, an image may be invested with a variety of meanings determined by the context into which the artist has placed that image – as the context changes then so does the meaning of the image. To cite one example, the American poet EE Cummings uses the image of the prostitute to suggest temptation and sin, natural sexual desire and fulfilment, charm, revulsion, innocence (of the narrator) and worldliness (of the woman) – but rarely do all of these aspects occur in one poem. It is in connection with this observation that I would like to consider one of Bob Dylan's lesser-discussed themes, that of the "hill" (or "mountain"), a theme which appears to have a wide variety of possible interpretations. It is my intent here to explore the different connotations that the image of the hill carries in various Bob Dylan compositions. I will outline <u>five</u> main groupings into which Dylan's usages of the hill image fall.[4] Once I have described and illustrated these five areas I will then go on to address some of the wider issues that this study raises.

Old Testament Imagery

The first manner in which Dylan uses the image of the hill in his songs is in connection with "Old Testament imagery", an unsurprising category considering Dylan's Jewish background and biblical influence. However, while one might expect to find a large number of clear references to Mount Zion, Sinai and other Old Testament mountain scenes among Dylan's many uses of the hill image, instead it becomes evident that most of the allusions to Old Testament hill scenes in Dylan's work are subtle and often inconclusive. For example in *'License To Kill'* Dylan sings:

> *Now, there's a woman on my block,*
> *She just sit there facin' the hill,*
> *She say who gonna take away his license to kill?*

Bert Cartwright suggests that these lines point to Mount Zion and the fact that "the custom of praying toward that holy hill is seen in 1 Kings 8:44-48"[5] – other hearers however might view the stanza as representing a devout Christian woman meditating upon the cross of Calvary as the solution for troubled humankind. Neither interpretation is wrong and both may even be intended by Dylan, but Cartwright has a tendency to prefer the Old Testament interpretations in these ambiguous instances. To provide a further example of Cartwright's preference towards Old Testament interpretations we might consider *'A Hard Rain's A-Gonna Fall'*, where Dylan declares that

> *. . . I'll tell it and think it and speak it and breath it,*
> *And reflect from the mountain so all souls can see it.*

Cartwright[6] sees this as referring to Horeb, the mountain of God in Exodus 3:16, but the image could just as easily be drawn from Jesus' teaching in the sermon on the mount about a bright city on a hill (Matthew 5:14-6) or from Jesus' transfiguration in Mark 9:2ff. Cartwright has elected to adopt the Old Testament allusion, but in the final analysis, it is inconclusive. Once again, in *'Is Your Love In Vain?'* Cartwright[7] views the line

> Well I've been to the mountain and I've been in the wind,
> I've been in and out of happiness".

as referring to Deuteronomy 34:1-57, but I prefer to read the stanza as originating in the account of the temptation of Jesus in Matthew 4:1-11, especially as Dylan continues straight on with the lines:

> I have dined with kings, I've been offered wings,
> And I've never been too impressed.

Part of the beauty of poetry and verse is that various readers and listeners carry away different nuances from certain words and phrases, and thus arguments that attempt to prove whether Dylan might be drawing from Deuteronomy or Matthew in a given instance are perhaps futile. What I <u>am</u> trying to show though is that when it comes to Dylan's use of Old Testament mountain imagery there is often ambiguity and an almost deliberate unwillingness on the poet's part to be clear and specific concerning the exact source of that metaphor. It would be speculative to suggest whether this allusiveness on Dylan's part concerning his use of Old Testament imagery might be in some way due to a coyness concerning his Jewish background at certain points in his life.

New Testament Imagery

The second category of hill image covers the various New Testament hill scenes excluding the death of Christ, for example the temptation and transfiguration of Jesus and the sermon on the mount. I have already noted that a line from *'A Hard Rain's A-Gonna Fall'* may allude to the transfiguration of Jesus in the gospel stories[8] and Dylan returns to the transfiguration later in his career in *'Jokerman'*:

> You're a man of the mountains, you can walk on the clouds,
> Manipulator of crowds. . .

and in *'Don't Fall Apart On Me Tonight'*:

> . . . if I could, I'd bring you to the mountaintop, girl,
> And build you a house made out of stainless steel.

(The latter couplet appears to me to be a modern comic rendering of Peter's words to Jesus at Mark 9:5 where the disciple offers to erect tents for Jesus and the prophets on the transfiguration mountainside.) However, while I have suggested that both of these examples represent a possible reinterpretation of the transfiguration scene by Dylan, there are other plausible New Testament interpretations. The figure of the "Jokerman" is a *"manipulator of crowds"* whose realm is the hills, and so there is probably an implied nod towards the sermon on the mount.[9] Indeed, as I move into our next classification of hill image, that of "Future Hope and Judgement", I will show how the idea of the hills as being representative of the future and of judgement also may be present in *'Jokerman'* and *'Don't Fall Apart On Me Tonight'*.

Future Hope and Judgement

The description in *'Jokerman'* of the "mountain-man" walking upon clouds could be regarded as referring to the *"one like a son of man, coming with the clouds of heaven"* (an important passage for many Jews and Christians, from Daniel 7:13 and quoted by Jesus in Matthew 24:30), and if this nuance is accepted as influencing the *'Jokerman'* lyric then the mountains become a symbol for the sky or heaven and the path of the apocalyptic judge. Likewise, the reference to the house of steel on the mountaintop in *'Don't Fall Apart On Me Tonight'* may (in this context) be a reinterpretation of Jesus' description of his Father's heavenly home in John 14:2, an argument which is strengthened by comparing another song from the *"Infidels"* album, *'Sweetheart Like You'*, where Dylan says

> . . . *in your father's house, there's many mansions,*
> *Each one of them got a fireproof floor,*

again using poetic language to suggest the durability of the eternal home. There are a great many other instances in Dylan's work where he uses hills or mountains to represent either heaven or future judgement. For example, the apocalyptic theme of the coming of the son of man may be present in *'Romance In Durango'* in the lines

> *Look up in the hills, that flash of light. . .*
> . . . *we may not make it through the night,*

a passage that echoes back to Dylan's quotation of Matthew 24:27 in *'I Shall Be Released'*:

> *I see my light come shining,*
> *From the west unto the east.*
> *Any day now, any day now,*
> *I shall be released.*[10]

The image of hills makes a further appearance in Dylan's musings on eternity in his rendering of the traditional folk song *'House Carpenter'*, where heaven and hell appear as hills on the horizon:

"Oh, what are those hills yonder my love?
They look as white as snow".
"Those are the hills of heaven my love
You and I will never know".
"Oh, what are those hills yonder my love?
They look as dark as night".
"Those are the hills of hell-fire my love
Where you and I will unite".

In *'Highlands'* Dylan also uses hills as a metaphor for heaven when he sings

Well, my heart's in the highlands, at the break of day,
Over the hills and far away.
There's a way to get there and I'll figure it out somehow,
But I'm already there in my mind,
And that's good enough for now.

and both *'House Carpenter'* and *'Highlands'* remind the listener of the fact that Dylan is part of a long tradition of artists who have made such a comparison. Stephen Scobie notes that Dylan may be quoting Scottish poet Robert Burns when he sings the line *"my heart's in the highlands"*, and although Scobie is uncertain of the underpinning religious message of the song, he is certain that heaven is pictured in the hills.[11] The correlation between heaven and hills is made in many areas of the arts, not merely in poetry and song but even in such a genre as popular American film – for example in Tim Burton's *"Edward Scissorhands"* the "Christ-figure" Edward comes from and returns to his mountain home, a symbolic heaven, and in westerns such as *"Shane"* or *"Pale Rider"* the Christ-figure heroes ride away into the hills at the end, a symbol of eternity[12] – Dylan's natural use of the hill/heaven metaphor makes plain to the listener his familiarity with the symbolic language of the arts.

Metaphor for Life

I will deal briefly with the fourth characteristic use of Dylan's hill motif, that of the "Metaphor for Life". Dylan often compares life to climbing a hill, a metaphor sometimes infused with biblical allusion. In *'You Ain't Goin' Nowhere'* Dylan says

We'll climb that hill no matter how steep;

the lyrics to *'Coming From The Heart'* read

. . .the road is long, it's a long hard climb
I been on that road too long of a time;

and in *'Minstrel Boy'* he says:

> *. . . Lucky's been drivin' a long, long time*
> *And now he's stuck on top of the hill.*

'*Cold Irons Bound*' also contains an example of the hill as a metaphor for life:

> *The road is rocky and the hillside mud,*
> *Up over my head nothing but clouds of blood.*

In a manner similar at times to John Bunyan's *"The Pilgrim's Progress"*, Dylan pictures certain challenges of life metaphorically, often using the image of the hill to represent difficult times. Although the 'hill of life' is the over-ruling metaphor in the above lyrics, there is however some link with the fifth category of hill image, that of 'Calvary Hill', with the writer comparing his road through life with the road that Christ took to the cross[13] – it is to this important fifth section that I now turn.

Calvary Hill

The most interesting way in which Dylan uses the image of the hill in his writings is in his portrayal of Calvary (also traditionally called Golgotha), the place of Christ's execution. There are two main instances in Dylan's work that provide the listener with a primary basis for reading "Calvary" into Dylan's use of "hill". The first is in '*Sign On The Cross*' (1985 *"Lyrics"* version) where Dylan says

> *. . . see the sign on the cross just layin' up on top of the hill.*

thereby linking "hill" firmly with "cross". The second is in '*Idiot Wind*', in the comparison of the original studio (out)take of '*Idiot Wind*' with its official album version. While the third line of the third verse of the album version reads

> *There's a lone soldier on the cross, smoke pouring out of a boxcar door.*

the earlier version is rendered

> *There's a lone soldier on the hill, watchin' fallin' raindrops pour.*[15]

Dylan thereby uses "cross" and "hill" synonymously.

From this basic supposition (that Dylan regards Calvary as a hill) one may go on to note many other songs where Dylan has used the word "hill" to suggest "Calvary" – these include '*Billy*', where the cowboy messiah figure is told that

> *Up to Boot Hill they'd like to send ya;*[16]

'*Foot Of Pride*', where Dylan meditates on Christ,

247

Yes, I guess I loved him too,
I can still see him in my mind climbin' that hill,
Did he make it to the top, well he probably did and dropped
Struck down by the strength of the will.

and *'Shelter From The Storm'*, a song full of biblical imagery and which climaxes:

In a little hilltop village, they gambled for my clothes,
I bargained for salvation an' they gave me a lethal dose.
I offered up my innocence and got repaid with scorn. . .

These songs show how Dylan sometimes represents Calvary as a hill and how this conventional image is used to trigger religious connotations in songs that at first might not appear particularly religious (this is especially the case with the lines in *'Idiot Wind'* and *'Billy'*). However, when one looks into the New Testament accounts of the death of Jesus Christ then an interesting factor in this debate becomes apparent – that Calvary may not have been upon a hill at all. So two questions must be answered: firstly, how has the image of a hill come to represent Calvary, and then how has this tradition filtered down into Bob Dylan's songs? I shall go on now to suggest some answers to these questions.

Origin and Transmission of the Tradition of Calvary Hill

Three of the New Testament gospel accounts (Matthew 27:33, Mark 15:22, John 19:17) name Christ's execution site *Golgotha* (from the Aramaic/Hebrew word for *skull*) while Luke 23:33 links it to the Latin for skull, *Calvaria* (and hence *Calvary*). While it is clear that the crucifixion site is connected in some way with the notion of a skull,[17] the name in itself certainly does not contain any hint that the place was a hill, unless one reads into "Place of the Skull" a hillock with a "round and skull-like contour", but this seems unlikely.[18] On top of the lack of any real biblical evidence for a hill, the apocryphal Acts of Pilate has the governor ordering that Jesus be *"hanged . . . in the garden where you were seized"*.[19] So how does one account for the rise of the hill as an image for representing Calvary when there is no direct New Testament support?

Scholars cite two main explanations for the rise of the hill tradition (although neither is conclusive). Firstly, there is the idea that the Place of the Skull *"was visible from some distance"* according to Mark 15:40 and Luke 23:49 and has *"led many to think of it as a hill"*.[20] Secondly, the Johannine motif of Jesus being *"lifted up"* (eg, John 12:32) has been used to suggest crucifixion on a hill, although "lifting up" most likely functions either to emphasize the height of the cross itself or as a metaphor for the exaltation of Jesus. It is likely that a combination of these factors led to the tradition of Calvary as a hill, along with notions of a "skull-shaped" hill as discussed in the previous paragraph.

While it is difficult to locate the exact source of the hill tradition, it is thankfully easier to discover the means by which this tradition has reached Bob

Dylan. For this, it is necessary to look not to theology but to the arts, as it is largely by this medium that the Calvary hill tradition has been passed on. Gertrud Schiller[21] notes that early Christian pictorial symbolism equated Golgotha with Mount Zion, the future place of Paradise, and this may account for the hill image that developed in narrative art, the earliest known example being carved into the wooden door of Sta Sabina, Rome, circa AD 430. The depiction of Calvary as a hill has thereafter been ever-present in art – just a few noteworthy examples might include *The Crucifixion and Iconoclasts* in the Chludov Psalter (folio 675, c. AD 850-75, State Historical Museum, Moscow), *Crucifixion* by Andrea Mantegna (1456-9, The Louvre, Paris), *The Entombment* by Raphael (1507, Galleria Borghese, Rome), *The Entombment of Christ* by Rembrandt (1639, Munich, Alte Pinakothek), and *The Archangel Michael Foretelling the Crucifixion* by William Blake (c. 1808, Tate Gallery, London). It is highly likely that Bob Dylan was influenced by fine art's image of the cross on the hill, especially if (as Ledeen suggests[22]) his trip around Europe in 1962 involved visits to various art galleries.

Literature may also have been an important vehicle for the transmission of the hill tradition which itself then became an important theme in Dylan's writings. Such an influential work as John Bunyan's *"The Pilgrim's Progress"* contains the image of a cross at *"a place somewhat ascending"*[23] and certainly left its impact upon literature that followed. An even earlier (Old English) reference to Calvary hill comes from the poem *'Dream of the Rood'* (which some commentators attribute to Cynewulf); written from the perspective of the cross, one stanza begins

The soldiers on their shoulders bore me,
until on a hill-top they set me up.[24]

Of course before the writing of *'Dream of the Rood'* certain church fathers had alluded to Calvary hill[25] and modern poets have also used this image in their writings. For example, in *"Ecce Homo"* David Gascoyne writes:

. . .here is the hill
Made ghastly by His spattered blood. . .
. . .Where on he hangs and suffers still,[26]

while Dylan Thomas, in *"Altarwise by Owl-Light"*, writes:

This was the crucifixion on the mountain.[27]

Bob Dylan's awareness of various forms of artistic expression offered ample opportunity for the image of the hill to become closely associated in his mind with the cross of Christ.

Spiritual music would also have played its part in this process. Apart from the obvious influence of hymns such as *'There Is A Green Hill'*, the blues/gospel tradition that the youthful Dylan immersed himself in reinforced the image of Calvary hill. Refrains setting Christ's sufferings on a hill were common – James H. Cone cites a good example:

> *Oh, dey whupped him up de hill, an' he never said a mumbalin' word,*
> *He jes' hung down his head an' he cried.*[28]

One should also remember to acknowledge the power of the movies on Dylan: if he had failed to see some of the earlier classics, including Cecil B. DeMille's 1927 *"King of Kings"*, then he surely would have seen 1959's *"Ben Hur"* – both films that depicted Calvary on a hilltop.

Applications

I have so far established that Dylan refers frequently to the image of a hill in his songs, and that out of the five broad categories into which this image tends to fall the most important one of these and the one that has had the greatest amount of exposure through the arts is the image of Calvary hill. It is now important to ask what this all means when one approaches the music and lyrics of Bob Dylan – what can these observations tell the listener about Bob Dylan's work? I would suggest that there are two main areas of importance, which I shall discuss as a consequence: firstly, Dylan's self-identification as Christ, and secondly Dylan's use (or omission) of imagery during certain periods of his career.

Dylan's self-identification as Christ

One of the most distinctive features of Dylan's poetry is the way in which he regularly pictures himself as a messiah figure, a phenomenon that has been labelled by Roos & O'Meara as Dylan's *"obsessive identification with Christ".*[29] One important way in which Dylan signals to the listener that he intends to identify with Christ is through the appearance of the hill metaphor – for example in *'Minstrel Boy'* Dylan pictures himself as 'Lucky'

> *. . . stuck on top of the hill*

and uses both the image of the hill and the irony contained within the name 'Lucky'[30] to signal the poet's empathy with Christ. A similar point may be observed in a number of Dylan's other songs: in *'Shelter From The Storm'* the reference to

> *a little hilltop village*

is a major signifier of the connection between the artist's struggles and those of Christ; in *'It Takes A Lot To Laugh, It Takes A Train To Cry'* the lines:

Well, if I die,
On top of the hill,
And if I don't make it,
You know my baby will.

function in a similar way to those in *'Shelter From The Storm'*; and in *'Tombstone Blues'* Dylan's reference to Samson in DeMille's 1949 epic might easily double as a melancholy commentary on the cross if one reads the hill reference in a dual sense:

Now I wish I could give Brother Bill his great thrill,
I would set him in chains at the top of the hill,
Then send out for some pillars and Cecil B. DeMille,
He could die happily ever after.

Of course it is not unusual for an artist to compare his or her life with that of Christ, a fact possibly due to the constant cycle of public praise and rejection that any artist undergoes. To provide an example from another popular musician who uses the motif of the hill to signal a Christ-likeness, the final verse of Bruce Springsteen's *'Darkness On The Edge Of Town'* (1978, *Colombia Records*) reads:

Tonight I'll be on that hill 'cause I can't stop,
I'll be on that hill with everything I got . . .
I'll be there on time and I'll pay the cost.

In this example from Springsteen and in many of Dylan's lyrics it is only through the device of the hill that any possible comparison between the artist and Jesus becomes apparent to the listener. This then is the first main importance attached to studying Dylan's use of this imagery.

Use (or omission) of imagery during certain periods of Dylan's career

The second reason for taking an interest in Dylan's use of images such as the hill is that his use of imagery may reveal something of the artist's personal feelings towards his subject at certain times. Generally speaking, included within an artist's use of an image is a clue to the artist's disposition toward the subject to which that image relates; in this case, Dylan's use of the hill motif should tell the reader something of what the artist at various points in his career thinks of Jesus Christ and the cross of Calvary. Of course one must always beware of over-extracting an artist's life and personal feelings from his works (this has happened with a number of readings of *"Time Out Of Mind"*[31]), but it is still true to say that an artist's frame of mind towards a matter may be perceived in some way through the images in his works.[32] It then also becomes important to note the places where an image is omitted from a work where it might normally be expected to appear, as that may also tell the reader something about the artist's disposition. So the question arises: does Dylan's use (or omission) of the hill motif throughout his career offer any clue as to his understanding of and relationship with Jesus?

The answer to the above question is 'yes'. Prior to Dylan's 1978/9 Christian conversion his references to Calvary are often either seeped in despondency and doubt (the above examples from *'Minstrel Boy'*, *'Shelter From The Storm'*, *'It Takes A Lot To Laugh, It Takes A Train To Cry'* and *'Tombstone Blues'* serve as good examples of this[33]) or else are used with some irony, for example during the "preach" in *'Sign On The Cross'*:

Ev'ry day, ev'ry night, see the sign on the cross just layin' up on top of the hill.

(It may be interesting, although probably stretching the point, to suggest that the lines from *'When I Paint My Masterpiece'* that read

Yes, it sure has been a long, hard climb,
Train wheels runnin' through the back of my memory,
When I ran on the hilltop following a pack of wild geese,

also form a subtle and ironic reference to the cross and it's apparent fruitlessness [noting also the common spiritual context of "train"].) There is little doubt though that 1978's *"Street Legal"* reveals a true reconsideration on Dylan's part of the meaning of Calvary, and with this comes a change of tone in the use of the hill image. Whereas pre-1978 references to the hill on the whole are often obscured by metaphor and indicated defeat, *"Street Legal"* shows Dylan warming to a more open and positive view of Calvary. A pivotal point is a new understanding of the resurrection of Jesus, an event that transformed Christ's death from an outright embarrassment and failure into a victory laden with hope[34]. For Bob Dylan, signs of this belief in the resurrection first appear in *'Changing Of The Guards'*:

She wakes him up,
Forty-eight hours later, the sun is breaking,
Near broken chains, mountain laurel and rolling rocks.

and shows a use of the hill image in the new context of faith. References to Jesus' sacrifice now exhibit a certain dignity, such as in *'Where Are You Tonight (Journey Through Dark Heat)'*,

If you don't believe there's a price for this sweet paradise,
Remind me to show you the scars,

and Dylan appears to be more at ease with offering literal and straight-forward images of Calvary to his audience. Indeed from 1979 Dylan has little desire to hide behind the metaphor of the hill and instead is confident to refer explicitly to the mount of crucifixion – the road leads positively to the cross (from *'Saving Grace'*):

There's only one road and it leads to Calvary,
It gets discouraging at times, but I know I'll make it,
By the saving grace that's over me.

If it is true to say that the hill image (and some other aspects of Dylan's poetic language) is eclipsed by more traditional biblical terminology during Dylan's so-called "gospel years" then this is probably as a result of his new confidence to speak directly of the resurrected Jesus. However, Dylan's literal-biblical approach was swiftly attacked by the critics (even by many Christian ones) who asked *"Could it be that for Dylan, bluntness is the only way to approach the Good News?"*[35] and commented that *"Dylan was able to reveal much more religious truth prior to his conversion. Now, because of the noted lack of poetry and subtlety, what is communicated seems so flat".*[36] Possibly due to some of this public pressure, and no doubt also to a maturing of his own faith, Dylan gradually ceased to state explicitly his views on Jesus' death. And with that shift of emphasis came the reintroduction (with *"Infidels"*) of Dylan's use of less literal, more metaphoric language. On *"Infidels"* the motif of the hill returns powerfully and his poetry brims with mystery once again. Calvary retreats into ambiguity, as in the lines quoted earlier from *'Jokerman'* and *'License To Kill'*, and in the reference to the *'Neighbourhood Bully'*

. . . standing on the hill,
Running out the clock, time standing still.

In some cases the hill is even tinged with apathy; this is especially the case in *'Foot Of Pride'*, where the lines

Yes, I guess I loved him too,
I can still see him in my mind climbin' that hill,
Did he make it to the top, well he probably did and dropped
Struck down by the strength of the will

provide perhaps the strongest recorded evidence from that time that Dylan was experiencing some doubts over his faith. Of course a line such as

Say one more stupid thing to me before the final nail is driven in[37]

also helps to affirm this point of view.

Conclusion

"Infidels" marks the re-emergence of a songwriter who feels that his song-writing may not be able to survive merely on the direct assertions of faith and which to some extent again requires the shield of poetic language. That is <u>not</u> to say that I agree with the false dichotomy that asserts that "songs of faith" should

be free from metaphoric language while "secular songs" should only discuss religious topics when obscured in ambiguity. However, I would suggest that by tracing the path of a common religious motif such as the hill through the works of an artist that the reader may to a certain extent detect patterns of usage that may lead to insights into the spiritual disposition of that artist. However, to make any dogmatic assessment of Dylan's religious life from his lyrics would probably be to go too far. In his book about Dylan's spiritual quest, Scott M. Marshall remarks that *"it would certainly be a difficult task to divorce Dylan's essence from biblical tradition"*.[38] Bob Dylan and biblical language are inextricably linked, whether the writer himself be a believer or not. However, there can be no doubt that the language that Dylan consistently employs in his songs certainly continues to reflect upon and engage with the deep well of imagery that arises out of Christian tradition.

Notes:

[1] Gray, Michael. *"The Art of Bob Dylan"*. New York: *Hamlyn*, 1981, pages 43-6, 128.

[2] Ledeen, Jenny. *"Prophecy in the Christian Era"*. St Louis: *Peaceberry Press*, 1995, has discussed Dylan's apocalyptic theme with special emphasis upon the motif of the storm (especially pages 11-25).

[3] Jeffrey, David Lyle. *"People of the Book"*. Grand Rapids: *Wm B Eerdmans*, 1996, pages 322 and 318.

[4] It should be noted that these five categories often overlap and are therefore only useful as guidelines.

[5] Cartwright, Bert. *"The Bible in the Lyrics of Bob Dylan"*. Bury: *Wanted Man*, 1985, page 56.

[6] Ibid, page 43

[7] Ibid, page 51.

[8] Matthew 17:1-13; Mark 9:2-13; Luke 9:28-36.

[9] Although note that Yudelson, in the web-page *Bob Dylan: Tangled up in Jews* (at http://www.well.com/user/yude/Dylan, winter 1998) suggests that the *"man of the mountains"* line speaks of either Abraham (living in the hill country) or of Dylan himself (from the mountain country of Minnesota).

[10] As noted by Bert Cartwright in his article *'I Shall Be Released'* (in *On The Tracks* vol. 5, no 2, October 1997, page 24).

[11] See Scobie's review of *"Time Out Of Mind"* in *On The Tracks* vol. 5, no 3, February 1998 (pages 22-7, especially page 27).

[12] For more information on Christ figures in modern film see *"Explorations in Theology and Film"*, edited by Clive Marsh and Gaye Ortiz, (Oxford: *Blackwell*, 1997).

[13] Note that the lines quoted in *'Cold Irons Bound'* also make use of the powerful biblical-apocalyptic image *"clouds of blood"*.

[15] This earlier version appears on *"The Bootleg Series Volumes 1-3"*; the original take is on *"Blood On The Tracks"*.

[16] Included in this suggestion is the idea that Dylan sees Billy as some type of Christ figure – Dylan is of course known to use mythical or outlaw figures to depict certain aspects of the Messiah.

17 The most likely reason being as a symbol of death.

18 James Hastings points out that *"the expression 'Mount Calvary' appears to have come into use after the 5th Cent[ury]"*, thus suggesting that the idea of Golgotha as a "Mount" did not arise until well after the writing of the Gospels and therefore a Calvary hill motif was not the reason behind the name "Skull". See Hastings, *"A Dictionary of the Bible"* (vol. II, 1899, Edinburgh: *T&T Clark*, page 226.

19 In Schneemelcher, Wilhelm (editor). *"New Testament Apocrypha, Volume One: Gospels and Related Writings"*. Philadelphia: *Westminster Press*, 1963, page 459 [italics mine]. Note though that the Acts of Pilate is a far from reliable account.

20 Tenney C, Merrill. *"The Zondervan Pictorial Encyclopedia of the Bible"*. Grand Rapids: *Zondervan*, 1975, page 772.

21 In Schiller, Gertrud. *"Iconography of Christian Art"*. London: (volume 2, *Lund Humphries*, 1968, page 7.

22 Ledeen, Jenny. *"Prophecy in the Christian Era"*. Exeter: *Peaceberry Press*, 1991, pages 121-2.

23 Bunyan, John. *"The Pilgrim's Progress"*. London: *Penguin*, 1978, page 35. Michael Gray (op cit, pages 48-9) demonstrates how Dylan's language was influenced by Bunyan.

24 Jeffrey, David Lyle (op cit, page 117).

25 For references see Hastings (op cit), page 226.

26 To be found in Gardner, Helen (editor). *"The Faber Book of Religious Verse"*. London: *Faber and Faber*, 1972, page 333.

27 Thomas, Dylan. *"Collected Poems 1934-1952"*. London: *DIM Dent & Sons*, 1973, page 68. Bob Dylan told Anthony Scaduto that he *"knew about Dylan Thomas"* (in *"Bob Dylan"* [New York: *Helter Skelter*, 1974], page 27).

28 Cone, James H. *"The Spirituals and the Blues: An Interpretation"*. New York, *Orbis Books*, 1972, pages 47-8.

29 Roos and O'Meara, *'Is your love in vain – dialectical dilemmas in Bob Dylan's recent love-songs'* in *"The Dylan Companion"* (edited by Elizabeth Thomson and David Gutman. London: *MacMillan*, 1990, page 33.

30 Dylan is linked with 'Lucky' in the *"Travelling Wilburys' (vol. 1")* album credits (*Wilbury Records,* 1988) and in *'Idiot Wind'* (verse 1, line 5).

31 At the time of its release *"Time Out Of Mind"* was largely thought to reflect Dylan's fragile state both emotionally and spiritually, although Paul Williams has rejected the notion of a tormented Bob Dylan on *"TOOM"* and has instead described the album as *"an expression of joy in the face of hard times"* (see *"Bob Dylan Performing Artist 1986-1990 and Beyond"*. London: *Omnibus Press*, 2004, page 311).

32 This is certainly the theory that underlies many of the most interesting studies of Dylan's lyrics so far. One work that stands out in this respect is Paul Williams' 1979 extended essay *"Dylan – What Happened?"* (reprinted in *"Bob Dylan: Watching The River Flow"*. [London: *Omnibus Press*, 1996], pages 63-133), which interprets Dylan's 1970s lyrics in a strictly autobiographical manner – quite unlike the method that underpins Williams' writings on *"Time Out Of Mind"* (see note 31).

33 Cartwright describes *"Shelter From The Storm"* as picturing *"Jesus' experience on earth . . . as ending in utter frustration"* (1985, op cit, page 23).

34 Part of a letter Dylan wrote in May 1980 emphasises the importance he placed on the resurrection around this time: *"...You're also talking about Christ, the resurrected Christ; you're not talking about some dead man* [who] *had a bunch of good ideas and was nailed to a tree – who died with those ideas – you're talking about a resurrected Christ who is*

Lord of your life". (quoted in Heylin, Clinton (ed.), *"Saved! The Gospel Speeches of Bob Dylan"* [New York: *Hanuman Books*, 1990], page 111).

[35] Rose, Stephen C. *'Bob Dylan meets Jesus'* in *"Christianity and Crisis"* (number 39, 1979), page 288.

[36] MacKenzie, Jnr, Donald M. *'The Conversion on Bob Dylan'* in *"Theology Today"* (volume 37, 1980/1), page 358.

[37] Lyrics published in *"Bob Dylan: The 30th Anniversary Concert Celebration"*. (Spanish lyrics edition. Madrid: *Celeste Ediciones*, 1993), pages 24-9. Note that in the Spanish edition of the words, "nail" is rendered "day", contrary to the recorded lyric. This rendering, although most likely an error, interestingly places a different (and apocalyptic) nuance within the line.

[38] Marshall, Scott M. *"Restless Pilgrim: The Spiritual Journey of Bob Dylan"*. Lake Mary: *Relevant Media Group*, 2002, page 147.

Published in *ISIS* issue #82, January, 1999. Re-worked, for inclusion in this Anthology, June 2005.

Bob Dylan 1984

In Search of Jokerman

D. R. Neyret

Bob Dylan once said, *"I just know in my mind that we all have a different idea of all the words we're using . . . like if I say the word 'house'. . . we're both going to see a different house. . . "* There is truth in these words and as I sit here thinking of *'Jokerman'* I see a shimmering and ever-changing row of houses before me. Who really knows what Dylan wants to say in this song? I am not usually one of those pedants who delves into endless speculation on the meanings of Dylan's lyrics. For the most part, I think that's pointless; but this piece of work is too intriguing and has plagued me for years. The mysteries in this song run deep, and the key lies in figuring out who the Jokerman is. Some say he's Jesus, some say it's Dylan himself. I say the Jokerman is a fusion of mythological and mystical figures from throughout human history and culture.

Most people know about Dylan's so-called gospel years. After years of touring, drug-abuse, philandering and a divorce, in 1978, Dylan the Jew found Jesus. He became a preachy and somewhat dogmatic character. A believer in an imminent apocalypse and end of the world prophesy. But the zeal started to wane after three or four years and around 1982 he visited Israel. Dylan seemed to have simultaneously reconfirmed his Jewishness while maintaining his newfound faith in Jesus. Dylan's entire world seemed to be expanding and in 1983 he released *"Infidels"*, which contains the song *'Jokerman'*, one of the most confounding, multi-faceted and mysterious songs of his career.

This feeling of expansion is evident in *'Jokerman'*, both in the lyric as a whole and in who the Jokerman is and represents. Joseph Campbell's *"The Hero With a Thousand Faces"* may or may not have been a direct influence on Dylan, and we may never know, but for me, the Jokerman is indeed an ur-hero the way Campbell describes him. He is a prototypical being. An Avatar constructed from many different characters, a hero and god coming from all time and all cultures. A personal God. Nearly all human cultures have myths and stories of these god/heroes who share so much in common. Nearly all start out as commoners, charismatic and bright. They experience a deep spiritual or supernatural interaction with something powerful and transcendent. It calls them into action, sends them on a quest. They face and overcome moral dangers. Many have a twin or rival who is often an aspect of the hero himself, the twin within, which is a common theme in Dylan's work (*'I And I'*, *'Tweedle Dee And Tweedle Dum'*, *'Frankie Lee And Judas Priest'*, the joker and the thief).

Many of these hero/gods take on the form or aspect of certain animals. Dylan's own name, one he chose himself, comes from Welsh mythology via Dylan Thomas. Dylan was the son of the Welsh god Aranrhod who was born, baptized and went off to sea whereupon he took on its nature, swimming as far and as deep as any fish. An apt description for Bob. It is also possible that Dylan took his name from an American mystical-heroic figure, Matt Dillon, from the '50s TV series *"Gunsmoke"*, a figure many young people Dylan's age at the time were fascinated by.

Some hero/gods die only to come back resurrected and carry their story and the fruits of their quest to their people. They encounter other figures such as the mother, the lover and the guardian who watches over the object of their quest creating obstacles. They all pose problems that the hero/god must solve, sometimes through upright behaviour, sometimes through trickery and other times through seeming departure from their religion, principles or cause. And then there are those who represent the spirit of all that is wild or natural in the world and within us.

Think of the stories of Jesus, Moses, Abraham or the Buddha who was born an ignorant prince and went out to discover the suffering masses and subsequently went through several moral and physical tests to find truth. The violent Heracles was sent into exile only to later repent at the hands of Apollo. Gilgamesh went through struggles, battles and a perilous quest to find immortality. Pan, who represents all that is wild within us, speaks to man's lower nature yet is divine and wholly connected to the universe. His music moves mountains and feeds knowledge into us. Then there is Loki, a provider, trickster and instigator of conflict who manages to solve the tricky situations only to pay a price himself–another example of the twin within, the good/bad entity Dylan deals with so frequently.

This song is about yearning, searching for understanding, all the while superimposing religious doubts and fears. Dylan weaves all these great god/hero characters into one, purposefully trying to personalise his, or the narrator's, God. Humanity has always instinctively understood that all creation, all beauty, all knowledge and survival itself balances on the razor's edge between structure and randomness. The ur-hero, whether he's Jesus or the Trickster, shows mankind how to keep that balance, as well as the risks of losing it. That's why the Jokerman is such a compelling figure. But what Dylan is reflecting here, through an unknown narrator, is what many mere mortals fear and worry over. He explores those doubts, and fears that the Jokerman is simply not paying attention and not listening. He perhaps believes that this ur-hero, this god or God, is indifferent and even cruel and sadistic.

Most of this song is immersed in Biblical, Jewish and Christian tradition, and their sense of book learning. It is filled with repeated instances of Biblical, end-of-the-world prophecy, but we also see a deep and profound respect for the earth, nature, and their power. There is also a shown respect for the Ancients and their mythology. All this gives us a rounded sense of earthly and mystical knowledge. Common sense and intuition walk beside the revealed wisdom of the scriptures and we can recall Dylan's famous quote (no doubt inspired by English poet

William Blake), *"I can see God in a flower"*. But this song also contains a certain randomness of expression and more importantly, timelessness. There are lines in this song which are perhaps there because Dylan simply had them lying around in his little box of phrases, a storehouse of lines and verses he keeps around with the purpose of using them in a song one day. They sound good and invoke a certain feeling consistent with the overall theme and so he drops them into place. Not to make it sound so easy, we do know that this song, maybe more than most, was written and rewritten many times. Here are a few comments Dylan made during an interview in the early 1980s:

"A lot of times you'll just hear things and you'll know that these lines are the things that you want to put in your song. Whether you say them or not. They don't have to be your particular thoughts. They just sound good, and somebody thinks them. Half my stuff falls along those lines . . . I didn't originate those kinds of thoughts. I've felt them, but I didn't originate them. They're out there, so I just use them . . . It's more or less remembering things and taking it down . . . songs are just thoughts. For the moment they stop time. To hear a song is to hear someone's thought, no matter what they're describing . . . It's happened, it's been said, I've heard it: I have proof of it. I'm a messenger. I get it. It comes to me so I give it back in my particular style".

The song opens with a reference to Ecclesiastes:

Standing on the waters casting your bread
While the eyes of the idol with the iron head are glowing.
Distant ships sailing into the mist,
You were born with a snake in both of your fists while a hurricane was blowing.
Freedom just around the corner for you
But with the truth so far off, what good will it do?

"Cast your bread upon the waters, for after many days you will find it again" – Ecclesiastes 11-1. This reference is contrasted with images of what could be Babylonian idol-worship and right off we see opposing forces, turmoil. This is followed by the distant ships, the Ancients, lost in the mists. He calls upon them and there is Heracles who was born with snakes in his fists during a wild storm. His mother Hera put the snakes in his crib hoping they would kill him. Heracles was a son of God, not unlike Christ, and he killed the snakes with his supernatural strength. *"Freedom just around the corner for you"*. Every hero struggles for perfection and redemption, freedom from re-birth. But the ultimate good, Truth, is so far off that the world is a doomy and gloomy place. The doubts and fears in the narrator's world become apparent. What good would all this enlightenment and freedom do if our ur-hero is simply sadistic and absent? Truth is not enough to save.

Jokerman dance to the nightingale tune,
Bird fly high by the light of the moon,
Oh, oh, oh, Jokerman.

What is this tune he dances to? He seems lost in it and the narrator seems to be yearning to be a part of it. There's urgency there. We can surely call upon Keats for his use of the nightingale, a symbol of immortality, *"thou wast not born for death"*, but there is perhaps a more profound relevance for the nightingale tune. In medieval Spain, Christian, Muslim and Jewish mystics would gather together. They were poets and seers and sang of God, weaving their prismatic, mystical traditions together. They called this the Nightingale Song. The song of knowing. One of these great poets was Judah Halevi, *"the Sweet Singer of Zion"*, someone Dylan, I have a feeling, is familiar with. What this might be saying is that these three great religions, the world's mythology and great works of classical poetry form a whole, as the Nightingale Song itself attests to and is mirrored with the idea of our ur-hero. It encompasses all humanity and divinity. The mystic tradition has validity and force and the Jokerman is here for all of us, singing his blissful tune for everyone.

As a side note to the Nightingale Song, these mystical ideas, songs and poems from medieval Spain spread up to the southern regions of France and became seed for the medieval troubadours who in turn called themselves Nightingales. Of this, Dylan could be quite aware as he had delved in that world several years earlier (in the mid '70s), inspiring the heavily mystical, gypsy-cowboy album *"Desire"*.

But we will see later in the song that the narrator feels that the Jokerman is getting too wrapped up in his own bliss and is becoming apathetic to the troubles mortal mankind is experiencing. The hero/god became disinterested in the formation of evil in the world. This reminds me of a Hindu story of the battles fought with the demon Raktabija. Many gods were fighting, trying to destroy Raktabija but could not, so they went to find Shiva to ask him for aid but Shiva was lost in ecstatic meditation and could not join in the conflict of good against evil. There is a constant implication in this song that the end of the world is near and that the Jokerman is not paying attention, he's lost in his own bliss. The narrator calls and pleads, trying to bring the Jokerman's attention to all that's going on and has gone on in the world but this hero/god keeps losing himself in his nightingale song.

In the second verse we have our first sign of clear belief that the end is nigh, the sun is setting, it's the end of time and it's coming fast.

So swiftly the sun sets in the sky,
You rise up and say goodbye to no one.
Fools rush in where angels fear to tread,
Both of their futures, so full of dread, you don't show one.
Shedding off one more layer of skin,
Keeping one step ahead of the persecutor within.

Is the Jokerman saying goodbye to no one? Or is he simply not saying goodbye? Then comes a very tricky line in the song, *"Fools rush in where angels fear to tread"*. It is pregnant with Dylan's tomfoolery (I am sure he plays tricks on us) and his affinity for lifting lines from interesting places full of meaning. It may simply be part of this randomness of expression that was mentioned earlier. A line dropped into place because it sounds good. This phrase comes from Alexander Pope's, *'An Essay on Criticism'*. It is actually a poem riddled with an *'It's Alright Ma (I'm Only Bleeding)'* like cadence, which deals with the question of taste when judging poetry and criticizes those people who believe they know something of art, especially poetry. It also says that for true judgement we must look back to the Ancients and to Nature, themes that are very present in this song. This particular line of Pope's that Dylan uses deals specifically with the absurdity of talking about or judging something that we don't understand. Just because we may read and know the right books, does not make us wise or give us any intuitive insight into the true meaning of a particular poem or work of art. So in this particular line Dylan, via Pope, is saying that an unwise person would rush into critical analysis of something without consulting the wisdom of the Ancients and of Nature, unlike the wise, such as an angel, who would know better. I feel that this song cannot be understood without consulting the Ancients or Nature as we will see further on. Or perhaps I am a fool. So the world is inhabited by fools and angels but both of their futures are *"so full of dread"* that the Jokerman doesn't even show one (a future).

Then there's a quest for reinvention, transformation, purification as we drop any excess baggage *"shed skin"* and keep ahead of *"the prosecutor within"*, head for salvation as our own judge.

And once again the narrator tries to catch the Jokerman's attention as he dances in his ecstatic song of knowing. He's in the world, but not of it.

> *You're a man of the mountains, you can walk on the clouds,*
> *Manipulator of crowds, you're a dream twister.*
> *You're going to Sodom and Gomorrah*
> *But what do you care? Ain't nobody there would want to marry your sister.*
> *Friend to the martyr, a friend to the woman of shame,*
> *You look into the fiery furnace, see the rich man without any name.*

In the third verse, the Jokerman is seen as a god of the mountains and a dream twister. This is easily recognizable in many cultures as is the power of walking on clouds or water or having other supernatural powers. Mountain gods can be fierce and powerful or they can be healers, ridding people of disease. If we look to the Ancients again we see many mountain gods, the Ourea, who were the first born elemental gods. They include Kithairon, Helikon, Tmolos and Olympos who are all tied into the realm of music. Zeus had authority over all the mountain gods and with him they came to rule the universe.

Then there were the Oneiroi. They were personified dream gods, each an embodiment of different aspects of dreams. The most distinguished of these gods is Morpheus who visited the dreams of kings and chieftains. At his command, his brothers and all the other Oneiroi would send forth the various shapes that arise in the dreams of the common man, twisting them, so to speak.

The Gospels express clearly that Jesus compared the cities of Tyre and Sydon to Sodom and Gomorrah. He visited these evil places and washed his hands of them. Many miracles were performed in the former two cities and Jesus considered that if the miracles performed there had also been done in Sodom and Gomorrah, they would have repented long before. So in a sense, Jesus would have gone there too, but what does he care now? The Jokerman would be immune to evil, but now he is becoming indifferent and uncaring about a place condemned, debatably, for homosexual practices and other sinful behaviour. Therefore, these people would not be interested in Jokerman's sister, being allegedly homosexual. Even these places have become prototypical and symbolic, spawning many mythological tales of evil and indecency.

The martyr could be John the Baptist who was very close to Jesus. The woman of shame could be Mary Magdalene or the woman caught in adultery whom Jesus rescued from stoning by saying, *"He that is without sin among you, let him cast the first stone at her"*. But there is also the prophet Hosea who spoke of compassion for the martyred people of Israel who married Gomer who was a prostitute. It could be all or any of these figures.

Also from The Gospels is an unnamed rich man who, upon death, enters the fiery realm of Hell. He was visited by the poorly Lazarus, who wished to eat the food that fell from the rich man's table. Lazarus was ill and covered with sores. He suffered tremendously but never lost sight of God and spiritual riches, unlike the greedy rich man whose only wealth was worldly. When Lazarus died, he went straight to the bosom of Abraham. When the rich man died, he went to Hell. This parable composes a dramatic scene of contrasts – riches and poverty, heaven and hell, compassion and indifference, inclusion and exclusion, much of what this song is about.

But this line in the song also evokes the story of Nebuchadnezzar of Babylon casting into the fiery furnace three Jews; Shadrach, Meshach and Abednego who would not bow down before his image of gold. Nebuchadnezzar then looked into the fiery furnace and saw not three, but four men. The fourth man being described as a son of the gods. Obviously he is a protector, an angel or according to some translations and interpretations, Christ himself: an unnamed, spiritually rich man.

And the narrator once again calls out to the Jokerman before we come to another very Biblical fourth verse.

> *Well, the Book of Leviticus and Deuteronomy,*
> *The law of the jungle and the sea are your only teachers.*
> *In the smoke of the twilight on a milk-white steed,*
> *Michelangelo indeed could've carved out your features.*
> *Resting in the fields, far from the turbulent space,*
> *Half asleep near the stars with a small dog licking your face.*

Leviticus and Deuteronomy are books very much sacred to both Jews and Christians. Leviticus is mostly concerned with priestly rituals and religious observances. It's also about creating sacred space apart from the day-to-day world and finding contact with God. We could presume that this is what launches our hero/god, the Jokerman, into action in the first place. Leviticus also contains the phrase engraved on the Liberty Bell, *"Proclaim liberty throughout the land unto all the inhabitants thereof"* –Leviticus 25:10. Spreading this message of truth and salvation to his people is the Jokerman's goal and also his ultimate challenge. But we can surmise that the narrator now feels confused and deceived by this. He feels that the Jokerman has given up this quest.

Much of Deuteronomy is the personal farewell address of Moses, who is one of the references underlying the Jokerman's characterization as well as one of the classic examples of Campbell's ur-hero. Moses' address to the Children of Israel in Deuteronomy carries a major theme: that God is One. *"Hear, O Israel: The Lord your God, the Lord is One"*. –Deuteronomy 6:4-7. Like the Jokerman looking into the fiery furnace, seeing the rich man with no name, Moses has climbed Mount Sinai and received the Ten Commandments from One whose name is *"I am that I am"*, the One who says, *"No man sees My face and lives"*. Another crucial element in Deuteronomy is that human beings have free choice. We can accept or reject God's Law. Moses says, *"I set before you this day life and death, a blessing and a curse. Choose life"*. Leviticus, Deuteronomy and the whole Pentateuch is about responsibility. It's about the individual, who is free to make good or evil choices. The Law is about creating a social, moral and ethical structure that will both increase the probability of good choices while minimizing the damage of bad ones.

The Books of Leviticus and Deuteronomy are grouped together with the mythological, pagan domain of the law of the jungle and the sea. All living things came from the sea and shall return to the sea. Many people have written of a negative connotation concerning *"the law of the jungle and the sea"* thinking of chaos, disorder and fear; the horrible consequence of un-Godly living. I feel though that Dylan's intent here is a positive one. He is expressing the sentiment that all these elements somehow fit together; the revealed wisdom of the scriptures and the general wisdom and order of nature. All these things are the ur-hero's teachers and ours as well. This gives a very rounded sense of learning, book knowledge and intuitive, involving a lot of common sense. As Rudyard Kipling once wrote:

Now this is the Law of the Jungle
As old and as true as the sky
And the wolf that shall keep it will prosper
But the wolf that does break must die
Just like the creeper that girdles the tree-trunk
The Law it runs forward and back
That the strength of the pack is in the wolf
And the strength of the wolf is in the pack.

"In the smoke of the twilight on a milk-white steed" is another flagrant look into the apocalypse. As we read through the pages of the Book of Revelations, we see

the Lamb of God opens all the seven seals in John's vision, the words hidden behind each seal burst into light, the world's history is revealed beginning with the appearance on earth of Jesus Christ on a white horse. King David was also prophesied to enter Jerusalem on a *"milk-white steed"* and Michelangelo indeed carved the features of both these historical figures but for now this amalgam is away from all that. Resting like a wandering troubadour with a dog at his heels finding his own sacred space; his own meditation room under the stars; oblivious that mankind is in a world that is about to come to an end.

Jokerman dance to the nightingale tune,
Bird fly high by the light of the moon,
Oh, oh, oh, Jokerman.

Well, the rifleman's stalking the sick and the lame,
Preacherman seeks the same, who'll get there first is uncertain.
Nightsticks and water cannons, tear gas, padlocks,
Molotov cocktails and rocks behind every curtain,
False-hearted judges dying in the webs that they spin,
Only a matter of time 'til night comes steppin' in.

Now the world has become so corrupt that the rifleman and the preacherman have the same goal; to prey on the sick and the lame. There's a race on to take advantage of the weak and destroy souls but who will win? Who will get there first? Who is worse? Both are judging with corrupted vision; blindness. Debauched systems filled with violence and greed, finger-pointing and side-taking; spinning webs of untruth and blame when all the while the end of the world is coming.

It's a shadowy world, skies are slippery grey,
A woman just gave birth to a prince today and dressed him in scarlet.
He'll put the priest in his pocket, put the blade to the heat,
Take the motherless children off the street
And place them at the feet of a harlot.
Oh, Jokerman, you know what he wants,
Oh, Jokerman, you don't show any response.

In the last verse Dylan merges this sense of doom with accumulated Biblical allegory. The sky darkens. The world is shadowy and mysterious, full of darkness and obscurity. Somewhere a prince is born; a future king, a future leader of people, a president or prime minister. The woman dresses him in scarlet, the colour that is associated with sin, the devil, the beast, the Whore of Babylon. *"Hereafter I will not talk much with you: for the prince of this world cometh, and hath nothing in me"*. – John 14:30. This woman, the mother of this "prince" is an enabler to a corrupt and Godless leader, one who buys off priests and prepares for waging war. He may gather up *"motherless children"* but he places them *"at the feet of a harlot"*, Mystery, Babylon the Great, Mother of Harlots and

Abominations of the Earth. This leader will partake in her world of false religion, power, control, tyranny and greed. He will drink from her *"cup of abominations"* and be drunk with licentiousness and spiritual adultery. We could name any number of leaders from past and present and fit them into this realm: Pisistratus, Herod, Caligula, Mao, Stalin, Hitler, Pinochet, Than Shwe, BushCo. As with most of this song, the meaning is timeless, the sentiments ever present, perpetual, cyclical.

And then the narrator pleads once again with our ur-hero, yearning once again that the Jokerman wake up and hear his plea, that he must see what this "prince" wants and who he is, must see what he's after and what he will do. He is utterly saddened and perplexed, afraid even, that the Jokerman is not listening. *"You know what he wants! You don't show any response!"* It's an angry tone, full of helplessness and exasperation. It is a terribly emotional moment in the song. The narrator may wonder why we should even believe in any sort of hero, god or prophet. Is the world a Godless place? A fall from grace? Or is God simply withdrawn, indifferent and sadistic? Why create this place of turmoil, corruption, evil and greed and then wander off under the stars enjoying the bliss and all but ignoring mankind's suffering?

I am reminded of the story of Narada. He is a quintessential jokerman, a trickster and powerfully noble holy personage. He is a celestial musician, wise advisor and is respected by gods and demons alike. One great talent he had was as a quarrel-monger. He would go to both gods and demons and tell each of the others' secrets, purposely pitting one against the other. Gods and demons naturally despised each other and Narada knew that this would stir up much hatred and the demons would take some kind of action. What was the purpose of this? To bring evil to the absolute brink. Only with an almost overflowing amount of wickedness could evil entities attract punishment and destruction. This is the purpose of all the trickster/joker gods the world over, and usually it works out that evil is banished and destroyed.

But now this song is expressing the feeling that something is out of kilter. Everything is broken. Something has happened, some inexplicable event or phenomenon that has prevented any sense of balance or righteous revenge to occur. Jokerman, or the hero, god, prophet or holy personage of one's choice, or even God, has become unable or unwilling to partake anymore. The sentiment here in this song is that this planet is being left behind, forgotten about by the gods or God; sadistically left to come to an end. The narrator still believes they're out there, he sees them and calls to them, but he feels they've forgotten about the balance that needs to be kept in check; forgotten to come when evil overflows; forgotten everything while absorbed, dancing to that blissful nightingale tune.

Published in *ISIS* issue #119, March, 2005

Bob Dylan 1998

A Close Encounter of the Fifth Kind
Bowled over by the Bag Lady

Patrice Hamilton

Many years and even more shows have passed since that amazing evening when I met Bob Dylan in the South of France. I had four-and-a-half fabulous hours in the delightful company of a man whose music has meant so much to me and many others. After my initial nerves settled it was just like talking to a mate down the pub. No superstar trip from Bob.

To begin with, bass player Tony Garnier and a Personal Assistant, Suzie Pullen, were sitting at the table with Bob, myself and my ex-husband Michael, but Tony and Suzie soon wandered off.

Indeed to set the record straight on one count – Jim Callaghan sat at another table some distance away with Claude Angele Boni who did not take part in the conversation at any time – she was kept well away from Bob at <u>his</u> request.

She wrote a book in the 90s and referred to Michael and me as an *"English couple"* who were waiting for her to give us a lift back to her house so preventing her from staying with Bob and that Jim had offered us a room at Bob's Hotel Juana. None of this was true. She was not waiting for us and we already had a room at a nearby hotel. This account is how it really happened.

***

I'd met Jim Callaghan, Bob's minder, about 18 months previously. He'd been impressed by my drawings and paintings of Bob and had been very kind and sympathetic about my missed opportunity of meeting Bob during the filming of *"Hearts of Fire"*. I had the feeling he was weighing me up almost like an 'assessment' for the fairly remote possibility of a future meeting with Dylan. At that stage it was nothing more than a distant dream. Then, in July 1992, we decided to go to the South of France for a week's holiday and to take in a concert as the icing on the cake.

Juan Les Pins was like Paradise. It was scorching hot, Mediterranean blue sky, turquoise sea, palm trees and Bob – what more could you want? The concert was to be held in a beautiful park, which was adjacent to an equally beautiful beach. We'd wandered around all day meeting up with old friends in the Dylan fraternity and looking forward to the evening ahead. We'd been told that the park closed at

6 o'clock and that everyone would have to queue outside the gates and that it would be every man for himself when the gates opened.

We were in a small party of eight friends, so instead of leaving through the gates at 6 o'clock, we wandered onto the beach where there was no gate. We were eating fruit and enjoying a paddle in the crystal clear water, when I was aware that someone was calling me over to some tables set with food and wine under umbrellas. It looked very inviting.

It was Jim Callaghan sitting with his wife and friends and members of Bob's band; he invited us to sit down and help ourselves to wine and strawberries. He then said to me if it was possible to meet Bob what would I prefer: a quick handshake backstage before the concert when Bob would be fairly uptight (also I wouldn't be able to get in the front to watch the concert); or wait and take a chance.

I had to be quick in replying but without hesitation I said: *"I'll take a chance"*. I asked: *"How will I know?"* He replied: *"You'll know when the time is right"*. I didn't dare hope; I felt a bit sick and a knot lodged in my stomach. Our group wandered back from the beach into the empty park and we positioned ourselves along the rail right in front of the stage and waited in a state of high tension. The gates opened and the massive crowd thundered into the park and headed for the same rail we were already bracing ourselves against. The night was starry-warm and perfect. The venue was also ideal – the stage framed by palm trees and the beach. Heavenly!

It was a blistering show. We just stared up at the amazing phenomenon that is Bob Dylan, all of us knowing there was nowhere on earth we'd rather be. As the last notes of *'Blowin' In The Wind'* died away I knew I had to act fast. Jim Callaghan had given me a backstage pass so I shot round to the back of the stage, on the beach, and, in the crowd and confusion, there I saw Dave Stewart, whom I had met earlier in the day. I asked: *"Dave, has Bob gone back to his hotel?"* He said: *"Yeah, I think he must have"*. Right, Plan B had to be put into operation. Problem was I didn't have a Plan B! Jim's words kept coming back to me *"You'll know when the time is right"*.

OK, how the hell would I know when the time was right? I was feeling slightly panicky now and not nearly as confident as I'd felt an hour earlier. It was about 11.30pm and I didn't have much idea of what to do next except wait. I was clutching a bag of T-shirts, Dylan prints of my drawings, and books on Somerset – just in case. I must have resembled some sort of neurotic bag lady as I stood on the grass verge just hoping there'd be some sort of sign or vision that would point me in the right direction.

We'd come out of the park, which was opposite Bob's hotel (Hotel Juana), a beautiful white building standing majestically, framed by palm trees and fronted by a large open terrace, lit up and deserted except for a few small figures sitting at a table in the corner chatting and sipping wine. I recognised one of the figures as Dave Stewart . . . then realised one of the others was Bob Dylan!

We stood motionless on the grass verge opposite the terrace. People were still milling around from the concert; the town was lit up and busy, people eating, drinking, talking, laughing . . . several of our friends wandered off to eat but Michael and I stayed put – almost rooted to the spot.

One friend in particular said: *"You've got two chances of meeting Bob. Bob's chance and no chance"*. He walked away laughing and shaking his head. It was near to midnight. I could still see Bob and Dave deep in conversation. I could also see past them up the steps to the hotel into the chandelier-lit reception area. Then I saw Jim and his wife having a drink. This was my signal and I knew that the time was right. I said: *"Let's go"* and we walked very purposefully across the road, through the hotel gate across the terrace – taking care not to look to our left, tempting as it was – up the steps and into the reception area where Jim said: *"Hi. Come and have a drink!"* I felt I was nearly there.

We chatted for a few minutes and I have to confess I wasn't concentrating too closely on what was being said. Out of the corner of my eye, I saw Bob and Dave Stewart walking towards the gate, my heart sank. Just my luck to come this far and now they were going off somewhere together. But then I saw them stop by the gate. Dave went off and Bob walked back to his table. I couldn't believe my luck. *"Right"*, said Jim. *"I reckon the time is right, follow me"*. And with that I picked up my carrier bag and followed. I didn't have time to be nervous or even to think about what was about to happen after those few short steps. I was standing in front of Bob who was sitting at a small round table and I could hear Jim saying: *"These are friends of mine, Bob, she's an artist"*. I could have died of embarrassment but thankfully I survived my blushes.

There sat the living legend – about two feet away from me, cap on freshly showered familiar curls, dark glasses, black voile shirt and denim jeans, head on one side looking quizzical and every inch Bob Dylan. I plonked myself down on the nearest chair. I felt the need to keep talking to try to hide the fact that I was very nervous. I decided the only way I could deal with the situation was to talk to him as if I was talking to a friend in my local pub. I had to forget who I was actually talking to and keep everything as normal as possible. I have to say it worked very well.

I dived into my plastic bag and drew out the book on Somerset. I thought if I met Bob it could possibly be a talking point, something that I thought he would find interesting, which it proved to be. He picked it up from the table and started leafing through it, commenting that Somerset seemed like a nice place. I replied it is quite a mysterious place that had many myths and legends attached to it like that of Joseph of Aramathea who had visited on more than one occasion and legend had it that he planted a thorn tree. Bob expressed an interest in King Arthur. Did he exist? Guinevere and the knights of the round table? We talked very generally about Somerset. We also talked about the house I lived in and the garden where wild ducks waddle up from the stream and tap on the French windows. He seemed genuinely enchanted. He asked me to write my name, address and phone number in the front of the book. My hand was shaking so much I started laughing, it was a real effort to write legibly. I said: *"I'm sorry, my hand is shaking"*. He laughed and said that's OK as long as you write it. He said he would like to visit Somerset some time. *"Well that's fine, we've got a spare room"*, I quipped.

269

Me: *"Do you like tea?"*
Bob: *"Yes, I love tea".*
Me: *"Well I'll put the kettle on".*

He seemed to be really enjoying the banter. I felt I needed to keep the momentum going, he seemed very relaxed and I felt I had his full attention, so into my trusty plastic bag I dived again and this time brought out my 'piece de resistance!' A book of cut-out-and-make-your-own model of Stonehenge! We thought it was hilarious when we saw it in the shop because after all of that cutting out and gluing tab A to tab B, etc. all you'd end up with is a load of little cardboard cubes and oblongs, which you then arrange into a stunning model of Stonehenge.

Before I handed it to him I said: *"This is for all those long, lonely nights in hotel rooms when you're incredibly bored and wondering what to do".* I then thrust it into his hands. He looked really puzzled, probably wondering what on earth I was going to bring out next. He flipped over the pages and a broad grin spread across his face, then he threw his head back and really laughed. That moment was absolutely wonderful, I'd made Bob Dylan laugh. It was time to dip into the bag again, this time out came a T-shirt with a 1966 image of Dylan with the dark glasses and wild hair; the lyrics to *'Mr Tambourine Man'* were swirling all around his head. His face lit up.

Bob: *"Wow is this for me?"*
Me: *"Yes, if you'd like it".*
Bob: *"It's great".*

He grinned like a little kid at Christmas; he wanted to know how I'd done it. I explained. I like to think of him wearing it when he's mowing the lawn! At this point I realised that my mouth was incredibly dry as I'd been talking non-stop. Seeing a full glass of white wine in front of me, rather cheekily I asked if he'd mind if I had a glass of wine as I was really thirsty. He grinned at me and said: *"Only if you share it with me"*, and pushed his empty glass towards me. Oh dear, I thought, my hand was never going to be steady enough to perform the feat of pouring half the wine out of my glass into his! I picked up my glass and started to laugh and said: *"I don't think I can do this".* He laughed, took my glass and said: *"Give it to me, I'll do it"*, and poured it into his own. Boy did that wine taste good! He started to talk about the show that we'd seen a few hours earlier.

Bob: *"What did you think of the show tonight?"*
Me: *"Brilliant. Great concert!"*
Bob: *"Oh really, you think so?"*
Me: *"Yes, you did a lot of my favourite songs".*
Bob: *"I couldn't hear much crowd reaction".*
Me: *"Oh, it was there, believe me everyone around me enjoyed it".*
Bob: *"Was the sound OK? I was really worried about the sound".*
Me: *"The sound was fine to me. I'm no technician but it sounded great".*
Bob: *"The sound didn't seem right".*

Me: *"Maybe it's different when you're at an outside venue, the sound gets lost into the air".*
Bob: *"You really think it sounded OK?"*

Why would Bob need reassurance about a concert when performing is what he's always done, and especially from me who knows nothing about the technicalities of it all?

Me: *"Maybe when you're in an enclosed place, like say Hammersmith Odeon, the sound is more intense".*
Bob: *"Yeah, Hammersmith. That's a good place, I like it there".*
Me: *"So do we! It's fantastic. I can remember the first moment you appeared on stage at Hammersmith (1990). The tension in the crowd just before you appeared was electric, I felt I was going to explode and little bits of me would fly all over the room".*
Tony Gamier: *"So that's what hit me in the eye!"*

I said it amused me the way the press often referred to him as a moody recluse and we fans as middle-aged hippies. I don't know which is worse.

Me: *"Mind you, at some of those shows you looked a really miserable bugger".*
At which point, he switched to *'Dont Look Back'* mode.
Bob: *"Me, miserable? I'm never miserable. You don't see me being miserable".*
(which amused me greatly)
Me [grinning]: *"You cheered up as the evening wore on!"*
Bob: *"That was a good place, I enjoyed playing there. We're gonna be doing 24 shows, maybe in England next year".*
Me: *"Great! I'll have to sleep out on the pavement again for the tickets".*
Bob: *"No, no, you can have tickets. You shouldn't have to do that".*
Me: *"It was a laugh. We slept out on deck chairs and in sleeping bags on Hammersmith Odeon steps and even had a barbecue, it was great".*
Bob: *"Really? You did that?"*
Me: *"Yeah, but it was winter, there was ice on the ground and it was bloody cold! It was worth it, though. They were great shows. We've made a lot of good friends; it's like a huge family on the move".*
Bob: *"That's really good!"*

At round about this time, Charlie Quintana (who was drumming for Bob on this tour) came running across the terrace waving his drumsticks in the air.

Bob: *"Hey Charlie where you going?"*
Charlie: *"We're playing with some guys on the corner of the street and Victor's passing the hat!"*

He cracked up laughing. Bob was incredulous.

Bob: *"Victor? No! Victor? Passing the hat? Not Victor? I've gotta see this! Busking, that's sick man, sick".*

By this time he was laughing, too. He got up from the table so we followed him like mates going for a night out. Across the terrace, out of the gates we proceeded to walk down the road together. How bizarre was this? Pinch me. There I was, walking by Bob's side down the road in the South of France on a beautiful, warm starry night, having already had an amazing time chatting with him and drinking wine, definitely the stuff dreams are made of. As we walked, he with his familiar rolling gait, people were sitting around idly looking up and doing a double take. Hey, that guy looks like Bob Dylan. It was really weird. I imagined some journalist ending up with a picture on the front page of a Sunday newspaper with the headline 'Dylan: Who's the mystery blonde?' We reached a considerable crowd of people on the corner of the street, all enthralled by Bob Dylan's band playing guitars with some Irish boys, probably no older than 17 or 18, who were also playing guitars and Charlie Quintana seated on the pavement crashing away on an upturned tin. What a scene!

I was standing next to Bob watching this, still not really believing it was all happening and wondering whether anyone would actually believe me if I told them! A good friend of ours, John Hume, was taking photos of the band and obviously thoroughly enjoying the occasion. He looked across, saw me, saw Bob, couldn't believe his eyes and snapped a great photo, which I treasure even if at that angle he could only capture half my face and half Bob's. It's a very precious reminder of a great night. I thank you, John.

Incidentally, I had a camera in my bag the whole time I was talking to Bob, but felt if I asked for a photo it may have burst the bubble. I didn't want to risk spoiling things by behaving like a besotted fan. I think he might have agreed if I'd asked but I didn't want to take that chance. And anyway, the whole thing is like a movie in my head, which I can re-run whenever I like.

We hadn't been there very many minutes when a German woman standing in front of us suddenly turned round, saw Dylan and said *"Hi Bob"* really loudly right in his face. I felt him jump. Bob turned to me said: *"I can't handle this, I'm gonna have to go"*. He grabbed my arm and said *"Let's go back through the park"*. As if I'd say no! The same park that I'd seen the concert in a few hours earlier. As we walked back he began asking me if I was in Juan Les Pins on holiday. I said that we'd come down for a week and thought it would be good to take in a concert at the same time.

Bob: *"What have you been doing? Have you been to the beach?"*
Me: *"Oh yes, a bit of sun-bathing, sight-seeing, it's a great beach. We've also been over the border into Italy to see a ruined town called Bussana Vecchia".*

I told him it had been ruined in an earthquake sometime in the mid 1800s and now the ruins had been restored and taken over by artists and crafts people. It was a fascinating place that not too many people knew about and maybe he could get away with going up there and not being recognised. It made me realise how hard it was for him; he couldn't even go down to the beach. We'd seen the band there quite a bit, but I really felt quite sorry for him that there was a circus everywhere he went.

We crossed the road from the park to the Hotel Juana to find that all the lights on the terrace had been turned off and the gates were locked.

Bob: *"Oh this is good . . . we're locked out"*.

All of a sudden as if by magic, waiters appeared, scurrying about. Lights came on, the gates were opened and more bottles of wine appeared on the table. Three chairs at the table. I sat very close to Bob on his right and Michael sat across from us. Bob began pouring wine for us all. Being well brought up I said: *"Do you mind us drinking your wine, like this?"* He said: *"No, help yourself"*. Jim said afterwards he would have appreciated I said that as so many people take him for granted and think as he's a rich guy *'lets get what we can out of him'*. I pointed out I would have said the same to anyone! I noticed he lit cigarettes (Marlboro light) every so often but only took a couple of drags and then stubbed them out. We clinked our glasses together and said *"Cheers"* he added *"Bottoms up"* and giggled.

Bob seemed in such a relaxed mood. I kept thinking how lucky we were and that I should savour every moment. His curls were inches from my face and I remember thinking how many times I'd drawn that wonderful nose. Stupid or what! I'm a very tactile person and I was by now feeling quite relaxed, enjoying the whole situation. It could have been something to do with the wine of course! I'm sure during our conversation I touched his arm several times and was almost certainly guilty of calling him *"dear"* on a few occasions! What am I like? Anyway, he didn't seem to mind. In fact I think he was a little intrigued by this slightly eccentric English woman with her plastic bag of goodies!

He was interested to know who else in the music world we'd seen in concert. I mentioned that I'd first seen The Rolling Stones in 1964 and then for the second time in 1990! The first time, I couldn't hear it very well because all the girls there were screaming and crying; it was deafening. I remember my school friend Sarah wearing a big hat with badges bearing the names of the individual Stones. We'd both put on make-up to look older than our 13 years and when I looked at her face in the light of the foyer afterwards, she looked like Alice Cooper with long black streaks of mascara running down her face and dripping off the end of her chin! There was a list of people we'd seen in concert – Van Morrison, Eric Clapton, Burt Jansch, Martin Carthy (Bob had fond memories of Martin and commented on what a great guitarist and performer he is). He mentioned liking *'Banks Of The Nile'* and said he'd heard his latest album and liked it, and asked if Dave Swarbrick played with him often, such a good fiddle player.

Bob said that: *"We are living in the Age of Elvis."* I asked him what he meant by that. He said that once the old rockers had all gone what would be left? What would be coming along behind? Jim called from another table across the terrace and said *"your poems will be read out"*. Bob was laughing *"No, no, no"*. Then he quoted a few lines in a solemn voice.

Bob: *"It's all kid's music and videos these days. It's nothing".*
Me: *"It's completely rootless".*
Bob: *"Yeah, yeah that's exactly it, it's rootless. Once they're all gone what will there be? No-one like the Grateful Dead. Now they're really great, they're really big everywhere, bigger than me".*
Me: *"No, I don't think so, certainly not in England anyway".*
Jim: *"No, Bob. They couldn't get arrested in London, nobody's heard of them. They may be international but you're global Bob".*
Me: *"How does it feel to be 'Global Bob?"*

Bob couldn't really answer for laughing but still seemed unconvinced that the Grateful Dead weren't hugely recognised world-wide. He didn't think that World Music was going anywhere – he felt it would never really take off in a big way. He mentioned a couple of names of musicians. Many of whom I had never heard. When he asked me if I knew them I said *"No"*. That was just as well because we think he probably made them up just to see what we'd say!

We talked of seeing Eric Clapton in the early days when he played with The Yardbirds around small venues and pubs in the London area. Bob was surprised that we'd seen Clapton that far back.

Bob: *"With The Yardbirds? With Jimmy Page?"*
Michael: *"No, before Jimmy Page".*
Bob: *"Paul Samwell-Smith?"*
Michael: *"Yes. Chris Dreja".*
Bob: *"Oh yeah!"*
Michael: *"I saw him play once with Sonny Boy Williamson".*
Bob: *"Oh wow! I'd liked to have seen that. Did Keith Relf play harp?"*
Michael: *"No, he stood down".*
Bob: *"That must have been great".*
Michael: *"It's certainly something to remember".*

Then Michael asked him, in between more glasses of wine: *"Have you got another album planned".*

Bob: *"Yes, I've done one produced by David Bromberg. None of my songs just other people's, but after that I'm gonna do maybe one of all my songs. I've got them written on little bits of paper all over the place. It's difficult to get it all together, it's mind-boggling."* (Note the very English expression!).
Me: *"Stravinsky did that, things written on the back of bills, tickets etc".*
Bob: *"Yeah, yeah like that. Some days you don't know whether to write a song or make a phone call. Sometimes a phone call seems more important, there's just so many things to do".*

I asked him about the drawings and paintings that I'd heard might be coming out in a book.

Bob: *"They're drawings not paintings, just drawings, very conservative"*.
Me: *"How do you mean conservative?"*
Bob: (grinning) *"Just conservative"*.

John Jackson, the lead guitarist, ambled across the terrace and waved.

Bob: *"Hi JJ"*.

JJ grinned and waved and went inside the hotel.

Bob: *"He's always smiling and laughing, nothing fazes him. Santana comes on stage, Jimmy Vaughan and even Ron Wood, they blew the place apart. He wasn't fazed. He just carried on playing as if it was him. He's smiling, this sounds like shit and he's still smiling.*
He makes me laugh and forget the words to 'Tambourine Man', He's improved beyond recognition, though. He'll have 20 groupies in his room tonight – they all love JJ".

We talked very generally about a few other things like the French truckers strike that had nearly put an end to our trip and concert! What did we think of the Channel Tunnel and all agreed it was a terrorist's dream. He also asked us what we did for a living – all very ordinary questions, but he showed a great interest in what we did in our lives. I suppose in a way he felt comfortable talking to people who weren't asking him probing, personal questions. He mentioned he was working on producing a film and was getting the script together.

I said it was a shame that *'Hearts of Fire'* had been hacked about. He said he hadn't seen it but that the producer, Lain Smith, was a great guy and had sent him a case of Scotch. We even discussed the fact that I take herbal tablets called Devils Claw because I get a kind of arthritic pain in my hands sometimes, through painting day after day in my job as a ceramic artist. I said he may have experienced something similar through playing the guitar constantly. He didn't actually admit to anything but I gave him a packet of Devils Claw tablets anyway to try. He seemed totally bemused by the idea, and my eccentricity was probably confirmed!

Me: *"Have you seen the great film John Hammond Jnr. made about Robert Johnson?"*
Bob: *"No, what's this? A movie? TV? What?"*
Me: *"It was on television – a documentary about Robert Johnson, his life and music. They interviewed a lot of his old girlfriends, they were amazing people. Nobody seems to know exactly where he's buried. There are about six different burial sites according to who you speak to!"*
Bob: *"I'd really like to see that, is it going to be on anywhere, do you know?"*
Me: *"We've got it on tape at home"*.
Bob: *"Oh really. I'd really like to have that, could you get a copy to me?"*
Me: *"Yes of course. No problem"*.

Bob: *"That would be great"*.
Me: *"Where shall I send it?"*
Bob: *"To the Dylan Office"*.
Me: *"Jeff Rosen?"*
Bob: *"Yes"*.
Me: *"Could you give me the address?"*
Bob: *"Yeah, sure, that's really good. Thank you"*.
Me: *"That's OK, it's a pleasure!"*

We sent him a copy when we got home and it was later confirmed that Bob had received it and was very appreciative. It seemed like the night would never end. We'd had four-and-a-half-hours, chatting with someone who had been an important part of our lives for almost 30 years and, silly as it sounds, it felt like we could just arrange to meet the next day and carry on our conversation. Of course, I knew that would never be possible. But for those few hours we'd had something very precious and enjoyable – something that I would never forget.

At around 4.30am Bob rose from the table and said he was going to go upstairs. He shook hands with Michael and I was very lucky to get a goodnight kiss on the lips. We thanked him for a great evening and super concert and watched him amble into the hotel foyer and disappear.

We were both walking on air. What a wonderful evening it had been – quite unbelievable. In my hand I clutched a few souvenirs, a book of matches from the Hotel Juana, a cork from one of the wine bottles, an empty Marlboro packet and Bob's disposable lighter he'd left on the table. I couldn't resist being a daft fan after all!

Jim came across to me, beaming all over his face: *"What d'you think of that, then? Nobody, but nobody gets four-and-a-half hours with Bob Dylan"*.

Me: *"Maybe we outstayed our welcome?"*
Jim: *"Naah. If he hadn't wanted you there he'd have given me a signal and you'd have had to go. I'd have been the first to know and you'd have been the second. I could tell, he really enjoyed your company"*.

With that wonderful compliment ringing in my ears, we strolled back to our hotel, which was just a few doors down from Bob. We saw Bob and Jim sitting having coffee the next day on the same sunlit terrace but this time we kept our distance and just waved. What a time we'd had!

Note: It is interesting when reading the above account that a number of the words and phrases used by Bob when talking with the *"English couple"* were very English. The word holiday for example. This was noted by Patrice at the time.

First published in *"Brits & Bob's: Bob Dylan in the British Isles"*, edited and compiled by Steve Butterworth. These recollections are reprinted here with the kind permission of long-time *ISIS* subscriber and contributor Patrice Hamilton.

Bob Dylan 1999

Time on My Mind

Matthew Zuckerman

"Time Out Of Mind" is a journey made up of songs, eleven of them, written by Bob Dylan with the help of countless other singers and songwriters. Almost every song starts with the singer walking, always alone except for the many ghosts from his past. A restless hungry feeling haunts every track, and that room where his love and he laid is too far in the past to be seen. These lines plucked from *"TOOM"*'s eleven songs tell the tale; almost any other selection would tell the same story:

> *I'm walking through streets that are dead*
> *Gonna walk down that dirt road until my eyes begin to bleed*
> *The light in this place is so bad making me sick in the head*
> *I'm drifting in and out of dreamless sleep*
> *I've been wading through the high muddy water*
> *With the heat rising in my eyes*
> *Boys in the street beginning to play*
> *Girls like birds, flying away*
> *Rolling through the rain and hail, looking for the sunny side of love*
> *Shadows are falling and I've been here all day*
> *It's too hot to sleep and time is running away*
> *I'm waist deep, waist deep in the mist*
> *It's almost like, almost like, I don't exist*
> *I'd go hungry, I'd go black and blue*
> *I'd go crawling down the avenue*
> *All the laughter is just making me sad*
> *Skies are gray, I'm looking for anything that will bring a happy glow*
> *Night or day, it doesn't matter where I go anymore, I just go*
> *The sun is beginning to shine on me*
> *But it's not like the sun that used to be*

To some listeners, the music is swamped by the trademark Lanois ambience, and to others it is notable only for its three or four standout tracks (by general agreement 'Standing In The Doorway', 'Trying To Get To Heaven', 'Not Dark Yet' and – possibly – 'Highlands'), but to many, myself included, *"Time Out Of Mind"* is the first great rock album to look old age unashamedly in the face.

'Love Sick'

Back in the summer of 1997 when I first played the hissy, pre-release tape of *"Time Out Of Mind"* on my daughter's tiny (and tinny) cassette deck – my audio equipment being in storage at the time – and I first heard the opening bars of *'Love Sick'*, they immediately brought to mind Screamin' Jay Hawkins' *'I Put A Spell On You'*. (The song could almost be subtitled *'You Put A Spell On Me'*).

'Love Sick' brings to mind the song-cycle *"Winterreise"* by Schubert (music) and Wilhelm Müller (words). This series of twenty-four songs (written between 1822 and 1827 and set to music in 1827) tells the tale of a man broken by love walking through a winter landscape, observing the world from a distance and "talking to himself in a monologue". In the first song, *'Good Night'*, the singer asks:

> *Why should I stay any longer until I am driven away?*
> *Leave stray dogs to howl in front of their master's house.*
> *Love loves to rove –*
> *God made it so–*
> *From one to another;*
> *Dear love, good night.*
>
> 'Good Night'

Every line in *"Winterreise"* could have come from *'Love Sick'* – or any song on *"TOOM"*, for that matter – and every verse of every song on *"TOOM"* would sit comfortably in *"Winterreise"*.

> *Frozen tears are falling from my cheeks.*
> *Did I not notice that I was weeping?*
>
> 'Frozen Tears'

> *The chill wind blew straight in my face;*
> *My hat flew off my head.*
> *I did not turn back.*
>
> 'The Lime Tree' (inspiration for the "Good As I Been To You" cover?)

> *It is burning hot under my two feet, although I am walking on ice and snow.*
> *I do not want to breath again. . .*
>
> 'Retrospect'

On and on through every song, the singer tramps through a silent and desolate world, seeing futility, broken love and Godlessness on every branch and signpost.

> *I see one signpost standing there,*
> *Steadfast before my gaze.*
> *There is one road that I must take,*
> *Which no one has ever travelled back.*
>
> 'The Signpost'

Finally, he espies an organ-grinder, a figure not unlike that tambourine-wielding man from Dylan's past.

> *There beyond the village stands an organ grinder,*
> *And with numb fingers he grinds as best he can.*
> *Strange old fellow, shall I go with you?*
> *To my singing, will you grind your organ?*
>
> 'The Organ Grinder'

Is the similarity of theme and treatment between *"Winterreise"* and *"TOOM"* a coincidence? There seem to be no specific musical or lyrical connections and I have never come across anything about Dylan expressing an interest in Schubert or lieder. When a BBC interviewer brought up Schubert in a talk with Dylan in 1986 during the shooting of *"Hearts of Fire"*, he showed no particular spark of interest at the mention of the name.

All the same, it would not surprise me in the slightest to find that he is familiar with this work, or even that he wrote *"TOOM"* under the influence of it. If *"Blood On The Tracks"* can be seen as a descendant of Petrarch (the Italian poet from – almost – the 13th century), then *"TOOM"* can certainly be viewed as a successor to Schubert and Müller. (And the above lines from *'The Organ Grinder'* do suggest that Dylan might have been familiar with this song cycle as far back as 1964 when he wrote *'Mr Tambourine Man'*.)

It is interesting to note that Müller is not generally regarded as a first rate, or even second rate, poet. The words to *"Winterreise"* do not amount to great poetry, but as part of the song cycle – a medium in which the effect of the music and words become inseparable – they become a powerful, and a great, work of art. It's worth keeping this in mind when discussing the lyrics to *"TOOM"*. The few dissenting voices among the choruses of praise for the album have focused on the seeming lack of originality and sophistication in some of the language. These criticisms are valid, but what looks hackneyed on paper can come alive in the music.

As Dylan said back in 1968:

"It's the difference between the words on the paper and the song. The song disappears in the air, the paper stays. They have little in common. A great poet, like Wallace Stevens, doesn't necessarily make a great singer. But a great singer always – like Billie Holiday – makes a great poet".

There are many fine versions of *"Winterreise"* in the catalogue. Peter Pears and Benjamin Britten recorded a much loved version in 1963 and Dietrich Fischer-Diskau recorded it masterfully a number of times. My own favourite, however, is a 1954 recording on *EMI* by German baritone/bass Hans Hotter, with the great Gerald Moore on piano.

'Dirt Road Blues'

This is a song that at first listen would seem the most likely candidate to be a patchwork of old songs, but none of the words actually strikes any such bells in my mind. (As Michael Gray noted in *"Song & Dance Man III"*, most of Dylan's quotes of blues lyrics occur in songs that don't adopt the blues form.) The title, however, is a clear evocation of Charley Patton and countless other country blues singers. Patton recorded *'Down The Dirt Road Blues'* in 1929 and Arthur "Big Boy" Crudup recorded an unrelated song entitled *'Dirt Road Blues'* in 1945, and there are countless versions of other similarly titled songs: *'Dusty Road'*, *'Big Road Blues'*, and so on. Even more songs include the phrase *"down the dirt road"* – Bobby Grant's *'Lonesome Atlanta Blues'*, for example: *"I'm gonna walk down that dirt road till someone lets me ride"*.

When Dylan sings of *"rolling through the rain and hail, looking for the sunny side of love"*, it suggests not a blues, but the old country song *'Keep On the Sunny Side'*, written by Blenkhorn & Entwisle and recorded by The Carter Family:

The storm in its fury broke today,
Crashing hopes we'd cherished so dear,
Clouds and storm will in time pass away,
And the sun again will shine bright and clear.

Keep on the sunny side,
Always on the sunny side,
Keep on the sunny side of life,
It will help us everyday,
It will brighten all our way,
If we keep on the sunny side of life.

'Keep On The Sunny Side'

Musically, the song sounds like a meeting between Carl Perkins and the deep Mississippi blues, as if Charley Patton had lived long enough to make it to Sam Philips' Sun Studios in Memphis in the early 1950s.

'Standing In The Doorway'

Though it bears no lyrical or musical connection (except for the title), there is a blues song called *'Standing In The Doorway Cryin'* by Jessie Mae Hemphill, available on *"She-Wolf"* (*Hightone* HMG6508). There is also a wonderful song by William Harris recorded in 1928 called *'Bullfrog Blues'* that contains the line: *"I left you standin' here in your back door cryin'"*.

Don't know if I saw you, if I'd kiss you or kill you. . .

The dichotomy between love and hate is well documented in song, and this line brings *'Pretty Polly'* by Dock Boggs to mind:

She threw her arms around him and trembled with fear,
How can you kill the poor girl that loves you so dear.

'Pretty Polly'

I'm strummin' on my gay guitar, smokin' a cheap cigar. . .

Another Dock Boggs song, *'Danville Girl'*, shows its influence in a number of songs, including Jimmie Rodgers' *'Waiting For A Train'* and Dylan's *'New Danville Girl'/'Brownville Girl'*. The second verse of the song could be the origin of that cheap cigar Dylan is smoking:

I was standing on the platform,
Smoking a cheap cigar,
Listening for that next freight train,
To carry an empty car.

'Danville Girl'

As for the *"gay guitar"*, one version of *'The Gypsie Laddie'* (originally collected by Francis James Child, Child ballad #200) runs:

Of a rich young lady I'm going to tell,
Who lov'd a gipsy young laddy well;
While she was playing on her gay guitar,
The young gipsy laddy, the young gipsy laddy did her tender heart ensnare.

'The Gypsie Laddie'

However, it may be a "Gay" and not a "gay" guitar that Dylan is playing. According to guitarist Ed Gerhardt, Gay guitars were rather flashy instruments favoured by certain country singers in the 1950s. As he recalled, they were not particularly pricey – or good, for that matter – though they certainly looked the piece slung over a Nudie suit in a honky-tonk. Another informant said that they never really caught on because they had an unfortunate tendency to fall apart. So by the sound of it, a Gay guitar would go very well with a cheap cigar.

I eat when I'm hungry, drink when I'm dry and live my life on the square.

Back in 1963, Dylan recorded *'Moonshiner'* during the *'Times They Are A-Changin''* sessions. The last verse contains a close relative of the above line, and the song is strongly reminiscent in mood to *'Standing In The Doorway'* (and indeed the whole of *"TOOM"*).

Let me eat when I'm hungry,
Let me drink when I'm dry,
Dollars when I'm hard-up,
Religion when I die. . .

'Moonshiner'

When the last rays of daylight go down, Buddy, you'll roll no more...

This is another line that has many echoes in traditional song, one example being:

Hey Buddy, won't you roll down the line...
'Roll Down The Line'

(It's probably just a coincidence that in his Grammy acceptance speech, Dylan mentioned that he felt the spirit of Buddy Holly looking down on the sessions.)

You left me standing in the doorway crying, blues wrapped around my head.

This is yet another line that can be found in similar form in many a blues song, though I don't recall *"wrapped"* being used in such a context before. Here's one example, by Sonny Terry and Brownie McGhee:

Woke up this mornin', woke up this mornin',
Blues all around my head, Lord lordy...
'East Coast Blues'

'Million Miles'

This is a smoky blues with a loping beat, strongly suggestive of many others (particularly Robert Johnson's *'Stop Breaking Down Blues'*, though with a decided Tom Waits feel to it), without throwing up any specific models. There are hints of many different songs though, some probably intended, some not.

At two points in the song, Dylan sings *"That's all right, mama"*, which is a song by Arthur Crudup that Dylan himself recorded during the *"Freewheelin'"* sessions. The most famous version, of course, was by Elvis Presley in 1954, released along with *'Blue Moon Of Kentucky'* as his first single. Another song title that crops up in the song is *'Rock Me, Baby'* by B.B. King.

And that's not forgetting:

I'm just one too many mornings an' a thousand miles behind.
'One Too Many Mornings'

I'm trying to get closer but I'm still a million miles from you.
'Million Miles'

'Trying To Get To Heaven'

Alan Lomax's 1960 collection, *"Folk Songs Of North America"*, includes a song called *'The Old Ark's A-Moverin''* that contains the lines:

Look at that sister comin' long slow
She's tryin' to get to heaven fo' they close the do'.

'Trying To Get To Heaven' is a song that is almost a mosaic of traditional lines. Mike Daley wrote in a newsgroup that he was reading the above-mentioned Lomax collection and found that song on page 248. He started thumbing through the book and unearthed a number of other lines that appear in the song:

> *Seal up your book, John, and don't write any more.*
>
> *'John The Revelator'* (page 252)

> *This train don't pull no gamblers, no midnight ramblers, this train!*
>
> *'This Train'* (page 255)

> *'Ridin' in the buggy, Miss Mary Jane . . . Sally got a house in Baltimo'.*
>
> *'Miss Mary Jane'* (page 259)

> *I wanted sugah very much, I went to Sugah Town,*
> *I climbed up in that sugah tree an' I shook that sugah down.*
>
> *'Buck-eye Rabbit'* (page 266)

It is worth noting that these five quotes almost appear in the same order in the song as in the book, so it's not unreasonable to imagine that Dylan might have spent a night or two thumbing through this volume himself. (The *"train don't pull no gamblers"* line also appears in Curtis Mayfield's *'People Get Ready'*, a song Dylan has recorded three times over the years.)

Another clear correlation comes from *'I Will Turn Your Money Green'*, recorded by Furry Lewis on August 28, 1928:

> *When I was in Missouri, would not let me be,*
> *When I was in Missouri, would not let me be,*
> *Wouldn't rest contented 'til I came to Tennessee.*
>
> *'I Will Turn Your Money Green'*

'Till I Fell In Love With You'

This is another blues that, like *'Million Miles'*, is strongly reminiscent of many songs without throwing up any specific models. Interestingly, the song that this most reminds me of is not a blues at all but *'Crying'*, a beautiful number by the late Roy Orbison.

> *I was all right for a while, I could smile for a while,*
> *Then I saw you last night, you held my hand so tight,*
> *When you stopped to say hello,*
> *You were wishing me well, you couldn't tell,*
> *That I'd been crying over you,*
> *Crying over you,*
> *And you said "So long",*

And left me standing all alone,
Alone and crying. . .

'Crying'

'Not Dark Yet'

Christopher Ricks wrote on this song at length in *"Visions of Sin"* in one of the few chapters of the book I found I could appreciate without reservation (i.e. without wanting to throw the book to the ground, though I did keep picking it up). Little needs to be added, except the following observation:

She wrote me a letter and she wrote it so kind. . .

A letter from a loved one features in countless folk and blues songs – far more often than they appear in pop or rock songs. Maybe the presence of the telephone has made the arrival of the letter less of an event. Sonny Terry and Brownie McGhee's *'East Coast Blues'* not only refers to *"blues all around my head"* (see *'Standing In The Doorway'* above), it also has this to say about the receiving of a letter:

Woke up this mornin', woke up this mornin',
Blues all around my head, Lord lordy,
Woke up this mornin', blues all around my head,
Well I dreamed last night, the girl I loved was dead.

You can read my letter, you can read my letter,
You sure can't read my mind, Lord lordy,
You can read my letter, you sure can't read my mind,
Well when you see me laughin', I'm laughin' just to keep from cryin'.

'East Coast Blues'

However, the source of this quote was surely Slim Critchlow's *'Girl From The Red River Shore'*, collected in *"American Ballads & Folk Songs"* by John A. Lomax & Alan Lomax. The fourth verse goes:

She wrote me a letter, and she wrote it so kind,
And in this letter, these words you could find:
"Come back to me, darling. You're the one I adore,
You're the one I would marry on Red River shore".

'Girl From The Red River Shore'

A song of the same name has been said to have been recorded as an outtake from *"TOOM"*, but it has generally been referred to as an original composition. While that is possible, this is most probably the song that was recorded.

"I can't even hear the murmur of a prayer" is a phrase that must feature in many places, but *'Somebody's Darling'* by Marie Ravenal de la Coste and John Hill Hewitt has a turn of phrase that somehow sounds very familiar:

> *Give him a kiss, but for Somebody's sake,*
> *Murmur a prayer for him, soft and low.*
>
> *'Somebody's Darling'*

'Cold Irons Bound'

The most striking thing about this song is certainly the title, a phrase that conjures up a number of images and meanings without being pinned down by one – is he bound 'by' or 'for' cold irons? (Since writing this, I have heard Dylan performing the song in concert, and he sometimes sings *"in cold irons bound"*, suggesting that the former is what was intended.)

Again, there is an echo of many songs, if no specific model, one such being *'The Fields Have Turned Brown'* (quoted in the second line of the song) by the Stanley Brothers and another being the traditional Irish ballad, *'The Constant Farmer's Son'*.

> *I went to church on Sunday and she passed by. . .*

Dylan would surely be familiar with the traditional song *'Loving Hannah'*:

> *I went to church last Sunday,*
> *My true love passed me by,*
> *I could see her mind was a changing,*
> *By the roving of her eye.*
>
> *'Loving Hannah'*

'To Make You Feel My Love'

Somehow, it doesn't seem a fruitful enterprise to hunt for songs that contain sentiments such as *"I could hold you for a million years"* or *"I could make you happy, make your dreams come true"*. Perhaps the most striking achievement of this song is its avoiding the *"moon"* and *"June"* rhyme (though the one time Dylan did employ this hoary cliché, it was in the striking *"They're not showing any lights tonight and there's no moon/There's just a hot-blooded singer singing 'Memphis in June'"*.) Most people find it hard to understand why such a bland song made the cut, elbowing out the excellent *'Mississippi'* and *'Girl From The Red River Shore'*, but, as a friend of mine observed, this one works much better if you view it through David Lynch glasses. Seen in this way, *"I'd go hungry, I'd go black and blue, I'd go crawling down the avenue"* does not sound quite so insipid.

'Can't Wait'

This is the only song on the album that has been drastically rearranged in live performance, the sprightly rhythm of the stage version changing the mood from despair to sardonic anger. The studio version has a hypnotic groove that is strongly reminiscent of Howlin' Wolf's early recordings – *'Smokestack Lightnin'* or *'Evil'*. There are expressions that jab at the memory – *"trying to walk the line"*, *"I'm your man"*, *"the sweet love we knew"*, *"night or day"*, *"rolling through stormy weather"*, *"graveyard of my mind"* – that suggest other songs (such as – *"No, no, ma'ma, I can't wait. . ."* from the Mississippi Sheiks' *'Blood In My Eyes'*), but few specific models.

One thought that came to me after listening to *"TOOM"* was that *"Blonde On Blonde"*, *"Blood On The Tracks"* and *"Time Out Of Mind"* make a striking triptych – the same deeply romantic sensibility in youth, middle- and old-age, toiling through a surreal landscape that always tends toward the apocalyptic. When Dylan sings, *"I'm breathing hard, standing at the gate"*, it immediately suggests another gate, the one he was standing outside in *'Absolutely Sweet Marie'* three decades before – back when he was only half- and not utterly sick.

'Highlands'

In 1939 William Saroyan wrote a play entitled *"My Heart's in the Highlands"*, and Jack Kerouac mentioned it in his book *"Vanity of Duluoz"*. While Dylan could well be conversant with these works, the clear model for the song is *'My Heart's In The Highlands'* by Robert Burns:

> *Farewell to the Highlands, farewell to the North,*
> *The birth-place of valour, the country of worth!*
> *Wherever I wander, wherever I rove,*
> *The hills of the Highlands forever I love.*
>
> *My heart's in the Highlands, my heart is not here,*
> *My heart's in the Highlands, a-chasing the deer,*
> *Chasing the wild deer, and following the row –*
> *My heart's in the Highlands, wherever I go.*
>
> *Farewell to the mountains high covered with snow,*
> *Farewell to the straths and green valleys below,*
> *Farewell to the forests and wild-hanging woods,*
> *Farewell to the torrents and loud-pouring floods!*
>
> *My heart's in the Highlands, my heart is not here,*
> *My heart's in the Highlands, a-chasing the deer,*
> *Chasing the wild deer, and following the row –*
> *My heart's in the Highlands, wherever I go.*

Robert Burns (1756-1796)

287

This Scottish connection explains the *"Aberdeen waters"*, of course, though there is an Aberdeen in Mississippi that was sung about by Bukka White.

The most striking scene in the song is the conversation with the waitress, in particular the exchange in which she guesses that he doesn't read women writers and he counters that he's read Erica Jong. He evidently has, too. In *"Any Woman's Blues"*, published in 1990, Jong wrote:

"I am looking now at one of the paintings I painted to his design (he had scribbled a rough sketch on a napkin; I, of course, had painted it), and there's no denying that it's an abortion. Not my style at all".

"Any Woman's Blues"

And Jong is certainly aware of Dylan, too. In her *"Inventing Memory"*, published in 1997, the same year as *"TOOM"*, she talks at one point about the funeral of a rock star named Sally Sky, mentioning:

". . .a very rambling Dylan, who allowed as how much he had loved Sally, how he wished he could have saved her, how she was always her muse".

Inventing Memory

One last possible connection with this song, suggested to me by Pete Oppel, is the song *'The Beautiful Waitress'* by Terry Allen in 1978. The last (spoken) part of the song goes:

'A waitress asked me what I did.
I told her I tried to make art.
She asked me if I made any money.
I said no. . . I have to teach to do that.
She asked me what I taught and where.
I told her.
She told me she liked art, but that she
couldn't draw a straight line.
I told her if she could reach for something
and pick it up, she could draw a line that
was straight enough.
She said she wasn't interested in that kind
of drawing. . . but had always liked horses.
I said I did too, but they are hard to draw.
She said yes that was very true . . . said she
could do the body okay, but never get the
head, tail or legs.
I told her she was drawing sausages . . . not horses.
She said no. . . they were horses.

As for the musical influences on this song, Dylan has said that the riff is taken from a Charley Patton song. It certainly sounds like one, but after having worked my way through every song that Patton recorded, I haven't found an exact match. Many of the songs come close though, and *'Screamin' And Hollerin' The Blues'* or *'Down The Dirt Road Blues'* could well have been on his mind when he came up with the riff.

'Mississippi'

This is was an outtake from the *"TOOM"* sessions, left off, Dylan later related in an interview, because of a disagreement with Daniel Lanois on how it should be recorded.

Back in 1947, Alan Lomax (whose name crops up frequently in the discussion about *"TOOM"*) visited Parchman Farm and recorded many of the inmates there. On *"Prison Songs, Vol. 2: Don'tcha Hear Poor Mother Calling"*, there is a recording of a chain gang swinging their axes and singing *'O Rosie'*. The chorus of this song is the exact same line as the chorus to *'Mississippi'*:

Just one thing that I did wrong
I stayed in Mississippi a day too long

There is also an old freedom song, *'Keep your Eyes On The Prize'*, which contains the lines:

The only thing that we did wrong,
Is stayed in the wilderness a day too long.

'Mississippi' was re-recorded four years later and included on *"Love And Theft"*, Dylan's next album. It has been said by some that tracing the possible origins of phrases that appear in Dylan's songs is a futile exercise. They may well be right, but others who point to these 'liftings' as proof that Dylan is a plagiarist who compensates for his own failing muse by pilfering the works of others are, to my mind, wide of the mark.

A few years after *"Love And Theft"* appeared, it was discovered that a dozen or so lines had been lifted from Junichi Saga's book *"Confessions of a Yakuza"*, translated by John Bester. The media had a field day, declaring that Dylan had been caught with his hands in the till, though no lawsuit ensued from Saga.

What the accusers failed to notice was that in almost every case, Dylan had lifted a mundane phrase with little or no poetic content.

On pages 57 and 58, the yakuza (Japanese gangster) states:

"My mother. . . was the daughter of a wealthy farmer. . . (she) died when I was eleven. . . my father was a traveling salesman. . . I never met him. (my uncle) was a nice man, I won't forget him. . . After my mother died, I decided it'd be best to go and try my luck there".

This is plain reminiscence as bald as it gets, with no turn of phrase that would be worth stealing. In Dylan's *'Po' Boy'*, it becomes:

289

My mother was a daughter of a wealthy farmer,
My father was a travelin' salesman . . . I never met him.
When my mother died, my uncle took me in – he ran a funeral parlor,
He did a lot of nice things for me and I won't forget him.

This is still not great poetry. In fact, if you were to read it without having heard the song, you may well not notice that it is intended to rhyme or scan. When sung by Dylan, however, it becomes a magical creation, full of warmth for the people mentioned, and a multi-syllabic tour de force of singing.

As William Blake once stated:

"The difference between a Bad Artist & a Good One Is: the Bad Artist Seems to Copy a Great deal. The Good one Really Does Copy a Great deal".

All the translations of *"Winterreise"* are by William Mann, copyright 1986.

The seeds of this article were first published in *ISIS* issue #87, November, 1999. Revisited in June 2005 for inclusion in the Anthology.

Bob Dylan and his band 2000

Cold Irons Bound – The Failure of The Sun

Nick Train

"De pedicis et manicis insana cogitatio".

Diary entry – Samuel Johnson.

"An insane thought of fetters and handcuffs".

I'd be astounded if Bob Dylan is aware of this obscure quotation from Samuel Johnson's dark back pages, which reveals his mingled sense of guilt, fear of insanity and, some have speculated, masochistic longing. But it rose unbidden to mind as I reflected on the maelstrom of *'Cold Irons Bound'*. Indeed, *"an insane thought of fetters and handcuffs"* strikes me as the most concise summary of the song.

What a song this is! I know we shouldn't really play at song-ranking, but I was thrilled, or, perhaps, chilled by *'Cold Irons Bound'* on first hearing and my regard for it has not waned. For me, it's up there with *'Trying To Get To Heaven'* and *'Not Dark Yet'* as one of the three potentially great songs on *"Time Out Of Mind"* and offers layers of successively bleaker meaning.

First, we must firmly dismiss the wrong-headed suggestion, which has been propagated even by *ISIS* subscribers, that *'Cold Irons Bound'* is a *"pudding"* of a song, or misproduced, or even more bizarre, that the vocal is in any way inappropriate. On the contrary, the song and its performance are artful in the extreme and it achieves its disorientating ends convincingly. For once, the riff-fancying teen mags and the Grammy awarders have it right, more so than the erudite journals. *NME* praises its *"edgy rock and roll crunch"* and I believe Michael Gray was plain wrong in his review to suggest that the song would repel non-Dylan fans. Far from it, this is the most effective rocker that Dylan has delivered since, shall we say, *'Foot Of Pride'* and anyone who still loves rock and roll shouldn't be able to resist it.

Much more important, we must recognise why the song's backing surges, booms, and implodes, as it does, and why Dylan's vocal is at times smothered and lost. The effects convey the very sound of being *"waist deep in the mist"*, or of feeling that *"the universe has swallowed me whole"*. The melange of guitar paints the lowering *"clouds of blood"*; that failing, fading voice submits to falling *"on my bended knee"*. In other words, and indeed throughout *"Time Out Of Mind"*, the production and the performance are mutually reinforcing and, most certainly, artistically calculated. The sound of the album mirrors the poetic vision.

And that vision is overwhelming. In the song and the album, its constituents are as follows.

Disintegration of the personality – *"beginning to hear voices"*, *"one look at you and I'm out of control"*. There's a psychological dislocation here, a dislocation measured by a radical alienation from nature and humanity –

"the fields have turned brown", *"waist deep in the mist"*, *"up over my head, nothing but clouds of blood"*, *"oh, the winds in Chicago have torn me to shreds"*, *"friends of mine; I was wrong about 'm all"*, *"your love just hasn't proved true"* and *" you can't see in and it's hard lookin' out"*.

What we learn here is that the reported decay of "beauty" and turning away of the "heart" have distanced the singer, not only from his lover, but also from Creation. However, his response is not to rail against misfortune, but, far more disturbingly, to make helpless, penitent submission to the forces of nature and fate – *"almost like I don't exist"*, *"the universe has swallowed me whole"*, *"I'm on my bended knees"* and, of course, that recurring image – *"cold irons bound"*.

Back to Johnson's intimation of insanity, humiliation, thrall.

'Cold Irons Bound' is not just a "my baby done left me and I feel bad" lament. Indeed, I dispute whether there is any real value in interpreting the album itself from this perspective. Dylan agrees. During an interview with *MOJO*, he explicitly refuted an unduly literal interpretation of the ostensible subject matter of *"Time Out Of Mind"*.

MOJO: *"You talk about lost love"*.

Dylan: *"Well, I sang about lost love on my first album. I think this relates more to my first album than the last album"*.

Whatever Dylan's protestation, the morbidity of Bob Dylan, with its fixation on the romance of death, rather than, as he here suggests, on the death of romance, provides a closer link across the span of his recording career than admitted. The reason being that, rather than just a maudlin analysis of a failed affair or marriage(s), the final constituent of *'Cold Irons Bound'* and the real source of its and the album's poetic power is an exploration of the debilitating effects of accepting, then losing, faith. In particular, it analyses the perilous experience of confronting God, God incarnate and oblivion.

"One look at you and I'm out of control, like the universe has swallowed me whole". This phrase would be hyperbole and poor hyperbole at that, if we take it at face value, as applied to a glimpse of a former or current squeeze. No, it describes what happens when man sees God's face – *"No man sees my face and lives"*. In such circumstances, the ego truly is annihilated.

292

Elsewhere in *'Cold Irons Bound'*, Dylan's, by now, familiar trope of conflating erotic and metaphysical love is even more explicit. *"I went to church on Sunday"* and it's there, tellingly, that the first intimation of the waning of faith is located – *"Why my love for her is taking such a long time to die"*. Then in that abject penultimate line of the song, delivered in a whisper of submission, the narrator is found *"on my bended knee"*. On his knees in defeat, supplication, despair and the posture, at least, of prayer. Though, given that in *'Not Dark Yet'*, there's not even *"the murmur of a prayer"*, we know that the kneeling is sterile.

There is more to reveal about the song's devastating encounter with the Godhead, but first it must be put into the context of the vacillating nature of the singer's relationship with the Almighty.

My central proposition is that whenever Dylan sings about lost love on this record he is "really" lamenting his loss of faith in Jesus, or at least his unease at its weakening. In fact, developing a point made by Michael Gray in his review of the album, if Dylan isn't dealing with spiritual doubts, but is simply luxuriating in lost *"LURVE"*, then the album, to my mind, loses much of its interest and poetic force.

The evidence for this interpretation is manifold. Critically, there are the album's two recurring puns. The first, much to the delight, I'm sure, of Stephen Scobie, who identified and explored it in his book *"Alias Bob Dylan"*, is Dylan's pun on identity– I/eye.

The instances of it arise in *'Dirt Road Blues'*, – and I use the one reading only – *"My I's begin to bleed"*; *"Til I Fell In Love With You'*, *"My I's feel like they're falling off my face"*; *'Not Dark Yet'*, *"ain't looking for nothing in anyone's I's"*, and *'Highlands'*, most beautifully, *"I got new I's, everything looks far away"*. The reason for this overt admission of a compound, failing, or transmuting ego is that the singer is reporting on the experience warned of in *"I And I"*, of seeing God's face. It deranges you, maybe it destroys you, and it certainly changes you.

The second pun is more explicit in its relevance to the argument. It is, as Andrew Muir has already noted in *ISIS*, that venerable literary conceit, the confusion of Son and Sun. The *"glorious Son/Sun of York"*, etc.

The Son/Sun is a seen or unseen presence all the way through this record. In *'Dirt Road Blues'*, the singer is *"rolling through the rain and hail"* – no sun in that sky – looking for the *"Sonny side of love"*. In *'Standing In The Doorway'*, the singer is stranded in the *"dark land of the Son"*. Is this the vale of tears, or the domain of Antichrist? *"Til I Fell In Love With You'* notes, *"tomorrow night, before the Son goes down, if I'm still among the living, I'll be Dixie bound"*. This last song, while not the most successful on the album, has its moments. One I particularly relish is its nod to the eternal triangle of dependencies in Dylan's career: woman/muse, God and drugs. *"Junk is piling up, taking up space"*. Dylan is not singing about a storage problem here. He's sweating, staring catatonically, thinking about that girl (Jesus), who won't be back no more. Cold turkey for God. And that lovely, rueful payoff, *"I was alright, 'til I fell in love with you"*. Ye shall be changed, indeed. For the worse.

But, to return to the Son/Sun motif, as Muir notes, it is with terrible regret in *'Not Dark Yet'* that Dylan sports *"the scars that the Son didn't heal"*. And, presumably, won't or can't. Finally and most intriguingly, in *'Highlands'*, *"the Son is beginning to shine on me, but it's not the same Son it used to be"*. However, *'Highlands'* is audibly and philosophically apart and it's better to address its import later.

Meanwhile, let's pursue the Sun. It is notable by its absence, calculatedly so. In *'Lovesick'* *"the cloud's are weeping"* – no Son here. *'Standing In The Doorway'* is very deliberately set in the *"summer night"*, *"when the last rays of daylight go down"*, under a *"midnight moon"*. We note how frequently, through the record, *"midnight"* is invoked, that furthest moment from the Son's apogee. The narrator's sickness in the head is attributed to the *"bad"* light – presumably, *"bad light"* is what you get under a *"dark Son"*. *'Not Dark Yet'* deals even more explicitly with the imminence of night, the fading of the Son. Even *'Make You Feel My Love'* has its *"evening shadows"*. Boasting an aching melody and heartfelt performance, *'Make You Feel My Love'* is partly, but only partly, rescued from banality if you assume that the voice of the song belongs to Jesus and is addressed to an erring member of the flock – *"I could hold you for a million years"* and *"you ain't seen nothing like me yet"* are both at least reasonable claims, from the perspective of a Redeemer. *'Can't Wait'* is set where *"skies are grey"*, when *"it's way past Midnight"* and with the singer *"looking for anything that will bring a happy glow"* – the Son?

So, the ache we experience listening to *"Time Out Of Mind"* is the loss, or absence of, the Son/Sun. This interpretation puts me in mind of Matthew Arnold's great poem, *'Dover Beach'* and its *"Sea of Faith"*, receding with a *"melancholy, long, withdrawing roar"*. That's a wonderful description of the aural impact of the album, as the singer's faith recedes.

In addition to the puns, there is a deal of further corroborative evidence for this view of the singer's blasted state. *'Lovesick'* quotes 1. Corinthians in its account of emotional betrayal – *"I spoke like a child, you destroyed me with a smile"*. The betrayal here is so complete, the alienation described in *'Lovesick'* so extreme, that it's impossible to believe the song relates only, if at all, to an earthly love. The search for the Son in *'Dirt Road Blues'* finds the singer *"praying for salvation, laying round in a one-room country shack"*, which is as blunt a statement of unassuaged spiritual hunger as you could wish for. *'Standing In The Doorway'* resonates with apprehensions of Gethsemane, as the singer debates whether to kiss or kill his former lover, the Son, if re-encountered in this crepuscular setting. It also posits, somewhat unconvincingly, *"I know the mercy of God must be near"*, though offering no proof. Furthermore, what sort of *"fool"* do you think the singer is *"suffering like"*? I wager it's the fool in the Prayer Book, *"who hath said in his heart: There is no God"*.

By the way, just as I've always loved that amazingly honest *"You may call me Zimmy"*, line from *'Gotta Serve Somebody'* – who knows what humiliating school playground experience of anti-Semitism that harks back to? – so I admire the self-pitiless observation in *'Standing In The Doorway'*, *"even if the flesh falls off of my face"*. Because that's exactly what Bob Dylan's flesh is doing these days. The physical dissolution recognised and confronted in *"Standing In The*

Doorway", recalls the desperation in *'Can't Wait' – "that's what happens when things disintegrate"*. Not only is his ego shot, but so is the fleshy packaging.

Reverting to God, He scores another name-check, of course, in *"Til I Fell in Love With You' – "I know God is my shield and He won't lead me astray"*. For me, this is perhaps the most inconsistent line on the whole album – a ringing declaration of faith, amidst the doubt and despair. Perhaps it is only bravado. Elsewhere, the singer declares *"nothing can heal me now, but your touch"*. This is a plea for thaumaturgic healing, isn't it? He's waiting on a miracle. And, talking of anguished anticipation, *'Can't Wait'* is a new take on the *"Saved"* album track *'Are You Ready?'*, both with a crackling tension, awaiting the last days – *"it's late"* and *"the end of time has just begun"*. The miracle being awaited, with less conviction, it must be admitted, than in the earlier song, and for which the singer can't wait, is the Second Coming. *"If I ever saw you coming, I don't know what I might do"*. Maybe that last line is simply *'4th Time Around'* – type sexual crudity, but more likely it's the frustration born of endlessly deferred expectation of release and/or Apocalypse. The follow-up, *"I'd like to think I could control myself, but I know it isn't true"*, reminds us of the loss of *"control"*, engendered by the sight of God, that we found in *'Cold Irons Bound'*, In this context, the poetically unconvincing *"lonely graveyard of my mind"* takes on more resonance – the dead emerging from their graves at the Last Trump. The singer of *'Can't Wait'* is in an agony of apprehension, waiting outside the *"gate"*, that same closing door of *'Trying To Get To Heaven'*, that same doorway at which the singer has stalled in *'Standing In The Doorway'*. The theme of social exclusion, running through *"Time Out Of Mind"*, is crystallised here into spiritual panic. Is the singer permanently debarred from heaven, or, psychologically, from the consolation of faith? The tension raised by these doubts is screwed to fever pitch by the interplay between the song's bald title – *'Can't Wait'* and the repeated chorus, *"I don't know how much longer, I can wait"*. Here, *"can't wait"* means either, a: I can't possibly wait a moment longer, or, b: I am thrilled by the prospect of what is to come, or both. He can't wait, but until the weird release offered by *'Highlands'*, he's going to have to.

'Highlands' is itself replete with religious imagery. The encounter with the waitress/muse takes place on a *"holy day/holiday"*. The *"great white clouds, like chariots that swing down so low"* offer gospel comfort. The singer can only get to his highlands *"when I feel good enough to go"* – a morality test is requisite. In addition, there's that nonchalant line, *"I'm wondering what in the devil it could all possibly mean?"* As so often the case with Dylan, this is not so throwaway. Nonetheless, the answer is not going to be found on the sublunary world of the devil. If anywhere, the answer is in the highlands.

It is important to recognise what a different aural effect *'Highlands'* is striving for. Trilling, skipping and hypnotic, it is far removed from the gloom and fracture of *'Lovesick'* or *'Cold Irons Bound'*. And the lyric reflects this lightening of mood. Lightness and brightness prevail, contrasted with the dark of the previous tracks. That gloom fell as a result of the waning of the Son/Sun, but is dissipated in *'Highlands'*. Here it's *"the break of dawn"* and, later, *"the break of day"*, not

295

the gloaming. The singer *"can't see any other way to go"*, but at least there is a way, up out of the trackless wanderings of the Dirt Road valley of death.

Yet, *'Highlands'* is mysterious, because the comfort it offers is explicitly not a reaffirmation of Christian faith – *"not the same Son it used to be"*. The light in *'Highlands'* perhaps recalls for us Dylan's interview comment, quoted by Andrew Muir in *ISIS*:

Dylan: *"All my beliefs come out of those old songs, literally. . . 'Keep On The Sunny Side' – cf. 'Dirt Road Blues' "Sonny side of love"). . . I believe in Hank Williams singing 'I Saw The Light'; "I've seen the light too"*.

So, Dylan seems to be keeping, determinedly, to the sunny side of the street in *'Highlands'*. There's no more examination of the entrails of failed love. Like a voyeur, an outsider, he spies lovers in the park. These Young men and the Jong women (and don't Neil and Erica make a lovely couple?) are envied, but, ultimately, the distance between him and them is accepted. The song's close – *"that's good enough for now"*, hardly stands as an expression of religious ecstasy, but its undeniable wry humour represents a looking on the bright side, a lightening-up. I can't really conceive what nature of equanimity or resignation this love of old songs brings the singer in *"Highlands"*, but I'm glad it's on offer. In sum, then, *"Time Out Of Mind"* describes a journey away from faith towards, but not yet to, the highlands, where the loss, though still keenly felt, is supportable. In my final analysis, I guess that the "meaning" of Highlands is that the singer's faith has been replaced with a wary, but indulgent agnosticism, not fully-fledged atheism. That some sort of faith in faith has been retained and that, for now, this sufficeth.

The discussion has carried me far from my original intent, namely to account for the power of *'Cold Irons Bound'*. Perhaps the key line in the song, at least as it relates to my analysis, is that statement of total betrayal – *"I found my world, found my world in you. But your love just hasn't proved true"*. This breach of spiritual contract, as I would argue, has unhinged the singer, defenestrated him, his identity submerged, perhaps disintegrated, his ego shackled by its impotence. In truth, *"cold irons bound"*, back on the chain gang.

The religious context of *'Cold Irons Bound'* and the holy terror of the singer's predicament, is confirmed by consulting The Book Of Common Prayer, which provides gruesome detail about the actual meaning of being *"cold irons bound"*. It identifies those *"such as sit in darkness and in the shadow of death, being fast bound in misery and iron; because they rebelled against the word of the Lord"*. Elsewhere it threatens that God *"shalt bruise them with a rod of iron, and break them in pieces like a potter's vessel"*. In *'Cold Irons Bound'* the singer is caught in the shadows, being fast bound in misery and iron, having turned away from the Sun.

The only release from these straits appears to be death. Twice in *"Time Out Of Mind"* chains, of iron, are invoked and their breaking related not only to manumission, as in *'When The Ship Comes In'* and *'Ballad In Plain D'*, but to death. In *'Dirt Road Blues'* the singer's I's are bleeding and, suggestive of the nearing of the end, but also playing with the I/eye pun, there's *"nothing left to see"*, nothing but the wait for his *"chains to be shattered"*, then release. In *'Trying To Get To Heaven'*, the singer is aware of the hearts of men *"beating, like pendulums swinging on chains"*. Those men are, in one of Dylan's standard metaphors for death, *"waiting for the trains"*. We hear then the rumbling approach of *"Time Out Of Mind's"* other slow, death-delivering trains, the *"midnight train"* and the trains that pull no *"midnight ramblers"*. We sense the fragility of the chain of life, particularly in that wonderfully effecting delivery of the single word "beating", when all our corporeal fragility is exposed.

On this morbid note, I shall conclude. And not improperly, because, as all commentators are agreed, one of *"Time Out Of Mind's"* achievements is this level-eyed acceptance of death. Let me close with another quotation from Dr Johnson, this time a public one, from his epitaph for his friend, the physician Dr Robert Levett:

> *"Then with no throbbing, fiery pain*
> *No cold gradations of decay*
> *Death broke at once the vital chain,*
> *And free'd his soul the nearest way".*

Levett had been cold irons bound to life, until he found his way to the highlands.

Published in *ISIS* issue #78, May, 1998

Stories in the Press

For a few more Bob

Rolling Stone magazine estimated Bob Dylan's take-home pay for 2004 to be circa $10.5 million and ranked him as number 49 in their top 50 earners for the year.

During 2004 Dylan played 112 concerts, including 22 dates at minor-league baseball stadiums with Willie Nelson.

His exceptionally successful book, *"Chronicles: Volume One"*, sold more than 312,000 copies, earning him royalties of at least $1 million. Meanwhile, he is said to have earned a cool $1.25 million for his part in a *Victoria's Secret* television commercial.

With sales figures buoyed by *Columbia's* release of fifteen remastered SACD versions of his classic albums, Dylan sold circa 787,000 CDs from his catalogue in 2004. The bulk of the SACD series had, however, been sold in late 2003 and according to *Sony*, by October 2003 (one month after their release) the company had already shipped 700,000 Dylan SACDs. Combined sales for 2003 and 2004 must therefore have produced very good figures for Dylan. 2004 also saw Dylan earn $5.6 million in songwriting royalties.

Home Truths

A listener, Mark Vaughan of Redland was seventeen when Bob Dylan visited London in 1963. His parents knew Bob's manager and invited him to dinner. All went well until there wasn't enough peas for Dylan:

"There just wasn't enough peas for him: the pork, tomato and herb risotto was going down well. Yes, Robert Zimmerman, the Jewish boy from Duluth ate pork. But because there wasn't enough peas for him, he took a fork, and with a smile on his face said: 'These look good' and proceeded to take some peas from Mark Vaughan's girlfriends plate. No one complained, least of all, Alison. In fact, he could have done anything and got away with it. And he knew it".

Printed in issue #101 of *ISIS* March 2002
From John Peel's Radio-4 programme (26 May 2001)

Millions Seek Dylan Tickets

"A Staggering 20 million ticket applications have been received for Bob Dylan's 21-city tour of the US, the biggest in rock history . . . but only 651,000 seats are available for the 40 performances.

Top price for Dylan tickets is $9.50 (about £4.00) among the highest for a rock concert . . . The deluge of applications (an estimated five million envelopes, each containing an average application of four tickets per envelope) has caused a huge headache to the US Postal Service already snowed under by seasonal mail".

Extracts from a news cutting reprinted in issue #23 of *ISIS* February 1989
The article refers to Dylan's 1974 *"Comeback Tour"*

Dylan Lobs like a Complete Unknown

An airport assignment turns into an autograph hunt for reporter-cum-groupie Matt Price.

The bus between Perth airport and the city centre carries thousands of visitors each year, but it's safe to assume that none so famous as Bob Dylan has ever boarded the 24-hour shuttle. Yet there he was early yesterday walking down the aisle past a group of Asian tourists who only later would learn what all the fuss was about.

Dylan arrived from Singapore a little before 2am, to be greeted by two photographers and a couple of scruffy fans bearing dog-eared album covers.

There was no obvious security and no waiting limousine as the 59-year old strolled into the international terminal looking every bit the musical legend in a cowboy hat and leather jacket.

On seeing the flashbulbs, Dylan drew his duty free bag to his face and disappeared back into customs. He emerged minutes later, still shielding his face while wandering aimlessly towards the front of the terminal. Then it got really bizarre. Dylan, perhaps the most famous and influential musician alive searched for some transport, looked as if he might hail a cab, and then walked on to the airport shuttle. He sat down for more than a minute, and then meandered off the bus with the transport situation still in a state of confusion. Fellow passengers later went into convulsions on learning the identity of the odd looking midnight cowboy.

After the unusually polite entourage requested *The Australian's* photographer, Andy Tyndall, to stop taking pictures, a plainly unruffled Dylan sidled up to Tyndall and asked if he had a clear shot. Tyndall obliged by showing Dylan several of the digital images in his camera, after which the cultural icon suggested the other photographer take a snap of the pair.

Naturally, Tyndall obliged and, sensing an irresistible opportunity, the autograph hunters presented their LPs, to be rewarded with a signature and photograph. Dylan, who starts his Australian tour tomorrow night, then jumped in a van and disappeared. At this point it is probably prudent to disclose that my close friend Russell and I were the faintly embarrassed autograph hounds. Sadly, on being presented with such rare and entirely unexpected access to the notoriously reclusive musical icon, this overawed reporter and long-term Dylan fan – who now has a signed copy of *"Desire"* on his bedroom wall – abandoned all journalistic instincts and was unable to speak.

Printed in issue #96 of *ISIS* May 2001

Bob Dylan 2000

The Venusian Conservative

Peter Higginson

I'm watching Bob Dylan in conversation with a bearded man in a trailer in Canada in 1986.

It's a *BBC Omnibus* programme called *"Getting to Dylan"* and our hero is fending off some pretty clumsy questions with good grace.

Marlboro at the ready, drawing of interlocutor underway, Bob tries to be as accommodating as possible to the breathless questioner; and what is extraordinary is the amazing sequence of shifts from ordinary to other-worldly modes of being. We are watching a man perfectly at ease with his environment – he apologises at one point for flicking ash at an unfortunate off-stage character – and at the same time a man in touch with the most profound mercurial energies, as is evident from his flashing eyes, gorgeous speech-tones and wicked humour. *"A pipe?"* he asks at one point in response to some question about Schubert's muse, and the heart warms with pleasure at his impish shock.

On the one hand Dylan is a traditional conservative – wealthy family-man, moral, established. On another he is a strung-out Venusian genius, and I shall attempt here to sketch some aspects of this tension in his work.

It was Joan Baez, I think, that first used the Venusian conceit. Dylan blew into NYC *"from Venus"* in '61 and changed her world. The image is used of others too– Sting has described Jimi Hendrix as *"Venusian"*, it is common shorthand for a peculiar genius. But I want to use it here as shorthand for that *psychic* energy that rubs so roughly up against the demands of a domestic life. Carl Jung, for example, suffered a psychotic break in 1912 when he saw visions of a blood-soaked Europe, presaging the First World War. At the same time he was running a counselling practice in Basel and had a young family. The tensions nearly destroyed him– he had to retire to an island at Bollingen and build a mystical tower. Dylan suffers from the same tensions– as Larry Sloman points out in *"On the Road with Bob Dylan"*, much of *"Planet Waves"* is precisely about *"the balancing of domesticity with the concerns of a mystical artist"* (129) and a mystical life is a psychic life that invites much suffering.

The psyche is a poisoned chalice– promising growth and redemption, treasures of insight, it can also be a busted flush that delivers unstable disintegration. I take *Venus* to be a symbol of its unearthly strangeness, *conservatism* to be the antidote that grounds psyche but which never quite satisfies the soul.

It is worth pointing out that astrologically speaking, Bob Dylan's birth chart for May 24, 1941 (Duluth, Minnesota) places Venus in the constellation of Gemini. This is said to make him hard to pin down, but it also gives him a love of money. In the interview mentioned above Dylan claims to have started with *"no money"* but it didn't take him long to make it and he has been known to take a healthy interest in his financial affairs. *"The money's in the bank"* as he has it in *'Cold Irons Bound'* and this conservative, almost suburban, smallness contrasts greatly with the cosmic drama of *"beginning to hear voices"*– the shamanic-schizophrenic drama of the "Venusian" Dylan's mind. *"I went to church on Sunday"* sings Dylan in the same song– a small-town mid-American Protestant church I imagine, but *"reality has always had too many heads"*. You can't imagine the Methodist minister being too fond of that concept– a distinctly pissed-off swipe at the Gorgonesque spiritual psyche. What is God, then, Bob: Methodist or Medusa in this song? The conservative self (the rabbi, the member of the Vineyard Fellowship, the dad) answers *"the former"*.

The intrigued psychic poet knows that reality always contains a blast of the latter – the hideous blessing of the perfidious Venusian Muse. The roots of the drama go back to some of the earliest songs. The protest songs were deeply conservative in their moral tone and relied heavily upon concepts of justice for their effect. The call was not to overthrow the system but for it to live up to its ideals more fully. The cry at the end of *'Hattie Carroll'* for your tears to be shed at the six-month sentence reveals anger at the system's failure to be more powerful. In *'Only A Pawn In Their Game'* he contradicts himself and excuses from justice the white trash who killed the black person. But the underlying feeling is conservative Dylan wants the national institutions to be inclusively American. He abhors racism but is quite fond of Old Testament bourgeois justice: the judge in *'Seven Curses'* is a bad apple, not an institutionalised murderer. Dylan has never gone as far as Bruce Springsteen in naming *"Murder Incorporated"*. In the closest he ever came, *'Masters Of War'*, he is still looking to an unforgiving Jesus as his moral guide. It was not in his politics that he was ever to be radical. It is, rather, to his psychic perception that we must look for evidence of better worlds.

In *'I and I'* Dylan wrote, *"the world could come to an end tonight/But that's all right/She should still be there sleeping/When I get back"*. The merest echo of a John Donne sentiment in a way (*"What if this were the world's last night. . . ?"*) the lines more uniquely point to a paradox in Bob Dylan's life: that he is fully grounded amongst the things and values of this world (justice, money, power) but that he lives largely *"in another world"* (*'Dark Eyes'*) where the I is a not-I of Venusian otherness. The place where the girl is sleeping may as well be Venus since it is unaffected by the death of planet Earth. It is a place where the self that walks abroad is not empirically real but is made of the psychic stuff of dreams. Soul, we may say. And since we are discussing Venus we should say that it is also made of love, for love is the medium in which the dream-soul moves. *"When I get back"* does not mean from the railway-station to the bedroom. It means from the world of soul to the world of the body and its conservative concerns. Dylan feels so strongly related to this princess that he cannot envisage their bond being broken even by the end of the world. The bond is the girdle of Venus– a.k.a true love. Unbreakable, as the film has it.

And yet Dylan's beautiful soul is quite capable of the darkest and most vicious righteousness as he veers from love of the Song of Solomon, as it were, to the hate of that *"Book of Leviticus"*: *"Can they imagine the darkness/That will fall from on high/When men will beg God to kill them/And they won't be able to die?"* This is a completely other self– a violent angry redneck persona that wouldn't have disgraced John Wayne or Billy Graham. It is the self that counts the dollars and the dimes as signs of one's Calvinistic redemption. *'Yonder Comes Sin'*, *'Ain't Gonna Go To Hell For Anybody'*, *'Gotta Serve Somebody'* are phrases of selfishness, bondage and projection. Condemnation and rejection pour out in the "Conversion" period in the name of a savage justice that seeks to take the measure of a wholly rotten world. This deep conservative instinct runs quite counter to the tender psychic spirit that could write a *'Tomorrow Is A Long Time'*, say, with its sweet spiritual negativity:

> *I can't see my reflection in the waters*
> *I can't speak the sounds that show no pain*
> *I can't hear the echo of my footsteps*
> *Or can't remember the sound of my own name*

The other-worldly humility of that contrasts favourably with the conservative humility of *'Gonna Change My Way Of Thinkin'*'' which is all frontier righteousness.

One should not however be judgmental, so to speak. The conservative instinct is as vital a social resource as the wild spirit. We seek here not to prioritise one mode of being, merely to observe how it interacts with its Other.

"There's a white diamond gloom on the far side of this room", wrote Bob Dylan in 1977, *"and a pathway that leads up to the stars"*. He is very often concerned with rooms and their paraphernalia– windows, doors, floors. Not that odd for a Zimmerman, we might say. But we often feel that the conservative substance of rooms represents a psychic drama. *"Knockin' on heaven's door"*, *"Go away from my window"*, *"Each one of 'em got a fireproof floor"* all suggest that for Dylan the room is a scene of spiritual drama– perhaps a covert symbol of the house of the soul. In *'Where Are You Tonight?'* however, the drama is overt and the very solid room is open to the cosmos– perhaps literally the Venusian girdle. One might ask how one could live in such a situation– a room infested with stars.

This seems to have been Dylan's central predicament before his conversion– that his psychic life was erupting upon and destroying his domestic serenity. *"If you don't believe there's a price"*, he writes, *"for this sweet paradise/remind me to show you the scars"*.

The scars, again, are not physical but psychic. For sixteen years Dylan has been indebted to Psyche and for the last five years it has cost him his marriage. Psyche is a Tough Mama. She demands that the conservative days be given up and the wild spirit let loose again in the mind. *"The wailing of chimes"* in *"the empty rooms"* of *'Changing Of The Guards'* might be the protest of the soul at this predicament– torn so expensively between the quotidian human room and the beckoning Venusian pathway.

Bob Dylan is a true patriot. Though he may complain about how patriotism is used (*"steal a little and they throw you in jail/Steal a lot and they make you king"*) it is only because he believes in a higher patriotism– a true Jeffersonian democracy. Jefferson may be turning in his grave but for Dylan he is still the hero. The sun may be going down on the Union but the Founding Fathers are still the heroes of *'Tears Of Rage'* and there is still a patriarchal father who may dish out some very tough justice *'When He Returns'*. This is largely why Dylan is not popular with those post-modernists who have deconstructed the hell out of everything and who are no respecters of centralism. They would detest the secret agenda at the heart of Dylan's work– an agenda in which God keeps appearing, even at the darkest hour of *"Time Out Of Mind"*, to be a guide, at least, or (in *'Til I Fell In Love With You'*) a "shield". Post-modernists want the artist to dethrone God, but Dylan is too loyal. His "Joey" may have read Nietzsche and William Reich but Dylan is no Nietzschean, nor is he a psychologist. He has a much more tender and exotic faith than that. In its more conservative form it is a kind of patriotic spirituality– true to Jehovah, respectful to Yahweh, steadfast for Jesus. Dylan finds a kind of honour in being loyal to his patriarchs because the rest of us are *"breaking down the distance between right and wrong"*. How much suffering there must be for such a moral man, then, when his own stable world is broken down by the botched psychic emergence described in *"Time Out Of Mind"*.

If the psychic world of *"Street-Legal"* was disruptive and odd, it was at least exotic: *"she's smelling sweet like the meadows where she was born/on midsummer's eve, near the tower"*. But in *"TOOM"* the Venusian world has fragmented to the point where it is indistinguishable from empirical ruin. Though things are beginning to show signs of psychic emergence (*"the sun is beginning to shine, boys are beginning to play"*) the emergence is botched– it does not develop into a future vision but becomes a shocking disappointment (*"it's not the same sun that it was before"*, *"I feel like I'm coming to the end of my way"*). The stars have turned *"cherry red"*– a sign of exhaustion not promise. The Venusian Muse only *"passes by"*, the protagonist can hear voices presaging not inspiration but decay. *"I've got new eyes"*, claims one character in a moment of possible joy, only for us to be informed that *"the world seems far away"*. Everything indicates a period of psychic growth, such as would have produced a *"Blood On The Tracks"*, going wrong. *"World Gone Wrong"* is Psyche gone pear-shaped. It is no wonder that the writer borders on psychosis– something has come along to botch and butcher his psyche and this is an absolute disaster for Dylan who can only wring out a record of the physical effect upon him– *"all used up, eyes falling off face, sweat pourin' down"*. It is bad enough when Psyche appears full of fruit to tempt him from the conservative path. When she shows up raped and dishevelled Dylan almost dies of shock. As one contributor to the bobdylan.com discussion forum recently said, it is possible that *'Highlands'*, for example, is almost entirely about the consequent confrontation with suicide.

Bob Dylan is a torn man. He is pulled between the world of moral domestic patriarchy and the exotic world of his psychic artistry and love. He is a deeply conservative man who bears a Venusian curse– a curse that gets so bad sometimes it almost kills him. It is the curse first glimpsed perhaps in *'Visions Of Johannah'* where the psychic visions *"have taken my place"*, that is, eradicated the conservative quotidian self. At best the Venusian exoticism can be a thrilling creative ride, at worst it brings ruin and horror, which is when Dylan clings to the rather brutal but reliable staff of the Judaeo-Christian God. If I could do one thing for him it would be to grant him unreserved access to his *"other world"* which seems to have been most cruelly taken from him as from so many of us by unknown psychic forces leaving us only *"streets that are dead"*. There are three contenders for the identity of Morning Star and they are Christ, Lucifer the light-bringer and Venus.

Dylan has had plenty of contact with the first two. What about a new Bob Dylan album with the title *The Venus Redemption?* A kind of *"Street-Legal"* meets *"Time Out of Mind"*. A Gemini classic.

A previously unpublished article from the *ISIS* archive, reworked in June 2005

BENIER'S COMMENT
Out of this world...

"... And tell Mrs Dylan that Bobby stayed in Sydney."

Bob Dylan and his band 2000

Confessions of a Yakuza
and the Myth of Plagiarism

Derek Barker

The press, especially in the USA, has been working overtime with regard to Bob Dylan's apparent use of prose borrowed from a little known Japanese writer named Dr Junichi Saga. Don't worry though, this piece isn't about to employ headlines like *"They ain't his, Babe"*, *"Free-Stealin' Dylan"*, or worse still, accuse Bob Dylan of plagiarism. Nevertheless, it is always most interesting to discover Dylan's influences, especially when they include direct quotations. Plus, the extent of the usage here makes this instance more significant than most.

Dylan's latest muse came to light when Chris Johnson, a 29-year-old Minnesota native currently working as an English teacher in Kitakyushu, Japan, happened upon a copy of a book called *"Confessions of a Yakuza"* while browsing in a bookstore in Fukuoka, Japan. Johnson, a keen Dylan fan, instantly spotted the line *"My old man would sit there like a feudal lord, with his back to some fancy flower arrangement"*.

The line, which appeared on the first page of the book, immediately reminded him of a lyric from *'Floater (Too Much To Ask)'*:

My old man, he's like some feudal lord,/
Got more lives than a cat.

Chris didn't have to read too much further for confirmation that the line wasn't merely a coincidence. Just three pages later, he came across a second line: *"If it bothers you so much", she'd say, 'why don't you just shove off?'"* As Chris continued to read the book he searched for more phrases, turning the corners of pages as he went. By the time he had finished the book, he had folded no less than a dozen pages. Chris then emailed his findings to a Website devoted to Dylan's chords and lyrics, and in May 2003 the site, www.dylanchords.com, posted his findings. The post was spotted by a reporter for the *Wall Street Journal*, who, after contacting Dr Saga, got the story on to page one of the July 8th edition of the paper and from there the story ran and ran in the USA.

Obtaining a copy of *"Confessions of a Yakuza"* was a fairly arduous task. Although for a while the book appeared to be readily available in the USA (where the public seem receptive to foreign language translations) it soon sold out everywhere. The book, which had virtually been condemned to the remainder bins, suddenly jumped more than 20,000 places on the Amazon.com best-selling list.

Our story began when a terminally ill cancer patient, 73-year-old Eiji Ijichi, visited Dr Junichi Saga in the hope of getting some relief from the worsening pain of his illness. From the moment Ijichi removed his clothes, revealing extensive body tattoos, Dr Saga knew this patient was different. The former gangster knew that his time was coming to an end and he was willing to share the story of his life as a "yakuza" with the physician.

Dr Saga, who has a general practice in Tsuchiura, Ibaraki Prefecture, on Lake Kasumigaura, soon decided his elderly patient's reminiscences should be committed to tape and he began visiting Ijichi at least twice a week at his home. Each of Dr Saga's many visits, which usually lasted for about three hours, were punctuated every thirty minutes or so when his host, who tired easily, would break for a cup of tea. Over a period of many months the short pieces of conversation built into a fascinating account of the random events that had led the fifteen year old son of a prosperous country shopkeeper to become a member, and ultimately the leader, of a gang organizing illegal dice games in Tokyo. Ijichi talked about the first time he was raided by the police, his first love affair, and the girl he ran away with. He described his body tattoos (full body tattoos are a trademark of the yakuza) and how he cut off the little finger of his left hand as a ritual gesture of apology. He also told the doctor about the ties between members of "the brotherhood" and how he came to kill a man who worked for him.

Japan's yakuza criminal class can trace its beginnings back to the middle of the 17th century. *"Confessions of a Yakuza"*, however, is set around the time of World War II. The word "yakuza" originates from the Japanese card game Oicho-Kabu. The word is derived from the numbers 8-9-3 – Ya being 8, ku 9, and za 3. Unlike Black Jack, which the game closely resembles, the goal in Oicho-Kabu is to reach 19, not 21. The significance of the numbers 8-9-3 is that they add-up to 20, which in the game of Oicho-Kabu is worthless. The word "yakuza" therefore became widely used to denote something useless, including those people without worth in Japanese society.

Dr Saga, whose book was published in Japan to little acclaim or profit in 1989 and translated into English in 1991, said his book has sold about 25,000 copies in English and fewer still in Japanese. Indeed, at the time of writing, the Japanese edition is out of print and Dr Saga has only earned about 1 million yen, or £5,250 from sales of the book.

Dr Saga's publisher, *Kodansha International*, with offices in Tokyo, New York and London, told *Wall Street Journal* it was too soon to tell whether the controversy would significantly boost sales. Just ten days later, however, the book was at #117 among the best selling books on Amazon.com and was their eighth best selling biography! No one was more surprised than Dr Saga regarding the controversy:

"Bob Dylan is a very famous American country singer, yes? I'm not familiar with these things. . .

I had heard his name before, but I wasn't familiar with his music. I'm ecstatic that such an influential singer was inspired by what I wrote . . .

I remembered that I had heard 'Blowing In The Wind' in the 1960s on the radio".

After learning that Bob Dylan had used some of his prose on his album, Dr Saga, who usually favours opera, bought a copy of *"Love And Theft"*.

"I like this album, his lines flow from one image to the next and don't always make sense. But they have a great atmosphere".

Dr Saga says he's delighted that Dylan read his book and chose to adapt some of the text to fit his songs. Saga says he has no intention of suing:

"Why would I sue? To take something that made people around the world happy and try to exploit it for money – that's poverty", Saga said.

"I don't want this to become a bad thing, but it would be nice if Mr. Dylan acknowledged his source – perhaps with a note in future editions of the CD. That would be very honourable".

"Please say hello to Bob Dylan for me because I am very flattered and very happy to hear this news. I hope that Mr. Dylan's fans might go out and buy my book".

Dr Saga went on to say that in his book people find love despite bad luck and bitter lives. *"The two themes are love and the life of an outlaw – in other words love and theft".*

Although the essence of Dr Saga's book might have portrayed a sense of love and theft to Dylan, we already know the phrase itself came directly from another source, Eric Lott's 1995 book *"Love And Theft: Blackface Minstrelsy and the American Working Class. . ."*[1]

Dylan, however, is as tight-lipped as ever regarding his muse(s). When Dylan's publicist, Elliot Mintz, was asked if there was any connection between Eric Lott's *"Blackface Minstrelsy"* and *"Love And Theft"*, he simply commented that Dylan *"does not deny a connection".*

When Dylan's manager, Jeff Rosen, was asked the same question about *"Confessions of a Yakuza,* he said, *"As far as I know, Mr. Dylan's work is original"*, but that Mr Dylan couldn't be reached for comment.

Notes on Dylan's Source

"My old man would sit there like a feudal lord, with his back to some fancy flower arrangement".

"Confessions of a Yakuza" (page 6)

My old man, he's like some feudal lord/Got more lives than a cat.

'Floater (Too Much To Ask)' (verse 9)

309

"If it bothers you so much", she'd say, 'why don't you just shove off?'"
"Confessions of a Yakuza" (page 9)

Juliet said back to Romeo, 'Why don't you just shove off/If it bothers you so much?'
'Floater (Too Much To Ask)' (verse 11)

"My mother . . . was the daughter of a wealthy farmer . . . [she] died when I was eleven . . . I heard that my father was a travelling salesman who called at the house regularly, but I never met him. [My uncle] was a nice man, I won't forget him . . . After my mother died, I decided it'd be best to go and try my luck there".
"Confessions of a Yakuza" (pages 57-58)

My mother was a daughter of a wealthy farmer/My father was a travelling salesman, I never met him/When my mother died, my uncle took me in – he ran a funeral parlor/He did a lot of nice things for me and I won't forget him.
'Po' Boy' (verse 7)

"Break the roof in!" he yelled . . . [He] splashed kerosene over the floor and led a fuse from it outside".
"Confessions of a Yakuza" (page 63)

Yes, I'm leaving in the morning just as soon as the dark clouds lift/Gonna break the roof in–set fire to the place as a parting gift.
'Summer Days' (verse 14)

"I won't come anymore if it bothers you".
"Confessions of a Yakuza" (page 139)

I won't come here no more if it bothers you.
'Honest With Me' (verse 7)

"D'you think I could call myself a yakuza if I couldn't stand up to some old businessman?"
"Confessions of a Yakuza" (page 141)

What good are you anyway, if you can't stand up to some old businessman?
'Summer Days' (verse 5)

"I heard he caused some kind of trouble that put him on bad terms with the younger men . . . But age doesn't matter in that business . . . Age by itself just doesn't carry any weight".
"Confessions of a Yakuza" (part of a passage from pages 153-155)

The old men 'round here, sometimes they get on bad terms with the younger men, But old, young, age don't carry weight/It doesn't matter in the end.
'Floater (Too Much To Ask)' (verse 5)

"A good bookie makes all the difference in a gambling joint – it's up to him whether a session comes alive or falls flat . . ."
                    "Confessions of a Yakuza" (part of a passage from pages 153-155)

Things come alive or they fall flat.
                                        'Floater (Too Much To Ask)' (verse 9)

"But even kicking him out wasn't as easy as that . . . So I decided to wait a while and see how it worked out".
                    "Confessions of a Yakuza" (part of a passage from pages 153-155)

It's not always easy kicking someone out/Gotta wait a while – it can be an unpleasant task.
                                        'Floater (Too Much To Ask)' (verse 16)

"Actually, though, I'm not as cool or forgiving as I might have sounded".
                            "Confessions of a Yakuza" (page158)

I'm not quite as cool or forgiving as I sound . . .
                                        'Floater (Too Much To Ask)' (verse 16)

"Tears or not, though, that was too much to ask".
                            "Confessions of a Yakuza" (page 182)

Sometimes somebody wants you to give something up/And tears or not, it's too much to ask.
                                        'Floater (Too Much To Ask)' (verse 16)
                                        (plus the song's subtitle *(Too Much To Ask)*

"Just because she was in the same house didn't mean we were living together as man and wife . . . I don't know how it looked to other people, but I never even slept with her – not once".
                            "Confessions of a Yakuza" (page 208)

Samantha Brown lived in my house for about four or five months/Don't know how it looked to other people/I never slept with her even once.
                                        'Lonesome Day Blues' (verse 4)

"They were big, those trees – a good four feet across the trunk".
                            "Confessions of a Yakuza" (page 241)

There's a new grove of trees on the outskirts of town/The old one is long gone /Timber two-foot six across/Burns with the bark still on.
                                        'Floater (Too Much To Ask)' (verse 7)

"There was nothing sentimental about him – it didn't bother him at all that some of his pals had been killed".

"Confessions of a Yakuza" (page 243)

My captain, he's decorated – he's well schooled and he's skilled/He's not sentimental – don't bother him at all/How many of his pals have been killed.

'Lonesome Day Blues' (verse 8)

Quotations and page numbers are taken from the English language paperback edition of *"Confessions of a Yakuza – A life in Japan's Underworld"* published in 1995 by *Kodansha*. Lyrics from *"Love And Theft"* are quoted from the official *"Love And Theft"* songbook.

Some Other Possible "Yakuza" Connections

Something not previously mentioned by other commentators are the lyrics contained in *"Love And Theft"*, which are not directly taken from *"Confessions of a Yakuza"*, but might have been inspired by Dr Saga's book. While listening to the album recently this verse sparked my thoughts:

One of the boss' hangers-on,
Comes to call at times you least expect,
Try to bully ya – strong arm you – inspire you with fear,
It has the opposite effect.

'Floater (Too Much To Ask)' (verse 7)

This verse, from 'Floater (Too Much To Ask)', reminded me of one of the passages from *"Confessions"* so I continued to listen to the album with Eiji Ijichi's story in mind.

The next Dylan line I came across, again from 'Floater', was, *"If you ever try to interfere with me or cross my path again/You do so at the peril of your life".*

This line, from verse 13 of 'Floater', can only be construed as a threat, and is very definitely in keeping with sentiments contained in *"Confessions of a Yakuza"*.

Although less obvious, the penultimate verse of 'Floater' seems to reflect both Dylan's current mindset and that of the elderly gangster. It seems that both men have reached a point in their lives where they are choosing to reflect on their dreams and hopes – only some of which have been realised. Both men, in the book and song, brush the past aside, but can't escape it.

I had 'em once though, I suppose, to go along,
With all the ring dancin' Christmas carols on all of the Christmas Eves,
I left all my dreams and hopes,
Buried under tobacco leaves.

'Floater (Too Much To Ask)' (verse 15)

For all its southern American imagery, *'Floater'* is also a kind of extended meditative play on Saga's yakuza. With eight direct borrowings and several more possible allusions, *'Floater (Too Much To Ask)'* is undoubtedly the song most influenced by Eiji Ijichi and Dr Saga's *"Confessions of a Yakuza"*.

Other lines from *"Love And Theft"* that could have been inspired by *"Confessions of a Yakuza"* are: *"These memories I got, they can strangle a man"*. (*'Honest With Me'*). *"He's not a gentleman at all – he's rotten to the core/He's a coward and he steals"* (*'Lonesome Day Blues'*) and *"If it's information you want you can go get it from the police"*. (*'Summer Days'*).

The line *"I'm here to create the new imperial empire"* from *'Honest With Me'*, would seem to me to refer to the Japanese Imperial Empire. Dylan could of course be referring to an episode of *Starwars*, but I somehow doubt it.

Also from *'Honest With Me'* is the wonderful line *"Well, my parents they warned me not to waste my years/And I still got their advice oozing out of my ears"*. This sentiment is in keeping with Ijichi's feelings about advice given to him by his father.

Been workin' on the mainline – workin' like a devil,
The game is the same – it's just up on a different level,
Poor boy – dressed in black,
Police at your back.

This line from *'Poor Boy'* is interesting because although the situation has now changed with the modern day yakuza, traditionally most yakuza came from very poor beginnings and often dressed in black. The Police at your back reference is self-explanatory.

Blackface Minstrelsy

Although *"Confessions of a Yakuza"* appears to have provided Dylan with a lot of material for *"Love And Theft"*, especially *'Floater'*, the good doctor's book is just one of 'many' sources Dylan visited to create 'his' wonderfully kaleidoscopic album.

The inclusion of speech marks around the title *"Love And Theft"* quickly led to the supposition that Dylan might be acknowledging that he had borrowed the album's title from Eric Lott's book *"Love and Theft: Blackface Minstrelsy. . ."* The speech marks could be Dylan's way of conveying that the phrase was not original but merely a quotation.

Dylan certainly seems to have a fascination with minstrels and minstrelsy, and just prior to the release of *"Love And Theft"* he told Edna Gunderson of *USA Today*:

[*'Desolation Row'*] *"That's a minstrel song through and through. I saw some ragtag minstrel show in blackface at the carnivals when I was growing up, and it had an effect on me, just as much as seeing the lady with four legs".*[2]

In *Judas!* #3 Richard Jobes informs us that it was a common feature of the minstrel show to perform and transform Shakespeare's plays, often *"lampooning"* them in the process.

Jobes: [*'Po' Boy'*] *"borrows its opening verse directly from an 1866 minstrel performance of Othello, written by George Griffin. 'If for my wife – your daughter – you are looking', Othello says to Brabantio, 'You'll find her in the kitchen busy cooking'"*.[3]

In *'Honest With Me'*, Dylan sings *"The Siamese twins are comin' to town, People can't wait, they've gathered around"*. I assume these lines must refer to Chang and Eng, the 'original' Siamese twins who toured the USA and Europe with the minstrel shows for many years beginning in 1829.

Some Other Sources

Some of the other references are fairly obvious. Robert Johnson, Sonny Boy Williamson and a host of other Delta blues players, but also the upcountry white pickers like Dock Boggs, get plundered on *'High Water (For Charley Patton)'*. Boggs (and many others) also recorded a song by the title of *'Sugar Baby'* (it can be found on a several albums including *"Anthology Of American Folk Music"*, edited by Harry Smith). In the same way that he took the title of a Blind Willie McTell song, *'Lonesome Day Blues'*, in tribute to McTell, Dylan also borrowed the title of one of Patton's own songs, *'High Water Everywhere'* and used it in homage to the founder of the delta blues.

Throughout *"Love And Theft"* Dylan visits, or to be more precise revisits, classic American literature such as *"The Great Gatsby"* and *"The Adventures of Huckleberry Finn"*. He also takes inspiration from The Bible, Gaetano Donizetti's opera *"Don Pasquale"*, Shakespeare, William Blake, Ernest Hemingway, nursery rhymes, traditional folk songs, and let's not forget Dylan's own vast canon of work. A few of the more obvious (to me) usages are:

Oh the cuckoo is a pretty bird that warbles as she flies.
From *'The Cuckoo Is a Pretty Bird'* aka *'The Coo Coo Bird'* (trad.)
Performed by Bob Dylan at the Gaslight Café, October 1962.

I'll be standing on the corner,
On the corner of Twelfth Street and Vine
'Kansas City' by Wilbert Harrison

Upon my word and honour,
As I was going to Bonner,
I met a pig,
Without a wig,
Upon my word and honour
'A Pig Without A Wig' (nursery rhyme)

'I Cried For You (Now It's Your Turn To Cry Over Me')
Song by Abe Lyman

During the two years since its release, *"Love And Theft"* has certainly provided Dylan scholars with a plethora of material to sift through and the recent discovery, by Chris Johnson, of *"Confessions of a Yakuza"* has caused quite a stir, particularly in the American press. Dylan enthusiasts will, however, be very aware that Bob Dylan has been borrowing throughout his career, right down to the acquisition of his own surname. Moreover, he has never made any attempt to deny it. In fact, on a number of occasions he has spoken openly about it. As far back as 1962 Dylan was telling interviewer Edwin Miller of *Seventeen* magazine:

"I seem to draw into myself whatever comes my way, and it comes out of me. Maybe I'm nothing but all these things I soak up".

35-years later Dylan made this now often quoted statement to John Pareles:

"My songs come out of folk music. I love that whole pantheon. To me there's no difference between Muddy Waters and Bill Monroe. . .
My songs, what makes them different is that there's a foundation to them. . . That's why they're still around, that's why my songs are still being performed. . . they are standing on a strong foundation. . .
Those old songs are my lexicon and my prayer book . . . All my beliefs come out of those old songs . . . You can find all my philosophy in those old songs".[4]

Those who know or knew Bob Dylan well have reiterated those sentiments many times over the years.

"It was something, the way he was soaking up material in those days – like a sponge and a half".

Eric Von Schmidt

"All I can compare him with was blotting paper. He soaked everything up".

Liam Clancy

Obviously, Bob Dylan isn't the only artist to dip into a common cultural heritage. This type of borrowing has always been part and parcel of the folk process. Ironically, Eric Lott has stated in print, that in part, he took his book's title *"Love and Theft: Blackface Minstrels and the American Working Class. . ."* from Leslie A Fiedler's book of literary criticism, *"Love and Death in The American Novel"*.[5]

What I find remarkable about Dylan's usage of material from *"Confessions of a Yakuza"* is firstly the extent, and secondly that the borrowings are nothing more than commonplace dialogue. Lines like:

"My mother . . . was the daughter of a wealthy farmer. . .", and *"They were big, those trees – a good four feet across the trunk"*, have me wondering why would Dylan decide to utilise such simple prose?

On Plagiarism

Whilst the album's title may have been borrowed from a fairly obscure book, *"Love and Theft: Blackface Minstrelsy . . . "*, and it has taken almost two years for someone to come across the quotes taken from the even more obscure *"Confessions of a Yakuza"*, many of the other borrowings, Tennessee Williams' *"A Streetcar Named Desire"*, Willie McTell's *'Lonesome Day Blues'* and Robert Johnson's *'Dust My Broom'* to name but three, are so familiar to most people that there could not have been even the remotest intension of subterfuge on Dylan's part. Also, as pointed out by Jon Pareles, in writing songs for his album, Dylan was not claiming to present original research on the culture of the yakuza, and therefore it is nonsense to accuse him of plagiarism.

On at least one occasion – around the time of the release of *"Time Out Of Mind"* – Dylan spoke of jotting down quotes, phrases and lines of text and storing them in a box for use on future songs. Later, when asked how he wrote a particular song, Dylan replied, *"The box wrote that"*, meaning that he picked pieces of paper from the box and used them to construct the song. In the case of *"Love And Theft"*, it appears that a great deal of the album was constructed from quotes so maybe *"The Box"* wrote most of this album! In any event, *"Love and Theft"* is a heady mélange and this method of writing is an extremely intriguing way for a songwriter with such deep cultural and musical roots to compose songs. Ideas shouldn't be the exclusive property of one person: they are meant to inspire and stimulate the next idea. As Sean Wilentz points out in his piece, *'On "Love and Theft" and the Minstrel Boy'*, *"There isn't an inch of American song that he* [Dylan] *cannot call his own. He steals what he loves and loves what he steals"*. In any case, the key issue regarding appropriation and allusion is how the source is artistically transformed into something new and exciting. It is probably true that major sources, such as *"Confessions of a Yakuza"*, should receive credits and it is just possible that the September reprint of the album may rectify that situation, but cries of *"plagiarism"* are nothing short of ridiculous.

Notes and Sources used in this text:

[1] Lott, Eric. *"Love and Theft: Blackface Minstrelsy and the American Working Class (Race and American Culture)"*. *Oxford University Press.* Reprint edition May 1995 ISBN: 019509641X

[2] Gunderson, Edna. *'Dylan is positively on top of his game'*, interview, *USA Today*, published September 10, 2001. (This quote is also reprinted in *"Troubadour – Early and Late Songs of Bob Dylan"*, by Andrew Muir, *Woodstock Publications*, 2003, ISBN: 0-9544945-0-4

[3] Jobes, Richard. in *Judas!* Issue #3, October 2002. From *'Ethiopian Skits and Sketches'*, published in *"Inside the Minstrel Mask"*, edited by Bean, Hatch and McNamara (*Hanover University Press*, 1996. (This quote is reprinted in *"Troubadour – Early and Late Songs of Bob Dylan"*, by Andrew Muir, *Woodstock Publications*, 2003 ISBN: 0-9544945-0-4

[4] Pareles, John. Interview, conducted in Santa Monica, California, September, 1997, published *New York Times*, September 28, 1997

[5] *"Love and Death in the American Novel"*. *Jonathon Cape*, May 1967, ISBN: 0224611518. Reprinted many times in paperback. Last reprint January, 1998, Publisher: *Dalkey Archive Press;* ISBN: 1564781631

Published in *ISIS* issue #110, September 2003

Afterword

I read on a Dylan newsgroup that the line *"Samantha Brown lived in my house for about four or five months . . . I never slept with her even once"*, was a clear reference to impotency. That analogy made me smile a little and I remember thinking how endless the interpretations of Dylan's lyrics are. However, after reading an observation by Richard Jobes that the line *"I got my hammer ringin', pretty baby, but the nails ain't goin' down" ('Summer Days')*, might be an allusion to impotency, I was tempted to look again at some of the sexual allusions contained in *"Love And Theft"*.[3] Take a look for yourself and then make up your own mind.

For those that haven't seen the television series, Samantha Brown journeys around the USA for *Travel Channel,* hanging out in hotels and other people's holiday homes.

Bob Dylan 2000

A Close Encounter of the Shocking Kind

Derek Barker

"I was feeling like I was worthless, and maybe the root of it is a self-esteem issue. I felt like nothing, and I felt if I shot him, I would become something . . ."

Mark David Chapman never denied shooting John Lennon. He did not even attempt to run from the scene. He simply paced around for a few moments before sitting cross-legged to read a book. The book was J.D. Salinger's *"The Catcher in the Rye"*.

Mark Chapman was an emotionally and mentally disturbed young man. He had suffered delusions from childhood and in his early teens heard voices that he attributed to *"The Little People"* who lived in the walls of his bedroom. Later in life, his disturbed mental state led him to two suicide attempts and in 1979 and '80 he was receiving psychiatric counselling for severe depression and was also battling against paranoid schizophrenia.

Now a born-again Christian, he took a job as a hospital maintenance man and settled down to marriage. However, Chapman, who was now living in Hawaii, became erratic and obsessive and again started talking to "The Little People". He told his wife he was going to change his name to *"Holden Caulfield"* (the main protagonist in J.D. Salinger's novel) but, at the same time, signed himself out of work as *"John Lennon"*.

Chapman had visited New York, possibly in the late summer of 1980, with a view to killing Lennon, but he returned to his home in Hawaii without committing the act. However, he retuned to New York on December 6, 1980 and arrived outside the Dakota building on 72nd Street and Central Park West at about eight o'clock on the morning of December 8th.

According to Chapman, John Lennon came out of the Dakota building at around lunchtime (all other reports say 5pm) and signed an autograph for him before getting into a waiting car. Lennon spent the evening recording at *The Record Plant* studio on West 44th Street and returned to the Dakota apartment building at around 10.50pm. As he and Yoko Ono stepped from the car and made their way to the Dakota's entrance, Mark Chapman, still clutching the copy of the album *"Double Fantasy"* that Lennon had signed for him earlier, stepped out of the shadows.

Chapman: *"He walked past me and then I heard in my head. It said, 'Do it, do it, do it', over and over again"*.

In the time it took to fire five shots (four of which entered Lennon's body) from a .38-calibre revolver, the tortured 25-year-old fulfilled his macabre quest for identity. He had achieved what he had set out to do – he had made a name for himself!

Chapman pleaded guilty to the crime, thereby forfeiting his right to a trial. He was incarcerated in the Attica Correctional Institution near Buffalo, N.Y. where he remains in solitary confinement for his own protection. But what has this got to do with Bob Dylan?

Although I'm not aware of any "official" statement, there have been rumours that Bob Dylan's name might have been on a list of possible targets. Statements by Chapman indicate that he only planned to commit one murder and that the intended victim was always John Lennon. It seems, however, that he had compiled a "standby" list in case Lennon was inaccessible.

Chapman told his October 3, 2000 parole board:

"There was a list of people" . . . Probably – I thought he [Lennon] *wouldn't be an attainable type of thing, and I did think of harming some* [other] *people . . . a few other people.*
After premeditating the murder of him in my mind, I'm thinking, if I can't get him, here's, you know, a list of people".

When asked who else was on the list Chapman said:

"I can't think of anybody else. There was probably two or three others".

In an article about Chapman and Dylan, the British newspaper *Daily Mirror* said:

"Dylan was on a hit-list of celebrities drawn up by Chapman before he finally settled on killing Lennon".

In the same piece, titled *'The Hunter'* and published on Saturday August 15, 1981, the *Daily Mirror* featured a photograph of Dylan signing an autograph on a New York Street. The photograph, which was supposedly taken about a year before Chapman murdered Lennon, was discovered by accident when a freelance photographer noticed a striking resemblance between the autograph hunter and Mark Chapman, while going through some old photographs. The *Daily Mirror* quoted a NYPD spokesman as saying:

"We haven't been able to establish for certain that it is Chapman, but it certainly looks like him".

It is known that Chapman had previously been to New York with a view to committing murder. He told his parole board:

"I, um, flew to New York a few months before that to do that crime with full meditation in my heart. I then was able to somehow turn myself around and came back to Hawaii, and I told my wife that all was fine".

In *ISIS* #20, Patrick J. Webster speculated that one of the possible influences for the song *'Shot Of Love'* could have been the death of John Lennon.

"Like all of us, Dylan was extremely shocked and saddened by the events of December 8th and one month later – January 8, 1981 – he visited John's widow, Yoko Ono, to give her his personal condolences. Just eight weeks later – March 1981 – Dylan had written and recorded the title track for a new album, *"Shot Of Love"*, the cover of which would depict an explosive/shot impact almost certainly "borrowed" from a 1965 'Explosions Sketch' by Roy Lichtenstein".

If further confirmation is needed that Lennon's death was part of the motivation for the song, this is what Dylan told journalists at the Travemunde Press Conference in July 1981, shortly after the *"Shot Of Love"* album had been recorded.

Dylan: *"He [Lennon] was actually shot by someone who supposedly loved him. But what kind of love is that? That's fan love. That's what hero worship can breed, if you worship a man in that kind of way".*

Like many musicians and celebrities the world over, Bob Dylan has had his share of overly obsessive "fans". Soon after Lennon's death, however, Bob was plagued by a particularly malevolent wacko by the name of Carmel Hubbell. In early June 1981, Bob was rehearsing at Rundown Studio in LA when Hubbell walked in through a loading bay door. After a confrontation with Bob's office manager, Hubbell was ejected from the building and the police were called. Far from being the end of the confrontation, the problem escalated; threatening notes were left on office windows, including one that mentioned *"death devices"*.

According to biographer Howard Sounes, Hubbell was just one of several "fans" who regularly trespassed on Dylan's property at Point Dume.

Sounes: *"There were so many [trespassers] that Bob employed a full-time security team. Robert Kirby, head of security, kept a log of the people who came to the main gate. One man would frequently drive up and challenge the guards to a fight; the fellow claimed to have been a friend of Bob since he gave the singer a sack of potatoes".*

However, of all the obsessives that plagued Dylan, Hubbell was by far the most persistent. She was logged as trespassing on Dylan's property nineteen times in the space of four weeks (May-June, 1981). On the occasions that Hubbell didn't make it onto the property she left notes, some of which were described by Sounes as *"sinister"*. Then, in the early hours of June 21, one of Bob's ex- girlfriends, Helena Springs, received a telephone call stating that threats were being made to Bob's life and to those involved with him. Springs was told that the threat came from the KKK and from the Nazis. The voice said there was *"a chain reaction because Chapman is going on trial Monday and Manson is being released from prison"*. Springs was told that she was being watched and that she should leave home for her own safety. When Springs asked who was calling, she was told it was *"Carmel Dylan"*.

Hubbell then leased an apartment in a house next to Dylan's Point Dume home. Again, she gave her name as being *"Carmel Dylan"*. At the request of Dylan's lawyers, Hubbell was told by Los Angeles Superior Court to stop harassing Bob Dylan and his staff. She was also ordered to desist from using the surname Dylan.

The trigger for me to write this piece came about in 2003, when I stumbled across what I considered to be a rather macabre advert on the Internet. The item in question, which was advertised by the seller, Moments In Time, as *"a chance to own the ultimate in ghoulish memorabilia"*, was the copy of *"Double Fantasy"* that Lennon had autographed for Chapman only a few hours before Chapman murdered him. The album, which Moments In Time stated was *"the most important piece of historic rock memorabilia ever"*, was offered for sale for £312,500. The seller also stated that the album, which contained forensically enhanced fingerprints from Chapman, was instrumental in the case against him. Considering Mark Chapman pleaded guilty to the charge of murder, the seller seems to be applying a generous slice of 'poetic licence' here.

Patrick J. Webster's Lichtenstein – *"Shot Of Love"* article appeared in *ISIS* #20, July 1988

Roy Lichtenstein
"Explosion Sketch" (1965)

Pearl Beach
"Shot Of Love" (1981)

Bob Dylan 2002

Riffing With Larry Charles

Interview by Trev Gibb

Q: *I've got quite a lot of points to filter through and how I'll approach them I'm not sure, but I'll plunge ahead. . .*

A: We'll just riff around, I'm sure that something interesting will come out of it.

Q: *I think the movie speaks so much truth; it's been a long time since I've seen a film like that. Did you intend it to be a social commentary?*

A: Well you know, it's interesting; we never had any intention at all or any concern about results or consequences. We really started from a very purely organic place, just exchanging ideas, thoughts; sometimes a word or an expression in a very almost unconscious, automatic, writing it up technique, without imposing any order on it and letting the order and patterns emerge out of it naturally.

Q: *The film is very poetic in feel and very Shakespearian, especially in the case of the screenplay.*

A: I agree, that's you know . . . Bob inspires you to reach these heights you didn't think were possible.

Q: *It must've been an experience meeting Bob Dylan?*

A: There's nothing to describe it. It was the most life changing experience of my life. . . it's just meeting your guru, just holding a mirror to you and the world and saying look. That's what it's like being with him, just surprising you at all times, confounding you at all times, confusing you. But all with the end result of cracking open your head and just seeing more deeply and more clearly.

Q: *Dylan always seems discreet, but his discretion speaks a thousand things at the same time; he seems to evoke and provoke so much. . .*

A: He does and he's very enigmatic and very complex and very dense, which is no surprise. And so he will never say, *"This is what I think"*. He will have something and he will say it and I will say, *"Wow you really feel strongly about that!"* and he'll say, *"Well somebody does"*.

Q: *Very Dylanesque.*

Laughs

Q: *The film is so layered; it's colourful, provocative, like a puzzle.*

A: Yes, the last piece of the puzzle was you. That to me is the key. When I go around the country to these screenings I tell people it is a puzzle and the last piece is you. You have to kind of be involved and interact with it. And wherever you are in your life at that moment you're gonna see certain things in that movie like you do in a Bob Dylan song. And you may come back a year from now or ten years from now and be in a different place and see the movie in a different light as well.

Q: *The film has only really played in America. Is it going to play England any time soon?*

A: Yes it should be opening. I know there's a film festival in England that it's gonna open at. *BBC* films, was one of the financial partners, so it's definitely meant to open in England. It's gonna open all over Europe now; over the next couple of months, actually.

Q: *There have been rumours of a DVD release coming out soon, is there any plans finalised for what will appear on the DVD?*

A: There is a DVD that's going to come out I believe in February, with some deleted scenes and some other bonus stuff. But that's not the definitive version there's still yet my director's cut somewhere down the line, if we can get the financing together we'll put that out too, that's kind of more expensive to put together.

Q: *Will there ever be a definitive version? There's so much going on and so many scenes that didn't make it.*

A: Well right. By definitive I only mean like . . . everything, we shot everything that's in the script. And there is a version of that. From a historically archival position it might be worth having out there as well . . . I also have hours and hours of Bob rehearsing. I kept a camera rolling while he was doing all the music, never cutting, so I have all the between song patter and warm-up stuff, and I feel like there's a great historical archive there not to be exploited commercially, I think that would be wrong, but at some point down the line, way down the line perhaps, it should have some historical value.

Q: *It's very intimate . . . Most of those live scenes with the band. The camera perspective creates such an intimate feel.*

A: As far as the music goes, one of our earliest conversations was how to shoot the music. Bob had some very specific ideas about how he thought music should look and what's gone wrong with music on film and why he has felt that he had never actually been well represented performing on film. And we went back and looked at some things we both liked a lot. Like old *Johnny Cash* shows, and even *Ed Sullivan* and *The Grand Old Opry* shows with Hank Williams, and we found they basically used one camera and put you right there. There was an intimacy created between the musician and the home audience. And we really responded to that. Nowadays people are afraid to stay on that one shot – and we cut and we cut, and this kind of *MTV* style – and we made a conscious decision to go back to this more pure version of presenting the music and it wound up being very dramatic.

Q: *You get right in perspective-wise. It's very direct. The cinematography on the whole is so rich. One frame is like a photograph with so much going on in every part of the screen.*

A: I'm glad you noticed that. Thank you very much, that was an effort . . . we were both attracted to density and I tried to just fill the frame up at all times with a lot of information. The way Bob's songs are filled with references and allusions so that you could go back over and over again and listen to them and never get tired. I wanted this to have that same quality.

Q: *There appears to be layers at every level in the film. One of the sections on the website actually deals with the idea of allusions and references.*

A: Yes I've read that, it's great. The thing is I've been to about twenty cities where I've hosted screenings and answered questions and what's so great is that the audience, as I said, the audience being part of the puzzle, and the puzzle pieces can be moved around and create a different puzzle each time . . . people see things in the movie beyond even what was intended and those are often quite valid. I've heard interpretations of aspects of the movie that were certainly not conscious on our part. But when I looked back, I go: "Absolutely! That's a very valid interpretation of what's going on there".

Q: *The film is like a living art form and I'm sure it will grow through time and have a resonance like Dylan's songs do. Even politically some of the references in there could apply to now or ten years ahead.*

A: Or a hundred years ago, Yes. That was one of the themes. We didn't intend for it to be as prophetic as it turned out to be, it was again not our intention to comment or be topical in any way, we were more interested in talking about the idea of the cycles of history and how history repeats itself. We think we're unique, we think we're in a unique time, but really this is just another cycle of history that resembles every other one that's come before it and as it turned out it ended up being very prophetic and topical as well.

Q: *Were you thinking about W. B Yeats and 'Turning And Turning Within The Widening Gyre'?*

A: Yes, well when you're with Bob, you're with a Bard on that level. Someone whose job it is in life to be thinking about those things and commenting and writing about those things, so you're in that state of mind when you're with him and inevitably in the way Bob has throughout history – his own history – your tapping into things, into a certain psyche again almost unconsciously but inevitably.

Q: *I've seen this film countless times, I found it initially very overwhelming but it made me more willing to engage with it and to explore.*

A: Yeah, well people who are willing to engage with it, that's usually the reaction . . . Again, I've gone around the country to all kinds of obscure places and the audience is very willing to engage and they have that sense of being overwhelmed. And then they let it wash over them and they enter into it and experience it and they wind up having a great experience from it.

Q: *You've tapped into something that at this particular moment in cinema history is dwindling. Now, when you go see a movie its escapism and you sit back and let it do its things, whereas with this film you have to engage and take part.*

A: Yes, well most movies today are very cut and dry. It's a very risk-averse business now because there is so much money involved. They need people to come in and move on. And this is not a movie that's intended that way. This is a movie that's intended to be savoured and revisited like something you'd see in a museum or a poem you'd read in a book, rather than mass-market entertainment.

Q: *I do feel it will gain a Cult Status somewhere along the line. As I've said it has richness and a resonance.*

A: Bob was very clear about that. And his work, often a lot of his greatest work, has been met with disdain when it comes out. And then later on people go, *"Wow! You know "Slow Train Coming" is a brilliant album"*, or whatever. You know what I mean? And I look at this that way also. This is not done for a commercial acceptability; this is done to make a statement.

Q: *I think Dylan said, "What's wrong with being misunderstood?"*

A: Yeah that's Bob. I mean when we were working on it he had a line that he wanted to put in and he said he had a line and I said, *"Bob I have to say even in* the script I don't think people are gonna understand that line". And he said, *"Well what's so bad about being misunderstood?"* And I think he was saying . . . He's a person; he's been understood, he's done that, he's now willing to risk being misunderstood in order to reach a deeper level of understanding. And that's a very courageous place for an artist to go.

There was no commercial consideration in making this movie. This is a purely instinctive process, which is really an anathema to the making of movies today.

Q: *It is such a shame that the critics could not engage with this movie. They completely missed the boat.*

A: Well Bob again in his way told me that the critics wouldn't get this movie, but the audience would if they had a chance to see it and that has been borne out by my own personal experience. I think the critics are, for the most part, part of a larger system, a more corporate system. And this (the movie) just doesn't fit into any niche that they can really relate to.

Q: *"Masked And Anonymous" has a mood of the Carnivalesque, for example, 'Desolation Row goes to the Movies'. The colour, the lighting, the characters and so forth . . . There is a cartoon feel, especially in the case of the main soundstage.*

A: Yes, well it was a great synthesis of various things that were going on in our heads at the time and if we started today it might be totally different, you know.

Q: *The characters evoke a Shakespearian quality; each of the characters seems to act as a device in the story. One of my favourite performances is that of Luke Wilson, who seems to have a more moralistic voice in the movie.*

A: Luke was great . . . I mean people either understand how cool it is to make a movie with Bob Dylan or they don't and he was one of the people; he was the first person to commit to the movie. He just called me up and said look *"I will do anything in this movie"*, and he and I became very close friends through the making of this movie.

Q: *All the characters to me have this underlying cynicism that's rounded off with satire. In fact the film is full of dark humour and black comedy.*

A: Well right, the dark humour and black comedy, which is so much a part of Bob's music also, was missed by a lot of people, a lot of the critics I think. Whereas, the audience was able to see it.

Q: *One of the scenes that only got to me later on was the scene in the movie about the shooting gallery of world leaders. That's hilarious!*

A: Yeah, that was really funny, I agree. Again we initially set out to have different look-alikes and I couldn't find good look-alikes of the versions I wanted and finally . . . well at a least there's a good Ghandi, and it was like, let's use that. So it was again, you know, the synchronicity of it. You had to be very open to the synchronicity of it to take advantage of it.

Q: *A lot of key scenes in the film take place on staircases, such as Jack Fate's release from prison, his conversation with Oscar Vogel and his visit to his mother's grave. There are also references to stairs in the dialogue, like when Pagan Lace says, "We'll take the stairs" or when Fate says, "My fall from grace didn't end at the bottom of those stairs". What was the logic behind the staircase motif running through the film?*

A: Yes, yes, absolutely. Right that's true. You know something. What you just said actually was one of those things that happened at the screenings, I hadn't thought about that. There's a lot of staircases imagery in the film . . . When I went around scouting, I was attracted to the staircases in and around LA. There are a lot of dramatic staircases hidden from view. If you ever seen Laurel and Hardy's, *"The Music Box"*, there were incredible staircases in L.A., on the side of hillsides and I'd be struck by them as we drove by. And I'd say we could do the scene here, we could do the scene there. Something unconscious was drawing me to them. That's a very interesting comment, I hadn't even thought about that. But I actually see it now. It's totally valid.

Q: *The poetic feel of the movie and especially some of the lines in the movie are astounding. lines such as: "Hospitals built as shrines to the diseases they create" and "Vietnam War lost in the whore houses of Saigon", and importantly "We spend our time trying to kill time, but when all is said and done time ends up killing us".*

A: I know. Sometimes Bob would come in with a line like that and say, *"Do you think we should use that?"* and I'd go, *"You crazy!? It's such an amazing line, you just changed my life with that line"*, you know. But Bob is very irreverent in relation to his own work and he's very willing to . . . he doesn't like it to be pretty, he likes to twist it and push it and make it sound wrong, you know, *"Only time will tell who has fell and who's been left behind"*. You know, he really likes to sort of flirt with the wrongness of it, to see what might be elicited by that and with a lot of these lines he would play with them and you know where I might be really satisfied with the pretty version of it, he would want to push further and deeper and see if we could kind of twist it around somehow. It was a fascinating process to go through.

Q: *It's that subversive nature that makes the film so intense and so great. "Masked And Anonymous" totally subverts the notion of how a film should be. It isn't a movie as you would define a movie, it isn't a conventional movie, but that's why it's so great. Once you get into it there's so much.*

A: I totally agree, I mean I want to almost not call it a movie, because it's so Brechtian and so theatrical and so literary and so poetic. It seemed almost limiting to call it a movie.

Q: *So is it a work in progress? Every time it expresses something slightly different.*

A: Yes, well one of the things that I've said and I've felt a lot about this, is the concept of the finished product. We've come to believe in this society that something is finished, but that's really an illusion and this is a movie that really can be . . . if I could I would work on it for the rest of my life and change it and play with it and re-do it, and take the pieces apart and put it back together. Really it's a flowing fluid thing rather than a finished product.

Q: *But it's great that you and Bob can put up your receivers and allow this stuff to flow through you and for the art to seep through.*

A: Well again, that's the inspiration that he has been to me, I mean he is a purely instinctive person, he doesn't judge his thoughts. These are my thoughts and they might have levity they might not, lets find out. He really just follows his instincts. Look, they made him Bob Dylan so he has reason to trust those instincts and so that was the philosophy I adopted.

Q: *One of the phrases that strikes me, and seems to resonate through the movie, is the phrase "As long as I keep talking I know I'm still alive". All the characters seem to be governed by this idea, this frustration, in finding something real, such as Pagan Lace's tragic pleas of, "Save me, save me".*

A: Yes, exactly. That's exactly right. There is a sense of the film on one level being about communication and the breakdown of communication and how do we even hear what we do hear? What is the process by which we hear someone else, when the words come out of someone else's mouth? Things like that we were interested in. We're interested in language itself. Language itself becomes a theme of the film. What is the purpose of language? How is language used to transmit ideas? These are kind of interesting, complex themes that are there again, part of the fabric as well.

Q: *Of course the film itself uses language in many different ways, not just musically, or vocally, but its there visually, it's in what you hear and what you don't hear. It's everywhere. It's often only suggested. In fact there are suggestions everywhere in the film. And all of these things going on simultaneously can lead you off in so many different directions.*

A: Right, and even when your seeing a visually dense frame you are also hearing a cacophony usually in the background of that frame as well, that could be peeled away as well to hear a lot of different things going on too.

Q: *Even the reference to "Evil Doers" as spoken by Edmund certainly has a resonance with the 'here and now'.*

A: Yeah, and at the same time there's . . . almost quaintness to that expression. Bob is very interested in that and I think if you listen to *"Love And Theft"* it's there too. I think this is part of that same period in his work, which is the juxtaposition of the old, and the quaint and the old fashioned with the post-modern. He's trying to really juxtapose those forms and see what happens.

Q: *He seems to have retained – and it certainly shows in the film – or regained what he had in the '65-'66 period of stream of consciousness, but there's another element to it completely. I was wondering is there any connection between "Love And Theft" and "Masked And Anonymous"? Did either/or inspire the other? Did some of the lines from "Masked And Anonymous" appear in "Love And Theft" and so forth?*

A: Yes, what happened was, he was working on *"Love And Theft"* at the same time and in fact I had the privilege of going to the recording studio and what happens is, a lot of lines that didn't wind up in *"Masked And Anonymous"*, wound up in *"Love And Theft"* and vice versa. Again we're mixing and matching and sort of making our own puzzle. And so there were quite a few things like that, that emerged. Again, it was part of his interest at the time. I think from *"Time Out Of Mind"* through this movie you can almost look at now as a period, like the *born-again period*, or the *electric period*. And I think that now he's done that, the culmination is maybe the movie, now I think you're going to see him drift for a while until he finds that next thing that interests him.

Q: *This movie explores the idea of things that are not defined, in many ways and Dylan doesn't go for perfection.*

A: Right, he very much embraces the imperfect, and the beauty of the imperfect, the beauty of the flaw and he's not afraid of that. And that's part of his courage as an artist. Also, you know, he recognises the illusion of perfection . . . This goes back to the idea of the finished product also, which is why there is such a wealth of Bob Dylan bootleg material also.

Q: *And ultimately there's a message there, or as the editor states, "There is a story there" and it comes in many different ways in the movie, whether it be moralistic or not, there is a message.*

A: Yes exactly and again it depends who you are and where you are when you see the movie what you'll draw from

Q: *Exactly, and where you are in your life as well.*

A: Yes, yes.

Q: *The film will continue to grow; I know that in maybe ten years time a line in the film will jump out like never before, it will have a resonance. This even applies with "Love And Theft". I don't know if Dylan or anyone else is aware of this, though he probably chuckles to himself over it, but there are lines in "Love and Theft" that come from. . .*

A: The Japanese book?

Q: *Yes*

A: Yeah, the *"Confessions Of a Yakuza"* . . . Yeah, well a couple of things about Bob: First of all, he is like one of the last of the well-read people, you know what I mean? He's so well read and well read in the sense that he can quote anything. He can quote the Bible, he can quote Rimbaud, he can quote Yeats, he can quote whatever it is and he has just a really innate knowledge of literature, no matter what the source, in many different languages also. By the same token, he is constantly . . . he has these fragments, these bits rolling round in his head all the time and he's constantly – almost like a roulette wheel – trying different bits together and seeing what happens and so when people say, *"Oh this is from "Confessions of a Yakuza"*, I think he laughs, because he's taken a totally non-poetic sentence, perhaps out of the middle of a paragraph of *"Confessions Of a Yakuza"* and turned it into art.

Q: *In "Masked And Anonymous" that whole idea applies also, references, allusions and so forth and I guess therefore there's a lot of linkage to people like T. S. Eliot.*

A: Absolutely, well again we're talking about juxtaposing a lot of different forms, almost stripping them together, one after the other; a biblical reference might be followed by a reference to Shakespeare, which might be followed by a film-noir reference. Just constantly pushing and mixing and matching and seeing if they hold together.

Q: *There is definitely a noir influence there.*

A: Yes, that was a big influence. We talked about movies like *"Key Largo"* and I've described it as *'sci-fi-film-noir-musical-comedy'*. And I see Bob as this kind of post-apocalyptic Humphrey Bogart or Clint Eastwood. Yeah, and I think Bob is very much of that era also. Those were movies that probably really made an impression on him.

Q: *Well, "Empire Burlesque" is made up of lines from "The Maltese Falcon" and so forth.*

A: Yes, yes.

Q: *And of course while watching "Masked And Anonymous", the performances, and Dylan's performance as well as the use of lines in the film, harks back to that whole idea.*

A: Absolutely, that was again, very intended, very intentional.

Q: *Most of the critics who see the film don't see an art form. They have resentment to its experimentative nature and this whole Yakuza situation with "Love And Theft" only fuels their negativity and fuels controversy.*

A: Right, well people thought they had something, again, this sensationalistic aspect of the media today. People thought, *"We've caught Bob Dylan somehow"*. But instead what they did was – and this is why the story fell apart – because it was so much more complex and so much more enigmatic and ambiguous then the way it was presented, that the media couldn't handle it after a while. It's like, if you really want to enter this world, the world of Bob's head, you better take your shoes and get ready for a long journey.

When you're around Bob that's what's coming out of him. You know, he's somebody who's seen more than you have and knows more than you know and if your wise you listen and he will tell you everything you need to know, but your gonna have to do the work of interpreting it and that's how the movie is also, its like Bob is telling you everything, this is another aspect of the movie. This is Bob telling you everything about himself also, but it's not laid out clearly, you have to do the work of kind of putting the pieces together.

Q: *I think it may have been Andrew Motion, or perhaps Sean Wilentz who spoke of how in "Masked And Anonymous" Bob is able to say the things that as Bob Dylan he cannot say, but it can be done as Jack Fate. Of course when Bob is talking about himself he often refers to himself in the third person.*

A: Absolutely, well there is an aspect of Bob, you know, he needs to be called Bob for instance, because *'Dylan'* is our problem. Dylan is what we've imposed on him and he holds on to his Bob-ness his humanness in a way, his realness, because if he gets sucked into the Dylan part, that's the mythological part that everybody has kind of created, that is almost too gigantic a burden for him to carry.

Q: *In a documentary made about "Hearts Of Fire", Bob talks about looking through the windows of a pub and seeing people being very real, but once he's walked into the room, he knows that realness will disappear.*

A: Right, right. Well I think also when the time comes people will start to see the connection between Bob's cinema work. One of the things I realised after the fact, I was watching *"Dont Look Back"* recently and the scene where he has the argument with the English journalist, that's Jeff Bridges character forty years ago. And then wow! It started to connect to me . . . I watched it again recently and at the end of the movie Bob's sitting at the back of a limousine after a performance, staring out the window, driving away and the camera just stays on him and I'm thinking that's a parallel ending to our movie.

Q: *What gave you the whole idea for the Carnivalesque feel?*

A: It just started out with conversations about some images that we liked and slowly it began to emerge out of that.

Q: *The soundtrack itself is very clever, it has this multicultural aspect. The mixing of cultures is very apparent, that L.A., South American feel. Why did you go for that whole feel?*

A: Well, what I went for was a combination of things. First of all, I collected images, photographs; journalistic photographs from third world countries for a couple of years. And I just saw similarities in them and at the same time I really spent a lot of time in downtown L.A., which is this juxtaposition of various culture, the sort of crossroads of numerous cultures, African, Spanish, Mexican, Central America, South America, Eastern European, American, poor, rich and then I would look at the these pictures of third world countries and they looked a lot like downtown Los Angeles and I started to sort of get this idea of the cacophony of this country, that if you look at one direction in Los Angeles you see Beverly hills and the beach, but if you look in the other direction it's a third world country. This kind of weirdly cacophonous, multi-ethnic, third world country and so I loved that idea of exploring that a little bit more deeply, and then I started thinking about the cover songs in different languages and then Jeff Rosen was generous enough to just open the vaults to me and give me access to all those covers. There's thousands and thousands of these foreign covers and I just started listening to them and some just drew you in so powerfully like the Japanese version of *'My Back Pages'*. . . It also makes a statement in the movie that people don't realise the impact Bob Dylan has had on their lives, he's so pervasive its almost overwhelming.

Q: *Was the closing song going to be 'City Of Gold'?*

A: No. You know, again I only had a certain amount of input into the soundtrack and they felt they wanted to put some bonus tracks on that were not from the movie and I argued to put more stuff from the movie on the soundtrack. *'City Of Gold's'* a great song, which I loved, but I felt there were also songs from the movie we couldn't put on as well. They were pieces of songs that we used that we didn't get to put on the soundtrack. And maybe at some point again there will be a more, quote, *'definitive'* version of the soundtrack.

Q: *What were the songs you shot for the film that didn't make the cut?*

334

A: Yeah, well as I said when we filmed the music we kept the camera rolling. He was supposed to do six songs and he wound up doing twenty-two. I think there are four of his performances on the soundtrack, so that leaves like 18 songs that I have, fully filmed. There's probably a handful of those that are traditional songs that he reinterprets with the band.

Q: *Did he record 'Standing In The Doorway'?*

A: Yes he did and I think that will . . . I think that's going to make it onto the DVD actually. Beautiful version of it.

Q: *The film has a kind of Jazz element; it's experimental. Bob himself has that. People say he isn't a good singer or a good musician, but if you take away what people say, he is very much a Jazz musician. He works with improvisation, with phrasing. Even his melodies . . . He sings his songs differently each time, he does counter melodies in opposition to the original tune.*

A: Absolutely, he phrases things differently each time; he changes his voice. He has so much more control over his music than people recognise. Even now, he's doing this voice now, that's a kind of wizened old mans voice. Like a Muddy Waters, Howlin' Wolf voice. But it is a voice.

Q: *The thing about this voice is that, the words and the music if even 30 years old, they resonate completely differently, they take on wisdom and an experience, they become convincing. The voice adds the depth that the songs only hint at.*

A: Exactly, it changes the meaning of the song and that's one of the things he's always looking to do is reinvent the songs for himself . . . I was with Jesse, his son, one day and I was talking about how on *"Love And Theft"* he doesn't really play harp and that I had been listening to *'Pledging My Time'* on *"Blonde On Blonde"* and he does this avant-garde, Miles Davis sort of harp solo, and how brilliant that was. And Jesse says, *"From the day he walked out of that recording studio for "Blonde on Blonde", he has never listened to that record again"*. And that's the way he is you know, he needs to keep it fresh, keep it looking forward, don't look back. He needs to be constantly reinventing it; he can't get sucked into the nostalgia of it. This is the curse of Bob Dylan in a sense, in that he can't really enjoy his music like we do, he has to be continuingly be reinventing it and that's an interesting dilemma for him.

I respect deeply Paul McCartney and The Rolling Stones – but they have essentially become nostalgia acts and Bob is not a nostalgia act, he is still a vital artist, recreating and creating new work all the time, night by night, and that's one of the reasons now, over the last few years especially with this band he had, he became a great concert draw, again because I think he was inspired by groups like The Grateful Dead to come out every night and reinvent the show. So you never knew from night to night what you were gonna get.

335

Q: *That whole period from "Time Out Of Mind" to the film interestingly deals with the whole essence of time; in fact time with Dylan is something that I believe hasn't been studied enough. One of the lines Dylan says in the film is "We try to kill time, but in the end time ends up killing us".*

A: Yeah well and that's Bob, you see him exploring that theme in *"Time Out Of Mind"* and *"Love And Theft"* and this movie. And you see that in contrast to *"Dont Look Back"* or *"Highway 61"*, where mortality is kind of an abstract concept. Here there's a reality to it, a gravity – no pun intended – to it. And that's a big difference; you're seeing his thoughts through that prism.

Q: *The experimentation with time is something prevalent especially in "Time Out Of Mind" and in particular for me in my favourite Dylan song, 'Standing In The Doorway'– it stops time.*

A: Yes, that's really true. And we talk about time and dreamtime and things like that in the movie too and we're playing with that idea as well in the movie.

Q: *"In my dreams I'm walking through intense heat".*

A: Yes, and then he said, *"I don't pay any attention to my dreams"*. I mean Christian Slater has a line and it's been cut down now. There's a longer version of that scene where Christian Slater says to Chris Penn, *"Have you noticed when you dream a dream seems to last many hours, but only lasts a few seconds?"* and Chris Penn says, *"No not really"*. So we're discussing it and we're also having fun with it at the same time; we're playing with those ideas and exploring those ideas.

Q: *Are you hoping to experiment further with Bob?*

A: Oh even as we were finishing this movie we started working on a sequel so we have been talking about that for quite some time. Whether we will get a chance to sit down and get to work on it any time soon, I'm not sure. But we talked about that not long before we finished this one. I mean he had a great experience making the movie and I think he'd like to do it again.

Q: *When he's shaving at the mirror in the trailer and Jeff Bridges comes in I think that harks back to "Renaldo And Clara" in one sense where Renaldo is looking in the mirror. Very similar.*

A: Yes, yes, absolutely. And then Jeff is looking in that mirror also and they're both looking back at each other and reflecting on each other, almost like alter egos. A lot of that is almost Bob debating with himself in a sense. The journalist winds up being an interesting shadow figure for Jack Fate and vice versa.

Q: *There's also a part in the movie with a riff that sounds like 'Gotta Serve Somebody' as well.*

A: I had started with a gospel version of *'Gotta Serve Somebody'*. I think it might have been Mavis Staples actually. But as the sequences got more polished, I needed that riff and I dunno if we took the riff from the Staples . . . But, there were a couple of places where we were playing with that a lot, to fill in space in certain places and where the actual songs themselves could not be adapted and we would have to go back and create a piece based on that. Also in the hotel room when the young Jack Fate meets up with Angela Basset for the first time, we used a kinda dubbed version of *'Political World'* there that was kinda very interesting also, that was really fun to play with.

Q: *I thought that reminded me of something.*

A: Very, very far under the surface you'll hear Bob's voice going *"Political world, political world"*, but it's very mixed down . . . We recorded so many songs . . . he recorded a number of older songs and redid them in his way and a lot of that stuff just didn't end up making it into the movie. In fact I was just thinking as I said that, there is a rehearsal take of *'All Along The Watchtower'*. It's like an *'All Along The Watchtower'* jam without a vocal that I didn't find 'till after I finished the movie. I'd forgotten that he had done it and I thought, *"God, that alone is a fantastic kind of instrumental"*, almost like an Allman Brothers version of *'All Along The Watchtower'*; that was just great.

It's really something. I have to remember to mention this to Jeff Rosen, because that's something that should come out at some point it's really quite spectacular.

I think I'm gonna have to get going, I'm enjoying this so much, I could do this all afternoon.

Q: *Well I never thought I'd be able to speak to you as long as this.*

A: Oh that's my pleasure. I so deeply appreciate what you're doing and deeply appreciate your love for the movie and your devotion to it. I mean it's been a great experience talking to you. I can't thank you enough for all your hard work.

Reprinted in *ISIS* by permission of T. Gibb. Interview edited for *ISIS* by Derek Barker. The full Trev Gibb interview can be found at the unofficial *"Masked And Anonymous"* database website.
trevgibb.co.uk/Masked/riffing_larry.htm

Published in *ISIS* issue #113 March 2004

Bob Dylan 2003

It's Alright Ma,
It's Dylan's Fate and Dylan's Fate Only

R o n n i e   K e o h a n e

Dylan reportedly started writing *"Masked And Anonymous"* in July of 2000. Then in 2001, he gave three extensive interviews (Gilmore – *Rolling Stone*; Gunderson – *USA Today* and Hilburn – *LA Times*). The themes consistent in the interviews surface throughout *"Masked And Anonymous"*. Dylan comments on the character of celebrities, his own icon status, threats to national sovereignty, the right of self-defence, the selling out of the music industry, the malicious power of journalists turned advocates, to cite a few, and these concerns are voiced throughout the movie's script. Dylan also acknowledges that there has been a calling on his life. That in hindsight his career has not been a random act nor has his life been a series of random acts. Who he is and what he is to those who share this life with him no longer puzzles him. He is very accepting of the life he was given to live. He is resigned, he is content and he is reminiscent. Supposedly the script is based on a story titled *'Los Vientos Del Destino'* or *'The Winds of Destiny'* (by Enrique Morales). In *"Masked And Anonymous"* Dylan tells us that though it has been a wild ride full of treachery and loyalty, hatred and gracious love, callousness and compassion, violence and passion, he and his alter ego Jack Fate have ridden it well.

Throughout the movie there is the larger than life image of a father figure that Dylan/Fate can never escape. We first meet Dylan/Fate in the movie as he is let out of prison and we later find out it was the father that ordered his imprisonment. Their relationship is not just strained but non-existent, but you never see one without seeing the other. I believe that the father character represents "the sixties". Meaning the revolutionary mindset, the drug culture, the free love movement, the anti-war movement, the feminist movement, the environmentalist movement, the moral/silent majority and the global identity movement to name a few. Dylan as Jack Fate says that early on the father (sixties) was loving. But soon priorities changed. The father adopted political goals that became the focus. Dylan/Fate did not follow in his father's footsteps. The son had other voices calling him. He was more about *"playing music, you know!"*

There is a scene that appears in the script that never made it through the final edit for the theatre version. These are words written by Dylan:

". . . Alexander the Great. The cat who conquered all of Persia, Africa and Egypt. A lot of people don't know about him, but he was a great singer too. His mother – says to him, 'Is that all you're gonna do with your life? Just sing songs to the girls? You could be out there doing a lot more, son. You could be conquering this god-forsaken world'. You know what he got up and did?. . . Alexander the Great. That's who I'm talking about. He went out and raised an army, cooked all his enemies in crank case oil, rounded up all the wise citizens and doused them in canned heat, wiped his mouth, looked around and went home, went to bed, and died. Left every nation he plundered and conquered for his enemies to divide. Sure, he could've stayed home and strummed on his guitar, but you never would have heard of him. He would never have been Alexander the Great".[1]

As the sixties were coming to a close chronologically (since their impact continues today), there was great unrest in the United States. We were making great strides following the Civil Rights Movement but we were still stumbling in our attempts to walk righteously. The streets were full of anti-war demonstrations juxtaposed with groups referred to as the Silent Majority supporting U.S. foreign policy. Each night the American home was treated, during dinnertime, to film footage of injured soldiers or their body bags being transported from Vietnam. Many wanted a "messiah" to come and lead them out of this turmoil. Hadn't Bob Dylan shown that he was capable to be just that leader when he moved us all with songs like: *'Times They Are A-Changin'*, *'Blowing In The Wind'*, *'Masters Of War'*, *'Chimes Of Freedom'*, etc.? Where was he? Why did he choose to stay away and raise his family when society needed him? Did Dylan doubt that all he had to do was lead and we would have followed him? That may just have been what kept him home. Dylan's assessment of politics has always been right-on about its effect on people. In 1984 Dylan said:

"I think politics is an instrument of the Devil. Just that clear. Politics is corrupt; I mean, anybody knows that".[2]

This explains why Dylan has never ventured into a political arena. Just as he portrays that the destruction of Alexander the Great occurred when he stopped being just a song and dance man and went out to fulfil his mother's expectations. Alexander died in his twenties and Dylan is still rolling strong through his fifth decade as our premier musical genius. Dylan has not kept this a secret. In *'Wedding Song'* he told us via Sara that, *"It's never been my duty to remake the world at large, Nor is it my intention to sound a battle charge"*.

In a monologue Dylan/Fate portrays the mother figure as a woman who is not just disillusioned with the marriage but actually hates the spouse. If my theory that the father represents the sixties is correct, then the mother represents those who detest what they believe the sixties were and the societal changes that the sixties gave birth to. The mother turns her resentment and hatred on Dylan/Fate, the son. The son in a home movie is shown only wanting to entertain and play his music for the mother. But the voice tells us that her hatred for the father and their marriage made her hate the product or physical symbol of that marriage. The son was never able to overcome the mother's animosity to the father and be accepted as the son on his own merits. No matter how wonderfully he performed he would never get the accolades that a lesser talented individual would get. He would always be viewed negatively through a psychedelic prism glass.

Today, the mention of the name of Bob Dylan brings out extreme feelings in many people who could not name five songs or 1% of his catalogue, nor tell us anything about the man. But Dylan has been dubbed as the conscience or voice of the sixties generation, and for that he has endured worship by some and intense dislike by many more. Unfairly, this has prevented Dylan being viewed for his musical talent and product only. *"Masked And Anonymous"* allows everyone to hang out with Bob Dylan the man and musician for an hour and forty-five minutes. Since he wrote the movie we are exposed to his humour, his concerns and most importantly his love of music. In August 1969, several hundred thousand fans migrated to the Woodstock Festival and probably half of them emboldened by pharmaceuticals anticipated that they would be invited to Bob's house where Sara would make them pancakes for breakfast. That didn't happen. But this movie is probably the closest anyone will come to spending time with Mr Dylan.

Bobby Cupid & Mistress both truly love Dylan/Fate because they know him, know his heart. Over the years Dylan has found a few good friends who are loyal and true. They have resisted all temptations to sell Dylan out to the media and public. They know Dylan the man. Bobby Cupid (Luke Wilson) shares Dylan's love affair with music and those who were his teachers like Blind Lemon, Willie McTell, Leadbelly, etc. Bobby Cupid says in the movie that those who sneak to find out information should be hung or shot. Dylan has voiced this very same perspective about the people who look to sell personal information about him to the press. They are not friends. They are choosing to be spies and traitors. The following interview quote is paraphrased in the movie in one of several scenes where Bobby Cupid proves that his reason to be around Dylan/Fate is to be his friend and that he is not hanging onto Fate for personal gain. In 2001 Dylan was quoted saying:

"People tend to ingratiate themselves with other people by passing along information. I have the same feeling about them that Sherman and Lee had about people hanging around their tents. They're spies. All informers should be shot. A person should not rat on anybody. It's a principle I adhere to".[3]

Mistress (Angela Bassett) reminds Dylan that *"home should be a refuge and a warm place for the heart"*, a type of *"shelter from the storm"*. And for Dylan, his homes had a woman in everyone. These women know the real Dylan and he knows them as well. Joan Baez in *'Diamonds And Rust'* recalls how suddenly his voice would be heard after an absence of years. Mistress's expression when she opens the door to see Dylan/Fate is probably an expression that Dylan has seen on several women's faces over the years. Why do they let him in? Are they weak, dependent women? No, they are strong women. The women are not afraid to care for a man. They are not afraid to *"cook, and sew, and make flowers grow"*. And

Dylan is not afraid to let them know that he *"needs that woman"*. The women know that these relationships may not be looked on favourably by society, but when it is just Dylan and each lady, it is the two alone that count.

Fate visits the dying father. Fate tells Mistress that he needs the father *"to see me"*. In a sombre scene at the father's bedside Fate is momentarily glanced at, never really seen and the chance for reconciliation between the two disappears. Fate cries and lifts his eyes seemingly to heaven. In an earlier (and also a later) scene, a cross is visible above the father's deathbed where Fate sets his gaze. Accepting the fact that he will never change people's fixed misconceptions about him, Fate leaves to go play his music.

Uncle Sweetheart (Goodman) is typical of the powerful in today's music industry. A business that has no idea what its product and the value of that product is. It doesn't dawn on Sweetheart that four guitars and drums could be all that you need. He needs gimmicks, side-show freaks, sequins, false causes, prizes and awards. He does not share Cupid's, and Fate's, sentimentality about Blind Lemon's guitar. If it doesn't have immediate monetary value to Sweetheart, it has no value. In recent interviews with Dylan and throughout the *"Masked And Anonymous"* script, the music industry is portrayed as a world that exists only to honour itself and give itself prizes. There are several scenes with different characters mocking today's pop stars as being gutless, self-absorbed and shallow. Dylan in a *Rolling Stone* interview with Mikal Gilmore tells of his disappointment with several unnamed performers and states:

"Anyway, I got disillusioned with all the characters at that time – with their inner character and their ability to be able to keep their word and their idealism and their insecurity. All the ones that have the gall to thrust their tortured inner psyches on an outer world but can't be at least true to their own word. From that point on, that's what the music business and all the people in it represented to me. I lost all respect for them. There's a few that are decent and God-fearing and will stand up in a righteous way".[4]

Tom Friend (Jeff Bridges)(the press) is the type of person who, when he enters Dylan/Fate's proximity and space, sucks the oxygen out of it. Dylan has never weathered encounters with intrusive fans or inquiring minds very well. People like Tom Friend show the first thing they want from Dylan is for him to acknowledge that they too are as creative a genius and as entertaining as Dylan himself. Or they try to remind Dylan that he doesn't have all the answers. That he is nothing special. If there was just a simple twist of fate, they themselves could easily carry on in Dylan's place. The reporter sees his task, as exposing that Dylan is not the messianic type person that they the media, and never Dylan, have portrayed him as. Dylan comments on this very perception:

"I'm not sure people understood a lot of what I was writing about. I don't even know if I would understand them if I believed everything that has been written about them by imbeciles who wouldn't know the first thing about writing songs. I've always said the organized media propagated me as something I never

pretended to be…all this spokesman of conscience thing. A lot of my songs were definitely misinterpreted by people who didn't know any better, and it goes on today".[5]

Tom Friend shows no intention of being respectful or honest. He enters Fate's trailer while he is on stage and invades Fate's privacy. His interview is anything but an interview. The reporter waits for no response. His questions are attacks and presuppositions. After all, his editor has told him if he did not find a story that he should *"make one up"*. The reporter conducts a brutal one-sided interview with Fate, and when it abruptly ends, he proclaims that he got his story though Fate spoke not a word.

Dylan told Gunderson:

"That evil might not be coming your way as a monstrous brute or the gun-toting devilish ghetto gangster. It's the bookish-looking guy in wire rimmed glasses who might not be entirely harmless".[6]

In fact the first song that appears in Dylan's *"Lyrics"* book contains the line: *"some people rob you with a fountain pen"*. If anything Dylan is consistent with his foundational beliefs on human nature.

Nina Veronica (Jessica Lange) is a woman full of fear and looking for hope in all the wrong places. She believes that she will find fulfilment and success by winning the praises of those who would kill her for the price of a cup of coffee. She has no foundation but is tossed to and fro. Ironically, it is she who addresses the need that seeds of hope (a gospel or good news) must be planted so that they take hold and grow. Miss Veronica bends to whoever has the power at the moment.

One character is alluded to twice early on in the movie. Edmund the *"dictator in waiting"* (also referred to as the Pervert) chuckles when he and his male assistant remember a certain *"banjo player"* that they dealt with in the past. What did they do to this banjo player? Uncle Sweetheart, when showing Fate where the concert is to be held, tells him that this is the very stage where a *"jazz singer"* was disfigured. So now we know what made the Pervert and his assistant have a jocular moment. Immediately before the concert Fate seeks some quiet time. It is then that the disfigured jazz singer/ banjo player (Ed Harris) in black face greets Jack Fate. He tells Fate that since he had a forum years ago he felt he needed to speak out against Fate's father's brutality and evil. For this he was silenced. He gives his name as Oscar Vogel and reminds Fate that, *"it is not what goes into the mouth that counts but what comes out of a man's mouth"*. A teaching from Jesus recorded in the fifteenth chapter of Matthew.

The new dictator assumes power because the uniqueness of this country has been eroded. What was once a great nation has been destroyed from within. In the movie, Dylan/Fate pulls out the tune *'Dixie'*, a song idolizing the days of the past. It is interesting that the borders of this new country extend southward past Mexico and north into Canada, but it seems not to have within its grasp parts of the deep south, aka Dixie in today's America. Dylan, over decades, has spoken out against the movement in America that no longer saw America as the great melting pot, but sought to split the population according to ethnic lines. Dylan played a pivotal role in the Civil Rights movement of the sixties. He stood for a movement to bring all peoples together fitting the motto *"E pluribus unum/Out of many – one"*. Today the "rights" movement only separates people from anyone not in their group. In 1985 Dylan lamented:

"Now everybody wants their own thing. There's no unity. There's the Puerto Rican Day parade, Polish Day, German Week, the Mexican parades. You have all these different types of people all waving their own flags, and there's no unity between all these people".[7]

And what are we to speculate about this apocalyptic country? The boundaries include most of North America and stretch out. The country/state that includes today's United States of America is run by a two-bit dictator who has turned the country into a struggling third world wannabe. Shortly before 9/11 Dylan warned,

"If we're [America] not careful, we'll wake up in a multi-national, multi-ethnic police state".[8]

In this movie Dylan wakes to that very nightmare. Less than 36 hours before the first plane hit the World Trade Center, Dylan gave these warnings: The press and its audience are acting irresponsibly when, *"A celebrity is on Page One and on Page 10 you might see something about 100 trucks rolling in from Mexico carrying God-knows-what . . ."*[9] In October 2001 Dylan made a rare speech from the concert stage and asked the audience at Staples Arena to reject Madonna's post 9/11 call for everyone to *"think global"*. Dylan's concern is not only for the United States. Tom Friend attempts to rile Fate by pointing out that England, a country close to Dylan/Fate's heart, is not so English anymore. It would be really difficult not to connect all the anti-globalisation clues that Dylan gave us as he wrote this script.

On T-shirts that promote the movie is Bobby Cupid's line:

"The more you know . . . the more you suffer".

Dylan told us in *'A Hard Rain's A-Gonna Fall'* that he promised to sing about all that he would witness regardless of the retribution he would face.

On the movie posters is a quote from Tom Friend (press). In the movie he gets right in Dylan/Fate's face and asks him, *"Would you reach out your hand to save a dying man if you knew that he might pull you in?"* Gregory Peck at the Kennedy Center Honors in 1997 described Bob Dylan as a man who was, *"never about to get out of town when the fighting started"*. Through his songs and his comments Dylan has always spoken his mind regardless of the backlash. Whether it was ripping the masks off falsehoods or speaking the truth, Dylan never considered his own popularity a reason to remain silent. The most black and white example of Dylan risking it all to save a drowning man was the infamous 1979-1980 gospel concert tour. He devoted an entire year of concert set lists to speaking about Scriptural truths and the need for and way of salvation. He knew that this would not sit well with his fan base, this would not sit well with the sixties' survivors, would not sit well with the Jewish community, the rock community and even sit well among many Christians. But he did it. Why then did Dylan stop performing gospel shows? Three years after his last "all gospel" show Dylan remarked, *"I don't particularly regret telling people how to get their souls saved. Whoever was supposed to pick it up, picked it up"*.[10] In *"Masked And Anonymous"*, when Uncle Sweetheart attempts to defend Jack Fate and his ever-changing impact on the culture, Sweetheart exclaims, *"Does Jesus have to walk on water a second time to make a point?"*

There is a scene with Bobby Cupid and Uncle Sweetheart in which *'Drifter's Escape'* can be heard being played live by Fate and his band Simple Twist of Fate (Larry Campbell, Charlie Sexton, Tony Garnier and George Receli). The two men are trying their hand at analysing Dylan's lyrics. (It should be noted that the original script was written with the assumption that the song being played would be *'Tryin' To Get To Heaven'* and not *'Drifter's Escape'*). Cupid's interpretation of the song is pretty straightforward. It is about getting to heaven and knowing the path. Sweetheart develops an elaborate analysis involving Jekyll and Hyde, and the manipulation of evil for good. Throughout the movie Dylan wrote many humorous lines that use much of the media hype about him, turning the tables in a masterly fashion on the pundits. In the movie he does it with humour but in this interview he takes his lyrical analysts straight on:

"Unfortunately, people have been led down the wrong path by quasi-intellectuals who never really get the cultural spirit in the air when these songs are performed. 'Masters Of War' for instance, is supposed to be a pacifist song against war. It's not an anti-war song. It's speaking against what Eisenhower was calling a military industrial complex as he was making his exit from the presidency. That spirit was in the air, and I picked up on it. People focus on the Senators and Congressman in 'The Times They Are A-Changin'' but never the Nietzschean aspects. The spirit of 'God is dead' was in the air, but Nietzsche was the son of a bourgeois pastor. That turns the rationale on its head. And 'Desolation Row'? That's a minstrel song through and through . . ."[11]

In all of the three interviews in 2001 Dylan brought up *'Masters Of War'* and how it is <u>not</u> an anti-war song, but rather a call to be mindful of the military industrial complex. This thread also made it into the movie. Tom Friend, without revealing his sources, proclaims that the Vietnam War was lost in the whorehouses of Saigon and not on the battlefield. Just who would have been visiting those whorehouses? The Congressmen, Senators and Industrialists who came together to protect their own political or financial empires at the cost of sacred human lives.

But Dylan has found contentment. He like Fate does not struggle with what befalls him. This life is not all that he perceives. But he is also grateful that he has been given this life to live. Paraphrasing Dylan's interviews since 2001 he tells us that he knows the world may never see him, nor understand him, but he is always ready to play for us. *"It's all right Ma . . . it's my life and my life only"*.

In the movie's closing scene, Fate breaks up an assault by Tom Friend on Uncle Sweetheart with a punch to Friend's gut. Fate then breaks a bourbon bottle and places the shattered glass at Friend's jugular. He then casts the bottle away without killing Friend. Friend pulls out his gun threatening either or both Fate and Sweetheart. Suddenly Bobby Cupid slams Blind Lemon's acoustic guitar across Friend's back and proceeds to beat him to death with the instrument. The neck of the guitar delivers the same impact Fate's bourbon bottle would have done and severs Friend's jugular.

Both Dylan and his closest companions have endured savage attacks on Dylan's character by poisoned pens of the likes of Tom Friend. We may see a glimpse in this scene of the distaste Dylan holds for these vultures. What is interesting is that in the movie, Fate shows understanding to his friend who protected him. This may be Dylan telling his real friends that he does realize that his request for them never to go to the press to defend him is understood by Dylan. He knows how loyal and protective they have been to him and if he could lift that burden from them he would. So Dylan accepts the punishment for his friend Bobby Cupid. Dylan is grateful to his friends. In the song *'Mississippi'* from 2001 Dylan sings:

Well my ship's been split to splinters and it's sinking fast
I'm drownin' in the poison, got no future, got no past
But my heart is not weary, it's light and it's free
I've got nothin' but affection for all those who sailed with me.

Throughout the movie, a radio preacher is often heard in the background. In one scene saying, *"The only power the government has is to crack down on criminals. When there aren't enough criminals, you make them. You make so many things a crime that it becomes impossible to live without breaking laws. Who wants a nation of law-abiding citizens? What's there in that for anyone? You pass laws that can't be observed or enforced or even objectively interpreted. You create a nation of lawbreakers and then you cash in on the guilt. That's the system, that's the game"*. Dylan has warned this was coming for decades.

I can see the day coming when even your home garden
is gonna be against the law.

'Union Sundown' 1982.

The opening monologue by the radio preacher blares out this question: *"Are you humble before God?"* Jewish scholars debated long before accepting the Book of Esther as Scripture. No one denied that the story of Esther was not a good tale of the Jewish people, but it seemed to have one big flaw. It describes a great time of Jewish redemption without attributing that redemption to the God of Abraham, Isaac and Jacob. It was finally accepted because one cannot read the story without seeing the Master's hand. According to the film's Director, there is one more character to be mentioned: God. *"It's a lot about destiny and the serious forces that guide our lives that we don't understand"*, Charles explains during a 2003 interview in San Francisco. *"God's one of the main characters, actually. The role of fate, the role of predetermination, karma and afterlife and the Messiah – these are all Jewish concerns. It's a highly religious movie in a lot of ways, but not in a traditional, Cecil B. DeMille - sort of way".*[12]

"We would spend a lot of time alone together in enclosed rooms while he chain-smoked, talking about all kinds of things", Charles says. *"We are freethinkers, and our interest in God and our curiosity and our literary analysis (of God) are all what I would classify as very Judaic traditions. We had some talmudic dialogue that allowed us to explore these questions. When we talked about Martin Buber or Maimonides, that helped us deepen a certain thought that we were trying to express".*

"I think when he [Dylan] was 'born again' he was just expanding his feeling about religion and God". Charles muses. *"In his mind – this is my interpretation – I don't think he saw such a disconnect between his Judaism and his Christianity. I think he sees it all as streams running from the same source. His definition of religion, his definition of God, is a very broad one and encompasses a lot of traditions, and I don't think they are in conflict with each other".*[13]

Dylan also discussed God with Mikal Gilmore in 2001. Here is a part of the exchange:

Dylan: *"You hear a lot about God these days: God the beneficent; God, the all-great;, God, the Almighty; God, the most powerful; God, the giver of life; God, the creator of death. I mean we're hearing about God all the time, so we better know how to deal with it. But if we know anything about God, God is arbitrary. So, people better be able to deal with that, too".*

Gilmore: *"That's interesting because so many people think that God is constant, you know, and unchanging".*

Dylan: *"Oh, absolutely".*[14]

Dylan then advised the questioning reporter to look up the word "arbitrary" in the dictionary. I did, and here it is: *1: depending on individual discretion (as of a judge) and not fixed by law <the manner of punishment is arbitrary> 2 a: not restrained or limited in the exercise of power: ruling by absolute authority b: marked by or resulting from the unrestrained and often tyrannical exercise of power.*

The film that is in theatres ends with Dylan riding off to a wonderful rendition of *'Blowin' In The Wind'* with his 2001 band. *'Blowin' In The Wind'* is a song that allows one to be hopeful that something better may come. However, on the soundtrack CD *'Blowin' In The Wind'* does not appear. Instead Dylan's gospel song from 1980 *'City Of Gold'* is performed by the Dixie Hummingbirds. *'City Of Gold'* assures us that there indeed is something better to come. It is that belief that leaves Fate's demeanour in the final scene to be one of peace. Dylan once said that if this world is all that one believes in, then that person is kinda "stuck". Dylan's back may be up against the wall so often it *feels like it's stuck*, but actually he knows there's *a place with something going on.*

Get ready for the show!

[1] *"Masked And Anonymous"* Screenplay by Sergei Petrov & Rene Fontaine

[2] Loder, Kurt. Bob Dylan Interviewed (1984) *Rolling Stone*

[3] Gunderson, Edna. *USA Today*, September 10, 2001

[4] *"Bob Dylan by Mikal Gilmore" Rolling Stone* November 22, 2001

[5] Hilburn, Robert. *'How Does It Feel? Don't Ask' Los Angeles Times* Sept. 2001

[6] Gunderson, same as 3

[7] Cohen, Scott. *"Bob Dylan – "Don't Ask Me Nothin' 'Bout Nothin' I Might Just Tell You the Truth: Bob Dylan Revisited" Spin,* December 1985

[8] same as 5

[9] Gundersen, same as 3

[10] Hilburn, Robert. *Los Angeles Times* 1983

[11] Gundersen, same as 3

[12] Interview with Larry Charles, *San Francisco Bulletin* 2003

[13] same as 12

[14] same as 4

Published in *ISIS* issue #111, November 2003

Bob Dylan is bigger than Rock and Roll.

Pete Townshend

He should be accorded the same dignities as Yeats, Eliot, Stevens, Burling, Pound and other twentieth-century poetic peers.

Allen Ginsberg

He's a brutally honest guy. He loves to tell the truth. He even enjoys it . . . I'm like a B student of this fuckin' guy. He's the real thing.

Neil Young

It really was a question of everybody admiring Dylan. We'd go see him as the big guru.

Paul McCartney

I listen and love a lot of musicians but, Bob Dylan, Bob Dylan, Bob Dylan, Bob Dylan, Bob Dylan, Bob Dylan.

Jackson Browne

Bob Dylan is the greatest singer of our times. No one is better. No one, objective fact, is even close. His versatility and vocal skills are unmatched. His resonance and feeling are beyond those of any of his contemporaries. More than his ability with words, and more than his insight, his voice is God's greatest gift to him.

Jann Wenner

I always thought, and still do, that he's one of the best, if not the best white blues singers, ever. He has the phrasing of Charlie Patton and Robert Johnson, but it's based on country blues as opposed to urban blues. Dylan united everything. All American culture, from Mark Twain to Charlie Parker, are somewhere in Bob.

Dave Alvin

I don't think it is possible to overestimate Bob Dylan's contribution to the 20th century. He was the greatest influence on every singer/songwriter. On everyone with any job remotely like this. Anyone who denies it is lying. There is only Dylan.

Warren Zevon

He's the best at what I do

Jakob Dylan (Bob's son and leader of the Wallflowers)

People live with hope for green trees and beautiful flowers, but Dylan seems to lack that sort of simple hope, at least he did from 1964 to 1966. This darkness wasn't new to me. It became stronger as the years passed by.

Suze Rotolo (Bob's Greenwich Village girlfriend)

Appendices

Recommended Book Resources:

Books by Bob Dylan:

Dylan, Bob. *"Lyrics 1962–2001"*. *Simon & Schuster*, 2004
Dylan, Bob. *"Chronicles Volume One"*. *Simon & Schuster*, 2004
Dylan, Bob. *"Tarantula"*. *Macmillan*, 1971/*Scribner Book Company*, 2004
Dylan, Bob. *"Drawn Blank"*. *Random House*, 1994

Biographies:

Heylin, Clinton. *"Bob Dylan Behind the Shades: Take Two"*. *Viking*, 2000/*Penguin Books*, 2001
Scaduto, Anthony. *"Bob Dylan"*. *Abacus* 1972/*Helter Skelter Publishing*, 1996
Shelton, Robert. *"No Direction Home"*. *New English Library*, 1986/*Da Capo Press*, 2003
Sounes, Howard. *"Down the Highway – The Life of Bob Dylan"*. *Doubleday*, 2001/*Black Swan*, 2002

(Note: If the reader requires only one Dylan biography the choice has to be *"Bob Dylan Behind The Shades – Take Two"*, by Clinton Heylin.

Studies of Dylan's work:

Gray, Michael. *"Song & Dance Man III: The Art of Bob Dylan"*. *Continuum*, 2002
Ricks, Christopher. *"Dylan's Visions of Sin"*. *Viking*, 2003
Williams, Paul. *"Performing Artist 1986–1990"*. *Omnibus*, 2004
Williams, Paul. *"Performing Artist 1974–1986"*. *Underwood-Miller*, 1992
Williams, Paul. *"Performing Artist 1960–1973"*. *Underwood-Miller*, 1992

Tour Accounts:

Bauldie, John. *"The Ghost Of Electricity"*. 1988
Lee, C.P. *"Like The Night (Revisited)"*. *Helter Skelter Publishing*, 2004
Muir, Andrew. *"Razor's Edge"*. *Helter Skelter Publishing*, 2001
Sloman, Larry. *"On the Road"*. *Bantam Books*, 1978/*Helter Skelter Publishing*, 2002

Miscellaneous:

Barker, Derek (editor). *"ISIS: A Bob Dylan Anthology"*. *Helter Skelter Publishing*, 2001. Revised edition 2004
Dundas, Glen . *"Tangled"* (5th Edition). *SMA Services*, 2004
Engel, Dave. *"Just Like Bob Zimmerman's Blues"*. *Amherst Press*, 1997
Heylin, Clinton. *"A Life in Stolen Moments – Day By Day"*. private publication, 1996
Humphries, Patrick (text), Bauldie, John (notes). *"Oh No! Not Another Bob Dylan Book"*. *Square One Books*, 1991
Marqusee, Mike. *"Chimes of Freedom: The Politics of Bob Dylan"*. *The New Press*, 2003
Williamson, Nigel. *"The Rough Guide to Bob Dylan"*. *Rough Guides*, 2004

Photographic Books:

Cohen, John. *"Young Bob"*. *PowerHouse Books*, 2003
Kramer, Daniel; Feinstein, Barry; Marshall, Jim. *"Early Dylan"*. *Pavilion*, 1999
Kramer, Daniel. *"Bob Dylan"*. *The Citadel Press*, 1967

(For those interested in "Concert" pictures of Dylan, the years from 1984 onward are well covered in a series of four books by *ISIS* Staff Photographer John Hume)

Recommended Internet Resources:

Official Bob Dylan Site (General information and Tour information)
http://www.bobdylan.com

Expecting Rain by Karl Erik Anderson (Everything Dylan)
http://www.expectingrain.com

ISIS Magazine by Tracy Barker
http://www.bobdylanisis.com
P.O. Box 1182, Bedworth, Warwickshire CV12 0ZA England

Bob Links by Bill Pagel (Tour information)
http://www.execpc.com/~billp61/boblink.html

Bob Dylan's Official Albums:	RIAA Awards
Bob Dylan – March 19, 1962	G
The Freewheelin' Bob Dylan – May 27, 1963 *	P
The Times They Are A-Changin' – January 13, 1964	G
Another Side of Bob Dylan – August 8, 1964 **	G
Bringing It All Back Home – March 22, 1965 **	P
Highway 61 Revisited – August 30, 1965 *	P
Blonde on Blonde – June, 1966 **	P
Bob Dylan's Greatest Hits – March 27, 1967	5xP
John Wesley Harding – December 27, 1967 *	G
Nashville Skyline – April 9, 1969 *	P
Self Portrait – June 8, 1970	G
New Morning – October 21, 1970	G
Bob Dylan's Greatest Hits, Vol. 2 – November 17, 1971	5xP
Pat Garrett and Billy the Kid – July 13, 1973	G
Dylan – November 16, 1973 d	G
Planet Waves – January 17, 1974 *	G
Before the Flood – June 20, 1974	P
Blood on the Tracks – January 20, 1975**	2xP
The Basement Tapes – July 1, 1975	
Desire – January 5, 1976 *	2xP
Hard Rain – September 1, 1976	G
Street Legal – June 15, 1978 *	G
At Budokan – April 23, 1979	G
Slow Train Coming – August 20, 1979 **	P
Saved – June 19, 1980	

Shot of Love – August 12, 1981
Infidels – October 27, 1983 *   G
Real Live – November 29, 1984
Empire Burlesque – May 30, 1985
Biograph – November 7, 1985   P
Knocked Out Loaded – July 14, 1986
Dylan & the Dead – January 18, 1988   G
Down in the Groove – May 19, 1988
Oh Mercy – September 12, 1989 *
Under the Red Sky – September 11, 1990
The Bootleg Series Volumes 1-3 – March 26, 1991   G
Good as I Been to You – November 3, 1992
The 30th Anniversary Concert Celebration – August 24, 1993
World Gone Wrong – October 26, 1993
Bob Dylan's Greatest Hits, Vol. 3 – November 15, 1994   G
MTV Unplugged – June 30, 1995   G
Time Out Of Mind – September 30, 1997   P
The Bootleg Series Vol 4: Live 1966 – October 13, 1998   G
The Essential Bob Dylan – October 31, 2000
"Love and Theft" – September 11, 2001 **   G
The Bootleg Series Vol 5: Live 1975 – November 26, 2002   G
The Bootleg Series Vol 6: Live 1964 – March 30, 2004
The Bootleg Series Vol 7: – (proposed date of release August, 2005)

* Remastered: Hybrid Stereo SACD
** Remastered: Hybrid SACD with additional Surround Sound Mix
d Album deleted – currently not available.

"The Times They Are A-Changin'" is listed by Columbia Records as being released on February 10, 1964.

At the time this list was compiled (May 3, 2005), Bob Dylan had officially released forty-seven albums in the USA and the UK. In recent years, an increasing number of "best of" CDs of Dylan material have been released by his record label in selected territories only. These include "The Best Of Bob Dylan Volume 2" – Europe only and "Bob Dylan Live 1961-2000" – Japan only, to name but two. This list only covers albums released in the USA and the UK and therefore does not include the album "Masterpieces", which was released in March 1978 in Japan – and later that year in Australia and New Zealand – only, but does include "At Budokan", which was originally released in Japan only, but later gained world-wide release.

Notes: A complete list of oddities and variants is far beyond the scope of this appendix, but a few worthy inclusions are listed below.

"The Freewheelin' Bob Dylan": A very few copies of this vinyl record, containing four alternative tracks, 'escaped' from the LA record plant. This item is the most collectable of all of Dylan's albums and a mint condition stereo copy (only two copies are known to exist) has a value of circa £20,000.

"Bringing It All Back Home": This album was released in the Benelux countries as *"Subterranean Homesick Blues"*. As most European (*Columbia/Sony*) CDs were at one time manufactured in Holland, the album can often be found in other European countries, including the UK, with this erroneous title.

"Highway 61 Revisited": Japanese and early USA pressings had a different version of 'From a Buick 6'.

"Blonde On Blonde": *Columbia Records* lists the album as being released on May 16 1966. However, in his Dylan biography *"Behind the Shades: Take Two"*, Clinton Heylin states that a final overdub on the track, *'Fourth Time Around'*, was not recorded until June. Heylin also points out that the album did not enter the US charts until July 30, 1966, which would suggest a release date somewhat later than May 16. The Japanese pressings feature some slightly different mixes and extended fades on certain tracks.

The original UK and USA releases of this album on CD (April 1987) were nothing short of a disaster! The playing time of the CD was 71:00 minutes, which was a cut of almost two-minutes from the vinyl LP. The harshest cut of all was *'Sad Eyed Lady Of The Lowlands'*, which lost 32-seconds. The USA was quick to make amends and two subsequent pressings corrected the problem. The UK, however, was extremely slow to rectify the cuts. The album is now available in many excellent variants including an SACD release.

"Bob Dylan Greatest Hits": UK and USA releases of this title have slightly different track listings.

"Bob Dylan Greatest Hits Vol 2": Released in the UK under the title *"More Greatest Hits."* UK and USA releases have slightly different track listings.

The album *"Dylan"* was also available in certain territories as *"A Fool Such As I"*.

"Planet Waves": Originally released by *Asylum* in the USA and *Island Records* in the UK. Later re-released on *Columbia/CBS*. This album was available for a short time in quadraphonic.

"Before The Flood": Originally released by *Asylum* in the USA and *Island Records* in the UK. Later re-released on *Columbia/CBS*.

"Desire": Available for a short time in quadraphonic.

"At Budokan": Originally released on November 22, 1978 in Japan only. World-wide release April 23, 1979.

"The Essential Bob Dylan" was originally released in the USA only, as a double CD set (October 31, 2000). The set was later released in Germany as *"The Ultimate Collection"* (May 21, 2001). This was an expanded edition containing six extra tracks. This expanded 36-track European version was also released under its original title – *"The Essential Bob Dylan"* – in the UK, France, and the Far East in 2002. In November 2003, the 36-track version was released in Holland as a 3CD set with a "Limited Tour Edition Bonus Disc".

The first nine Dylan albums plus *"Greatest Hits"* were all available in mono. Note: The mono release of the *"Bob Dylan"* album sounds <u>far</u> better than the stereo release.

"Nashville Skyline" was not available as a mono release in the USA. The mono version of *"Greatest Hits"* actually features the stereo mix tracks with the left and right channels combined rather than tracks taken from the original mono mix albums.

September 15, 2003 saw the release of fifteen "classic" Dylan albums on the new hybrid Super Audio CD (SACD) format. These discs are the first recordings by any *Sony Music* artist to be issued in this format and can be played on both SACD players and standard CD players and offer remastered sonic performance on both platforms.

RIAA Awards

Now fast approaching its fiftieth year, the Recording Industry Association of America (RIAA) award programs are the longest-running objective measure of achievement for sound recordings in the United States of America. The awards were launched on March 14, 1958 when the first Gold Plaque was awarded to Perry Como for his hit single, *'Catch A Falling Star'* (*RCA Records*). Four months later, the cast album of Oklahoma, sung by Gordon Macrae (*Capitol Records*), became the first official Gold Award Album.

The Platinum Award category, for sales of one million units, was introduced in 1976 and by the mid-1980s the RIAA introduced Multi-Platinum awards for sales of 2 million or more units. The first Platinum album was The Eagles' *"Their Greatest Hits 1971-1975"*. Johnny Taylor's *'Disco Lady'* was the first single to be awarded Platinum status.

Assorted Facts

With sales of more than two million units each, *"Blood On The Tracks"* and *"Desire"* are Bob's best-selling "regular" albums. In a twist of fate, however, Dylan's first double-platinum award came not with *"Blood On The Tracks"* but with the release of *"Traveling Wilburys Vol 1"*. Released in October 1988, the album, which was immediately dubbed as one of the top 100 albums of all time by *Rolling Stone* magazine, remained on the *Billboard* chart for almost a year. The album has since gone triple-platinum. With sales of almost six million copies under its belt, Bob Dylan's best overall selling album is *"Bob Dylan's Greatest Hits"*.

Rated in all the music polls (#4 in *Rolling Stone's* *"500 Greatest Albums of All-time"* and #5 *Mojo's* *"100 Greatest Albums Ever Made"*) and by many musicologists as one of the finest albums of all time, Bob Dylan's groundbreaking release, *"Highway 61 Revisited"*, is a surprisingly slow seller. Released on August 30, 1965, the album peaked at #3 on the *Billboard* Chart and #4 on the UK Chart. However, it was almost two years to the day of its release before the album was certified Gold (500,000 units) and it was not certified as Platinum (sales of One Million units) until May 5, 1999, almost 24 years after its release!

These extremely sluggish sales figures also apply to *"The Times They Are A-Changin'"* (30 years to go Gold), *"Another Side Of Bob Dylan"* (35 years to go Gold), and *"The Freewheelin' Bob Dylan"* and *"Bringing It All Back Home"*, both of which took 36 years to go Platinum.

In contrast, the poorly recorded (but still wonderful) *"Street Legal"*, achieved Gold status in just two weeks. With god on its side, *"Slow Train Coming"* went Gold in four months and Platinum in just nine.

They say that absence makes the heart grow fonder and that was certainly the case when *Columbia* released the album *"Dylan"*, which went Gold in its first week of release. Even the much maligned *"Self Portrait"* took only two weeks to be certified Gold.

Only three of Bob Dylan's albums have so far reached #1 on Billboard. Discounting *"Before The Flood"* and *"The Basement Tapes"* (neither of which were *"regular"* releases and both of which were double LPs), these three studio releases came in succession; *"Planet Waves"* (1974), *"Blood On The Tracks"* (1975) and *"Desire"* (1976). However, Dylan got his first #1 album in 1970 when *"Self Portrait"* reached #1 on Cashbox (#4 on *Billboard*).

Incredibly, Bob Dylan has never had a #1 single on *Billboard*!

Recording Academy Grammy Awards

One year after the RIAA had introduced their Gold Plaque Awards, a group of US record executives calling themselves the Recording Academy, launched the Grammy Awards.

The inaugural Grammy Awards ceremony was held on May 4, 1959 in the Grand Ballroom of the Beverly Hills Hotel. The mission statement was to *"Cultivate a higher standard of popular taste"*. There were 28 award categories at the first event but the closest the organisers came to recognising rock 'n' roll music was one nominee each in the "Best Country & Western Performance" and "Best Rhythm & Blues Performance" sections.

Over the years conservative voting has led to a long list of absurdities and many of the best recordings of the last thirty-five years have failed to win, or in some cases even be nominated for a Grammy. This includes seminal records by Bob Dylan and the Rolling Stones. Grammy voters, meanwhile, have lavished awards on the likes of Toto, Christopher Cross, Bob Newhart and probably worst of all the truly appalling Milli Vanilli. The first award for rock music wasn't given until 1961 when Chubby Checker won the award for *"Best Rock & Roll Recording"*. Jimi Hendrix never won a Grammy; neither did the likes of Sam Cooke (albeit he was a frequent nominee) or Fats Domino, to name a few. In addition, British Grammy winners seem to be almost as rare as rocking horse s#*t.

In relation to Bob Dylan, the mid-sixties Grammy Awards can only be described as wholly perverse. The excellent *"Bringing It All Back Home"*, plus *"Highway 61 Revisited"* and *"Blonde On Blond"* (both of which would feature in virtually every musicologists all-time top 10 rock albums) received no commendations other than the latter two receiving nominations for *"Best Album Cover, Photography"*! It was a similar scenario in 1975 when *"Blood On The Tracks"* was nominated not for its musical content, but for Pete Hamill's liner notes! *"Blonde On Blonde"* and *"Highway 61 Revisited"* both received belated Hall of Fame Awards in 1998 and 2001 respectively. The Hall of Fame was introduced in 1973, assumedly as a way of compensating artists for previous shocking oversights. *'Blowin' In The Wind'*, *'Mr Tambourine Man'* and *'Like A Rolling Stone'* have all now been placed into the Hall of Fame after being totally overlooked by the Academy at the time of their releases. There are typically about half-a-dozen Hall of Fame placements each year. It's seems, however, that by the late nineties the Academy had realised that they had made so many oversights over the years that they might never catch up, and in 1997 they inducted no less than 143 records into Hall of Fame. It was in this bumper year that the song recently named by *Rolling Stone* magazine as the greatest song of all time, *'Like A Rolling Stone'*, was finally recognised by the Recording Academy.

Unbelievably, Bob Dylan had to wait until 1979 to collect <u>his</u> first golden gramophone, which was awarded to him for *"Best Rock Male Vocal Performance"* for *'Gotta Serve Somebody'*.

You might be excused for thinking that this win would be the turning point in Bob's Grammy achievements. Now that the Academy had finally discovered the existence of Bob Dylan there would surely be a flood of awards to make up for their past indiscretions. This, however, was not the case and Dylan had to wait another couple of decades before someone woke one morning and thought, "Hey, I know, let's give ol' Bob a Lifetime Achievement Award"; which they did in 1991. Afterwards, Dylan said that collecting a Lifetime Achievement was like attending your own funeral. Bob's partner to the Grammy party was . . . his mother. Now, how cool is that! Good on ya Bob.

The Grammy Awards are now telecast to an international audience of over 1.5 billion people in 170 countries.

Bob Dylan's Grammy History

1962: Best Folk Recording (nomination)
"Bob Dylan" (Bob Dylan)
(winner) Peter, Paul & Mary – *"If I Had A Hammer"*

1963: Best Documentary, Spoken Word or Drama Recording (nomination)
"We Shall Overcome (The March on Washington, August 28, 1963)"
Dr. Martin Luther King Jr. (with Joan Baez, Marian Anderson, Odetta, Rabbi Joachim Prinz, Bob Dylan, Whitney M. Young, John Lewis, Roy Wilkins, Walter Reuther, Peter, Paul & Mary, Bayard Rustin, A. Philip Randolph)
(winner) *"Who's Afraid of Virginia Woolf?"* – Edward Albee, playwright
(note)*"Best Folk Recording"* and *"Best Vocal Group Performance"* was won by Peter, Paul & Mary for their version of *'Blowin' In The Wind'*

1964: Best Folk Recording (nomination)
"The Times, They Are A-Changin'" (Bob Dylan)
(winner) Gale Garnett – *"We'll Sing In The Sunshine"*

1965: Best Album Cover, Photography (nomination)
"Bringing It All Back Home" – Daniel Kramer (Bob Dylan)
(winner) Bob Jones; Ken Whitmore – *"Jazz Suite On The Mass Texts"* (Paul Horn)

1966: Best Album Cover, Photography (nomination)
"Blonde On Blonde" – Gerald Schatsberg (Bob Dylan)
(winner) Robert Jones; Les Leverette – *"Confessions Of A Broken Man"* (Porter Wagoner)

1967: Best Album Cover, Photography (winner)
"Bob Dylan's Greatest Hits" – Roland Scherman with John Berg, Bob Cato (Bob Dylan)

1968: Best Folk Performance (nomination)
Bob Dylan on *"John Wesley Harding"*
(winner) Judy Collins – *"Both Sides Now"*

1969: Best Album Notes (winner)
Johnny Cash for *"Nashville Skyline"* – (Bob Dylan)

1969: Best Country Instrumental (nomination)
'Nashville Skyline Rag' – Bob Dylan
(winner) *"The Nashville Brass Featuring Danny Davis Play More Nashville Sounds"*
– Danny Davis & the Nashville Brass

1972: Album of the Year (winner)
"The Concert For Bangla Desh" – George Harrison & Friends (including Bob Dylan)

1973: Best Original Score – Motion Picture or a Television Special (nomination)
"Pat Garrett & Billy The Kid" – Bob Dylan
(winner) *"Jonathan Livingston Seagull"* – Neil Diamond

1975: Best Album Notes (winner)
Pete Hamill for *"Blood On The Tracks"* (Bob Dylan)

1979: Best Rock Male Vocal Performance (winner)
Bob Dylan on *'Gotta Serve Somebody'*

1980: Best Inspirational Performance (nomination)
Bob Dylan on *'Saved'*
(winner) Debby Boone – *'With My Song I Will Praise Him'*

1981: Best Inspirational Performance (nomination)
Bob Dylan on *'Shot Of Love'*
(winner) B.J. Thomas – *'Amazing Grace'*

1985: Record of the Year (winner)
'We Are The World' – USA For Africa (various artists, including Bob Dylan)

1985: Album of the Year (winner)
"We Are The World" – USA For Africa (various artists, including Bob Dylan)

1985: Best Pop Vocal Group (winner)
USA For Africa, (various artists, including Bob Dylan)

1986: Best Historical Album (nomination)
"Biograph" – Bob Dylan
(winner) *"Atlantic Rhythm And Blues 1947-1974, Vols. 1-7"* – various artists

1988: Best Traditional Folk Recording (winner)
"Folkways: A Vision Shared – A Tribute To Woody Guthrie And Leadbelly" – Bob Dylan
and various artists

1988: Best Traditional Folk Recording (nomination)
'Pretty Boy Floyd' from *"Folkways: A Vision Shared – A Tribute To Woody Guthrie And Leadbelly"* – Bob Dylan
(winner)*"Folkways: A Vision Shared – A Tribute to Woody Guthrie and Leadbelly"* Bob Dylan and various artists

1989: Best Album of the Year (nomination)
"The Traveling Wilburys, Volume I" – The Traveling Wilburys (including Bob Dylan)
(winner) *"Nick Of Time"* – Bonnie Raitt

1989: Best Rock Performance by a Duo or Group (winner)
The Traveling Wilburys for *"The Traveling Wilburys, Volume I"*

1991: Best Album Notes (nomination)
John Bauldie for *"The Bootleg Series, Vols. 1-3 (Rare and Unreleased), 1961-1991"* – (Bob Dylan)
(winner) James Brown, Cliff White, Harry Weinger, Nelson George, Alan M. Leeds for *"Star Time"* – (James Brown)

1991: Best Music Video – Short Form (nomination)
'Series Of Dreams' – Bob Dylan. Meirt Avis, director
(winner) *'Losing My Religion'* – R.E.M. Tarsem, director

1991: Lifetime Achievement Award
Bob Dylan
(along with the late John Lennon, Marian Anderson and Kitty Wells)

1993: Best Contemporary Folk Album (nomination)
"Good As I Been To You" Bob Dylan
(winner) *"Other Voices/Other Rooms"* – Nanci Griffith

1993: Best Rock Group Vocal Performance (nomination)
(Bob Dylan, N Young, R McGuinn, T Petty, G Harrison, E Clapton) – *'My Back Pages'*
from *"Bob Dylan – The 30th Anniversary Concert Celebration"*
(winner) Aerosmith – *"Livin' On The Edge"*

1993: Hall of Fame
'Blowin' In The Wind' – Bob Dylan (1963)

1994: Best Traditional Folk Album (winner)
"World Gone Wrong" – Bob Dylan

1995: Best Male Rock Vocal Performance (nomination)
Bob Dylan for *'Knockin' On Heaven's Door'* (*"MTV Unplugged"*)
(winner) Tom Petty – *'You Don't Know How It Feels'*

1995: Best Rock Song (nomination)
'Dignity' (*"MTV Unplugged"*) – Bob Dylan
(winner) *'You Oughta Know'* – Glen Ballard, Alanis Morissette

1995 Best Contemporary Folk Album (nomination)
"MTV Unplugged" – Bob Dylan
(winner) *"Wrecking Ball"* – Emmylou Harris

1997: Album of the Year (winner)
"Time Out Of Mind" – Bob Dylan

1997: Best Contemporary Folk Album (winner)
"Time Out Of Mind" – Bob Dylan

1997: Best Male Rock Vocal Performance (winner)
Bob Dylan on *'Cold Irons Bound'*

1997: Hall of Fame
'Like a Rolling Stone' – Bob Dylan (1965)

1998: Best Country Song (nomination)
'To Make You Feel My Love' – Bob Dylan
(winner) *'You're Still The One'* – Robert John "Mutt" Lange, Shania Twain

1998: Hall of Fame
"Blonde On Blonde" – Bob Dylan (1966)

2000: Best Male Rock Vocal Performance (nomination)
Bob Dylan on *'Things Have Changed'*
(winner) Lenny Kravitz for *'Again'*

2000: Best Song Written for a Motion Picture, Television or Other Visual Media
(nomination)
'Things Have Changed' for *Wonder Boys* – Bob Dylan
(winner) *'When She Loved Me'* for *Toy Story 2* – Randy Newman

2001: Album of the Year (nomination)
"Love And Theft" – Bob Dylan
(winner) *"O Brother, Where Art Thou?"* – soundtrack

2001: Best Male Rock Vocal Performance (nomination)
Bob Dylan on *'Honest With Me'*
(winner) Lenny Kravitz for *'Dig In'*

2001: Best Contemporary Folk Album (winner)
"Love And Theft" – Bob Dylan

2001: Hall of Fame
"Highway 61 Revisited" – Bob Dylan (1965)

2003: Best Pop Collaboration with Vocals (nomination)
Bob Dylan, Mavis Staples on *'Gonna Change My Way Of Thinking'*
(winner) Sting, Mary J. Blige on *"Whenever I Say Your Name"*

2003: Best Male Rock Vocal Performance (nomination)
Bob Dylan on *'Down In The Flood'*
(winner) Dave Matthews on *'Gravedigger'*

2003: Best Traditional Soul Gospel Album (nomination)
"Gotta Serve Somebody – The Gospel Songs Of Bob Dylan" – various artists
(winner) *"Go Tell It On the Mountain – The Blind Boys of Alabama"*

2004: Best Album Notes (nomination)
"The Bootleg Series Vol 6 – Live 1964" – Sean Wilentz (Bob Dylan)
(winner) *"The Complete Columbia Records Of Woody Herman And His Orchestra &
Woodchoppers (1945 – 1947)"*

Note: The above listings are for recordings released during the eligibility year October 1
through September 30. This means that albums such as *"Good As I've Been To You"*
(released October 27, 1992) and *"World Gone Wrong"* (released October 26, 1993) were
nominated for Grammy Awards in 1993 and 1994 respectively. This scenario means that
although *"World Gone Wrong"* was released in 1993, the Grammy was awarded for the
year 1994. Awards for 1994 were not presented until the Grammy Ceremony on March 1,
1995.

Selected Bootleg Recordings:

The first rock music bootleg was born in the summer of 1969 when a white-labelled record
in a plain white sleeve hit a hand full of record stores in Los Angeles. This untitled

360

collection of unreleased Dylan songs, which was soon to become known as *"Great White Wonder"*, was to spawn an industry that has survived to the present day. Since sound recordings did not receive copyright protection in the USA until February 15, 1972, these products received a wide distribution and business flourished. Even so, claims that various early incarnations of *"Great White Wonder"* sold 350,000 copies are a vast exaggeration!

The mystic and beauty that was the vinyl bootleg record has long since given way to the compact disc, and it is a selection of titles from this digital medium that are featured here. This list contains circa seventy entries. Seventy CDs might seem a little excessive. However, since the arrival of the bootleg CD in 1986/'87 almost 1,000 Dylan titles have emerged! These discs have been chosen for a number of reasons including historical significance, sound quality, performance, and packaging. Plus, I happen to like them!

I Was So Much Younger Then *Dandelion* 4CD 1958-65
The Dylan's Roots *Skeleton* 1CD 1961
The Bootleg *Wanted Man Music* 1CD 1961
Finjan Club *Yellow Dog* 1CD 1962
Folksingers Choice *Yellow Dog* 1CD 1962
Live In New York 1963 *Black Panther* 1CD 1963
All Hallows Eve & More *Midnight Beat* 2CD 1964
From Newport To The Ancient Empty Streets In LA *Dandelion* 2CD 1964-65
At The Beeb *MainStream* 1CD 1965
Thin Wild Mercury *Music Spank* 1CD 1965-66
Genuine Live 1966 *Scorpio* 8CD 1966
The Genuine Basement Tapes Vols 1-5 *Scorpio* 1CD each 1967
The Dylan Cash Sessions *Spank* 1CD 1969
Blood On The Tapes *Columbus* 1CD 1975
Songs For Patti Valentine *Wanted Man Music* 1CD 1975
Flagging Down The Double E's *The Razor's Edge* 2CD 1975
Tell It Like It Is *Spacematic* 1CD 1975
Creatures Void Of Form *The Razors Edge* 1CD 1976
Hold The Fort For What It's Worth *Wild Wolf* 2CD 1976
The Rundown Rehearsal Tapes *White Bear* 4CD 1978
Stop Crying *Red Sky Records* 1CD 1978
Contract With The Lord *Silver Rarities* Parts 1 & 2 1CD each 1979
Solid Rock *Wanted Man Music* 2CD 1980
Born Again Music *Flashback* 2CD 1980
Avignon *Moonlight* 2CD 1981
You Can't Kill An Idea – Part 1 / Part 2 *Silver Rarities* 1CD each 1981
Birds Nest In Your Hair *RattleSnake* 2CD 1981
Rough Cuts *Gold Standard* 1CD 1983
Live At The Palaeur *Shamrock* 2CD 1984
Clean Cuts *Sick Cat* 1CD 1985
True Confessions For Carol *RattleSnake* 2CD 1986
Precious Memories *Three Cool Cats* 1CD 1986
The Final Night And More *Dandelion* 2CD 1987
Temples In Flames 1987 European Tour Anthology *White Bear* 5CD 1987
Stuck Inside Of New York *Kiss The Stone* 2CD 1988
Golden Vanity *Wanted Man Music* 1CD 1988-92
The Deeds Of Mercy *The Razors's Edge* 1CD 1989
All The Way Down To Italy *Great Dane* 2CD 1989

Staying Here With You *Wanted Man Music* 2CD 1990
Toads Place Vol 1 / Toads Place Vol 2 *Wanted Man Music* 2CD each 1990
Paradise, Hawaiian Style *Q Records* 2CD 1992
The Supper Club Soundboard *RattleSnake* 1CD each 1993
Great Woods *Wild Wolf* 2CD 1993
Blue-Eyed Boston Boy *Razor's Edge* 2CD 1994
The Pedlar Now Speaks *The Razor's Edge* 2CD 1995
F*** The Playlist: Briton II *Sterling Sounds* 2CD 1995
Loving Of Liverpool *Mainstream* 2CD 1996
White Dove *Dandelion* 2CD 1997
San Jose '98 *Dandelion* 2CD 1998
Eating Caviar In a King Sized Bed *RattleSnake* 2CD 1998
Highlands Of Worcester *Wild Wolf* 1CD 1999
The Lonely Graveyard Of My Mind *Dandelion* 2CD 1999
Across The Borderline *Wild Wolf* 2CD 1999
Ace Of Clubs *Scorpio* 5CD 1999
Horsens Teater *Crystal Cat* 2CD 2000
Cardiff 2000 *Crystal Cat* 2CD 2000
Portsmouth - First Evening *Crystal Cat* 2CD 2000
Portsmouth - Second Evening *Crystal Cat* 2CD 2000
Telluride Town *Mr. Tambourine Man* 2CD 2001
The Genuine Bootleg Series *Scorpio* 3CD various
The Genuine Bootleg Series Take 2 *Scorpio* 3CD various
In The Garden 2001 *RattleSnake* 2CD 2002
Red Bluff 2002 *Crystal Cat* 2CD 2002
Romance In Durango *Tambourine Man* 2CD 2003
Bonnaroo 2004 *Black Dog* 2CD 2004
Deep Beneath The Waves *Tambourine Man* 2CD 2004
Walk Like a Duck Smell like a Skunk *Hollow Horn* 2CD 2004
Now You Mouth Cries Wolf *Hollow Horn* 2CD 2004
A Dog That Talks, A Fish That Walks *Hollow Horn* 2CD 2005
Blood On Your Saddle *Hollow Horn* 2CD 2005
Where The Monkey Dances *Hollow Horn* 2CD 2005

Bob Facts

Most Covered Songs: (As of May 2005)

Blowin' In The Wind – 380
Don't Think Twice, It's All Right – 222
I Shall Be Released – 185
Mr Tambourine Man – 178
Like a Rolling Stone – 174

Knockin' On Heaven's Door – 153
All Along The Watchtower – 146
It's All Over Now, Baby Blue – 133
I'll Be Your Baby Tonight – 121
Quinn The Eskimo – 118

Still on the Road

Since Dylan began what as become know as the Never Ending Tour (on June 7, 1988) he has played an average of 100 concerts per year. The total number of concerts between June 7, 1988 and December 31, 2004 is 1,692.

1988 – 71	1992 – 92	1996 – 86	2000 – 112	2004 – 112
1989 – 99	1993 – 80	1997 – 96	2001 – 106	2005 – ?
1990 – 93	1994 – 104	1998 – 110	2002 – 107	Still on the Road
1991 – 101	1995 – 116	1999 – 119	2003 – 88	

The
Classic Interviews
1965 - 1966

This CD is a fascinating, previously undocumented look at what Dylan was thinking during this evolutionary and pivotal stage in his career. Bringing together recordings of press conferences held in San Francisco and Los Angeles during late '65, and completing the package with the notorious interview undertaken by Martin Bronstein while in Canada early the next year; this is a timely reminder of what was going on in the Dylan camp during his most creative period.

The Classic Interviews
Volume 2
The Weberman Tapes

The *'Weberman Tapes'* are the stuff of legend. Recorded in 1971 during two telephone conversations between Alan Jules Weberman (the guy who raided Dylan's dustbins) and Bob Dylan. They were heard by only a tiny minority of fans who managed to search out one of a handful of copies that escaped when the LP was withdrawn before its planned release in the seventies. Now available officially for the first time (licensed personally by AJ to Chrome Dreams) and elaborately presented, as always, with a 16-page booklet featuring rare photos and an introduction by Weberman, this is a release that every Dylan fan will want in their collection.

Available at all good record stores and online at
www.chromedreams.co.uk (and) www.bobdylanisis.com

Songs That Dylan Loved

CD featuring original versions of songs that Dylan recorded or performed live during his awesome career.

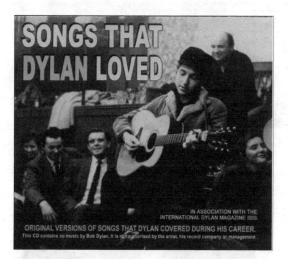

This CD brings together, for the first time, the original versions of songs that Dylan recorded on albums ranging from his first record in 1962, *'Bob Dylan'*, which was largely made up of folk and blues standards, right up to albums recorded in the 90's such as *'Good As I Been To You'*, which again went back to his earliest influences.

Featuring 27 tracks from artists as diverse as Woody Guthrie and Leadbelly through to Frankie Laine and The Ink Spots, this collection illustrates what an eclectic range of music has affected one of the most influential artists of the rock era.

Features deluxe slipcase and 16-page booklet

**Available at all good record stores and online at
www.chromedreams.co.uk (and) www.bobdylanisis.com**

Tales From A Golden Age
Bob Dylan 1941 - 1966

The first ever documentary charting Dylan's childhood, youth, early success and global dominance. From his birth to his motorcycle accident

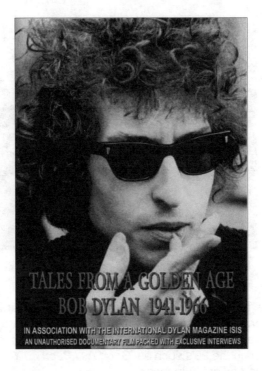

* A biography of Bob Dylan from birth through such classic albums as *'Highway 61 Revisited'* and 'Blonde on Blonde' to his motorcycle accident

* An documentary exploration of the creative genius of the man who changed the face of popular music

* Over 80 minutes of in-depth interviews from more than a dozen contributors

* Rare photographs of Dylan from private archives

An Independant production unauthorised by the Artist

Available at all good record stores and online at
www.chromedreams.co.uk (and) www.bobdylanisis.com

After The Crash
Bob Dylan 1966 - 1978

A truly superb two-hour documentary film charting Dylan's middle years from his motorcycle accident through to his accepting Christ into his life

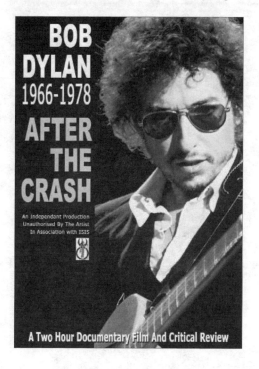

* A biography of Bob Dylan from his motorcycle accident through such classic albums as *'Desire'* and *'Blood on the Tracks'* to his accepting Christ into his life in 1978

* Two hours of in-depth interviews from fifteen contributors including Bruce Langhorne, Scarlet Rivera, Rob Stoner, Jacques Levy, and the infamous A.J. Weberman

* Rare photographs and film footage of Dylan; many items from private archives

An Independant production unauthorised by the Artist

**Available at all good record stores and online at
www.chromedreams.co.uk (and) www.bobdylanisis.com**